EROTIC
FANTASIES

D<small>RS.</small> P<small>HYLLIS</small> and E<small>BERHARD</small> K<small>RONHAUSEN</small> have worked
together in their analytic practice and psychological
research for the past fifteen years. After postgraduate
work at Columbia University, they specialized in family
therapy and group guidance in Califor
hausens now live in Paris and have gaine
nition for their efforts to liberalize cens
their work in the field of sex education
written *Pornography and the Law* and

…ny

…nia. The Kron-
…ed world recog-
…sorship laws and
…. They have also
…*Erotic Art*, Vol-
…has been in the
…ngth documen-
…opened in the

EROTIC
FANTASIES

A
Study
of the
Sexual Imagination

Drs. Phyllis and Eberhard Kronhausen

GROVE PRESS, INC.   NEW YORK

Library of Congress Catalog Card Number: 76-84895

First Evergreen Black Cat Edition 1970

Third Printing

Manufactured in the United States of America

DISTRIBUTED BY RANDOM HOUSE, INC., NEW YORK

GROVE PRESS, INC., 53 EAST 11TH STREET,
NEW YORK, NEW YORK 10003

Contents

INTRODUCTION   *xi*

I

Sex Fantasies in Early Erotic Literature

L'Ecole des Filles   *3*

The Whore's Rhetorick   *7*

Dialogues of Luisa Sigea   *9*

Merryland   *18*

Arbor Vitae   *23*

Gilles de Rais   *25*

THE EARL OF ROCHESTER

On King Charles   *27*

Sodom   *27*

The Why and the Wherefore   *32*

2
The Folklore of Sex

POGGIO

A Frenetic Woman   47
Giovanni Andrea . . .   48
A Young Woman Balked . . .   48
Witty Reply . . .   49
An Inexperienced Youth . . .   49
A Young Florentine . . .   50
A Man Had to Do with His Sick Wife . . .   51

RABELAIS

The Cause and Wherefore the Leagues Are So Short . . .   55
How Gargantua's Wonderful Understanding . . .   56
How Pantagruel Likewise with His Farts . . .   59

ARETINO

Dialogue on the Life of Married Women   60
A Trick   64
The Bawd's Trade   64

ANONYMOUS FOLK TALES

A Crop of Cocks   66
The Magic Ring   69
The Comb   73
The Pope and the Soldier   76
La Dame Excitée   79
Returning Home from the Market   81
The Prudish Lady   82
The Injured Finger   85

3
Erotic Writings in the Style of Folklore

Tenth Trial of the Ring—the Cocker Spaniels   90
Sultan Misapouf and Princess Grisemine   94
Little Red Riding Hood   99

ANDREA DE NERCIAT

Mon Noviciat 108
Les Aphrodites 114
Le Diable au Corps 117

4
Homosexuality

FEMALE HOMOSEXUALITY

Deux Gougnottes 128
Gamiani 130
Les Cousines de la Colonelle 134

MALE HOMOSEXUALITY

Teleny 138
Notes and Souvenirs from an Old Biblioprick 143
Ernest 147
L'Apprenti Sorcier 156
Hyacinthe, ou Les Milles Plaisirs 159
Pédérastie Active 162

5
Transsexualism and Bondage

Tableaux des Moeurs 171
"Frank" and I 173
Monsieur Venus 174
Amours Invertis 179
Gynecocracy 181
Miss High-Heels 189

6
The Bondage Problem

Aux Pieds d'Omphale 201
Fort Frederick 204
Arènes Olympiques 208
Unpublished Masochistic Story 211
Josiane et Son Esclave 219

L'Aveu 220

Le Club des Monteurs Humaines 223

7
Sadomasochism

The Passionate Lash 228

The Revocation of the Edict of Nantes 231

Le Pont 239

Anonymous Flagellation Story 242

Helena 244

Selma 246

8
Incest Fantasies

The Loves of Venus 250

The Modern Eveline 258

The Power of Mesmerism 261

More Forbidden Fruit 266

Initiations Voluptueuses 267

9
Juveniles

The New Epicurean 278

Child Love 285

Flossie 291

Débauchées Précoces 297

L'Amoureuse de Jeunes Garçons 305

School Life in Paris 307

Initiations Voluptueuses 311

Ange Dumoutier's Amorous Escapades 312

10
Bizarre Fantasies

DILDOES

School Life in Paris 322

ANIMALS

Dog's Tongue with Special White Sauce 327
Coralie and Régine 327
La Femme aux Chiens 327
Gamiani 328
Le Diable au Corps 329

FETISHISM

School Life in Paris 337
The Modern Eveline 339
Les Tableaux Vivants 341
Dévergondages, Souvenirs Erotiques 341

II
Miscellaneous Bizarre Fantasies

Harlequin, Prince Cherrytop 349
Le Surmâle 354
Le Docteur Lerne, Sous-Dieu 358
La Femme Endormie 362
Adollizing 384
Female Belly 387
Le Bain d'Amour 387
Le Keepsake Gallant 406
The Romance of Lust 408
Sept Péchés 418
La Liberté ou l'Amour 422

INTRODUCTION

It was our old teacher and control-analyst, Dr. Theodor Reik, who frequently pointed to the significant role of fantasy in human sex psychology. Among the first things he would try to elicit from a new patient were his favorite masturbation fantasies. Reik was less interested in the actual behavior—for instance whether the person masturbated once or three times a week on the average, or how he did it—than in the accompanying fantasies.

Perhaps Reik underrated the importance of a person's complete sex history, which is usually revealing of his whole style of intimate life. Without knowledge of an individual's sex fantasies, however, any information about his sexual behavior would be one-sided and perhaps totally misleading. A person may, for example, have no actual incidence of homosexual or sadomasochistic acting out in his sex history, and yet his entire fantasy life may revolve around such situations or be tinted by them.

The fact that a person may not have had the opportunity, courage, audacity, or disregard for consequences necessary to carry out his favorite sex fantasies does not mean that his sex psychology is equally bland or "normal." Among persons with colorless personalities one finds some of the most gaudy sex fantasies, though they would be horrified at the mere idea of acting out any part of them in real life.

It is in the nature of sex fantasies that they are, to a large extent, so unrealizable that they are seldom acted upon. And that is exactly their therapeutic function. They serve as mental aphrodisiacs and psychological stimulants, underlying "normal" sexual behavior. They are not "how-to" guides for sexual psychopaths. On the contrary, they serve as safety valves for bottled-up sex feelings, strivings, and wishes that are socially unacceptable or directly antisocial and inimical to the physical or mental welfare of the individual or his sex partners.

The fact that a few severely disturbed individuals, such as the fifteenth-century sex murderer Gilles de Rais, have acted out antisocial sex fantasies actually confirms the general rule. In these cases, the ego controls of the person concerned were not strong enough to withstand the persistent pressure of primitive, antisocial demands of the unconscious. But for the average individual, even the wildest and most antisocial sex fantasy serves only as a substitute outlet and control mechanism of the ego to keep actual behavior within socially tolerable limits.

There is widespread belief that sex fantasies are apt to lead sooner or later to acting out in real life. This is one of the rationales behind censorship moves to suppress erotic fantasies in literature and the arts. But this fear is ill directed and self-defeating, if the purpose is to control antisocial sex behavior and not— as we suspect—sexuality in general.

In this area, practical experience has proved to be contrary to popular belief. In decisions concerning the discharge of mental patients from the hospital, for example, their performances on certain clinical projective tests, such as the Rorschach and the Thematic Apperception Test, are frequently taken into consideration. Experienced clinicians know that the patient with a bland and fantasy-poor test record is frequently more likely to commit antisocial acts than one with hair-raising fantasies that might make him appear to be a dangerous sex maniac. An individual is less likely to commit the antisocial acts he fantasizes about simply because—having his fantasy outlet—he does not need to resort to direct action, as does the person with no other means of gratification.

Aside from projective tests, sex fantasies are difficult to elicit. A person may speak freely about his sexual behavior, but block at relating his favorite sex fantasies. This is understandable when one realizes that the sex fantasies of "perfectly normal" people are often embarrassingly bizarre and deviant, involving incestuous and otherwise taboo activities and target objects.

Guilt and shame reactions in connection with sex fantasies can, indeed, be so severe that the individual represses the fantasies almost immediately after their occurrence, a process similar to the forgetting of dreams. If such a person is asked what he thinks of during masturbation or other sex activities, he may sincerely report that he thinks of nothing. What he is saying, in reality, is that he is not *aware* of any erotic thoughts or fantasies. Although this is how statements of this sort are usually interpreted, there is no doubt that individuals differ widely in their ability to fantasize, and some people are richer in this respect than others. Nevertheless, we must warn that the ability to fantasize, while not tending to lead to behavioral acting out, is not without its mental health hazards. In some exceptional cases, the sex fantasies may take on an almost hallucinatory intensity (as was undoubtedly true for the Marquis de Sade). In that case, they may be experienced as ego-alien and result in a feeling of estrangement and depersonalization. It is this factor which may have led people to associate insanity with masturbation, as Jule

Nydes has pointed out.* However, it is only the more seriously disturbed individual for whom sexual fantasies may become hallucinatory. For the average person, they simply remain the necessary stimulus to the initiation of "normal" sex activities, whether masturbatory or sociosexual (that is, involving other people).

It is precisely this factor of sexual fantasy that distinguishes human sexuality from that of the lower species. We have little cause, therefore, to be either afraid or ashamed of our sex fantasies, as aberrant, deviant, and bizarre as they may be. The more intelligent the individual, the greater the role of fantasy in his sex life. This does not mean that he (or she) will be governed by sex fantasies to the exclusion of social sex contacts and intense involvement with real (non-imagined) sex partners. But it does mean that a free fantasy life will contribute to creative thinking, whereas mental blocks or inhibitions will interfere with the creative process.

The factor of inhibition (mental blocking) is especially important with regard to women. They report, as a group, considerably fewer sex fantasies than men. But they are, as a group, "less" in just about every category of sexological measurement, such as the frequency of masturbation, premarital and extramarital sex experiences, and response to erotic literature and art. Their lesser proneness to fantasize about sexual matters is therefore not surprising and should not, in any case, be taken as an indication of lesser potential in all these respects, but as an indication of a considerably greater degree of inhibition and repression.

Noting the great importance of sexual fantasy for human sexuality, we have, for many years, tried to gather as much information on it as possible. Research in this matter was, however, not easy. The method of interviewing people about their sex fantasies yielded, for the very reasons elaborated above, relatively meager results. So did, surprisingly, a thorough review of psychiatric and psychoanalytic literature. True, sex fantasies

---

* "The Magical Experience of the Masturbation Fantasy," *American Journal of Psychotherapy,* IV (1950), 303–10.

are touched upon in the course of certain case histories, e.g., in Krafft-Ebing (*Psychopathia Sexualis*), the writings of Wilhelm Stekel, Havelock Ellis, and others. However, emphasis is usually placed on deviant behavior and not fantasy.

Contemporary clinicians seem to have given the subject little attention, and what we found, even in psychoanalytically oriented articles and monographs, mostly of the 1920's and 1930's, was not particularly enlightening, although there are several isolated descriptions of sex fantasies in some of Freud's own cases. However, since these are readily available in inexpensive editions of Freud's work, they are not included here.

We therefore embarked upon a systematic review of erotic underground literature, both ancient and modern, and from all parts of the world. For the purposes of this book, we have restricted ourselves to Western literature of the last five hundred years, omitting classical Greek and Roman as well as Oriental erotic writings, because a limitation had to be set on the quantity of material to be included in a single volume. Then, too, classical and especially Oriental literature contains such different erotic fantasies that they would deserve a separate treatment and analysis.

This approach immediately yielded a rich harvest. Sex fantasies of the most fascinating nature came to light almost immediately, a phenomenon which one might have expected, since erotic literature—with the exception of what we call "erotic realism"—depends almost entirely on sex fantasies for its subject matter. A word on erotic realism is in order here. We first adopted the term to distinguish realistic literary descriptions of sexual events and their accompanying emotions from the reality-divorced fantasies of pornography. Later we included under the term those erotic writings of a fantasy nature which do not follow the usual structure and deliberate reality distortions of "hard-core" pornography—e.g., surrealistic literature, erotic wit and humor, and folklore. The distinction between erotic realism and "hard-core" pornography was made in response to current legal practice, that is, to distinguish between different types of erotic writings before the law. The distinction is otherwise of little use, since in a society that is free of all forms of sexual censorship, pornography—i.e., writings designed primarily or exclusively to serve the purpose of sexual stimulation—as well as other kinds of erotic literature, would enjoy the same protection before the law. Of course, erotically realistic writings are often as sexually stimulating as deliberate pornography. The distinction made is therefore a purely practical and legalistic one, relevant only under conditions of official censorship.

Another rich source of sex fantasies turned out to be folklore material, a fact which the great specialist in this field Gershon Legman has pointed out in various highly interesting and clinically (as well as bibliographically) important publications.* As to our own research for this volume, we have focused on hitherto almost inaccessible material of this type and have sought to bring it into the mainstream of clinical literature and experience and to interpret it in terms of its allegorical and symbolic content. Most of the selections in this volume are cited from extremely rare editions that are generally not available even at large libraries. However, during the past two years, several of the titles have been issued in inexpensive editions. Those published by Grove Press are *"Frank" and I* (1968), *Miss High-Heels* (1969), *The Modern Eveline* (1970), *The New Epicurean* (1969), *The Power of Mesmerism* (1969), *The Romance of Lust* (1968), *School Life in Paris* (1970), and *Tableaux Vivants* (1970). *The Whore's Rhetorick* is available in a hardcover edition (New York: Astor-Honor, Inc., 1961). Other works available in a variety of paperback editions are: Aretino's *Dialogues of Sisters, Wives and Courtesans*, Chorier's *Dialogues of Luisa Sigea*, Rochester's *Sodom*, Wilde's *Teleny*, and the anonymous works *Flossie* and *Gamiani* (the latter often attributed to Alfred de Musset).

As one might have expected, most of the thousands of sexual fantasies which we gathered from all these sources fell into several major categories: homosexuality, incest, sadomasochism, animal contacts, fetishism, pedophilia, bondage fantasies,

---

* *The Horn Book: Studies in Erotic Folklore and Bibliography* (New Hyde Park, N.Y.: University Books, Inc., 1964).

and transsexualism (reversal of sex roles), to name some of the most recurrent ones. Others were too difficult to classify in these broad terms. We have therefore put them in a separate group of bizarre fantasies, though they usually contain elements of one or the other or of several of the major categories. Nor are they necessarily any more bizarre than fantasies in the more general categories, though some of them are. Still, we found the creation of this special category of fantasies both expedient and clinically meaningful. Such fantasies are different in the sense that they are more personal or idiosyncratic than the recurrent, easily identifiable fantasies in the general categories.

Having done this research, which took several years, and organized the presentation here, we were surprised as much by the immense clinical implications of this material as by its initial shock value, which must be considerably more pronounced for the average reader than for psychologically trained professionals. But the shock effect of the material is, in our opinion, of therapeutic value. The person who lives in a limited and sheltered world will be faced with the immediate choice of either laying down the book or accepting the intrusion of these potentially rather disturbing fantasies. If he chooses the latter course, he will, in the end, be rewarded not only by a vastly enlarged vision of man's secret inner world, including his own, but by the assurance that he is not alone in what he may have considered as quite unacceptable in himself.

Bringing these hidden fantasies out into the open should therefore have the effect of reducing the person's anxiety, broadening his understanding, and making him more tolerant toward himself and others than he might have been before this confrontation with some of the darkest recesses of the mind.

It is in this sense that we present this unusual and possibly upsetting book, first of all to the clinical professions and students of human behavior, especially the sexologist, psychologist, psychiatrist, and cultural anthropologist. They will, we sincerely believe, find study of the material richly rewarding for their theoretical research, and for their practical work with "normal-neurotic" as well as more severely disturbed patients. We

recommend its careful study especially to the beginning thera-
pist in the firm conviction that it will help him to a quicker and
better understanding of human sex psychology than he could
have gathered from dozens of professional texts and years of
clinical practice.

To the layman with the moral courage to look at his own
unknown psyche and that of his fellow men, to the person with
literary interests and a sense of humor, we likewise recommend
this reading. But to those who are easily offended in their moral
sensibilities or who are disturbed by the unusual, we do not
recommend a reading.

ACKNOWLEDGMENT

We wish to thank Mr. Noel Burch of Paris for his valuable and
much appreciated help in gathering and translating some of the
French-language material for this book. Likewise, we would like
to express our thanks to Marie and Jose Simoes of Paris for additional translation work and for other assistance.

EROTIC
FANTASIES

1

Sex Fantasies
in Early Erotic Literature

L'ECOLE DES FILLES

One of the earliest specific references to a pornographic book in the English language is an entry in Samuel Pepys's diary.* On January 13, 1668, he "stopped at Martin's, my bookseller, where I saw the French book which I did think to have had for my wife to translate, called 'L'escholle des filles,' but when I come to look in it, it is the most bawdy, lewd book that I ever saw, rather worse than 'Putana errante,' so that I was ashamed of reading in

---

* See David F. Foxon, "Libertine Literature in England, 1660–1745," *The Book Collector*, XII (1963), 21–36.

3

it." Nevertheless, he did not seem to be able to get his mind off the book, for on February 8 he was back at Martin's, "and there staid an hour, and bought the idle, rogueish book 'L'escholle des filles,' which I have bought in plain binding, avoiding the buying of it better bound, because I resolve, as soon as I have read it, to burn it."

Next morning he read a little in it, finding it "a mighty lewd book, but yet not amiss for a sober man once to read over to inform himself in the villainy of the world"—the typical excuse of any timid, hypocritical soul and of many persons occupied in censorship drives, clean-up campaigns, and smut-hunts.

Pepys confides to his diary on the evening of the same day that after "mighty good store of wine," he went to his chamber, "where I did read through 'L'escholle des filles,' a lewd book, but what do no wrong once to read for information sake. . . . And after I had done it I burned it, that it might not be among my books to my shame." Again the attitude of the sexually conflicted person who cannot accept his natural interest in sex.

But what was the content of this book which so scandalized Her Majesty's Secretary of Naval Affairs in the seventeenth century? It was a book that had been in trouble from the very beginning. Its author—a certain Millot or Milliot—was hanged in effigy and his book burned beneath the gallows. All this, presumably because its main theme deals with the fantasy discussion of two girls, Fancine and Susanne, about various sexual topics and activities in which the older of the two takes the role of instructing the younger one.*

SUSANNE: Well, my dear, it is exactly with this [their penis and testicles] that men afford us this pleasure. For if a young man likes a girl, don't you know what he is likely to do if he happens to find her alone? He kneels in front of her and asks her in the nicest possible way whether she does not love him, for "I love you so," and while he thus speaks to her, he looks at her so desperately and longingly as if he was about to take his life on her account. And if the girl listens to him favorably, he

---

* Unless otherwise specified, all translations have been especially prepared for this volume.

quickly gets up and carries her in his strong arms to the bed, lays her down on her back, takes off her blouse and skirt and opens wide her thighs. At the same time he too opens his breeches and gets undressed. And when he is lying nude on top of the girl, this long thing penetrates with the greatest lust and pleasure into her little hole with which she makes peepee.

FANCINE: I cannot marvel enough about what you are telling me, dear Cousin. But how does he manage to get into it with this thing of his which is so soft and wobbly? Is it that he has to get it in with the help of his fingers?

SUSANNE: Oh you poor little dumb-dumb! It isn't always that soft. To the contrary! At the moment that he shows it to the girl, it completely changes its appearance and has no more in common with the way it was before. It gets much thicker and longer, as well as hard and stiff like a rock. There is also a skin which usually extends to the tip, but which is now pulled back toward the belly and reveals a sort of red, heart-shaped cherry which increases the man's pleasure if you touch it.

FANCINE: And it only gets bigger and harder, as you say, to enter into the little hole of the girl, is that right?

SUSANNE: Certainly, because otherwise it wouldn't be possible at all. But already the difficulty in entering causes pleasure, for you can imagine that it doesn't just suddenly get into it, but that it advances only little by little, and the young man is often covered with sweat by the time he gets his whole pride and joy into the girl, because the girl's hole just isn't very big. But that too gives a lot of pleasure to the girl, because she can feel how the boy's tool with which he opens her so forcefully moves back and forth in her vagina and tickles her most agreeably.

FANCINE: I would be rather afraid that he'd hurt me.

SUSANNE: Not at all, darling. The girls are very pleased with it. Of course, the first thrust, when he first enters, does hurt a little, simply because she isn't used to it yet. But immediately afterwards it changes to the nicest kind of tickling sensation and goes on to transport her into the greatest pleasure on earth.

FANCINE: And what is the girl's thing called?

SUSANNE: I call it vagina. Others give it all kinds of other names.

FANCINE: I see.

SUSANNE: When a young man does this with a girl it is called sexual intercourse, or just simply fucking. Anyway, the boys teach us all these expressions when they are at it with us. But don't use any of these words in polite society, because they are supposed to be dirty words that make young girls blush.

FANCINE: Oh, I'll certainly keep it to myself. But what does the young man do to get this stiff thing into the vagina?

SUSANNE: He can only get into the girl's hole if he first pushes forward and then pulls backward, then again pushes forward, and so on, and the girl responds by pushing on her part to help him get more easily into it until he is altogether inside. Lying underneath the young man, she can feel the violent movements of his behind.

FANCINE: Do you mean that he has to keep moving like that all the time and cannot stop at all?

SUSANNE: Yes, that's the way it is.

FANCINE: But how does he do it then that he only gets in little by little?

SUSANNE: Come here, look how I am doing it. And while she sees him move like this, she embraces him, kisses him on the mouth, pets him on his stomach, behind, and thighs, calls him her sweetheart, her love, her all, and experiences all the while that unspeakable happiness as his member enters into her womb.

FANCINE: Really, dear Cousin, the way you are describing it to me, I wouldn't mind trying it myself. And it seems that some girls ought to be thankful to their young men for all that they are doing with them, for they have, after all, been working hard at it and not gotten much for it themselves.

We see that *L'Ecole des Filles* is mild by contemporary standards and could hardly be considered "mighty lewd," as it seemed to Pepys. Since it has a certain sex-educational aspect, it might be considered an early erotic sex manual, similar in that respect to the *Kama Sutra* or to some of the classical Chinese and Japanese sex manuals which always combined erotic and educational elements.

Charming too is the naïveté of the dialogue. The content is by and large realistic, though not always clinically accurate, but the eroticism derives from the fact that two young girls are discussing sex matters. Further on, the text departs even more from reality and indulges openly in erotic fantasy, for instance, as Susanne relates the experiences of her wedding night:

Then he ejaculated and he strewed one hundred rose-colored pearls on the floor and asked me to collect them nude as I was. I was lying in the midst of it, wallowing from one side to the other, and made all kinds of movements in the light of the fire and the candles, while he kissed me, lifted me up, massaged my whole body as well as his own with jasmine ointment, until we lay down on the bed again and played around with each other. After that, he asked me to kneel in front of him, looked at me ecstatically from top to bottom, praised my stomach, my thighs, my breasts, and most of all my little "Sanctuary" that was round and closed. Sometimes he put his hand on it, and I must confess that I thoroughly enjoyed all these little games. Then he turned me around, examined carefully my shoulders, then the two cheeks of my behind, and finally made me bend over, supporting myself on my arms and hands, while he mounted me like a rider and asked me to move along on all fours. But soon he got off his little "horsie," not sideways but gliding down from behind (because he was not afraid, as he said, that I might hit him with my hind legs), and while still getting off, he immediately put his thing between the cheeks of my behind and entered my vagina that way . . . pushing in and pulling out again alternately and delighting himself in the contemplation of this game. All this in-and-out of his thing made a noise, dear Cousin, like when the baker kneads wet dough, or when little children shoot with toy cannons or pop little paper balls.

After the fantasy of the girl rolling around in the man's semen, which is referred to as "one hundred rose-colored pearls," we have the fantasy of horse and rider, the man imagining the girl to be his horse, which is a frequent sex fantasy. It occurs, for instance, in Jean Genet's play *The Balcony*, where a prostitute in the brothel enacts the role of a pony, prancing up and down in front of her customer, complete with pony tail, bridle, and bit. This fantasy may also be the hidden erotic meaning of the pony-tail hairdo, which is usually associated with youthful, robust women.

THE WHORE'S RHETORICK

The style of dialogues was popular in Pepys's time and much earlier, and some of the oldest erotic works in the Western world are in this literary genre. There were, for instance, the *Ragionamenti*, or *Dialogues*, of Pietro Aretino (1492–1557). Divided into three parts—the life of nuns, the life of married women, and the life of whores—Aretino's *Dialogues* have for the most part a serious philosophical and moral point and are less concerned with sex fantasies. More on Aretino appears in Chapter 2, "The Folklore of Sex."

La Retorica delle Puttane (*The Whore's Rhetorick*), another example of the dialogue genre, was first published in 1642. Ferrante Pallavicino, the author, was beheaded two years later at the age of twenty-eight for his anticlerical writings. In the form of a textbook of rhetoric, it describes a whore's life and the arts of persuasion she needs to learn. As Foxon rightly observes, "It is a satire not only on rhetoric, the Jesuits, and religion but also on sex and mankind."

The English adaptation, *The Whore's Rhetorick, calculated to the Meridian of London and conformed to the rules of art. In two dialogues* (London, 1683), did not fare too well with the English authorities either. Foxon reports a couple of contemporary convictions on account of its sale, though no one was executed for it. The English edition follows the Italian original quite closely, but differs mainly in that most of the material was turned into a dialogue between Dorothea and Mother Creswel, the bawd, and that many contemporary London references were added. At one point, the discussion takes a turn which is of particular interest with regard to sex fantasies.

MOTHER CRESWEL: In like manner the Female Orator must strive to make the best use and advantage of substantial Flesh and Blood, solid Kisses, and sensible Touches: but if these do not sufficiently mortifie an obdurate Lover, nor make him drop any golden Tears, she must not be unprovided of lascivious Pictures, obscene Images and Representations to raise her own and her Lover's joys.

DOROTHEA: This is a thing I never dreamed of.

M.C.: When you are detained in ugly, sordid, or ungrateful embraces, it would be difficult without the artificial aid of a picture to counterfeit those ecstasies which every comer may expect for his money. Therefore on these occasions you must frame in your mind the Idea of some comely Youth who pleases you best, whose shadow will create a greater lust than could be raised by a nauseous though real enjoyment. The

Picture of this charming Boy may very fitly be placed near your Bed, to imprint the fancy deeper in your imagination, and enable you to fall into those sweet transports, which do singularly gratifie the enjoyer's heart.

DOR.: This gallantry does almost ravish me, because it is altogether new.

M.C.: The dexterous acting this dying part, the artificial counterfeiting an immoderate passion, will ever produce very advantageous effects: the deceived Gamester, believing these amorous pangs created by himself, will be apt to fall into the like trance, will approve of the ardour of his own flame, and be ready to comply in the generosity of a grateful return.

DOR.: That is still the burthen of the Song.

M.C.: In this act young Ladies do oft forget their interest, and when the person does not please, it is a piece of self-denial my Scholar must learn, to make it appear he does. To prevent then any discovery of nauseating the present Bedfellow, a continual mindfulness of her own interest and the assistance of a handsome Picture are the best and most easy remedies. The whole series of carnal satisfaction does purely consist in fancy, and he effectually enjoys most, whose imagination is strongest, who frames in his mind the highest conceptions of joy and content. This artifice therefore is principally necessary in conjunction with certain credulous humours, who believe themselves adored by the whole Female Sex: such will as it were force their Mistresses to dissolve in pleasure, and give sense of a sincere delight, in regard their own fancies are high and elevated. They would otherwise count her dull and insensible of that weight of bliss she enjoyes in the circumference of their Arms.

DIALOGUES OF LUISA SIGEA

Around 1660 fell also the first publication of Nicholas Chorier's *Dialogues of Luisa Sigea*. This Luisa Sigea actually existed in the form of a noble Spanish lady of the time, but there is no more than a satirical connection between the *Dialogues* and the real lady herself.

This book resembles *L'Ecole des Filles* and is likewise divided into several parts, featuring such topics as "The Skirmish," "The Tribadicon," "Fabric," "The Duel," "Pleasures," and "Frolicks and Sports." Some of these contain considerable portions of pure erotic fantasy.

TULLIA: I cannot express how greatly refreshed I feel after so long a sleep; my limbs have reposed seven consecutive hours. And thyself, Ottavia?

OTTAVIA: As for me, I am awake since the moment that a horrible dream roused me from sleep, all frighted and trembling.

TULLIA: Relate to me the dream, please.

OTTAVIA: Tullia, methought I was with Caviceo [her fiancé] strolling along the shady and verdant banks of the Po, under the spreading willows which were protecting us from the heat of the sun. Caviceo was importuning my ears and soul with his most plaintive strains, which he uttered out of love; he was suing for a tender kiss, I refused him; thou was persuading me to give it, so I gave it to him; he took it. As he was then slipping one hand into my bosom, while entwining me with the other arm, I could scarcely free myself from his grasp, owing to thy influence and thy teachings. Being disentangled, I fled, he ran after me; but just as he was going to lay hands on me, I turned round . . . Ah! Tullia, what a ghastly object do I behold?

TULLIA: Had wolves set upon Caviceo, were they quartering thy love? Had he turned the sword on himself?

OTTAVIA: Softly! he would rather pierce me with his own dagger!

TULLIA: O pleasant and witty girl!

OTTAVIA: I behold him changed into a most frightful beast, as like the Satyrs we see in pictures, as unlike himself. His body was covered all over with bristles, a pair of goat's horns shot out on his head towards his forehead, ending in sharp points. But the ears, forehead, eyes, nose and countenance were all like Caviceo. He threatened me with a javelin twice longer and thicker than becomes a man fighting under Venus' banner; the rest of the body ended in a goat. He rushed at me, endeavouring to rape me and approached his mouth to mine; in fine, so unusual a sight startled me. Now, what evil does it forebode me? thou who art so learned, canst tell me?

TULLIA: I can indeed, cousin, and shall tell thee in its own time; but it is none of thy present business to know it.

OTTAVIA: Suffer me not to be any longer tortured with the desire of knowing, my lady.

TULLIA: This dream portends to thee, blooming and tender maid, the delicious fruit of another love; whilst it portends to Caviceo not grief, but the profaning of the conjugal bed.

OTTAVIA: Far from me such infamy!

TULLIA: It is a common saying, that those men whose wives allow themselves to be seduced by other men . . . pass into the ranks of goats and cuckolds.

Ottavia protests that she would never allow such a thing to happen. Her instructress, the older and much more experienced Tullia, then asks her just to wait and see what will happen to her in time. Meanwhile she tells her young cousin about her wedding night and what to expect of her own:

TULLIA: "Thou art up for killing me, Callias [her husband]," I cried, I roared in a pitiful voice. I no longer roared, but yelled. This did not move him much. I thrust the dagger aside; he grows angry, and falls to rebuking me for the disgraceful and impertinent liberty I was taking, as he said. He finally compels me to put the weapon back into the place out of which I had plucked it. But I presently felt a milky shower, a sweet alleviation for the wound he had just inflicted, flow from that tube into my garden. The unbridled and furious organ fell languishing. I was afforded a short truce.

OTTAVIA: Did that shower drop into the further end of thy garden?

TULLIA: Not at all, sweet maid, not a single drop. It merely bedewed the outer edge. As soon as Callias alighted, he besought me to wipe him; he then began to expostulate with me. "Tullia," he says, "if thou didst love me, thou wouldst not refuse, as thou dost, wretched me, who am burning with love for thee, the true fruit of thy love." "I do love thee," I answered, "and am mad in love with thee; but what wilt thou have unhappy me do in this carnage?" "Knowest thou not," he added, "that this part of thy person is no longer thine, but mine by full and lawful right? Why dost thou prevent me from freely enjoying my own goods? . . . My truncheon is getting very angry with thee. When I throw myself upon this beloved breast, squeeze me in thy arms, let nothing make thee slacken thy hold; do exactly whatever I bid thee, if thou wilt have me for husband; whatever I ask and require of thee, if thou wilt have me for thy lover. Now then, raise thy legs as high as ever thou canst, so that thy neat feet may with thy heels drawn together fondly kiss thy exceedingly smooth buttocks." I promised I would.

OTTAVIA: And thou kept thy word?

TULLIA: "Cheer up," he says, "I would willingly brave death for thy sake, and yet thy impatience baffles my love. So it is now entirely in thy power, and wholly thy duty, to show thy love for me in this conflict." "I should rather incur Venus' anger than thine," I answered. He interrupted me with kisses, and nimbly mounted me again. I raised my thighs as high as they can go; I hold him like a leech; he then sets the firebrand at the door of the love altar, removes inside with his fingers the lips of the vulva out of his way, puts the head in, next drives at me with all his might, thrusting the bludgeon into the gaping quarter. The point got stuck at the first shocks: for I felt it had gone much farther in now than before. I thought I was split open; I broke out in a long ejaculation; the tears rushed abundantly from my eyes. Callias stopped a while.

Finally, of course, Callias manages to deflower his bride. But she tells him that she has had so far only pain from it and no pleasure. They renew the battle, and this time they experience simultaneous orgasm. After that, attracted by the noise the couple has made, Tullia's mother and sister rush into the room and congratulate both the victor and the vanquished:

TULLIA: My mother ran into Callias' arms: "My son, hast thou fought gallantly? The shouts of my darling Tullia proved that thou wast victorious; I congratulate thee and Tullia on thy victory. Hadst thou not conquered, the bride would remain a widow." But Pomponia, having thrown her arms round me, was embracing me and sprinkling me with tears. "How cruelly this butcher has treated thee!" she whispered in a very low voice. "On hearing thee, sister, bemoaning, I pursued with my maledictions the unbridled lust of the scoundrel. But how goes it?" "Very well," I answered, "yet I arrived at the pleasure I was seeking by an exceedingly rough road. I reached the complete and supreme joys of life, on passing through the midst of the pangs of death." "Thou art now a woman?" she added. "As for me," said I, "I am one, and when I reflect in my own mind on the enjoyments I have had, my virginity was frittered; I wonder how so much happiness can be sold so cheap. I would prefer henceforth a day bereft of the light of the sun, than a night without the pleasures of Venus." "All right, that will do," she replied, "and certainly the girl that does not enjoy those gifts of Venus, I guess she does not enjoy life while alive."

In the sixth dialogue, "Frolicks and Sports," Tullia's interpretation of Ottavia's dream is coming true—she lets herself be seduced by a certain Lampridio, though not without the help of Tullia herself:

TULLIA: Lampridio, embrace Ottavia; and thou, Ottavia, embrace Lampridio. I shall play my little part in this comedy: with my hand I shall aim the male weapon at the female butt. It is well: the whole thing is buried within. How the privy parts of the one are admirably adapted to those of the other. Now, do not spare thy companion, Lampridio.

OTTAVIA: What are you up to? How you do squeeze me! How you shame me! How you thump me! Take away thy hand, Tullia; why art thou tickling me? Oh! oh! oh!

TULLIA: Raise thy buttocks. Raise it, I say, raise it higher. Shake it quicker, harder, more fiercely. Bravo, bravo! . . .

LAMPRIDIO: How happy you both make me! how you feed my voluptuousness, thou Tullia, with thy nectar! and thou, Ottavia, with thy ambrosia! Lo! lo! Now, now, Ottavia, lift, lift thy reins. Sturdily, sturdily!

TULLIA: Thou art fainting, Ottavia, thou art fainting.

OTTAVIA: I feel! . . . I feel! . . . How scalding this flood! How impetuously it is shot off! Kiss me, kiss me. And now I, too, am melting. The veins of my Venus are distilling. Oh! oh! I felt the effect of Jupiter's copulation with Juno. This pleasure comes from heaven. Oh! oh! the bottom! . . . I am fainting.

Later, Ottavia is introduced to anal intercourse, after Tullia again prepares her with a vivid account of her own experiences in that respect:

TULLIA: . . . The licentiousness of a degrading pleasure exceeds, in the eyes of scurvy frowzy Sodomites, all the sweetness of true glory. "I shall not be sufficient for it," I shouted. "I desire a respite, not a very long one." They then proceeded along the straight way of the honest Venus. The coitions that took place in this manner amounted to eight.

Continuing her story on how she was debauched by three men at a time, Tullia goes on:

After this, Aloisio places a bolster across the couch under my buttocks. "Now turn flat upon your face and expose to our eyes and affections the darling breech." "Well, what would you have?" said I. "Have a regard for a woman in a fright. You forget I am a girl and not a boy." "Pho!" replied Fabrizio; "what not a single one of the Roman girls, out of so many of those conspicuous for their accomplishments and beauty, has dared refuse, a witty and hand-some young lady like you dares refuse?" "But my spirit shudders at the idea of such a thing," I answered; "I could never bear it; you would kill me unaccustomed to this sort of warfare." "You could bear it," added Aloisio. "Much younger girls become famous among us men, owing to this corporeal intercourse. The taking away of your fore-part virginity cost you more." Seeing there was no help for me, I yielded to the raging mad fellows. Thereupon, Aloisio bends downward over my buttocks; he applies the ram to my back door; he batters it; he makes it totter; with a final effort he breaks it in. I groaned. He immediately plucked the tool out of the wound, buried it in the womb, and sent forth a heavy shower of seed into the lubric avenue of my matrix. The deed being done, Fabrizio goes through the same process. With eager impetus he pushes his spear-staff, and in less than no time he buries the whole in my guts. He keeps a good while going and coming back by the same road; and, what I did not think was possible, such a fit of some sort of itching or other came over me that I no longer doubted but I could accus-tom myself to this sort of thing, if I only wished. God forbid the like folly should ever mislead Callias! He did not, however, abuse beyond measure my submission throughout the secret senses of my womb, nor did the rascal's intemperance prevent me in the least from taking my pleasure.

OTTAVIA: Now tell me of Callias, please; did the naughty fellow ever gibe thee about that spot?
TULLIA: I guess he did, my dear Ottavia.
OTTAVIA: The same thing happened to me, my dear Tullia.

As it turns out, Ottavia has had experience with anal inter-course as well, but the hypocritical manner of speech adopted by Tullia, a device commonly encountered in erotic writings, may shed some light on public sex morality in general. Certain tabloid newspapers, especially in England, thrive on this moral-istic approach to "reporting" sexual matters, which enables their readers to both enjoy and condemn the titillating morsels of social scandal printed daily.

In the end, the *Dialogues* go into descriptions of sexual threesomes and foursomes:

OTTAVIA: Well now, Lampridio, assist me, assist me.
LAMPRIDIO: Assist thou likewise, Ottavia; assist, Tullia.

TULLIA: What would thou have both of us do?

LAMPRIDIO: I wish Ottavia, while I am conversing with her paps, to swing her buttocks in a measured and slow kind of motitation. And that tickling left hand of thine, Tullia, to excite by a salacious friction my scrotum and testicles to a complete enjoyment.

TULLIA: Play thy own part, thou jack. We shall each act ours admirably well.

OTTAVIA: Thou art giving me a cruel thumping, Lampridio. But thou shalt not get off with impunity. To these thrusts I shall reply by redoubted jerks. Here, here, here. Am I pleasing thee?

TULLIA: Lampridio, thou art showing thyself a truly notable warrior. After having driven alike dagger right home to the hilt, how thou causest not the death but the delights of expiring Ottavia! One would imagine, Ottavia, that thou art on for giving up the ghost, whilst this amorous hero looks as if he would remove his whole being into thy very bowels.

OTTAVIA: What idle talk! Why distract me in the height of so agreeable a sensation of an insatiable pleasure? But . . . but . . . there is burning within me a liquid mass of quick fire.

TULLIA: Ay, from the firebrand that Lampridio's love, concentrated in thy penetralis, is brandishing inside of thee. I will, nevertheless, kiss thee, my own Lampridio.

LAMPRIDIO: O fond kiss, pleasing augmentation of my delight! Come close to me also with those orbed breasts of ivory, that I may kiss them. Now . . . now, Ottavia, Tullia, there are escaping from me libidi . . . libidinous streams!

OTTAVIA: I feel, I feel them running into my pond. Go on. Oh! oh! Go on. And I, and I!

TULLIA: And thou, and thou, mayest thou melt into a flood. Help each other. It's all right, by the God Subigus! It is admirably well. Eh, Rangoni! What art thou musing over all the while, mute and still?

RANGONI: This thou mayst have conjectured.

TULLIA: Thou showest the mentule. How big it has become in a moment for the duel! Thou art a wonderful warrior. A taste of no repose is granted the poor creature as far as I can see. . . .

RANGONI: I shall be as lenient to each of you as I possibly can. O what an alluring posture! I hereby bury this rude javelin in this divine beauty. I beg thee, Ottavia, to take it in good sense.

OTTAVIA: Make haste, my kind; I feel a fresh titillation rising in the bottom of my reins. Is that right, Tullia? How funny! how funny!

TULLIA: Wag thy buttocks, Ottavia, as I am wagging mine. Keep time with me: it will be most agreeable to him and thee. Admirably! Admirably! How the quivering lubricities of thy loins are stirred up!

RANGONI: Endeavor to move up and down in rapid successions; I understand the language of the voluptuous flood issuing out of the lake in his loins. Make thy buttocks vibrate upwards to him, Ottavia, while I am assisting him, now that he is gasping.

OTTAVIA: Tullia! Tullia. . . . Thou, Rangoni, thou art transporting me with fury. I cannot help giving utterances to my frenzy. I feel it fall down drop by drop . . . Ah! ah!

TULLIA: The rain . . .

OTTAVIA: Which Danaë, the daughter of Acrisius, would prefer to her dear Jupiter's golden shower. Act, Tullia, act!

TULLIA: I have my own part to act, and I am acting it.

OTTAVIA: Twice already, twice, thou, Rangoni, Eh! eh! . . . and I three times. Ah! ah! ah!

Rangoni then speaks of wanting to introduce the girls to a "new posture":

TULLIA: Well now, what sort of one will it be? Ah! one just presents itself to my mind, they call it Hector's horse. Stretch thyself flat on thy back, Rangoni, and let that fulminating spear seek out the enemy it intends to stab. Exactly! But why toss up thy head so haughtily, thou lascivious tail?

OTTAVIA: Thou wilt be punished, swaggerer, thou wilt. What shall I do, Tullia?

TULLIA: Rise and get Rangoni in under thy thighs on turning thy back to him. Let the dagger of him lying down correspond with the sheath of thee bent over him. Thou art in a suitable position. It is all right.

RANGONI: O thou back of Dione's daughter! O ye loins of ivory! O ye incendiary buttocks!

TULLIA: Cease this abusive language. Whoever lavishes too much praise on the buttock rails at the conch. I see where this design thou hast on the buttocks is tending. I hate such prevaricating eulogies. Thou at least art wise, Ottavia: the greedy conch has swallowed thy unruly mentule, Rangoni.

OTTAVIA: Come, Rangoni! here! here! . . . Come, Rangoni, to my help! This hook which thou hast cast into my lake is drawing out of the bottom of my belly an extreme amount of voluptuousness. Come, Rangoni!

RANGONI: Here I am, Ottavia, here I am, here I am. Art thou coming? Art thou coming?

OTTAVIA: So I am, so I am, so I am! Ah! Ah!

In the seventh dialogue, "A New Kind of Pleasure," the discussion concerns oral eroticism:

OTTAVIA: The day before yesterday, Crisogono came to see my mother in the afternoon. All was quiet and silent. He had scarcely begun to wanton a little with her, when he became very importunate. "Yesterday morning," he said, "I learned a new kind of pleasure. One of our grand personages (who had certainly tasted it), says that there is nothing so disgusting and repulsive as those parts of his wife which stamp her as a woman—and he has a very pretty wife, mind! In that sink every thing is foul, while in this"—kissing my mother on the mouth—"dwells the true Venus. He therefore abominates that ill-favoured cavern, and adores that pure mouth, that charming head. He looks to nothing else, his member rises for nothing else. His wife is as spirited as she is beautiful, and even more obliging. She knows no other pleasure than her husband's; what he thinks right she thinks proper, and abets all the caprices of her husband; so she lends him the service of her mouth." . . . Crisogono persuaded my mother to what she was willing to do without persuasion. "Oh!" she said, smiling, "what an air you want me to play, and upon what a flute, in our concert!" taking in her hand his member, which began to rise. She seized the point of his dart between her lips and, turning her tongue around it, caused novel transports of delight to the member that slid into its new receptacle. But feeling that the fountains of the brine of Venus were on the point of bursting forth, she recoiled with horror. "You should not degrade me so far," said my mother, "as to make me drink a man in a liquid form?" She had scarcely spoken, when an abundant shower fell upon her robe. He showed some anger. "How could you be so foolish," he cried, "as to spoil such good work!" She replied: "Forgive me, the next time you will find me more obedient." She kept her word, and actually drank men in a liquid state—a spicy thing, for indeed the seed is spicy with salt!

The main fantasy in the *Dialogues*, as in *L'Ecole des Filles*, is the idea of two young women discussing supposedly taboo sexual topics. Additional fantasies in both books include defloration, anal intercourse, oral eroticism, group activities, and the introduction of a permissive parent figure, in this case Tullia's mother, who takes more than a casual interest in her daughter's wedding night, as well as Ottavia's mother, whose devotion to her lover is cited in the passage above.

Further, the *Dialogues*, as is true for many older erotic works, is rich in allegorical language. For the psychologist this is of special interest, since the same symbols—door, garden, rain, lake, flood, etc.—frequently occur in dreams and free associations of patients. The technique of allegorical language is pushed still further in *Merryland* and in other pieces of the same period.

MERRYLAND

There is no better source of information on ancient erotica than the old records of prosecution against publishers and booksellers. It is from such a source that we first hear of the curious book *Merryland*. In 1745 a deposition was made by a certain bricklayer, Edward Scudamore, of St. George's, Hannover Square, in London, identifying copies of a collection of engravings entitled "A Compleat Set of Charts of the Coasts of Merryland wherein are exhibited all the Ports, Harbours, Creeks, Bays, Rocks, Settings, Bearings, Gulphs, Promontories, Limits, Boundaries, etc." He told the court that he had bought copies at 5 shillings a time from John Brett on April 3 and from Mary Torbuck on April 5.* As a result, warrants were issued on April 5 for the authors, printers, and publishers of the *Charts*, who were also said to have published or sold two other classical erotic works, *Aretinus Redivivus* and *The School of Venus*.

Bibliographer Foxon cites a note from the office of the Secretary of State to the Attorney General in which the former says, "I send you inclosed . . . two very obscene and infamous books which seem calculated for corrupting the youth of the nation . . ." and asks for the Attorney General's opinion on

---

* Foxon, *op. cit.*, pp. 33 ff.

whether he thought the State's case good enough for prosecution. The Attorney General did, of course. But as Foxon remarks, "It is good to learn from Plomer's *Dictionary* that by 1748 he [the principal accused] was printing orders for the Middlesex Sessions."

The original edition of the *Charts* is not known to exist today. As Foxon points out, the name Merryland seems to have been a pun on Maryland and was most likely related to the Ancient and Most Puissant Order of the Beggar's Benison and Merryland, a phallic club started at Anstruther, Fife, in 1732. This club had an offshoot, the Wig Club—the wig being an allusion to the merkin, a pubic wig such as were then actually worn by some women of fashion. (A pubic wig owned by the club was said to have been made from the pubic hair of Charles II's mistresses and was added to by all new members.) Both clubs are described in Louis C. Jones's *The Clubs of the Georgian Rakes* (New York, 1942), and it appears that their membership included George IV, four dukes, seventy-three peers and law lords of Scotland, thirty baronets, and two bishops.

The diploma of membership of the Beggar's Benison contains a clear reference to the *Charts*, in that it confers "our full powers and privileges of Ingress, Egress, and Regress from and to, and to and from all the Harbours, Creeks, Havens and commodious Inlets upon the Coasts of our said extensive Territories [that is, of Merryland]."

Although there are no copies of the original *Charts* extant, we did have occasion to examine an early edition of *A New Description of Merryland*. First published in 1740, it was so popular that it reached a tenth edition by 1742. Both works had been preceded by the *Description of Bettyland* (possibly written by Charles Cotton, *ca.* 1683), *The Natural History of the Frutex Vulvaria*, and its companion piece *Arbor Vitae* (first published in 1732), and all these works feature the same allegorical, tongue-in-cheek style which characterizes the *New Description of Merryland, Containing a Topographical, Geographical and Natural History of that Country*.

In a "Preface by the Author" we read:

I need not say how useful and necessary a work of this nature will
be to the World. I shall only observe that nobody has ever attempted it before in this Method; and it is somewhat surprising that
all the modern Geographers . . . should be entirely silent about so
remarkable a Country, which was discovered many years ago and
was well known to the Ancients. I cannot imagine these gentlemen
so ignorant as to be entirely unacquainted that there is such a
Country; but as it is not my Business to account for their Omissions,
I shall say no more of them, but that their Silence has rendered this
work of mine the more necessary.

I shall decline adding anything more of myself, but lay before
my reader the following opinion of that truly learned Right Reverend Prelate the Bishop of London, who says, "Of all the Studies to
which men are drawn, either by Inclination or Interest, perhaps no
one can pretend such an agreeable Pleasure as the Description of
Countries."

Following are excerpts from various chapters sufficient to
give a general idea of this work.

Chapter II.

There is something very remarkable and surprising as to the
Longitude and *Latitude* of this Country, neither of which could
ever yet be fixed to any certain Degree, and it is pretty evident,
however strange it may seem, that there is great *Variations* both of
the Latitude and Longitude in Merryland as of the Mariner's
Compass in other Parts of the World. . . . Know then, courteous
reader, soon after my first Entrance into this wonderful and delightful Country (having as prying a Curiosity as most Men) I en-
deavoured to get the best Insight that was possible in every Thing
relating to the State of Merryland—Among other Things, I made
very accurate Observations both of the *Latitude* and *Longitude*, and
may venture to say, there could be no considerable Mistake in my
Observations as they were made with a proper *Instrument* of a *large
Radius,* and in perfect good Order, nay, I have been assured, when I
was in Merryland, that my Instrument was inferior to none: But
some years after, happening to be there again, and repeating the
Experiment, I found both Latitude and Longitude increased many
degrees, tho' I tried in the same Spot, and with the same Instrument
as before. . . .

This extraordinary Alteration of the Latitude is not at all agreeable but the greater degree it extends to, the less delightful is the Country to its inhabitants. . . .

I need say no more of the Situation of this Country, but—that the *Antipodes* to Merryland is by some said to be that prominent Part of the Continent called PDX 1 known in High Dutch by the Name of der Arsz-back, but as it is not my Intention to concern myself in these Disputes, but stick as close as may be to my Subject, I shall leave the Affair of the *Antipodes* to those that have a *Taste* that way; only shall observe, there are some people who very preposterously (as I think) give the Preference to the PDX: The *Italian* Geographers are very much inclined that Way, some of the Dutch have likewise come into it, and of late years a few in Great Britain have appeared not altogether averse to it.

Chapter III. Of the Air, Soil, Rivers, Canals, etc.

The air in Merryland is very different, being in some Provinces perfectly pure and healthy, in others extremely gross and pestiential; for the most part it may be said to be like the Air in Holland, "generally thick and moist, by reason of the frequent fogs which arise from its Lakes and Canals," yet it is mostly very pleasant to the Inhabitants, tho' it cannot always be said to be wholesome. . . .

The Climate is generally warm, and sometimes so very hot, that Strangers inconsiderately coming into it, have suffered exceedingly. . . . But this dangerous Heat of the Climate, with all its dreadful Concomitants, is not so very terrible, but it may be guarded against by taking proper precautions, and People might venture into it without much Hazard, even at the Worst Seasons, and in the most unhealthy Provinces, they need no more to avoid the Danger, but be careful always to wear proper *Cloathing*, of which they have a sort which is most commodious, and peculiarly adapted to this Country. It is made of an extraordinary fine, thin substance, and contrived so as to be all of one Piece and without a Seam, only about the Bottom of it is generally bound round with a scarlet Ribbon for Ornament.

Sometimes the Climate is as much on the other Extreme, *cold*, to a great Degree; but this rarely happens nor has it any bad effect on the Inhabitants, otherwise than by being disagreeable and uncomfortable to live in.

In general, the Country is warm enough, and so exceedingly delightful that every Man at first coming into it is transported with Pleasure; the very Sight of Merryland, or any Approach to it, puts one in Strange Raptures, and even in dreaming of it, people have enjoyed a most pleasing kind of Delirium: In short, it is the loveliest and sweetest Region of the World.

The Country lying very low (as Mr. *Gordon* says of *Holland*) *its Soil is naturally very wet and fenny,* the Parts that are best inhabited are generally the moistest; and Naturalists tell us, this Moisture contributes much to its Fruitfulness: where it is dry, it seldom proves fruitful, nor agreeable to the Tiller: The Parts which have never been broke up nor had spade or Plough in them, are most esteemed, and so fond are People of having the first Tilling of a fresh spot, that I have known some Hundreds of Pounds given to obtain that Pleasure.

Chapter IV. Of the vast Extent of Merryland, its Divisions and principal Places of Note:

1st, At the End of the Great Canal, toward the *Terra Firma*, are two Forts called LBA, between which every one must necessarily pass, that goes up the country, there being no other Road. The Fortifications are not very strong, tho' they have *Curtains, Hornworks* and *Ramparts,* they have indeed sometimes defended the Pass a pretty while, but were seldom or never known to hold out long against a close and vigorous attack.

2nd, Near these Forts is the Metropolis called CLTRS: it is a pleasant Place, much delighted in by the Queens of Merryland, and is their chief Palace, or rather Pleasure Seat, it was at first but small, but the Pleasure some of the Queens have found in it has occasioned their extending its Bounds considerably. . . .

6th, Here I Must not omit to mention a famous pleasant Mount which overlooks the whole Country; and lastly round the Borders of M. is a specious forest, which (as Mr. Chamberlayne says of the Forests of England) "seems to have been preserved for the Pleasure of Variety, and Diversion of Hunting."

Chapter V.   Of the Ancient and Modern Inhabitants, their Manners, Customs, etc.

M. is well known to have been inhabited soon after the Fall, and Adam was the first Adventurer who planted a Colony in this fruitful and delicious Country. After him the Patriarchs were industrious Tillers of the Soil. David and Solomon were often there and many modern kings and princes have honoured this Country with their Royal Presence and Protection. King Charles II in particular, was in close Alliance with it, and it flourished exceedingly in his Days. . . . We have had *Ministers* who preferred its welfare to that of their own Country, and Bishops who would not be displeased to have a small *Bishoprick* in M.

Chapter VI. Of the Product and Commodities such as Fish, Fowls, Beasts, Plants, etc.

Tho' this Country is so plentifully watered, by so fine a River and Canal, it is but indifferently stored with *Fish*, yet when a Stranger comes to it he would imagine by the smell of the Air, that the Country abounded with *Ling* or *Red-Herrings*—so strong is the Smell sometimes, that it is very offensive; but there are no such fish to be seen. *Cod* indeed are often found about the lower end of the great Canal, and *Crabs* in plenty on its banks. I never heard of any other fish in M., except *Mussels*, *Gudgeons* in abundance, some *Dabs*, and a few *Maids;* these last are rarely met with, and it is the Difficulty of catching them, I suppose, makes them much valued by Persons *of nice Taste.* I have indeed heard of a *Mackerel* being found here, by Mr. R. Surgeon of *Plymouth;* but this was purely *accidental*, it being only one single Mackerel, brought to M. by a young woman merely for the sake of *trying an experiment.* However, this scarcity of Fish is the less to be lamented as in this Country a *Flesh Diet* is most delighted in, and with that they are generally pretty well supplied.

For *Fowls*, here are *Cocks*, *Wagtails*, *Buzzards*, *Widgeons*, and *Gulls*, besides *Tom-tits*, which being small insignificant creatures are of no Esteem, and *Capons*, which are likewise held in great Disrepute.

Of *Beasts*, here are plenty of *Asses*, some *Bears*, *Dromedans* and *Mules*, and many sly, old *Foxes.* I have heard likewise of *Baboons*, *Monkeys*, and *Spaniels;* but as it is unnatural to find them here, I believe it is likewise more uncommon than reported.

ARBOR VITAE

The descriptions in *Merryland* and *Bettyland* (the latter refers to Queen Elizabeth, the former to Queen Mary) rely on geographical and topographical terminology to convey the obvious sexual meanings. In the same manner, *Arbor Vitae* uses biological terms:

Arbor Vitae, or the Tree of Life, is a succulent Plant; consisting of one straight Stem, on the Top of which is a *Pistillum*, or *Apex*, at sometimes *Glandiform* and resembling a May-Cherry, tho' at others, more like the *Nut*.

Its *Fruits*, contrary to most others, grow near the Root, they are usually no more than two in Number. . . .

The *Tree* is of slow Growth, and requires Time to bring it to Perfection, rarely seeding for any purpose before the Fifteenth year; when the Fruits coming to good Maturity, yield a viscous juice or balmy Succus, which being from Time to Time discharged at the *Pistillum* is mostly bestowed upon the open *Calykes* of the *Frutex Vulvaria*, or *Flowering Shrub*, usually spreading under the Shade of this Tree, and whose Parts, are by a wonderful Mechanism, adapted to receive it, etc.

This roundabout mode of expression, the flowery, allegorical language and the many puns, can result in a style which does not lack charm and interest. It is, however, a form of sexual repression, which may have more serious and less amusing effects. We have known individuals who by the same mechanism had obsessively sexualized their whole environment and who consequently found sexual symbols and meanings in the most commonplace objects and circumstances. One is reminded in this connection of the joke about the sex-obsessed patient who takes a Rorschach inkblot test. Having looked in silence at the cards which allow for various interpretations, he nudged the attending psychologist, winked an eye, and confidentially inquired, "Say, Doc, where did you get them dirty pictures?"

But there is a serious side to this. Our culture is, to a greater or lesser extent, suffering from a mild form of sex obsession, based on archaic superstitious beliefs from man's primitive prehistory when he endowed sexuality and the organs of generation with magical powers. Early man both feared and venerated these natural forces, an ambivalence which may form the background for all later taboos, prohibitions, and rationalizations concerning sexuality.

In some unfortunate individuals the latent cultural sex neurosis fulminates in acute and bizarre forms, and society is lucky if this kind of madness expresses itself merely in literary or artistic form rather than in overt antisocial action. For us there is no doubt that without such sublimated outlets, psychotic breakdowns and sex crimes would be even more prevalent than they have been. A mere look at the record of those periods of history when the natural sex drives were most suppressed should convince anyone that precisely in those times matters were at their very worst in these respects. Would Gilles de Rais, for example, have been driven to the brutal murder of scores of young boys, whom he first homosexually assaulted, had he been able to accept his sexual desires and had his mind not been twisted by the inculcation of unbearable shame and guilt?

GILLES DE RAIS

An excerpt from J. K. Huysmans's book *La Magie en Poitou: Gilles de Rais* (1899) will illustrate the connection between repression and the return of the repressed in the form of obsession, psychotic breakdown, and violent acting out:

He [Gilles de Rais] flees into the woods like a hunted animal, while his brothers-in-crime are washing the floor and carefully dispose of the corpse and the pieces of clothing. He staggers around aimlessly in the woods, the thick, deep woods, such as they still exist in Bretagne around Carnoët. He sobs as he walks, haunted by ghosts that rise up unexpectedly before him, looks around and suddenly discovers the obscenity of age-old trees. It is as if nature transforms itself before him, as if it was his presence that spoils it; for the first time he understands the unchanging lasciviousness of the woods, discovering obscene images in the towering trees. He sees a tree as a living thing, but reversed, head down, buried in the hair of the roots. The legs of this being stick up in the air, spread themselves, divide once more into so many crotches that become smaller and smaller, the farther they get from the trunk; there, between those legs, a branch is buried in frozen debauchery, and this repeats itself on a smaller and smaller scale to the very top of the tree; over there, that shaft appears to him an erect phallus which disappears in a skirt of leaves, or rather which sticks out of a green bush of hair and which buries itself in the velvety soft belly of the earth.

He sees threatening images. In the smooth, pale bark of the beech trees he recognizes the skin of the boys, this shimmering parchment-like white skin; in the darker wrinkled sheath of the old oaks he sees the elephant skin of the beggars; in the splitting of the branches appear holes and orifices whose oval incisions are surrounded by sullen rims of bark-scar tissue; he sees puckered cracks,

looking like unclean organs of evacuation or like the yawning sex
organs of animals. . . .

Everywhere obscene forms come out of the ground and rise
chaotically to the sky which takes on hellish shapes; clouds swell
into nipples, split into asses, round into fruit-bearing tubes, melt into
pools of semen.

THE EARL OF ROCHESTER

From the period of the Restoration in England (1660–85)
dates another symbolic and allegorical work which in many
ways is unique—the play *Sodom* by the Earl of Rochester.

John Wilmot Rochester was a man of exceptional talent
and fascinating personality. He was born in 1647 in Oxfordshire,
the son of Henry Wilmot, a close friend of the King, who
conferred the earldom on him for his military services. It may be
significant for the son's psychological development that he lost
this strong father figure when he was only eleven years old and
that, like the legendary "Walter," author of *My Secret Life*,
two centuries after him, he was educated during his formative
pre-adolescent years by private tutors, in relative isolation from
the rest of the community and its mores. Later he attended a
grammar school and then Wadham College, Oxford. It was
there that King Charles came to know him, perhaps attracted by
his charm and ready wit.

Although Rochester acquired at an early age the reputation
of a rake, he married when only twenty years old; his personal
correspondence indicates that, in spite of his unorthodox way of
life, he loved his wife and that his marriage was not a failure. He
soon became a favorite at court, though he frequently strained
the King's patience and forbearance with witticisms directed at
various court personalities, not excepting the King's mistress
Nell Gwynne, about whom he is supposed to have penned the
following epitaph:

> She was so exquisite a Whore,
> That in the Belly of her Mother
> Her Cunt was placed so right before,
> Her father fucked them both together.

Even the King himself was not safe from Rochester's satirical pen, as in the poem entitled "On King Charles by the Earl of Rochester, for which he was banish'd from the Court and turn'd Mountebank":

In the Isle of Great Britain long since famous known,
For breeding the best Cully in Christendom;
There reigns, and long may he reign and thrive,
The easiest Prince and best bred Man alive:
Him no ambition moves to seek Renown,
Like the French Fool to wander up and down,
Starving his Subjects, hazarding his Crown.
Nor are his high desires above his strength,
His Scepter and his Prick are of a length,
And she that plays with one may sway the other,
And make him little wiser than his Brother.
I hate all Monarchs and the Thrones they sit on,
From the Hector of France to the Cully of Britain.
Poor Prince, thy Prick, like the Buffoons at Court,
It governs thee, because it makes thee sport;
Tho' Safety, Law, Religion, Life lay on't,
'Twill break through all to its way to C--t.
Restless he rolls about from Whore to Whore,
A merry Monarch, scandalous and poor.
To Carewell the most Dear of all thy Dears,
The sure relief of thy declining years;
Oft he bewails his fortune and her fate,
To love so well, and to be lov'd so late:
For when in her he settles well his Tarse,
Yet his dull graceless Buttocks hang an Arse.
This you'd believe, had I but time to tell you,
The pain it costs to poor laborious Nelly,
While she employs Hands, Fingers, Lips and Thighs,
E'er she can raise the Member she enjoys.

SODOM

From the point of view of sexual fantasies, Rochester's most important work is his play *Sodom*. The play consists of five acts in rhyming couplets, with two prologues, two epilogues, and a short final speech by one of the characters. The cast of characters:

> BOLLOXINION, *King of Sodom.*
> CUNTIGRATIA, *Queen.*
> PRICKET, *Prince.*
> SWIVIA, *Princess.*
> BUGGERANTHOS, *General of the Army.*
> POCKENELLO, *Prince, Colonel and Favorite of the King.*
> BORASTUS, *Buggermaster-general.*
> PINE and TWELY, *Two Pimps of Honour.*
> FUCKADILLA,
> OFFICINA,   } *Maids of Honour.*
> CUNTICULA,
> CLYTORIS,
> FLUX, *Physician to the King.*
> VERTUOSO, *Merkin- and Dildo-maker to the Royal Family.*
>
> *With Boys, Rogues, Pimps and other Attendants.*

The first Prologue informs the audience that they are out of their minds to have come to the play, warns the women in the audience that they will probably depart more frustrated and unsatisfied than they came, and cautions the men to beware of loose wenches from whom they are likely to catch "a damn'd swinging clap." The "lustiest pricks in all the room" are invited to take their pleasure with the actress who best plays her part.

The second Prologue is even more unflattering to women, attacking their alleged inconstancy, fickleness, and deceitfulness. However, it may be that here, as later in the play, Rochester is merely assuming this misogynistic stance as a matter of parody.

Act One is set in a room in the royal palace, decorated with "Aretino's postures." (This refers to the famous set of drawings by Giulio Romano, meant to illustrate Aretino's sonnets and showing various intercourse positions. Of the original set only one or two drawings seem to have survived, while several later sets of similar illustrations have been wrongly attributed to Romano.) Immediately, King Bolloxinion delivers a speech, full of bitter cynicism and lese-majesty sentiment:

> Thus in the zenith of my Lust I reign;
> I eat to swive, and swive to eat again:
> Lett other Monarchs, who their sceptors bear
> To keep their subjects lesse in love than feare,
> Be slaves to Crownes, my Nation shall be free—
> My Pintle only shall my Scepter be.

This speech is applauded by the King's "Pimps of Honour." Soon the debauched potentate decides, however, that he's had enough of women and their wiles, and that henceforth he will tolerate no other kind of sexual relations than homosexuality, especially since the promiscuous conduct of the Queen has rendered her favors noxious to him. He takes two catamites, Pine and Twely, as his lovers, has Borastus proclaim the great news throughout the land, and instructs General Buggeranthos to enforce the edict.

Pockenello then informs His Majesty that one of his two lovers, Pine, has been in bed with the Queen, which he explains is partially the reason why the lady is no longer enjoyable. But Bolloxinion does not take the matter seriously and laughs it off as if it was no more than a witty quip.

Act Two takes place in a garden in which stands a statue of "a woman representing a Fountaine standing on her head and Pissing bolt upright."

The ladies have begun to feel the effect of the new law and bitterly complain about their lack of satisfaction. They try to console themselves with the dildoes that Vertuoso has provided for them, but they succeed only partially.

Act Three concerns the efforts of Princess Swivia to seduce her brother, the completely inexperienced young Prince Pricket. Lyrically she describes to him the seat of her passions in a manner calculated to arouse his own desire and at the same time allay any fears he may have:

> It is the workhouse of the world's chiefe trade;
> On such soft anvills all mankind was made.
> Come, 'tis a harmless thing, draw near and try,
> You will desire no other death to die.

Pricket hesitates, but his sister manages finally to excite him and leads him step by step to have intercourse with her. The Prince still does not really understand the whole process—he is apparently not too bright—but decides that the feeling he experienced was not unpleasant, though he is not yet satisfied. While the couple are preparing for another round, the inebriated maid Cunticula enters. Seeing that the Prince is having an erection problem, she begs permission to bring his tool back to life, but clumsily overdoes her manual ministrations so that the princely seed is spilled without benefit to either lady. This last exertion, however, proves too much for the young man, and the two girls have to carry him off to bed in the hope that sleep may restore his vigor.

In Act Four, the Queen tries hard to arouse General Buggeranthos, but, as his name might lead one to expect, she meets with little success. Meantime, the King enters and gives a speech in praise of sodomy which is heartily appreciated by Pockenello. Women, they say, are all the same: they are incontinent and subject to venereal disease which they pass on to men (a typical homosexual attitude which one hears occasionally expressed even today).

General Buggeranthos enters to report to the King that his prohibition of women is working well with the soldiers. They are now enjoying each other, he says, instead of squandering their money on prostitutes. But with the women things are not so well, the General admits, and he tells the story of a certain lady he has seen on his tour of inspection:

> Dildoes and dogs, with women do prevail
> I caught one frigging with a bob'd Cur's tail
> My Lord, said she, I do it with remorse,
> For I had once a passion for a Horse,
> Who in a moment, griv'd and pleas'd my heart

I saw him standing pensive in a cart;
With padded eyes, and back with sores opprest
And heavy halter hanging on his crest,
I griev'd for the poor beast, and strook his Main,
Pitty'd his daily labour and his pain;
Then on a sudden from his scabbard flew
The stateliest Tarse, that ever mortal drew,
Which clinging to his Belly, stiff did stand.
I took, and graspt it in my loving hand,
And in a passion mov'd it to my cunt,
But he to woman kind not being wont
Drew back his Engine, tho my cunt could spare
Perhaps as much room as his Lady Mare.
At length I found his constancy was such,
That he would none but his dear Mrs touch.
Urg'd by his scorn, I did his right depart,
And so despair surrender'd up my heart.
Now wand'ring o'er this vile cunt starving land
I am content with what comes next by hand.

Bolloxinion is much moved by the speech and promises to provide an elephant for the unfortunate lady.

The scene now changes completely as Twely enters, announcing the arrival of a delegation from Tarsehole, the King of neighboring Gomorrah, together with a letter and retinue of forty beautiful boys. Bolloxinion is delighted, and promises to send the friendly neighbor-King a supply of "modern Virgins" (a highly dubious present, in this context).

The last act begins with a scene between the court ladies and dildo-maker Vertuoso, who is accused of having fashioned the instruments on the measure of his own—in other words, far too small. To clear himself, Vertuoso demonstrates his member, which so impresses the ladies that they throw away their dildoes. But again the maladroitness of one of the women, this time of Fuckadilla herself, makes him ejaculate prematurely.

During an interlude set in a grove of cypress trees, "cut in the shape of Pricks," a little song, "Gentle Venus ease a Tarse," is sung.

In the final scene, the court physician, Flux, warns the King that the homosexual regime has raised untold havoc in the land:

many women have fallen ill, some have even died, and the people are beginning to complain "sorely of their fundament." He reminds the King, who seems to be oblivious to everything, that the Queen is already dead, the Prince has got the clap, and the Princess has gone mad. The only remedy, Flux counsels, is to restore Nature her proper rights: "Fuck women, and lett Bugg'ry be no more."

However, the King refuses to listen. Thereupon the clouds break open, fiery demons appear in the air, and the ghost of Cuntigratia rises and delivers a warning. "Dreadful shrieks and groanes are heard and horrid apparitions seen." Still, Bolloxinion remains adamant and announces that he will retire to a darker cavern, there to expire in the act of sodomizing his beloved Pockenello. The stage instructions are for the curtain to fall "amid fire and brimstone."

THE WHY AND THE WHEREFORE

One of the most curious pieces of erotica we have come across is a quaint little volume *The Why and the Wherefore: Or, the Lady's two questions resolved, . . . taken from the Priapeian Collection of the Chevalier Marino. By Dr. B——. London: printed for J. Lamb, in the Strand, 1765.*

In a preface we are told that a certain Chevalier Marino "lived upon terms of the most unreserved intimacy with a young lady at Turin." However, the pair kept separate houses, though it was the Chevalier's custom to visit his beloved mistress frequently and at almost any hour of the day or night when opportunity arose or the fancy struck him. For that reason, the door to the lady's bed chamber was never locked.

It so happened that one fine summer morning the Chevalier once again came unexpectedly to visit his mistress. He immediately went upstairs and quietly opened the door to the lady's boudoir. What met his sight surprised him: the young woman, completely naked, was straddling a chair upon which she had placed a mirror and was in the act of examining her private parts. Inflamed by the sight, the Chevalier quickly revealed himself and wanted to make love to her immediately. But the lady was sorely vexed for having been thus taken by surprise and in an unflattering position. She therefore addressed him thus:

Chevalier, do not take it ill, but I am not pleased with myself, consequently nor with you either. How could you surprise me so? I am paid however for my curiosity; but I am determined it shall cost you the trouble of giving me the reason of what I have discovered. I had a mind, with my own eyes, to satisfy myself what external charm of figure there is in that part of us, which is so much the center of attraction to your sex. I fairly own that nothing ever appeared to me less sightly, less inviting, less . . .

Despite her remonstrations, the Chevalier insisted he be allowed to make love to her: "See! Nay, more than see! My condition brooks no delay! We will talk more of this in cooler moments."

The lady began to weaken, but before giving in to him completely, she extracted a promise from him:

Ah Chevalier! there is no holding out against you. I catch your warmth; yet give me a moment's respite that I may tell you what is in my head, before you drive that, and everything else out of it, but yourself. Your condition, and indeed my own, forcibly reminds me of another question, I have often had in my thoughts to put to you. My present resistance then is not from waywardness, nor from whim, nor from want of good will, but purely from an excess of curiosity. Allow me therefore to use all the power of the moment over you, to exact from you a promise that you will gratify me in the solution of these two questions:

First, Why Men have not much to boast of their greatness, nor women of their beauty, in certain very interesting parts?

Secondly, Wherefore is it that both sexes are so eternally dear lovers of that same?

The Chevalier was unable to resist her demand and would have promised anything to obtain the satisfaction he sought. This being so, "the fair one no longer held out against his desires and her own."

A few days later, the Chevalier acquitted himself of his

word by sending her the following treatise: "History, Political, Natural and Moral of a Primitive Commonwealth. In answer to The Question of a Lady, Why Men have not much to boast of etc. . . ."

In the introductory remarks, he states his thesis clearly:

The subjects I propose to treat of are the terrible wars, the high exploits, the revenge, the blood and carnage, which pride and ambition caused long before the creation of the world, among those renowned tribes, the Poles (Cocks), the Flats (Cunts), and the Twinballians (Balls).

The Chevalier explained that in the beginning there was a paradisical state of peace between the various members of the human body. They all respected and loved one another, without ever thinking that the one was superior and the other inferior.

This was doubtless the first image of the golden age [continues the Chevalier], but whether vices grew with years, or that, as some pretend, the Devil delights in spreading disturbances to divisions, or that, according to what seems the best opinion, pride, so destructive to everything related to humankind, crept in among them; the several members who constituted their harmonious commonwealth, began by degrees to contend for authority and pre-eminence among themselves, and this baneful ambition became at length the cause of the perishing of numbers among them.

Leaving aside the natural history of the other members about whom, he says, there is nothing unusual to relate, the Chevalier begs his lady friend to consider only the fate of the Poles, Flats, and Twinballians, since it is only through their history that one is able to understand the present state of affairs and arrive at a satisfactory answer to the lady's questions. The Chevalier's history follows:

The Tall-Poles enjoyed incontestably the highest rank of honor among their own tribe; while those who composed it in general were persuaded, according to their constitutional pride, that in all the whole scale of beings, at that time, the Poles were the noblest, because without them no other could be produced. The consequence which they drew from this was that they had a right of dominion over all the other members. . . .

The Flats are naturally soft, and open to persuasion, but are not without their own ends in yielding. They have the art of making others, and even sometimes themselves, believe that they are doing a favor in the very act of their receiving one from those, who give them at least as good as they bring. . . .

The Flats, however, on this occasion, did as they generally do, submit to the strong solicitation of the Poles. They declared themselves content with the subaltern part they would allot them, on condition, however, of being the associates of their pleasures and of their honors.

This treaty being concluded it was easy to bring the Twin-ballians into their measures; who are a good hum-drum sort of people, and naturally formed to depend upon others. These, notwithstanding their round unthinking countenances, were not without a kind of duplicity, prefiguring, perhaps, their double service to the Poles and Flats. . . .

The Poles, seeing their affairs in so good a posture, and their authority so well established, held a grand council, in which, after mutual deliberation, it was resolved to elect one of their own body, on whom they would bestow the title and ensigns of empire, that no formality might be wanting to give a lustre to their authority.

The choice fell upon one of their grandees, called Maypole, chiefly through the cabals and influence of the Flats, whose staunch friend he had ever stiffly stood, and whose servant he was, every inch of him; so that, at once smitten with his colossal figure, and captivated by his high deeds, they had effectually solicited his election. Which being carried, they themselves performed the ceremony of the inauguration of Maypole, by handing their garlands on him, which was the essential investiture of the empire.

The mighty Maypole, being thus, by common consent, raised to the imperial dignity, signalized the beginning of his reign, by giving to the Tall-Poles, or grandees, the title of most high, renowned, and puissant princes: declaring at the same time nobles, all the commoners or Small-Poles. To the Twinballians, he assigned the office of treasurers to the Low-Countries.

But these were not his only gracious acts of sovereignty. To put an end to all doubt of his good intentions and his dear subjects, the Flats, he chose from among them for his empress one named Ingulpha, a monstrous beauty of prodigious parts, whose capacity was, at least, a match for his penetration.

This election being declared, the Small-Poles, who had not been at all consulted in it, looked on this neglect of theirs as a sort of slight put upon them, which they did not deserve, since in point of vigor and activity, some of them did not yield to the proudest of those huge, overgrown grandees. However, the thing being done, they acquiesced in it; without much admiring, and less yet envying the choice. . . .

I am not, however, clear whether the Poles and the Flats ever fairly had the faculty of speech, though their respective mouths, and other parts of their bodies, might authorize such an opinion; nor do I know whether they explained themselves in dumb show, as the mutes do. It is enough to be satisfied that they understood one another perfectly, as indeed to this day they do. As for example: when there is a treaty of union one foot between a Pole and a Flat, the happy couple soon know each other's meaning; the Pole swells, stiffens, and stands up; the Flat glows, tears, shudders amorously, and, in a sensible agitation, trembles to its Pole with a magnetic tendency. In short, it is a terrible taking. . . .

To resume the thread of this most interesting history, I am to observe, that the first days of this beginning empire were celebrated by rejoicings, in which love, union, and felicity supremely reigned. The Poles, great, small, or middle-sized, whom they commonly called the Hunting-Poles, more proud of proving their appetite than their taste, made hearty meals, without distinction of whether the Flats who kept open house for them were ugly or beautiful. Satisfied with their promiscuous fare, they acted just as the fancy took them, without troubling or envying the pleasures of their neighbours. For that cruel jaundice-faced monster jealousy, which under the appearance of love has since diffused its venom and rage over the whole world, was in those happy times an evil unknown.

But, at length, prosperity and power worked that effect upon them, which they now commonly have upon mankind, of rendering the more insolent such as were the more exalted above others.

That mighty potentate Maypole, and the grandees of his court, seeing their authority universally established, began to swell enormously upon it, and to take more state upon them. Giving themselves up to their mutual stiffness and arrogance, they would scarce acknowledge the Small-Poles to be of the same kind as themselves, and grudged them the common benefit of their reception from the Flats, whom they proposed to engross for their own pleasures.

In pursuance of their oppressive plan, their high-mightinesses, the Tall-Poles, prevailed at length to drive the Small-Poles out of the field, after having overwhelmed them with contempt; treating them as giants would do pigmies, that should stand in competition with them. They forbid them, under penalty of being treated as interlopers, all commerce with the Flats in general; as being meat for their masters.

The disastrous Small-Poles, finding themselves in so distressful a situation, were ready to burst with resentment, and yet could obtain no relief. For even the Flats took part with those cruel oppressors: nay, they went so far as to make bitter jests upon them, which redoubled their rage and affliction. The Flats, who had made comparisons and drawn conclusions not to the advantage of the Small-Poles, held them cheap, and would have no dealings with them. They even employed the powerful credit they had with the king and his grandees, to have them forbid the court as unworthy of their standing in their presence.

This greatly indisposed the Small-Poles, especially against the Flats of the greatest distinction, and it is observed to this day, that they are not thoroughly reconciled; as they never cordially agree when they meet.

The Small-Poles then lived a considerable time in this forlorn state; always ready for a revolt, as the bad treatment of them every day increased. Yet durst they not hoist the standards of rebellion; they dreaded the strength of the Tall-Poles and the Flats combined against them.

But while they were waiting for the end of their misfortunes, the friendly Hands would occasionally offer them some relief; but nothing could supply the place of what they had lost.

Those powers, however, who make the punishment of injustice their case, and can never endure ingratitude, soon chastised the Flats for the contempt they had shewn for these unfortunates. The Tall-Poles, whose insolence augmented every day, began to add a spirit of luxury to it, and consequently to make distinctions between a Flat and a Flat. Soon they came to pick out for their use the most beautiful of them, and to load with insults and irony such as had not that quality. In virtue of this new nicety, they then totally renounced these, and reserved all their favors for the choice pieces. The exultation and triumph of the happy favorites, both in their enormous bliss, and in the preference shewn them, redoubled the rage of those who were slighted and deserted.

It was then that they felt, with pain and regret, that hatred which they had given to Small-Poles cause to conceive against them. The base usage these had received for them was so present to the memory of the sufferers, that they would not vouchsafe the disgraced Flats so much as a civil salute; and would rather bear their own wants, than relieve them by affording any charity to such as had been capable of using them so ill.

Then it was that the Flats very seriously reproached themselves, they having been such improvident fools, as to admit of odious and exclusive distinctions among the Poles, since few of them were without their merit, and that after all something was better than nothing. But, in short, the past not being to be recalled, they had recourse to caresses and tears to bring back to them the affronted Small-Poles. Some of the sensiblest, and least ugly of the Flats, employed their whole act upon those who had formerly dealt with them, or were their old acquaintance.

The Poles are naturally disdainful and choleric, but their passion is soon over, and they rarely bear malice. They are sensible as well to pity as to tenderness; when once they are taken in a melting mood, it is easy to bring them to the lure. Besides, nothing on earth can entirely destroy that sympathy which nature has established between the Poles and the Flats. But what had doubtless a great share in determining them to forgiveness, was a desire of revenging their common misfortune. For this was a point upon which the deserted Flats had opened themselves to them explicitly, in a proposal to exterminate the Tall-Poles, against whom they were grown implacable, not only for their having preferred other Flats to them, which was of itself an unpardonable injury; but for their having set up a distinction past all endurance, by giving to them the name of the Ugly-Flats, and to their happy rivals that of the Beautiful-Flats, against whom they also vowed unremissible vengeance. They succeeded then in inspiring some of the Small-Poles with the desire of confederating with them towards the execution of their project. A place of meeting was appointed for consulting more deliberately and effectually the good of their common cause, and especially for promoting their schemes of revenge.

The first care of these reconciled Small-Poles, on returning from their interview, was to acquaint their fellow sufferers with what just happened to them. These received with joy the glad tidings, and looked on the purport of them as an occasion, which fortune seemed to present to them for their deliverance from tyranny, and for the revenge of their wrongs.

But to avoid discovery, they agreed that the leaders only among them should drop in singly and by different ways into the rendezvous which the malecontent Flats had appointed them, for deliberating on the measures that were to be taken.

With a view to strengthen their party, they brought over the Twinballians, who had reason to complain of the Tall-Poles, in whose service they had been unconscionably squeezed and drained.

The deputies of these three tribes repaired with the greatest secrecy to the place of rendezvous at the time appointed. The sad situation in which they saw themselves, their affliction, and even their pathetic silence, might have drawn tears from the most obdurate, or have split the flintiest heart.

At length Ingulpha, the empress of the Flats, whom Maypole had ignominiously driven from his court, on pretence that she was not only oversized even for him, but ugly, insatiate, and insipid, made a mouth as if she would speak; at which the whole assembly trembled, on her looking as if she would swallow them all.

As soon as they were a little recovered, this famous Virago, or according to the chaotic orthography, this Vorago, let her fury burst out in a copious stream of eloquence; while the Small-Poles stood upright to hear her; and the Twinballians, not as yet traitors, hung enraptured upon her lips.

Ingulpha proceeds to recount all the woes, slights, and injuries they, the Small-Poles, Ugly-Flats, and even many of the Twinballians have had to endure from the haughty Tall-Poles and arrogant Beautiful-Flats. She exhorts her audience that only a sudden attack could regain them their former status and freedom.

All might have gone well if the Twinballians, who, the text says, are by nature "something double and slippery," had not betrayed their friends and informed the King of the impending plot. Consequently, when the Small-Poles and Ugly-Flats made their attack, they were thoroughly beaten by the Tall-Poles and would certainly have been utterly destroyed, had a goodly number of them not saved themselves by flight.

But after the heat of the battle, they seemed to have preserved some of their enemies, only that they might treat them with the more indignity.

The Ugly-Flats were especially the worst used, as being deemed the authors and ringleaders of the conspiracy. The Tall-Poles, provoked beyond all regard for the honor of being at once stout and merciful, committed such cruel insults upon them that to this day they bear very sensible marks of them. They began by making a great gash in the phyzz of them, and the wound was so deep and so venomous that it bred a great deal of proud flesh, and could never be closed again; but from time to time breaks out ableeding afresh.

After the passage above, which contains an interesting fantasy as to the origin of menstruation, the story goes on to tell that the Ugly-Flats became uglier, the insolence of the Beautiful-Flats increased, and the neglect and scoffing of the Tall-Poles became more and more intolerable. The scene for a new revolt having been set, it took, as it often does in such matters, only a spark to light the powder keg of resentment and discontent upon which the ruling classes were so confidently sitting.

One day that a Small-Pole was very busy with an Ugly-Flat, in a corner, a Tall-Pole happened to surprise them just on a point of coming to the closest of their dealings. Without more ado, and purely in the wantonness of power, he shouldered away the Small-Pole, but what was worse yet, he did not take his place. So that both parties were mortally offended. The injured Pole vented his rage in tears of disappointed love. The baulked Flat looked as spiteful as the Devil. Both instantly hastened away to their respective friends to acquaint them with the outrage.

All of them made the deplorable case their own, and shuddered with indignation. The alarm was instantaneous. With one voice and one spirit, they proclaimed aloud, "Liberty! Liberty! Let the tyrants die." All the Small-Poles, erecting their crests, stood to their arms with a fierceness that seemed to add some inches to their height. The Ugly-Flats joined forces with them; some boiling with rage, others foaming at the mouth with madness. Their fury gave them first strength. All animated with ardor alike, they separated, and formed different bands, which on every side fell upon the tyrants with amazing impetuosity and vigor, and without giving or taking any quarter.

The King Maypole, surprised at the noise of the combatants, was soon informed of this insurrection; but his presence of mind did not desert him. He assembled all those of his court who were near his person, and led them on towards where the battle raged the hottest; flattering himself that the revolt would have no sinister consequences, and that merely his own majestic preference, seconded by his trusty Tall-Poles, would be sufficient to reduce the rebels to their duty. He marched them fiercely and in good order. The combat was terrible and bloody. The forces of the gigantic Tall-Poles were doubtless the most formidable, in their personal appearance; but those of the Small-Poles surpassed them by much in number and fury. Those were defending their empire and life; these fought for liberty and revenge, and meant nothing less than to conquer or to die in the attempt, so that victory for a while hovered in suspense. The great actions done on each side exceed the power of a mortal's pen to do justice to them.

Be it then enough to know that the revolters, after a combat warmly disputed, began to flag and give way; but fortune, who often delights in giving victory to the weakest, became all of a sudden favorable to them.

The tremendous Maypole was at the head of his trusty train of followers, performing miracles of valor: when, lo! his career of conquest was stopped by the dreadful Ingulpha, who thwarted his way, with a corps-de-reserve, a battalion of the most monstrous Ugly-Flats that could be picked out for the purpose. That imperial spitfire herself, with all her bleeding wrongs about her, faces him, fierce as ten furies in her grizzly form, setting up her bristles, opening wide her voracious maw, and grinning defiance at him. At her appearance, all the courage of the mighty Maypole failed him. He could not stand the aspect of this Queen of terrors; but all a-ghast, crest-fallen, he felt every nerve relax, every sinew wither, and for the first time in his life flinched from a Flat. The like dismay seized his faithful peers, on Ingulpha's band of hob-goblins, coming open-mouthed against them, and presenting their hideously formidable front; they drooped spiritless, and robbed of their wonted vigor, declined the shocking encounter.

Of these moments of dejection and faintness, their enemies took the advantage; and returning to the attack with redoubled rage and fury, left them no time to rally their spirits. Revenge! Revenge! was the word. Each fought it for his particular injury or affront. The carnage made rivers of blood to flow. The conquerors set no bounds to their barbarity. Weakness and fear are often the harbingers of cruelty. They were then absolutely bent on exterminating all their tyrants, and while the Small-Poles were employed in mercilessly destroying all the grandees, the Ugly-Flats with greater joy yet, and not less policy, were tearing their rivals to pieces; being determined to make sure work of them, in the not unreasonable apprehension that, in colder blood, the Small-Poles might, in defiance of their oath of a general extermination, be inclined, for their own sakes, to spare them. A lenity in which the Ugly-Flats would hardly have found their account. Of this then they took good care.

Nothing, in short, could escape the rage of the revolters: the massacre was complete; and to the great misfortune of the women, the noble race of the Tall-Poles was totally extinguished. Nor have the men reason to remember with more pleasure that cruel day in which the Beautiful-Flats shared their fate.

This battle between the personified sex organs of the superior and inferior types contains a version of the classical Medusa myth. The Medusa myth, which concerns one of the three Gorgons whose hair was changed into snakes, and who turned into stone all who looked on her, was interpreted by Freud as a reference to the terrifying and paralyzing aspect of the female sex organ to the unconscious (of the neurotic personality) as visible proof of a prior castration—the female sex organ being seen as a gaping wound in exactly the place where (for the unconscious) there must once have been a penis.

Another extraordinary fantasy follows immediately upon these matters, in a story within the main story. The Chevalier, it seems, has come upon a specimen of the extinct race of Beautiful-Flats. He found it in an antiquarian shop and "the owner of this superb monument of antiquity," the Chevalier states, "was a man of profound literature." He assured the Chevalier that this was one that had escaped the general massacre above related, and had hidden itself in some cavern or grotto, "where the exhalations of the earth had petrified it, as it has often happened to fruits, wood, and other things. However that may be," the Chevalier adds, not without wry humor, "so much is certain, that it was the image of a Beautiful-Flat, of which no trace now remains in the world, according to the opinion of Aristotle, and of others the most learned and deep studied in these matters."

The Chevalier admits, however, with wise diplomacy, that "there are still very pretty and agreeable Flats to be found."

The book ends with another story which concerns the question of why Jupiter in all his wisdom and fairness should have bestowed more impressive male sex organs on some animals and given them greater power of endurance than he has granted man. It was therefore decided that Jupiter should be approached in the matter:

One of the women, who valued herself upon eloquence, said in very chosen and fine words, that the solidest arguments ought to be employed towards convincing Jupiter of the justice of their demand; for example, "I would say," continued she, "that man being the king of animals, that member which produces such a lordly creature ought to excel that of any of the brutes, as much as man excels them in other qualities."

There was more discussion, after which we read:

All these reasons appeared excellent, but while the assembly was weighing and discussing them, a woman whose judgment was remarkable for solidity spoke as follows: "I fancy," said she, "that it will be necessary too to insist upon another very important point. It should be asked, that the object of our desires should not only be of the standard for length and breadth on which we are agreed, but that its virtue, or power of action, should continue as long as the woman herself should wish it."

This proposal was also generally approved. In short, when they had added several other articles, some unreasonable, some impertinent to the subject, they pitched on some of their best heads to form the instructions to their intended deputies. Nor was it without much noise, clamor, and heart-burnings, that they at length accomplished the fixing of the choice of three of the beautifullest to be deputed to Jupiter, who was then in Crete, the place of his birth.

Jupiter listened to the three earth maidens who came to him with the petition of their community and showed himself very gracious to them. However, there was only so much he could do:

"The whole world is witness, ladies, of the attachment with which I love your sex, and knows what pleasure I take in serving it," he told them. "But I cannot repeal the laws of fate, whose decree it is, in order to diminish the pride of the men that their life should be checkered with good and evil, and that to make some difference between the gods and mere mortals, the pleasures you procure them should be embittered with some imperfection. But granting, as the truth is, that in the pleasures of love the males of all other kinds have more vigor and advantages than the men, the women ought not to complain of it. They ought, on the contrary, to be thankful on thinking what fate has done in their favor. Examine all nature, and you will find that the other females have comparatively few enjoyments in the course of the year only at stated periods or seasons. It is true that to make some amends for this stint, the males regale them then with superior vigor. But at the same time it was doomed that the women might at every moment enjoy the pleasures of love. You must then be sensible, that if to this happy facility were joined such a proportion and power in the men as should depend on your own will, you would no longer but with contempt look on all our glory, and the pleasure of the seven heavens. But even should I, to oblige you, set at naught the decrees of fate, which you know however not to be in my power, all the brute creation would be on my back, and petition me for the faculty of enjoying as readily and as repeatedly as the gift of it is granted to you. But though I can revoke nothing in the laws enacted by the council of the gods, to which the name and sanction of fate are given, I can, however, as sovereign of the gods, change some of the articles, especially where the alterations are not directly opposed to the general order of things. I could, for example, easily subject you to the laws imposed on animals who know no desires but once or twice a year; and who to make love must wait the permission of the season for it. But I consider that a ten months privation would appear unconscionably long to you. In short, to prove to you how much I love the pleasure of the fair sex, and the desire I have to oblige such pretty embassadresses, I will reduce to three months the duration of the intervals of enjoyment, and ordain, that every time before the sun enters the equinoctial line, and before the solstices, that is to say four times a year, three whole days shall be consecrated to the sports of Venus, but the rest of the time must be spent in perfect continency. If the women accept of this my proposal, the objects of your desire in the men shall not only be in point of size double the proportion of that of other animals, but shall surpass them in nervousness. This is all I can do for you; but not to give you the trouble," continued he, "of returning to bring me their answer, and to spare you the fatigues of the voyage, tell those who sent you, that the very next equinox shall be the time of commencement for this my grant. If I see that during such an interval the women from the age of twelve to fifty shall have faithfully executed the prescribed continency, and if they keep to these conditions without any impatience for breaking them, I shall take it for granted that my proposal is agreeable to them, and I swear by the river Styx that I will make good my word to them."

Having delivered himself of this mighty speech, Jupiter, always playing the role of the most gracious host, "and to do things in the completest genteelest manner, took their Excellencies aside, and from maids that they were, made them, one after another, women for the rest of their lives. Caressed then and treated to their hearts' content, eased of their maidenheads, and loaded with presents . . . they took leave of Jupiter, and returned with all expedition, and without any mischance, to their own country."

We need hardly add that Jupiter's conditions for an improvement in human sex powers were totally unacceptable to men and women alike.

2

The Folklore of Sex

POGGIO

Poggio Bracciolini was born near Florence in 1380. At the age of twenty-four, he was invested by Pope Boniface IX with the office of Apostolic Secretary. He had always had a reputation for profligacy, and this reputation grew worse with age. He went so far in flaunting public morality that having lived half a lifetime with a mistress by whom he produced fourteen children, he did not hesitate to marry, at the age of fifty-five, a girl of eighteen, by whom he had six additional children.

It was therefore with an eye to his own justification that he wrote the dialogue "Should an Old Man Take a Wife?" (There is a fine old Liseux edition of this work in French, prepared by Alcide Bonneau; Paris, 1877.) He also wrote a number of bawdy folk tales, some made up by himself, others overheard in the market place or the wine cellars, which he visited regularly. These tales reflect admirably the spirit of the times, and often contain remarkable sexual fantasies.

A Frenetic Woman

A Townswoman of mine, who was thought lunatic, was being taken, by her husband and friends, to a soothsayer whose assistance or treatment was expected to effect her cure. In order to wade the Arno, they put her astride of the strongest man's shoulders, when she immediately began to wriggle her buttocks, *similis coeunti*, shouting at the top of her voice, and repeatedly: "I want to be fucked!" She thus disclosed the source of her affliction. Her bearer was taken with such a fit of laughter, that he fell with her into the water. All the rest burst out laughing when they heard what was the remedy for that kind of insanity, and declared that incantations would do no good; something else was required to cure the patient. And, turning to the husband: "You will be the best doctor for your wife," said they. Thereupon, they all retraced their steps, and, as soon as the husband had performed his conjugal duty, the woman recovered her sanity. Such is the best salve for the mental sores of women.

This story is typical of the widespread belief, no less current today, that the cure-all of mental illness is to be found in remedying disturbances of the sexual drive. It lay behind the medieval belief in incubi and succubi, the evil spirits who came to plague sexually frustrated men and women in their sleep, seducing and polluting them. Ernest Jones, the Freud scholar and psychoanalyst, has devoted a fascinating study to this phenomenon, *Nightmare, Witches, and Devils*.

Freud, too, is often said to have "seen sex in everything" and to have wanted to trace back neurotic disorders, such as hysteria, to sexual repression. The same has been alleged for other clinicians who have concerned themselves with the nature of sexual psychology, including ourselves. The truth is that all these assertions are gross oversimplifications. Freud and some of his successors, notably Wilhelm Reich and Theodor Reik, have stressed the importance of the sexual drive in mental hygiene, and the same may be said of us. But neither they nor we have ever attempted to reduce so complex a phenomenon as mental disorder to the simplistic formula expressed in Poggio's tale.

True, almost all emotional disturbances do have decided sexual aspects, and without attending to them in treatment, there can certainly be no cure. But to trace all emotional disturbances back to sexual trauma or maladjustment would be no more intelligent than the present hue and cry of conservative politicians for "law and order" as the cure-all for modern society's ills.

Nevertheless, there is some truth in the old tradition that links mental disorders to sexual disturbances, and the following are representative of the folk wisdom passed on by Poggio.

Giovanni Andrea
Taken in the Act of Adultery

Giovanni Andrea, the far-famed Bolognese doctor, was taken by his wife in the very act of criminal intercourse with the maidservant. The lady, stupefied at the unwonted scandal, turned to her husband: "Where now, Giovanni," she asked, "where is that precious wisdom?" "Here, in this hole," was the cool reply, "and right comfortable too."

A Young Woman
Balked by an Old Husband

An elderly Florentine had married a young woman, who, instructed by matrons to resist the first onset, and not to surrender to one summons, declined the proffered conference. The husband had prepared for the cruise, and was carrying a press of sail; surprised at the denial, he asked why she would not comply with his wish; the girl having alleged a headache, he disarmed, turned round, and slept till daybreak. The young wife, seeing she was no further pressed, regretted that she had followed the advice given and repelled the advances made her; so she awoke her husband, and told him her head no longer ached: "Very good," he replied, "but now my head is ailing [he was no longer sexually able]," and he left her with her maidenhood. It is therefore but wise to take, when offered, a thing that is acceptable.

Witty Reply of a Lady
Whose Inkstand Was Empty

A highly respectable lady of our acquaintance was asked by a messenger if she had no letter to give him for her husband, who had been abroad for some time as Ambassador of the Republic: "How could I write," said she, "since my husband has taken away the pen, and left the inkstand empty?" A witty and honest reply.

Popular at the time were "dunce" stories about men or women too stupid to act appropriately in a sexual situation. Poggio tells several stories of this kind, of which the following is an example:

An Inexperienced Youth Who
Did Not Make the Acquaintance of His Wife
During Their First Wedding Night

A young Bolognese, a simple-minded ninny, had married a beautiful maiden. The first night, not being in the least up to his business, since he had never before frequented any woman, he did not succeed in consummating the marriage. The next morning, being asked by a friend how matters had fared overnight: "Sadly," he sighed, "for, after repeated endeavours, I could never find in my wife the aperture I was told of." Seeing his silliness: "Hush, for God's sake," said the friend, "speak not a word about it; how unpleasant, and what a shame for you if the thing were known!" The simpleton begged for his advice and assistance: "I'll undertake," said his interlocutor, "to bore that aperture for you, if only you stand me to a first-rate supper; but I shall require eight days to perform the operation, which is a very difficult one." The idiot assented, and, at night, secreted his mate with his wife, himself retiring to another bed. After the interval agreed upon, the road had been so well opened by friendly exertions that no more thorns were to be feared; the husband was sent for. "I have toiled and moiled for your service," said his obliging companion, "but the requisite orifice is at last made." The young woman, now thoroughly initiated, congratulated her husband, praising highly his friend's labor. The fool, overjoyed at his wife's perforation, gave his best thanks to his comrade, and paid for the supper.

Sexual suppression and lack of information in some quarters of the world make situations of this type possible even today.

For example, a young man in India, who worked for a government agency in Bombay, told us recently about a friend of his who came to him after having been married for a couple of weeks and asked seriously for advice on how to perform coitus with his equally ignorant bride.

The joke in this next story of Poggio's, on the theme of incest, reappeared in a much later tale from another part of the world.

A Young Florentine Who Fornicated
with His Stepmother

A young Florentine was sporting amorously with his stepmother, when his father, coming upon them unawares, caught them in the very act. Stupefied at the strange indignity, he began to clamor and to assail with the most violent reproaches his son, who endeavored to stammer out some excuse. The dispute waxed hotter and louder, and attracted a neighbor who, ignorant of what had taken place, but anxious to pacify the quarrel, inquired the cause of it. All kept silence, for fear of bringing down shame on the family; but the would-be mediator pressed for an answer.

"It is my son's fault," at last said the father.

"No, indeed," retorted the youth, "it is he who began; he has done it to my mother a thousand times, and I never said a word; and now, for once that I touch his wife, rather silly of me and indiscreet, I confess, he fills the air with his screams, as if he were a madman." The neighbor laughed at the funny reply, and led away the father, whom he comforted as best he could.

The later version is as follows: A father gives his teen-age son money to obtain his first sexual experience in a brothel. On the way, the boy meets his paternal grandmother, who asks him where he is going. Upon hearing the nature of his enterprise, she suggests he come with her and she will give him the experience he wants, thereby saving the money he would have to spend at the brothel. Since the old lady is still quite attractive, the boy agrees. Upon returning home, the father asks him how he liked his trip to the whorehouse. The son explains that he met the grandmother on the way and that she has taught him his first lesson in physical love without his having to spend a single penny. The father is outraged upon hearing this and bitterly reproaches the son for having sexual relations with his (the father's) mother. Thereupon the son quite naïvely answers that he cannot understand his father's objections, since many times the father has done the same with his (the son's) mother, without the boy ever having complained about it.

In the following tale sex now becomes the remedy *par excellence* for physical as well as mental illness.

A Man Who Had to Do with His Sick Wife,
and Thus Restored Her to Health

"The like happened in Valentia to a countryman of mine," said one of the assistants, in the same strain. "A girl, a mere child, had married a very young notary; she had been but a short time under her husband's roof, when she was taken so grievously ill that everyone began to think she would die. The physicians despaired of her life, and the poor young woman, speechless, her eyes closed, scarcely breathing, looked already like a corpse. The husband was distressed at the prospect of losing a wife he had been so little acquainted with, and whom he, of course, passionately loved; so he resolved to caress her once more before she departed, and having dismissed all bystanders, under pretense of some secret or other, he achieved his design. Immediately, as if new life had been infused into her body, she began to draw her breath, and half-opening her eyes, spoke, and called her husband with a gentle voice. He joyfully inquired what she wanted, and she asked for something to drink; soon after, she was given some food, and was restored to health. A result brought about by the exercise of the matrimonial function, and which tends to show that it is a sovereign remedy for female distempers."

There is a medieval story from France which complements this one of Poggio's in an interesting manner. It is entitled, "Of a Girl Who Was Ill of the Plague and Caused the Death of Three Men Who Lay with Her, and How the Fourth Was Saved and She Also."

The setting of this story is Rome in the year 1450, when that city was ravaged by the plague. Among those who had fallen ill with this dreadful disease was a young girl, beautiful and charming, but still a virgin. When she saw that she was on the brink of death, she went to an old neighbor lady and confided to her that she was sorry to leave this world without ever having tasted of its pleasures. Above all, she wanted to see again a certain suitor who had, for some time, pleaded with her to grant him her favors, but whom, like all others, she had in the past always refused.

The old lady set out, found the young man, and brought him to the house of the sick girl. Without realizing that his beloved was a victim of the plague and taking the high color of her feverish cheeks as the proof of her sensual excitement, he immediately got down to business and gave the girl a good measure of the pleasure for which she was longing.

In fact, the girl asked him to repeat the act so many times that finally the young man's powers gave out. "When she saw that," the story goes, "she was bold enough to say, 'My friend, you have often beseeched me for that which I am asking you now. I know, you have done all that is in you. Nevertheless, I know that I have not all I want, and I am sure that I cannot live unless someone else comes and does to me what you have done, and therefore I beg of you, if you value my life, to go to such a one and bring him hither.' "

The young fellow was astonished at the request, but realizing that he had quite exhausted his own physical resources, he fetched a friend and brought him to the girl.

The girl did to the second lover as she had done to the first and again asked him after the last bout to provide still another lover for her. A third young man was likewise found and he too labored until he could labor no more.

Meanwhile, the first young man had begun to fall ill with symptoms of the plague; he hastened to the priest, made his confession, and died in his arms. His friend, the second lover of the young lady, also fell ill and asked everywhere about his friend who had brought him to her. He finally met the priest who had confessed the first one, told him his story, and confessed himself. Afterward, though only hours from his death, he hurried to the girl and found her with the man whom he himself had fetched for her. He bitterly reproached her for having infected and killed first his friend and then certainly himself, left, and died shortly after.

The third fellow, who had been witness to all this, was wise enough to conduct himself so that he escaped the danger of which his two friends had died.

The girl was soon thereafter brought back to her father's house and put to bed. However, she managed to sneak out to the stable and there seduced the son of another neighbor.

Brought back to bed, "there soon appeared upon her body four buboes, of which she was afterward cured. And I believe," the story ends, "you will find her now amongst the whores at Avignon, Vienne, Valence, or some other place in Dauphiné."

The belief that sexual intercourse may cure a variety of ills, as lack of it may be the cause of them, is prevalent enough to cause one to wonder whether there isn't a grain of truth in it. The fact of the matter is that successful sexual intercourse—that is, any sexual activity leading to orgasm—does have a salutary effect on the organism. There is an increase in blood circulation, a toning up of the whole body, a revitalization of the respiratory system (improved breathing), and finally a general relaxation of muscle as well as nervous tension which is difficult to achieve in any other way, or at least as quickly and thoroughly. One may safely say that the tenacious and universal belief in the efficacy of sexual intercourse for the maintenance of physical and mental health is not altogether without some foundation in actual experience.

RABELAIS

Rabelais was born sometime between 1483 and 1494, the son of a well-to-do French lawyer. He was sent to convent school and seminary, and started a career as an ordained priest. However, it seems he was more interested in the classical languages, Greek and Latin, than in theology. At any rate, he soon gave up his ecclesiastical position for the study of medicine, becoming in time a full-fledged medical practitioner. But soon he tired of that métier and devoted himself fully to his literary interests and travel. He liked to think of his three main interests in life as being drink (or thirst, in the wider sense), travel (or voyaging), and laughter (in the sense of debunking or blasphemy, as it was then called).

The influence of his theological and medical studies is clear in his works. In the field of medicine especially, he was extremely modern for his time. He believed in psychosomatic medicine, holding that for human health a proper balance between the mind and the body was essential. He insisted that to remain healthy a person had to be able to enjoy life, to know happiness, gaiety, merriment, humor, pleasure, mischief, irony, exuberance, beauty. Among many other progressive and unorthodox ideas, he held that in the healing arts, the physician should go with nature, not against it.

He sang the praises of *Cannabis sativa*, or "hemp," as a way to gain mystical and metaphysical experience, which he could not find within the framework of organized religion. His love for marijuana definitely influenced his fantastic sense of humor, penchant for the absurd, and tendency to take nothing seriously, least of all that which society takes most seriously: family, class, nationality, church, state, and—sex! Centuries before Freud he intuitively sensed the absolute necessity for lifting the oppressive burden of guilt, or superego, and of freeing oneself from "the tyranny of logic" which prevents one from understanding on a deeper level.

A true visionary, he foresaw a federation of the world, a "transfer of reverence" from superficial values, such as family, sex, and religion, to a Schweitzerian reverence for life itself. He refused to be intimidated by either the conventional taboos of language, of literature, or of daily life. Thus it was that he quite consciously set out to make light of the very virtues upon which society places such deadly serious emphasis—cleanliness, orderliness, and logic.

Instead, he proclaimed the necessity for liberating laughter about these values, and he ridiculed society's fear of the bodily functions, of dirt, and all that is not clean, logical, and in its proper place.

The following selection is from an old English translation of Rabelais's works, "Printed for Richard Buddeley, within the Middle Temple-Gate" (London, 1653), which we use as our source because it best retains the quaintness of language and some of the inimitable style of the original.

The Cause and Wherefore the Leagues Are So Short in France

How Pantagruel in his journey, seeing that the leagues of that little territory about Paris called France, were very short in regard of those of other Countreys, demanded the cause and reason of it from Panurge, who told him a story which Marotus of the Lac, Mona-chus, set down in the acts of the Kings of Canarre, saying, that in old times Countreys were not distinguished into leagues, miles, furlongs, nor parasanges, until that King Pharamond divided them, which was done in a manner as followeth. The said King chose at Paris a hundred faire, gallant, lustie, briske young men, all resolute and bold adventurers in Cupid duels, together with a hundred comely, pretty, handsome, lovely and well-complexioned wenches of Picardie, all which he caused to be well entertained, and highly fed for the space of eight dayes: then, having called for them, he delivered to every one of the young men his wench, with store of money to defray their charges, and this injunction besides to go unto divers places here and there, and wheresoever they should biscot and thrum their wenches, that they setting a stone there, it should be accounted a league; thus went away those brave fellows and sprightly blades most merrily and because they were fresh, and had been at rest, they very often jum'd and fanfreluched almost at every fields end, and this is the cause why the leagues about Paris are so short; but when they had gone a great way, and were now as weary as poor devils, all the oile in their lamps being almost spent, they did not chink and dufle so often, but contented themselves, (I mean for the men's part,) with one scurvie paultry bout in a day, and this is that which makes the leagues in Britany, Delanes, Ger-many, and other more remote Countreys so long: other men give other reasons for it, but this seems to me of all other the best.

Rabelais deals ironically with the taboo on excrement and the bodily functions, to hide which civilized man takes such extraordinary and, no doubt, exaggerated pains.

How Gargantua's Wonderful Understanding Became
Known to His Father Grangousier, by the Invention
of a Torchecul or Wipebreech

About the end of the fifth yeare, Grangousier returning from the
conquest of the Canarians, went by the way to see his sonne
Gargantua. There was he filled with joy, as such a father might be
at the sight of such a childe of his: and whilest he kist him and
embrac'd him, he asked many childish questions of him about divers
matters, and drank very freely with him, and with his governesses,
of whom in great earnest, he asked amongst other things, whether
they had been careful to keep him clean and sweet? To this
Gargantua answered, that he had taken such a course for that himself, that in all the countrey there was not to be found a cleanlier
boy than he. How is that (said Grangousier)? I have (answered
Gargantua), by a long and curious experience, found out a means to
wipe my bum, the most lordly, the most excellent, and the most
convenient that ever was seen. What is that (said Grangousier)
how is it? I will tell you by and by (said Gargantua). Once I did
wipe me with a gentlewomans velvet-mask, and found it to be good;
for the softnesse of the silk was very voluptuous and pleasant to my
fundament. Another time with one of their Hoods, and in like
manner that was comfortable. At another time with a Ladies Neck-
kechief, and after that I wiped me with some ear-pieces of hers
made of Crimson sattin, but there was such a number of golden
spangles in them (turdie round things, a pox take them) that they
fetched away all the skin of my taile with a vengeance. Now I wish
St Anthonies fire burn the bum-gut of the Goldsmith that made
them, and of her that wore them: This hurt I cured by wiping my
self with a Pages Cap, garnished with a feather after the Suitsers
fashion.

    Afterwards, in dunging behinde a bush, I found a March-Cat,
and with it wiped my breech, but her clawes were so sharp that
they scratched and exculcerated all my perinee; Of this I recovered
the next morning thereafter, by wiping my self with my mothers
gloves, of a most excellent perfume and sent of the Arabian Benin.
After that I wiped me with sage, with fennil, with anet, with
marjoram, with roses, with gourd-leaves, with beets, with colewort,
with leaves of the vine-tree, with mallowes, wool-blade, (which is a
tail-scarlet), with latice and with spinage leaves. All this did very
great good to my leg. Then with Mercurie, with pursley, with
nettles, with comfrey, but that gave me the bloody flux of Lum-
bardie, which I healed by wiping me with my braguette; Then I
wiped my taile in the sheets, in the coverlet, in the curtains, with a

cushion, with Arras hangings, with a green carpet, with a table cloth, with a napkin, with a handkerchief, with a combing cloth, in all which I found more pleasure than do the mangy dogs when you rub them. Yea, but (said Grangousier), which torchecul didst thou finde to be the best? I was coming to it (said Gargantua) and by and by shall you hear the *tu autem*, and know the whole mysterie and knot of the matter: I wiped my self with hay, with straw, with thatch-rushes, with flax, with wooll, with paper, but,

> Who his foule taile with paper wipes,
> Shall at his ballocks leave some chips.

What (said Grangousier), my little rogue, hast thou been at the pot, that thou dost rime already? Yes, yes, my lord the king (answered Gargantua), I can rime gallantly, and rime till I become hoarse with Rheum. Heark what our Privy says to the Skyters:

> Shittard
> Squitard
> Crackard
>   Turdous:
> Thy bung
> Hath flung
> Some dung
>   On us!
> Filthard
> Cackard
> Stinkard,
>   St Anthonie's fire seize on thy toane,
> If thy
> Dirty
> Dounby
>   Thou do not wipe ere thou be gone.

Will you have any more of it? Yes, yes (answered Grangousier). Then said Gargantua,

A ROUNDLAY
> In shiting yesterday I did know
> The sesse I to my arse did owe:
> The smell was such came from that slunk,
> That I was with it all bestunk:

O had but then some brave Signor
Brought her to me I waited for, in shiting!
I would have cleft her watergap,
And join'd it close to my flipflap,
Whilst she had with her fingers guarded
My foule Nockandrow, all bemerded in shiting.

Now say that I can do nothing, by the Merdi, they are not of
my making, but I heard them of this good old grandam, that you see
here, and ever since have retained them in the budget of my
memory.

Let us return to our purpose, (said Grangousier). What (said
Gargantua) to skite? No, (said Grangousier), but to wipe our taile;
But, (said Gargantua), will not you be content to pay a puncheon of
Britton-wine, if I do not blank and gravel you in this matter, and
put you to a nonplus? Yes, truly (said Grangousier).

There is no need of wiping ones taile (said Gargantua), but
when it is foule; foule it cannot be unless one have been a skiting;
skite then we must before we wipe our tailes. O my pretty little
waggish boy (said Grangousier), what an excellent wit thou hast. I
will make thee very shortly proceed Doctor in the jovial quirks of
gay learning, and that, by G——, for thou hast more wit than age;
now I prethie go on in this torcheculatife, or wipe-bummatory
discourse, and by my beard I swear, for one puncheon thou shalt
have threescore pipes, I mean of the good Breton wine, not that
which grows in Britain, but in the good country of Verron. Afterwards I wiped my bum (said Gargantua), with a kerchief, with a
pillow, with a pantoufle, with a pouch, with a pannier, but that was
a wicked and unpleasant torchecul; then with a hat, of hats, note
that some are shorne, and others shaggie, some velveted, others
covered with taffities, and others with sattin, the best of all these is
the shaggie hat, for it makes a very neat abstersion of the fecal
matter.

Afterwards I wiped my tail with a hen, with a cock, with a
pullet, with a calves skin, with a hare, with a pigeon, with a
cormorant, with an Atturneyes bag, with a montero, with a coife,
with a faulconers lure; but, to conclude, I say and maintain, that of
all torcheculs, arsewisps, bumfodders, tail-napkins, bunghole cleans-
ers and wipe-breeches, there is none in the world comparable to the
neck of a goose, that is well douned, if you hold her head betwixt
your legs; and believe me therein upon mine honour, for you will
thereby feele in your nockhole a most wonderful pleasure, both in

regard of the softnesse of the said doune, and of the temperate heat
of the goose, which is easily communicated to the bumbut, and the
rest of the inwards, insofarre as to come even to the regions of the
heart and braines; And think not, that the felicity of the heroes and
demigods in the Elysian fields, consisteth either in their Asphodele,
Ambrosia, or Nectar, as our old women here used to say; but in this,
(according to my judgment) that they wipe their tails with the
neck of a goose, holding her head betwixt their legs, and such is the
opinion of Master John of Scotland, alias Scotus.

In the same vein, he ridicules not only the primitivistic
approach to the legends of Creation, but also the social taboo on
flatulence, against which Western society had developed such
hysterical aversion reactions, as against all body odors.

How Pantagruel Likewise with
His Farts Begat Little Men,
And with His Fisgs Little Women

. . . unto which answered Panurge, There is no shadow like that of
courtaines, no smoke like that of women's breasts, and no clattering
like that of ballocks: then forthwith rising up he gave a fart, a leap,
and a whistle, and most joyfully cried out aloud, Ever live Pantagruel: when Pantagruel saw that, he would have done as much; but
with the fart that he let, the earth trembled nine leagues about,
wherewith and with the corrupted aire, he begot above three and
fifty thousand little men, ill favoured dwarfes, and with one fisg that
he let, he made as many little women, crouching down, as you shall
see in divers places, which never grow but like Cowes tailes downwards, or like the Limosin radishes, round. How now (said Panurge), are your farts so fertile and fruitful? by G—— here be
brave farted men, and fisgued women, let them be married together,
they will beget fine hornets and dorflies; so did Pantagruel, and
called them Pygmies.

THE "DIVINE" ARETINO

We have already referred to Pietro Aretino in the discussion of Chorier's *Dialogues of Luisa Sigea*. At heart Aretino was
a moralist, though his personal life followed a more or less
debauched pattern. Yet we owe to him some fascinating discus-

sions on various questions of sex morality. These form the main body of his *Ragionamenti*, or *Dialogues*, on the lives of nuns, married women, and whores, in which the married women fare by far the worst. Through these discussions of moral problems Aretino challenged the society of his day, but for our purposes here, the selections below stress the sex fantasies he developed.

DIALOGUE ON THE LIFE OF MARRIED WOMEN

I chanced to go to my country seat [said Nanna], where I used to frequent a great lady, I say great, let it suffice, who was causing her husband's despair by always wanting to stay at the village . . .

Her idea tended to a certain priest, . . . he had as large a revenue as the sprinkler with which he used to spatter the holy water, in the noble lady's garden. . . .

Her ladyship, being in the country, saw him one day pissing under her window, quite unconcerned; . . . Seeing in him something long like the shaft of a white cod, the coral head of which was cleft by an artistic hand, with a lovely bar running along its back: a codpiece which was neither stiff nor hanging, but bent into a bow, and surrounded by a crown of crispied hair, as bright as gold, between two neatly finished, plumpy, living jingly-bobs far nicer than those silver ones which adorn the legs of the Aquilon, at the Ambassador's fate . . .

While keeping her hands upon the ground, she fell into such madness, owing to the longing she had for the squire's codpiece, that she swooned, and was carried off to bed. . . .

He heard his wife calling for the priest. "I wish to make my confession," said she; "and if it's the will of God that I should die, I am clearly obliged to come to a resolution over it. But it grieves me sorely to part with thee, my darling husband!"

Then she heaved a mighty scream, as if she was just going to give up the ghost, and again called for the priest whom a valet ran for at once. . . .

"The Lord restore you to health," said the priest on drawing near. She, with her eyes rivetted on the codpiece which was hanging below the edge of the short serge frock the priest wore round his hips, fell into a swoon for a second time. . . . The husband, a thorough jackass, made everyone clear out of the room and pulled the door after him, that nobody might hear the confession. . . .

The priest seated himself down quite comfortably at the foot of the bed . . . he was about to ask her how long it was since her last confession, when she, sticking her claws in his rope that had become stiff in a trice, applied him to her stomach. . . .

And what dost thou say of the parson who, with two slight digs, cured her of her numbness? . . .

The confession being ended, the priest went back and sat down. He was laying his hand upon the patient's head when the husband came. . . . He found her mien altogether brightened and cried: "Indeed, there's no better doctor than God Almighty!" . . .

Boor, that's quite true. Yet she fell madly in love with him, so she did, that pretty darling; but to confess the truth, we are all women to choose what is worst. Devising how she could speak to him, she entered one fine night upon a long-winded story with her spouse. "We are rich, thank God," she said to him, "without children and without hope of having any. This is what caused me to think of a charitable deed."

"And what have you been thinking of, my darling wife?" inquired the too kind husband.

"Of your sister," she replied, "burdened as she is with boys and little girls, I wish to bring up her youngest."

The husband agrees, fetches the child, and then hires the young priest as tutor.

Supper was over, the table cleared, and the household sent to bed, the husband's nephew included. "Dear little sister," she says to me, "as our husbands readily relish the whole year round the nice bits they meet with, why should we not taste tonight that good bit of the tutor's? If I may judge from his nose, he must have one like an Emperor. Nobody will be ever the wiser of it; he is besides, so ugly and so dirty that no one would believe him, though he were to brag about it." . . .

"That's a very dangerous thing," I said to her; "should your husband return, what would become of us?"

"Fool!" she answered, "what are you thinking of? Do you fancy I am so dull that, if my crackbrain did chance to walk in, I should not discover the means of making him swallow everything?" . . .

Having overheard everything and, with that presumption proper to pedagogues, lifting the door curtain, he marched in without further invitation. . . . The moment she beheld him, the lady shouted: "Master, keep the bridle on your mouth, your hands at rest, and for this night, use only your holy-water sprinkler."

The dunce, whose nose was not framed for scenting out the pistil of roses, nor his fingers for stopping the holes of a flute, cared very little about kissing or handling. He unsheathed his fuming-headed, all fiery, wart-bespangled stool-leg, and filliping it, cried: "It's wholly at your Ladyship's service."

She took it on the palm of her hand, saying, "My cosy ducky, my pigeon, my chaf-finch, enter into your aviary, your palace, your estates!" And introducing it under her belly, being propped against the wall, she lifted one leg up and wanted to eat the sausage standing. The rogue gave her a lusty shaking. During the while, I looked like a monkey that is chewing the sweet bit before it has it in its mouth; if I had not satisfied myself somewhat with an iron pestle which I found on a box and which had served, as I perceived by its smell, for pounding cinnamon, indeed I would have died with impatience at the pleasure of the others. The horse's head finished its work; the woman, being tired though not satiated, sat down upon the side of the couch and, seizing again the dog by the tail, turned him round and round so that he went back over the road; as she did not much like looking at the master's face, she gave him her back, and taking hold of the *Salvum me fac*, madly plunged it into her zero; she plucked it out of it and put it into the square, then again into the round, and thus finished the second assault, saying to me: "There is still enough left for you."

I, who was on the point of fainting, as a poor devil that is starving and cannot eat, was preparing to put my finger at a certain place on the old fox, to revive his sentiment (it's a little secret I had learned), when all on a sudden we hear a knocking at the door. At the second volley, she recognized her husband and burst into louder and louder fits of laughter, so that her husband should hear her. When she was quite sure that she had made herself heard, she asked, "Who is there?"

"It's I," replied he.

"Oh my husband, I am coming down; wait a moment. Let nobody go away," she added, and ran to open the door. The door opened, she cried, "A ghost said to me, 'Don't go to bed. Thy husband will certainly not sleep out tonight.' And for fear of giving way to sleep, I have got our neighbor to stop with me; the poor thing has quite overwhelmed me by relating her life in the convent; had I not called down our tutor, a regular sleepyhead, who completely cheered me up with his nonsense, it would have been a bad time for me."

She led upstairs the *Credo In Deum* who, without asking any further, began to laugh on seeing the pedagogue: being quite put out of himself by this sudden arrival, he resembled an interrupted dream. The husband, as soon as he had perceived me, fostered in himself the idea of entering into possession of my little domain. In order to have the opportunity of familiarizing himself with me, he took the tutor in hand and, pretending he was greatly pleased with his conversation, made him recite the ABC's backwards. The queer fellow, in reciting it the wrong way, made him laugh so loud that the other rolled over. Meanwhile, I had clearly perceived the wife's sheep's eyes and the signs she was making me by walking on my foot.

"Since your servant-maids are gone to bed," said I, "I am going to lie down with them."

"No, no," rejoined the husband, and turning to his wife, he said, "bring her into the bedroom. She shall sleep there."

As soon as said it was done. I was scarcely in bed when I heard him say to his wife in a very loud voice that I might have no suspicion: "My darling love, I must at once return to where I come from; send the sleepyhead to bed and go there likewise." He went downstairs with great bustle, opened the door, shut it again while remaining inside, as if he had gone out, then stealing up again very softly, entered the chamber I was sleeping in without sleeping, and came secretly to lie beside me. On feeling the hand laid upon my breast, I got into that delirium which one experiences sometimes, when one sleeps with the head downwards, and when it seems to you that something heavy, exceedingly heavy, weighs upon your heart, leaving you free neither to speak nor stir. . . .

He said to me: "If you do not utter a word, it will be a good thing for you." While speaking to me thus, he stroked my cheeks tenderly with his hand.

"Who's there?" said I.

"I am who I am," replied the invisible spirit. As he was endeavoring to part my thighs, which I kept squeezed tighter than a miser keeps his hands squeezed, thinking I was saying very low: "Madam, madam." I said it loud enough that she might hear me. The husband, who was engaged with me, jumped out of bed and ran to the hall at the same time as his wife was arriving with a candle in her fist to see what ailed me. He, on going into the room which she had just left, beheld that sot of a pedadogue lying on the bed, rubbing his vine-branch, until he should use it to make the lark sing; and just as the good setter of horns was saying to me: "What is the matter with you?" a holler, more like a donkey's braying than a human voice, interrupted the reply in my mouth. The husband was beating the tutor brutally with the fire shovel, and if the wife, having run to his help, had not plucked him out of his reach, he would have cooked his goose for him.

A play on the eternally popular notion of the insatiable female, the story is also a sarcastic commentary on hypocritical husbands, as well as a parody on false monogamy. It reminds us of a ditty in one of the underground magazines of old England, the *Bon Ton Magazine*, July, 1794.

A TRICK

> Nokes went, he thought, to Styles's wife to bed,
> Nor knew his own was laid there in her stead;
> Civilian, is the child he then begot,
> To be allow'd legitimate or not?

The next story from the *Dialogues* is a supplement to "The Life of Whores" and demonstrates how reputation is a potent factor in a person's becoming—through fantasy—a more desirable sex object.

THE BAWD'S TRADE

MIDWIFE: I know not how the Devil contrived to make a noted man's wife, famous for her beauty, elope; she fled, nor did anybody ever find out with whom. While people were talking of nothing else but her flight, I send for the favorite of a grand personage and I make him swear on the holy stone to keep secret what I am going to tell him; he swears he will. I then inform him, while he shook hands with me as a token of faith, that the friend's wife is in my room, but locked up in the dark, and that it would be a great misfortune if he revealed the fact to anybody. As he learns that I have her wholly at my disposal, he hastens to lavish his kind caresses upon me, he styles me mamma, madonna, little sister, mistress; while I say to him: "I should not like it to be known, for besides the poor creature would run the risk of being killed, I would break my neck, shoulder and thigh; I would be lashed, branded and perhaps burnt."

NURSE: The fellow goes and liquefies some servant maid; methinks I see the whole affair.

MIDWIFE: To what other dost thou think he would have to do it?

NURSE: Have I not told thee so?

MIDWIFE: Nurse, after much ado and not without wishing him good luck, I led him groping along in the dark to the arms of the maid as thou hast guessed; he paid her and rode her like a man. So, after having thanked me, he went off for an Ambassador; he exacted from him his word of honor; he gave him an account of the plot: and the Ambassador was obliged to come disguised to handle the servant. He handled and rehandled her ten times over, and not alone he, but a hundred Knights, Officers and Courtiers came to stick it into her: I won by this game nearly all I possess.

NURSE: Tell me: was the swindling detected?

MIDWIFE: Ay, so it was.

NURSE: How?

MIDWIFE: One morning as she chanced to have a tonsured pate on the top of her, the weather being very cold, a chafing-pan of lighted coals, which I had placed in the room, blazed up a little, and Monseignor beheld the damsel's face. Perceiving she was not the right one, he wanted to beat me and he called me most abusive names; he stuck his claws in my eyes twice or three times to pluck them out, nor could he forbear giving me a sound boxing. Had not my tongue come to my assistance, it was all over with me. Afterwards, when news of the trick I had played on so many fellows spread abroad, the husband of the eloped woman was nigh cutting me in pieces: he really fancied that this second story dishonored him more than the first. But whoever escapes once will escape a hundred times; so the swindle was turned into laughter.

ANONYMOUS FOLK TALES

Sexual stories are abundant in the anonymous folk tales of all peoples, from Siberia to the Dauphiné, from the Bretagne to Norway, as well as from the Near East, Asia, and the Pacific Ocean. There is so much of this material that it was necessary to exclude the Oriental and to focus on folk tales of Europe. However, many of these tales, especially the Russian, have undoubtedly come originally from the East.

For our selection we have relied primarily on the vast documentation known as *Kryptadia*, carefully prepared by collectors of folklore from various countries and published in Paris between 1897 and 1905. (This collection is multilingual; all of the stories here were translated by us either from French or German.)

Among the most interesting of these stories are those from

Russia, some of which we took from *Kryptadia*, others from a rare French collection entitled *Contes Secrets Russes* (*Rousskïia zavetnïia skazki*), published clandestinely by the Bibliothèque des Curieux (Paris, 1921).

Below are four extraordinary stories from the last-mentioned source which contain unique sex fantasies and are written in a quasi-surrealistic vein.

A CROP OF COCKS

Two peasants went out to sow rye, each in his own field. An old man happened to pass by that way. He hailed one of the peasants: "Good day to you, mouzhik!"

"Good day to you, little father."

"What are you sowing?"

"Rye, little father."

"Then may God assist you! May your rye grow high and full!"

Next, the old man went over to the other peasant. "Good day to you, mouzhik," said he.

"Good day to you, little father."

"What are you sowing?"

"What business is it of yours? I'm sowing cocks."

"Well, I hope you have a good harvest!" The old man went on his way; the peasants finished sowing, gave the soil a dressing, and went home.

When the spring rains had soaked the ground, the first peasant's rye grew straight and strong; but in the next field there grew only cocks—their red tips covered a whole dessiatine.

There were cocks everywhere—there wasn't even room to walk about! The two peasants came out to see if their rye had risen. The one was very satisfied at the sight of his field, but the other felt his heart sink. "Now what am I going to do with all those devils?" he wondered.

Harvest time came. The two mouzhiks went back to their fields: the one began to mow his rye; the other took one look at his field and saw that the cocks were now an *archine* and a half high. With their red tips waving in the air, they looked just like poppies. After contemplating this spectacle for a long moment, the peasant started home. When he reached his house, the first thing he did was to get a knife and sharpen it; he also fetched some string and paper and then went back to his field. Once there, he began to lop off all the cocks, wrapping them two by two in sheets of paper; he tied a string around each package and put them in his cart in order to take them to town and sell them. "Yes," he said to himself, "I'm going to put them up for sale; maybe there will be some fool who'll buy a pair."

As he drove his cart through the streets of the town, he shouted at the top of his lungs: "Who wants some cocks, cocks, cocks? I have lovely cocks for sale, lovely cocks, lovely cocks!" A lady heard him shouting his wares and said to her chambermaid: "Go quickly and ask that mouzhik what he is selling."

The girl rushed out into the street: "Listen, mouzhik, what are you selling?"

"Cocks, my girl!"

When she got back to the house, the chambermaid didn't dare repeat this to her mistress.

"Speak up, you idiot," her mistress commanded, "there's nothing to be ashamed of! Out with it, what is he selling?"

"Well, mistress, the fellow is selling cocks!"

"Silly girl! Hurry after him and ask him how much he wants for a pair."

The chambermaid called the peasant back: "How much does a pair cost?" she asked him.

"One hundred rubles, and it's cheap at the price."

As soon as the servant had brought this answer back to her mistress, the lady gave her a hundred rubles. "Here," she said, "go and pick out two fine ones, I want them long and fat."

The girl took the money to the peasant. "Please, mouzhik," she said, "give me the best you have."

"They are all very fine," he answered.

The chambermaid chose a pair of well-proportioned cocks and took them back to her mistress. The lady examined them, and as they were very much to her taste, she made haste to put them in the right place, but alas they wouldn't go in.

"Didn't the mouzhik tell you what to say to them to make them work?" she asked her chambermaid.

"He didn't say a word about that, mistress."

"How stupid you are! Go ask him right away."

The girl went back to the peasant. "Listen, mouzhik, tell me what to say to your wares to make them work."

"If you give me a hundred more rubles I'll tell you," answered the mouzhik. The chambermaid immediately informed her mistress of this new demand: "He won't tell for nothing, he wants another hundred rubles."

"Well, take them to him; two hundred rubles is a fair price for such fine instruments as these!"

When the peasant had pocketed the money, he told the servant: "When your mistress wants to use them, all she has to say is 'Giddiap!' "

As soon as this information was passed on to the lady, she lay down on her bed, lifted up her dress and gave the order: "Giddiap!" The two cocks immediately fulfilled their function; however, when the lady tried to remove them, she could not. The situation was becoming critical; the lady was so upset that once again she sent her chambermaid out into the street: "Run after that son of a dog and ask him what to say to them to make them come out again."

The servant rushed out, caught up with the mouzhik and delivered her message: "Mouzhik, tell me what to say to the cocks to make them come out of my mistress's body, for they are tormenting her greatly at this very moment."

And the peasant answered, "If she will give me another hundred rubles, I will tell her."

The girl rushed back to the house. The lady was lying on her bed, more dead than alive. "Take the last hundred rubles in the drawer," she commanded, "and give them to that rascal immediately, for I am at death's door!"

When the peasant had received his third payment of a hundred rubles, he consented to reveal the precious word: "All she has to say is 'Whoa!' They will come out immediately."

The chambermaid ran all the way home; when she got there, her mistress was unconscious and her tongue was hanging out. Thus it was she who shouted "Whoa!"

The two cocks came out. The lady was cured, she got up, took the cocks and put them away in a safe place. From then on, life became very pleasant for her: whenever she felt like it, she got herself fucked by the two cocks, and all she had to say was "Whoa" to make them come out of her.

One day, the lady went to visit some friends in the country and forgot to take her cocks with her. When evening came, she missed them sorely and was preparing to return home. Her hosts insisted on her staying the night. "That is absolutely impossible," she said, "I left a certain object at home and I could not possibly sleep without it."

"Well, if you like," answered her hosts, "we can send a reliable man to get it and bring it to you safely." Their visitor agreed to this. Immediately, a lackey was ordered to saddle a fast horse and fetch the object from the lady's house. "Just ask my chambermaid," she added, "she knows where it is."

When the lackey reached the lady's house, the chambermaid gave him the two cocks wrapped up in a piece of paper. He put them in his hip pocket and mounted his horse again to return to his master's house. On the way, he had to ride up a hill, and as the horse was not going fast enough, the lackey shouted "Giddiap!" Immediately, the cocks leaped out of the piece of paper and into the lackey's asshole. He was terribly frightened. "What are those monsters? Where did the accursed things come from?" he asked himself; he was on the verge of tears and did not know what was to become of him. However, going down the other side of the hill, the horse began to gallop so fast that the lackey had to shout: "Whoa!" Without further ado, the cocks evacuated the position they were occupying. The servant took them, wrapped them up in the piece of paper and, when he got back to the house, gave them to the lady.

"Well!" she asked, "have you brought them to me in good condition?"

"The devil take them!" he answered, "if I hadn't had a hill to go down, they'd have fucked me all the way!"

THE MAGIC RING

In a village there lived three brothers. As they were no longer on good terms, they decided to divide up their inheritance. However, the property was not apportioned evenly: chance favored the two elder brothers and left almost nothing to the youngest. All three were bachelors. One day when they were together in the street, they agreed that it was time they married. "That is all very well for you," said the third brother, "you are rich and you will find rich wives, but what am I to do? I am poor and in the way of riches I have only this cock of mine that comes down to my knees."

Now, a merchant's daughter was passing by just then; she overheard the three brothers' conversation and said to herself: "Ah! if only I could marry that young man! He has a cock that reaches down to his knees!"

The elder brothers married and the youngest son did not. However, the merchant's daughter went home obsessed with the idea of marrying him. Several shopkeepers asked for her hand, but she spurned them all. "The only husband I want," she said, "is so-and-so."

Her parents lectured her. "What are you thinking of, you silly fool? Be reasonable. How can you marry a penniless peasant?"

"Don't worry about that," she answered, "you won't be the ones who will have to live with him."

Then she got together with a professional matchmaker and sent her to tell the fellow to come and ask for her hand. The match-maker went to the peasant's house and said to him: "Listen to me, dear boy! What are you moping about like this for? Go and ask the daughter of such-and-such a merchant to marry you; she's been in love with you for a long time and would be glad to marry you."

Hearing this, the mouzhik put on a new smock and a new cap and went straight to the girl's father. As soon as she saw him coming, the daughter knew him as the man with the cock down to his knees. She was so insistent that her parents finally agreed to let her marry the young man.

On their wedding night, the bride discovered that her husband's cock wasn't even as long as a finger. "Ah, you rascal," she cried, "you boasted of having a cock down to your knees, what did you do with it?"

"Ah, dear wife, you know that before our marriage I was very poor; when I had to pay for the wedding feast, I had no money and nothing to borrow on, so I had to pawn my cock."

"And how much did you get for it?"

"Oh, not much: fifty rubles."

"All right. Tomorrow I'll ask my mother for fifty rubles and you can redeem your cock; you've absolutely got to get it, or never darken my doorway again!"

The next day, the young bride hurried to her mother's house: "Please, mother, give me fifty rubles, I need them very badly!"

"Why do you need them, pray?"

"Well, mother, this is why: my husband had a cock that came down to his knees, but on the eve of his wedding the poor man had nothing else to put up for security, so he pawned it for fifty rubles. Now my husband has a cock that isn't even as long as a finger. He simply must redeem his old one!"

The mother realized that this was a matter of dire necessity, and she gave her daughter the fifty rubles. The young woman immediately took them to her husband and said: "There! Now hurry up and go redeem your old cock: I don't want anyone else getting the benefit of it!"

The young man took the money and left with a heavy heart. "Now what is to become of me," he thought to himself; "how can I get such a cock for my wife? I shall go on walking as long as the earth will carry me."

He had been walking for some time when he met an old woman: "Good day to you, little mother!"

"Good day to you, young man! Where are you walking to?"

"Oh, little mother, if you knew how wretched I am! I don't know where to go!"

"Tell me your troubles, dear boy, perhaps I can help you."

"I would be embarrassed to tell you!"

"Don't be afraid, speak right out!"

"Well, little mother, here is how it is: I boasted that I had a cock that came down to my knees; a merchant's daughter overheard me and married me; but on our wedding night she discovered that my cock isn't even as long as a finger. So she got angry: 'What did you do with your long cock?' she asked me. I told her I had pawned it for fifty rubles. So she gave me the money and told me to redeem it or never to darken her doorway again. I don't know what is to become of me!"

"Give me the money," said the old woman, "and I will help you out of your trouble." The peasant immediately counted out fifty rubles to her and in return received a ring. "Here," she said, "take this ring and slip it over your fingernail, but no farther." The fellow did so and instantly his cock grew to a cubit in length. "Well," the old woman said, "is it long enough now?"

"But little mother, it still doesn't come down to my knees."

"All you have to do is slide the ring down your finger, dear boy."

He slid the ring down to the middle of his finger and he suddenly had a cock seven versts long. "Hey, little mother, what am I going to do now? A cock this long is a real calamity!"

"Slide the ring back up to your nail and your cock will only be a cubit long. Now I expect you'll be satisfied with that! When you use the ring, be careful not to slide it below the nail."

The young man thanked the old woman and started home again, happy at the thought that he was not returning empty-handed to his wife. When he had walked a long while, he felt the need to eat a morsel and, stepping off the road, he sat down by a stream, took some little biscuits out of his sack, dipped them in the water and began to eat them. After that, he lay back and admired the effect of the ring: he slipped it over his fingernail and his cock stood a cubit high; he slid it down to the middle of his finger and his cock rose to a height of seven versts; he took the ring off and his member returned to its former, modest proportions.

When the peasant had amused himself in this way for quite a while, he felt sleepy but he forgot to put the ring in his pocket before he fell asleep and left it lying on his chest. A gentleman and his wife happened to be driving by in a carriage. Catching sight of a peasant sleeping near the road with a ring shining on his chest, the gentleman stopped the carriage and said to his footman: "Go fetch that mouzhik's ring and bring it here." The servant immediately carried out his master's order, and the carriage got under way again.

However, the gentleman was fascinated by the beauty of the ring. "Look, darling, see how pretty this ring is," he said to his wife; "let's see if it will fit me." And he slipped the ring down to the middle of his finger: instantly, his cock shot out, knocked the coachman off his seat, passed over the horses' heads and stretched out seven versts in front of the carriage.

Seeing this, the panic-stricken gentlewoman shouted to the footman: "Go back to that peasant and bring him here!" The footman ran back to the mouzhik, woke him up and said: "Go to my master and hurry up about it!" Meanwhile, the peasant was looking for his ring: "The devil take you! Did you filch my ring?"

"Don't bother looking for it," replied the footman, "go to my master, he's the one who's got it; that ring of yours, my friend, has got us into a fine kettle of fish."

The peasant ran to the carriage in a twinkling of an eye. "Forgive me," began the gentleman in a plaintive tone of voice, "help me out of this predicament!"

"What will you give me, sir?"

"Here, take these hundred rubles."

"Give me two hundred and I'll help you." The barine gave the mouzhik two hundred rubles and the mouzhik slipped the ring off his finger. Instantly, the gentleman's cock returned to its former size. The carriage went on its way and the peasant went home.

His wife saw him coming from the window and rushed out to meet him. "Well!" she asked him, "did you redeem it?"

"Yes."

"Come on, show it to me!"

"Come into the house, I can't show it to you in the street." When they were inside, the wife kept repeating: "Show it to me! Show it to me!" He slid the ring over his fingernail and his cock grew to a cubit in length; he took it out of his trousers and said: "Look, wife!"

She started to kiss him: "Don't you think it's better, little husband, to keep such a treasure at home instead of leaving it with strangers? Let us hurry and eat dinner, then we shall go to bed and try it out!"

She immediately spread the table with dishes and bottles. The couple dined, then went to bed. Once the wife had tested the vigor of her husband's member, she spent the next three days peeking under her petticoats, for it constantly seemed to her that she could still feel it between her legs!

One day, she went to see her mother, while the mouzhik lay down for a nap under an apple tree in the garden. "Well," the merchant's wife said to her daughter, "did you redeem that cock?"

"Yes," answered the young wife, and she went into great detail on the subject.

As she listened, the merchant's wife became obsessed with the idea of slipping away during her daughter's visit, going to her son-in-law's house and testing that stupendous engine for herself. She managed to steal out and secretly hurried to the peasant's house. She saw him asleep in the garden. The ring was over his fingernail and his cock rose to the height of a cubit. "I'm going to perch myself on his cock," said the mother-in-law to herself as she took in the scene. No sooner said than done. Unfortunately for her, the ring on the sleeper's fingernail slid down to the middle of his finger, and all at once the merchant's wife shot up to a height of seven versts as the cock suddenly stretched. Meanwhile, the wife had noticed her mother's absence and, guessing what was behind it, she hurried home. There was nobody in the house; she went out into the garden, and what did she see? Her husband was sleeping with his cock in the air, and way up on top, so high you could hardly see her, was the merchant's wife, spinning in the breeze like a weather vane. What was to be done? How was she going to rescue her mother from such a dangerous predicament? A crowd gathered and an argument arose as to the best solution to the problem, with everyone giving his opinion. "There is only one thing to do," said some; "we must get an ax and chop down the cock."

"No," replied others, "you mustn't do that, it would mean the death of two people. If we chopped off the cock, the woman would fall to the ground and break every bone in her body. The best thing is for all of us to pray; perhaps God will work a miracle and save the old woman." In the midst of all this, the sleeper awoke, realized that the ring was in the middle of his finger and that his cock, which rose perpendicularly to a height of seven versts, was pinning him so firmly to the ground that he couldn't even turn over on his side. Very gently, he withdrew the ring; his cock shrank slowly, and when it was only a cubit high, the peasant realized that his mother-in-law was on the end of it. "What are you doing there, mother?" he asked her.

"Forgive me, dear son-in-law, I won't do it again."

THE COMB

A pope [priest] had a daughter who was still innocent. When summer came, he set about mowing his hay, but to each farm hand he stipulated that he would not pay him if his daughter could jump

over the stack of hay he had mowed. Several agreed to this arrangement and found themselves obliged to return home without being
paid for their work: as soon as one had finished his haystack, the
pope's daughter came along and jumped over it.

One day, a bold young fellow came to mow the churchman's
farm. The pope told him his conditions; the young man agreed to
them and set to work. When he had mowed a certain amount of
hay, he made a pile of it and lay down next to the pile. Then,
pulling his cock out of his breeches, he brought it to erection.
While this was going on, the pope's daughter came out to see how
the farm hand was working, and catching him in this position,
asked: "What are you doing there, mouzhik?"

"I'm fixing my comb."

"What do you comb with a thing like that?"

"If you like, I'll comb you. Lay down in the hay." The girl did
as he told her and the farm hand combed as one may well imagine.

"What a nice comb!" said the girl, sitting up again. Then she
tried to jump over the hay, but she could not, and succeeded only in
wetting her underclothes in a most shameful way.

She went to her father and said: "The haystack is very high, I
couldn't jump over it."

"Ah, daughter, one thing is sure, we have a fine worker there. I
am going to hire him for a year."

When the mouzhik came for his wages, the pope would not let
him leave. "I want to keep you for a year, dear boy."

"All right, good father." So the farm hand stayed on with the
pope, to the great satisfaction of the daughter, who visited him
every night. "Comb me a little!" she began.

"No, I won't comb you for nothing; give me a hundred rubles,
that way you'll have bought the comb."

The girl went to get the hundred rubles and gave them to the
peasant; from then on, he combed her every night. However, some
time later, the mouzhik quarreled with the pope, demanded his
wages and went away. The daughter was away from home at the
time. When she came home, she asked after the farm hand. "He quit
his job," answered the pope. "I paid him what I owed him and he
left a moment ago."

"Ah, father! What have you done? He's taken my comb with
him!" So saying, the girl set out in pursuit of the peasant; she caught
up with him near a stream. He had rolled up his trousers and was
fording across. "Give me back my comb!" she shouted.

The mouzhik picked up a stone and threw it into the water.
"Take it!" he said, and then, having reached the opposite bank,

hurried on his way. The girl lifted up her dress, waded into the water and began looking for the comb, but no matter how hard she searched the river bed, she could not find it.

A gentleman happened to be passing by in his carriage. "What are you looking for, dear girl?" he asked.

"A comb; I paid our farm hand a hundred rubles for it, but when he left the farm, he took it with him; I came after him and he threw it in the water."

The man got down from his carriage, took off his trousers and waded into the river to help the girl look for the comb. Suddenly, his cock attracted the girl's attention; she immediately seized it with both hands and shouted: "Oh, barine, you should be ashamed of yourself! That's my comb, give it back to me!"

"What are you doing, shameless girl?" said the man. "Let me go!"

"No, it is you who are shameless! You are trying to make off with something that does not belong to you. Give me back my comb!" And, still holding the gentleman by the cock, she took him back to her father's house.

The pope was at the window; he saw his daughter dragging the gentleman by his most sensitive member and shouting: "Give me back my comb, you scoundrel!" while the poor man pleaded: "Good father, save me from a death I have not deserved! I'll be grateful to you ever after!"

What was to be done? The churchman took his pope's cock out of his trousers, showed it to his daughter and shouted: "Little girl, little girl, here's your comb!"

"Yes, indeed, that is my comb, for the tip is all red. And I thought the gentleman had taken it!" Immediately she released her victim and hurried into the house. The man took to his heels as fast as he could go.

As soon as she was inside, the pope's daughter asked: "Papa, where is my comb?" Her father scolded her severely: "You little good-for-nothing!" And he shouted to his wife: "Look, little mother, she has lost her virtue!"

"Enough of that, little father," answered his wife, "take a look yourself and put matters to rights."

The pope immediately took off his trousers and fucked his daughter; as he came, he whinnied and shouted: "No, no, our daughter hasn't lost her virtue."

"Little father," said the wife, "stuff her virtue back in good and tight."

"Don't worry, little mother, it won't fall out, I've just wedged it into place. But our daughter is young yet: she doesn't know how to lift her legs the right way."

"Lift them higher, little girl, higher than that!" said her mother."

"Ah! little mother," the pope went on, "it's still all in a pile!" Thus it was that the daughter got her comb back, and from that day forward the pope carried on conjugal relations with both his wife and daughter.

THE POPE AND THE SOLDIER

A soldier wanted to fuck a pope's [priest's] wife; how was he going to manage? He put on his fanciest uniform, took up his rifle, and went to see the pope. "Well, friend, a ukase has just been issued ordering us to fuck all the popes; get ready!"

"Oh, soldier, can't you make an exception for me?"

"What an idea! Do you think I'm going to risk being punished just for you? Off with your pants, quick! And get into position!"

"Oh, now, soldier, couldn't my wife take my place?"

"Well, all right! But no one must know, because I would get into trouble! And you, friend, what will you give me? I won't take less than a hundred rubles."

"Take them, soldier, but have pity on me."

"All right, now come and lay down in your wagon, and put your wife on top of you. I'll get on top of her and it will look like I'm fucking you."

The pope lay down in the wagon and his wife lay down on top of him; then the soldier pulled up the wife's skirts and started to fuck her. As the scene progressed, the churchman lying on the bottom of the wagon became wildly excited; his cock stood up vigorously, bore a whole through the bottom of the wagon and came out all red on the other side. At the sight of it, the pope's daughter shouted: "Oh, what a sturdy cock that soldier has! It ran my mother and father through and through, and the end is still wagging!"

"A Crop of Cocks," the first tale, is a commentary on the whole concept of usefulness. The supposedly stupid mouzhik happily plants what seems to be a totally useless crop. Instead of wheat, barley, or some other valuable grain, he reaps a harvest of cocks, which turns out to be worth more than any conventional crop. The story is also a commentary on sexual greed, as represented by the rich townswoman who cannot get enough sex, then has to pay the mouzhik to learn how to stop the extreme overstimulation she is subjected to.

On a deeper level, the cocks represent the raw sex drive, for they do not distinguish between male and female, as the coachman, who fetched them for the lady, was to find out. In other words, we are told that the sex drive is blind and undiscriminating, sexual preference being due solely to upbringing and conditioning. Perhaps neither the original tellers of these stories, nor the audiences who have listened to them and repeated them to each other for centuries, have ever made such conscious connections. These are hidden meanings, produced by the unconscious and understood by the unconscious, and it is this appeal to deeper layers of understanding which provides the special enjoyment that one experiences with regard to stories of this type.

"The Magic Ring" is, in the first place, a reminder that sexual attraction is at the base of man-woman relations, no matter how many other considerations may enter into them. The rich merchant's daughter wants the poor boy solely because she thinks he has an extra large organ. For that she is willing to forget about his lack of financial resources.

This emphasis on the sexual organs (that is, on pure biological sexuality) is a frequent theme in sexual folklore, but is quite distinct from the emphasis given the male sex apparatus in pornographic writings. In folklore, it refers more to primitive human nature, in pornography it is a mere exaggeration of the male sex organ, meant to evoke sexual excitement (that pornography often fails to achieve its end in this way, especially with regard to women, is quite another matter).

Symbolically, the magic ring which makes the poor boy's penis grow is the vagina. The fact that it is given to him by an old woman signifies that the boy's sexual development and potency depend primarily on the influence of a benign, protective, non-castrating mother figure.

The interlude with the rich man misappropriating the poor boy's only asset, the magic ring, is again a commentary on greed, especially sexual greed. The same holds true for the last part of the story in which the wife's mother wants to try the son-in-law's large organ. There is a hint here of the common sexual rivalry between mother and daughter, as well as of the not infrequent attraction between mother-in-law and son-in-law.

"The Comb" is about the farmer's virginal daughter who is so athletic that she can jump over any stack of hay that the farm hands set up. Thus she robs (castrates) them, with the help of her (incestuous) father, of their pay (sexual rewards), for they are only paid if their stack (penis) is so big that the girl cannot jump over it (subdue or castrate it). When the girl finally comes upon a really potent male, she is promptly deflowered and her exclusive attachment to the father is broken, together with her hymen. It is now she who is humiliated (the soiling of her undergarments), just as she had humiliated the men before. The girl, however, does not mind this humiliation, indicating that—from the story's point of view—every dominating woman secretly longs for a man who is able to dominate her and free her from her own masculinization.

The sexually naïve girl persists in calling her lover's penis a comb just as he had taught her to do. When he finally leaves her, taking his comb (which she considers her own) with him, she runs after him to get it back. She returns hanging onto a substitute comb in the form of the penis of a mere passerby, but her father convinces her, by showing her his own organ, that his is the one she is looking for. The girl immediately accepts the logic of this proposal and—with the help and consent of the mother—the ideal incestuous family is established in which mother and daughter share the father without jealousy or rancor. The fact that the father happens to be a pope, that is, an Orthodox priest (Greek Orthodox priests are allowed to marry), is expressive of an anticlerical attitude common in folk tales and makes the situation even more ludicrously humorous.

The last story, "The Pope and the Soldier," has the same anticlerical cast as the previous one, but plays also on the priest's fear of homosexuality. Hypocritically, the soldier suggests the priest lie down under his wife so that it will look as if he is having intercourse with him, rather than her—the exact reversal

round and still the dervish shows not the slightest sign of tiring. Suddenly the woman excuses herself to go and relieve her bladder. As she gets up, she quickly erases, as if by accident, some of the chalk marks. A quarrel ensues, the dervish accusing her of erasing some of the marks, and the woman denying it with equal vehemence. After a while, the dervish says, "Ah well, have it your way, let's start all over again from the beginning!" Upon this the woman concedes the victory to him and the dervish returns the young man's money to him.

There are several variations to this old story, as well as numerous contemporary jokes, which feature the same punch line, "Ah, well! Let's start all over again!" Many recent jokes have their origin in folk tales which date back centuries and which come from cultural environments far removed from the setting of the later versions. Such is the case with the next story from the Ukraine, which has a counterpart in a recent American joke in which a married couple driving their carriage down a lonely country road are stopped by a tough highwayman, who —at the point of a gun—forces the woman to have intercourse with him and the husband to hold his testicles so they won't get dirty on the ground. But when it is all over and the hold-up man safely gone on, the husband brags to his wife that he got the better of the highwayman after all: "He was scared of me—I let his balls drop in the dirt when he was fucking you and he didn't say a word!" The original version follows:

RETURNING HOME FROM THE MARKET

A Cossack was riding one day behind the coach of a farmer who was driving home from market with his wife and mother. It so happened that the Cossack overheard the farmer say, "I would never allow my wife to do like other men's wives, making bastards even in front of their husbands!"

The Cossack immediately stopped the farmer and ordered him to get out of the wagon. The farmer obeyed. "Here, hold my horse!" The farmer did as he said. The Cossack then said to the wife, "And you! What are you doing there? Get out and come here too!" The wife got out as the Cossack had ordered, leaving only the mother in the coach, who was holding on to a pot she had bought at the market. The Cossack thought, "When I start fucking, I might soil my balls on the sand!" He therefore said to the old lady, "Get down here too! But since you are old, I'll give you an easy job!"

Having put the farmer's wife on the ground and getting ready to fuck her, he told the old lady to hold his balls in the kettle so he would not get them dirty.

Having finished, he got on his horse, and rode off.

After he was some distance away, the farmer said to his mother, "Well, mother, even though he's fucked my wife, I've had my revenge: I've sure tired out his horse!" And the mother said, "I, too, my son; I've done him even worse yet. He told me to hold his balls in the pot while he was fucking. But just as he was coming, I let his balls slip out of the pot and onto the dirty road!" As for the farmer's wife, she kept quiet and did not say a word.

The story below is interesting in that it deals with the hypocrisy of those who must use euphemisms to disguise their sexuality.

THE PRUDISH LADY

A certain rich lady had one by one dismissed all her menservants, because they had used what she called bad language. Hearing this, a young servant went to her, offering his services. "Listen, my little pigeon," the lady said, "I'll pay you well, only don't use bad language."

"Use bad language!" said the young man. "I wouldn't think of it."

One day, the lady inspected her country estate with the servant and they came upon a herd of pigs. One of the boars jumped on a sow and started working away so energetically that he foamed at the mouth. The lady turned to her servant and said, "Listen, what are they doing?"

The clever boy replied, "I think the pig that's underneath is most likely a sister or an aunt of the male above. That one I take to be seriously ill and believe he is being taken home by the kind female relative."

"Yes, yes," said the lady, laughing heartily, "that's no doubt what is going on!"

They came upon a steer mounting a cow. "And this," asked the lady, "what could this be?"

"This?" said the young man. "That's a blind cow who has eaten all the grass around her and can't find any more nourishment; so the kind steer is trying to push her to a fresh place in the pasture."

"That's nice," said the lady, and they walked on.

Next they came upon a stallion getting on top of a mare. Again the lady asked what it was, and the young servant said, "Does Milady see the smoke coming up from the woods beyond? Well, the stallion is mounting the mare to see where the fire may be."

"Yes, no doubt, that's it," said the lady, laughing so hard that the tears rolled from her eyes.

They continued, and arrived at a river. The lady took a notion to bathe. She commanded the servant to stop, undressed herself, and got into the water. The servant remained on the river bank and looked on. "If you want to bathe with me," said the lady, "get undressed quickly and come into the water!"

The servant undressed and got in with her.

Seeing his instrument of procreation, the lady thrilled with joy and, showing him her crack, said, "Look, what have I got here?"

"That's a well, Milady," said the servant.

"That's right," said she. "And that which hangs down from you, what is that?"

"That's called a horse," said the servant.

"Very well," said the lady, "horses have to drink, don't they? Is yours perhaps thirsty?"

"Yes, Madam," said the young man, "would you mind letting him drink at your well?"

"Not at all," said the lady, "let him drink; only make him drink at the top and not at the bottom!"

The young servant let his horse drink at the lady's well and she got excited. Soon she was beside herself and cried, "Let your horse get in deeper, my boy, so he can drink properly!"

That was how the lady of delicate sensibilities amused herself with her clever manservant.

As noted, incest is a common theme in folk tales, as in this story from the Ukraine, entitled "How Three Brothers Were Fucking Their Aunt": Unknown to each other, three brothers are having sexual relations with their aunt—one in the early evening, one at midnight, and one at early dawn. To each one, the aunt afterward gives a slice of bread. The last one, coming home in daylight, sees the other pieces of bread on the table and realizes that they have come from the same loaf. The brothers talk it over and admit that they have all had intercourse with the aunt. They feel that this state of affairs is not desirable and decide that the one who manages to have intercourse with the aunt in the presence of the uncle should in future have her alone. One of the boys achieves this by tearfully telling the uncle that he is to be married and does not know how to perform on his wedding night. The uncle decides to teach him by letting him have intercourse with the aunt, a proposition which the aunt readily accepts, and the uncle actually helps the young man insert his penis.

The countless stories of this type would indicate that incest, though not officially approved, was not considered a serious moral offense, and was probably more or less tolerated among the peasant classes of Eastern Europe as recently as a century ago. Today in almost all primitive regions of the world, as well as among lower socio-economic classes of the most highly developed countries, though probably not in Communist-dominated Eastern Europe, incest is not infrequent and is more or less tacitly tolerated.

A similar attitude, likewise reflective of a lower-class, peasant milieu is expressed in "The Child Who Was Too Young to Know": One summer night a farmer said to his wife: "Wouldn't you like to fuck?" She said, "Little John isn't asleep yet!" "Ah, never mind," said the farmer, "he's still too young to understand anything." Saying so, he started to work on his wife. All of a sudden, there was a thump on the door and it flew open. The husband jumped up to see who was coming, but from his bed in the corner, the little boy simply said, "Don't worry, Papa, go on fucking. It's only the pig!"

Adultery, like incest, is treated in the folklore of all peoples with an indulgent smile. A Scottish tale tells of a mistress who grew suspicious when her two sons began to cast eyes on her fair and fascinating maid. One day, the boys were busy at some work outside the house. The mistress used this opportunity to become quite confidential and gracious with the maid, and at last asked her which son she liked best. The lassie in her simplicity answered: "I like both the laddies well enough, but commend me for a straight stroke to your own man."

Honor, another recurrent theme, is the subject of this tale from Norway:

THE INJURED FINGER

A young country girl was suffering from an abscess on her finger and went to the city to see the doctor. The doctor, who was too busy to see her, asked his assistant what her trouble was, and on hearing that it was nothing more serious than a sore finger, he yelled out, "Let her stick her finger up her cunt!"

The innocent young girl heard the doctor's remark and started home, putting her finger in her vagina whenever she could. In that manner, the abscess actually broke before she had reached home, and was soon healed entirely.

When the girl's mother saw that the doctor had done the girl so much good, she sent her back to town to take him a keg of fresh golden butter which she had just churned.

This time the doctor was not so busy and let the girl come inside. At first he did not remember her at all and asked what advice he had given her to cure the sore finger. When she naïvely told him what had happened, the old fox said, "My dear, you can today render me an even greater service than I have rendered you."

"What is that?" asked the maid.

"My dear," said the old rogue, "I have myself got an abscess on the eleventh finger."

"But why can't you then follow the same advice you have given me?" asked the girl.

"You see, my dear," said the doctor, "I unfortunately don't have an instrument like the one that cured your finger."

"Well," said the girl, "in that case, I can lend you mine, if you like."

The doctor accepted her offer enthusiastically and used her instrument to best advantage. As they were thus going about it, the girl groaned with pleasure and said, "Now I know your finger is getting better, because I can feel that the sore has broken!"

When she came home, she told her mother what had happened. "Oh, my child," cried the good lady, "you have lost your honor!"

"In that case, I don't care," replied the girl, "for I shit on an honor that is seated so close to my ass!"

The battle of the sexes forms the basis of the American joke about the Texas rancher who is visited by a city couple. While taking the wife around the ranch, the rancher points to his prize bull and says that he is able to function as a male several times a day, every day of the year. The city lady is much astonished and exhorts the rancher not to fail to mention this fact when taking her husband around the ranch. The rancher does as the lady has asked him and repeats the observation to the husband. "And he does that with the same cow every time!"

"What are you talking about!" cries the rancher. "Of course, he's got a different cow each time!"

"I see," replied the husband. "Next time you take my wife to the bull pen, please don't fail to mention that as well."

While this at first seemed to us to be an original American joke, we have subsequently come upon several versions of it in folk tales from Picardy which date from the seventeenth and eighteenth centuries.

A curious tale from England, entitled "The Eel Pasties," complements these bull stories. It is about an important medieval lord who had among his servants one especially loyal, diligent, and prudent servant from whom he consequently had no secrets, including his many private love affairs. In fact, the young servant frequently acted as messenger and go-between in these affairs, as long as his master remained unmarried.

However, upon the advice and insistence of his friends and family, the master one fine day got married to a charming, beautiful, and rich lady. Everyone was happy about this, especially the young servant, who now hoped that his master would change his ways and remain home with his wedded wife, as other men of low and high office seemed to do. The young servant's disappointment was therefore keen when the master explained to him that although he very much loved his new wife, he had no intention of abandoning all his love affairs and that he would continue to rely on the servant's able and discreet services in these matters. But the lord encountered unexpected resistance on the part of his good servant, who simply refused to serve his master to those ends, as he thought it would be against his mistress's and his master's welfare. He pointed out to the master that his wife was far superior in beauty, as well as other respects, to any of the master's other ladies.

It would have been easy for the master to dismiss this servant and engage one less scrupulous who would have gladly and without question rendered him the services demanded. However, the lord was reluctant to get rid of so good and faithful a servant, hoping still to win him over to his side by means of persuasion. So one day he asked the young man what dish he preferred above all others. Without a moment's hesitation, the young servant replied that no dish pleased him as much as eel pasties.

"By St. John, it is a good dish," said his master. "You have not chosen badly."

Thus the master had the young man served eel pasties day after day, until the poor fellow could no longer stand the sight or smell of them. When the young man complained to the steward about it, he was only told that there was nothing to be done, since he was following orders from the master himself.

The servant went to see the master and asked why the cooks had been forbidden to serve him any dish other than eel pasties.

In reply, the master said, "Did you not tell me that eel pie was the dish that you most liked in all the world?"

"Yes, my lord," said the servant.

"Then, why do you complain now," said the master, "since I cause you to be served with that which you like?"

"I like them," answered the young man, "in moderation. I like exceedingly to have eel pies once, or twice, or even three times a week. But to eat it always, and nothing else besides—I cannot stand it! Anybody would get sick of it. For God's sake, my lord, command that I be given some other food that I may recover my appetite, otherwise I am a dead man."

"Ah!" said the master. "Yet it seems that you do not think I shall be a dead man if I content myself with the charms of my wife. By my soul, you may believe that I am as weary of them as you are of the pasties. In short, you shall eat no other food until you consent to serve me as you did before, and bring me a variety of women as you would have a variety of dishes."

The young man was persuaded, and promised he would carry messages and conduct his master's love affairs as before.

All these folk tales and traditional stories communicate hidden meanings, morals, and attitudes by means of parable and allegory. By listening for the sentiment behind the spoken or written words, they become psychologically meaningful, perhaps more for their sex attitudes than for their fantasy content. Yet they offer precise formulations of very widespread sex fantasies, as in the tales concerning an unusually large penis and in the incest stories.

In the chapters that follow, it will be seen that in erotic writings of more recent times, the sexual acts depicted (i.e., the fantasy content) exceeds in importance the attitudes toward those acts.

3

Erotic Writings in the
Style of Folklore

Since the style of folklore is so charming and lends itself so well
to sexual symbolism, it is not surprising that some more recent
writers, like Poggio, Rabelais, and Aretino, have employed it for
erotic subject matter. Such is the case in *Les Bijoux Indiscrets*
(*The Indiscreet Jewels*), by Denis Diderot (Paris: Bibliothèque
des Curieux, 1920). The story, which was first published in
1748, is a rather heavy satire on the mores of eighteenth-century
French high society, thinly disguised, in the fashion of the day,
as a mythical Oriental court. One episode contains a remarkable
sexual fantasy, told as a sort of fairy tale. The gimmick of this

story within the main story is a magic ring, given to the Sultan Mangogul by a genie, a ring which enables him to make women's "jewels" (sex organs) talk, thereby revealing all their guilty secrets.

Here is a slightly condensed translation of Chapter 26.

TENTH TRIAL OF THE RING—THE COCKER SPANIELS

Mangogul immediately went to the apartments of Haria; and as he was often wont to talk to himself when alone, he said: "This woman never goes to bed without her four watchdogs; and either jewels know nothing of such animals, or hers will tell me something of them; for, thank Heaven, it is well known that she loves her dogs to distraction."

As he was finishing this monologue, he reached Haria's antechamber and deduced that Milady was resting with her usual companions. These consisted of a small cocker, a great Dane, and two pugs. The Sultan took out his snuff box, fortified himself with two pinches of Spanish tobacco, and went toward Haria. She was asleep; but the pack, whose ears were on the alert, heard a noise and began to bark, waking her. "Hush, children," she said in a tone so gentle that she could never have been suspected of speaking to her daughters; "sleep, sleep, and let us all rest in peace."

Once Haria had been young and pretty; she had had lovers befitting her station, but these had vanished even faster than her charms. In order to compensate for this abandonment, she began to indulge in eccentric ostentation, and her lackeys were the handsomest in all of Banza. She grew older, and as the years went by she reformed her ways, limiting herself to four dogs and two brahmins, and becoming a model of virtue. Indeed, even the most vitriolic satirist could find here no grist for his mill, and for more than ten years Haria had been able to enjoy peacefully a reputation for chastity alone with her animals. In fact, her affection for her cockers was known to be so intense that even the brahmins were no longer suspected of sharing it with them.

Haria repeated her request, and the animals condescended to obey. Then Mangogul touched his ring, and the superannuated jewel began to relate its latest adventures. Its earliest ones were so far in the past that it could hardly remember them. "Get away, Medor," it said in a hoarse voice, "you tire me. I prefer Lisette:

she's gentler." Medor, unfamiliar with the voice of the jewel, went on with what he was doing; but Haria woke up again and pursued her speech: "Get away from there you little rascal, how can I get any rest? There are times when that is nice, but enough is enough." Medor withdrew, Lisette took his place, and Haria went back to sleep.

Mangogul, who had suspended the effect of his ring, twisted it again and the ancient jewel heaved a deep sigh and began to prattle, saying: "Oh, how sorry I was when the big greyhound died! She was the sweetest little woman in the world, the most affectionate creature imaginable; she kept me amused all the time, she was all wit and tenderness; you're nothing but brutes by comparison. That nasty man killed her. Poor Zinzoline; whenever I think about her, I'm moved to tears. I thought my mistress was going to die. She went two days without food or drink; her brain reeled; you can imagine her anguish. Her confessor, her friends, even her cockers refrained from approaching her. Her servants had orders to keep her husband out of her apartments. 'That monster took my dear Zinzoline from me,' she cried, 'keep him out of my sight; I never want to see him again.' "

Mongogul was curious to learn the circumstances of Zinzoline's death, and rubbing the ring on his coattail in order to increase its electrical power, he directed it at Haria and the jewel went on: "When Haria's first husband, Raladec, died, she became infatuated with Sindor. This young man, though well-born, was not very rich; he had, however, a talent which is agreeable to women and which constituted, after her cockers, Haria's chief passion. Sindor's poverty helped him overcome his aversion to Haria's age and her dogs. Twenty thousand crowns of *rente* made him oblivious to his mistress's wrinkles and the inconvenience of her cockers, and he married her.

"He felt sure that he could outdo our animals by means of his talent and tractability, and have them dismissed from favor at the very beginning of his reign; he was, however, mistaken. After several months, during which he imagined that he had done well by us, he took it into his head to point out to his wife that her dogs were not such pleasant bedfellows for him as they were for her; that it was absurd to keep more than three and that she was turning their conjugal bed into a kennel by taking in more than one at a time. 'I advise you,' answered Haria in an angry tone of voice, 'never to speak to me like that again! Indeed, it ill becomes a wretched Gascon cadet whom I rescued from an attic that wouldn't have been fit for my dogs, to put on such airs here! It seems they must have perfumed your sheets, my little lord, when you were living in furnished rooms? Get it through your head once and for all that my dogs had the run of my bed long before you did, and that you can either get out of it now or resolve to share it with them.'

"This declaration was perfectly clear, and our dogs remained at their posts; however, one night when we were all asleep, Sindor rolled over and gave Zinzoline an unfortunate kick. The greyhound was not used to such treatment and bit him on the fleshy part of the leg; Haria was instantly awakened by Sindor's cries.

" 'What is the matter, sir?' she asked. 'You sound as though your throat were being cut. Did you have a bad dream?'

" 'Your dogs, Madame, are devouring me,' answered Sindor, 'and your greyhound has just taken a bite out of my leg.'

" 'Is that all?' said Haria as she turned over. 'You're making much ado about nothing.'

"Sindor was stung by her words and got out of bed, swearing he would never set foot in it again until the hounds were banished. He resorted to mutual friends in an attempt to have the dogs sent into exile; all, however, failed in these momentous negotiations. Haria answered that Sindor was a whippersnapper whom she had rescued from an attic which he shared with rats and mice; that he could scarcely afford to be choosy; that he slept all night long; that she loved her dogs; that they amused her; that she had grown accustomed to their caresses from early childhood; and that she was resolved not to part with them until death. 'Tell him also,' she went on, 'that if he does not humbly submit to my wishes, he will rue it for the rest of his life; that I shall withdraw the settlement I made over to him and add it to the sum I have set aside for the care and sustenance of my children after my death.'

"Just between us," added the jewel, "Sindor must have been a fool to hope that she would do for him what she had refused to do for twenty lovers, a director, a confessor and a whole string of Brahmins, all of whom were at their wits' end. Still, every time Sindor came upon one of our animals, he could scarcely hide his irritation. One day, the luckless Zinzoline happened to cross his path; he grabbed her by the neck and flung her out the window: the poor creature died from the fall. That made quite a stir. Haria's face was aflame, her eyes were bathed in tears."

The jewel was about to repeat itself, as jewels are often wont to do. But Mangogul cut it short and it remained silent for a long while. When the sovereign felt that he had sufficiently confused that prating jewel, he restored its power of speech, and with a laugh the chatterbox began to reminisce again: "But by the way, I forgot to tell you what happened on Haria's wedding night. I've seen many ridiculous things in my life, but nothing so ridiculous as that. After a huge supper, the newlyweds were escorted to their bedchamber; everyone withdrew, except for the two ladies-in-waiting who were to undress the bride. Finally, she was undressed and put to bed, and Sindor was left alone with her. Realizing that the cockers, the pug, and the greyhounds had been quicker than he and had already taken possession of his wife: 'Allow me, Madame,' said he, 'to put aside these rivals of mine.'

"'My dear, do what you can,' said Haria. 'I, for my part, do not have the heart to send them away. These little creatures are devoted to me; and it has been so long since I've had any other company.'

"'This evening, perhaps,' Sindor went on, 'they will be so courteous as to surrender a position which I, by rights, should occupy.'

"'You will just have to see,' answered Haria.

"At first, Sindor used gentle means, and begged Zinzoline to retire into a corner, but the intractable animal began to growl. The rest of the troop took alarm, and the pug and the cockers began to bark as though their mistress's throat were being cut. Losing patience with all this noise, Sindor knocked the pug head over heels, thrust aside one of the cockers and grabbed Medor by the leg. Medor, the faithful Medor, seeing himself abandoned by his allies, attempted to compensate for this loss by exploiting the advantages of his position. Clinging to his mistress's thighs with blazing eyes, bristling hair, and gaping jaws, he puckered up his muzzle and showed his enemy two rows of very sharp teeth. Sindor made several assaults and each time Medor drove him back with nipped fingers and torn sleeves. This scene had lasted over a quarter of an hour with a perseverance that only Haria found amusing, when Sindor decided to resort to ruse in order to overcome an enemy whom he despaired of conquering by force. He titillated Medor with his right hand and Medor was so attentive to this maneuver that he failed to see what the left hand was doing until it seized him by the scruff of the neck. The extraordinary efforts he made to free himself were of no avail; he had to abandon the battlefield and give up Haria. Sindor took possession of her, but not without bloodshed; Haria seemed to have resolved that her wedding night should be a bloody one. Her animals put up a splendid struggle and lived up to all her expectations."

SULTAN MISAPOUF AND PRINCESS GRISEMINE

Still more in the style of folklore is the story "Le Sultan Misapouf et la Princesse Grisemine," which is included in the collected novels* of the Abbé de Voisenon (1708–1775).

It is impossible to give a succinct résumé of this extremely complicated libertine fairy tale. In the following excerpt, Misapouf, still a boy, is about to attempt to fit his "little finger" into the "ring" of Princess Muchtoomuch, in order to help break a spell cast over her and her sister Nevertrustalady by a bad fairy; according to the terms of the spell, Misapouf will then marry the Princess.

I was surprised by her [the Princess's] height; she was nearly six feet tall, and yet she was beautiful and well-formed.

"Wonder of our days," said I, tenderly clasping the tip of her left foot, "can it be that I am the happy mortal who shall succeed?"

"Prince," she answered, "I hope with all my heart that you shall succeed in this difficult endeavor."

At that moment, I saw Cerasin, the high bonze, enter the room with all the other bonzes of the land; he was carrying a book bound in gold leaf. He and his cortege bowed low to us, he recited something by turns under his breath and out loud, read a moment in his book and then, turning to me, addressed me as follows: "The Princess will lie on this sofa, and you may then attempt the adventure which is in store for you. Such good fortune will never befall a poor priest; however, one must abide by the will of fate. I must warn you of one essential point: the Princess's ring must not be forced in any way, for the fairy contrived such a perfect fit between the person and the ring that any awkward efforts on your part would cause the Princess horrible suffering. I will remain present during this test. I shall observe the eyes and the movements of the Princess and, according to what I see, I shall let you know whether to stop or to continue."

And so saying, he signaled to me that I could begin. I wanted to comply without further ado, but I do believe the fairy must have cast a spell over my little finger, for as I brought it near the ring, it began to swell; this disturbed me greatly, I nevertheless went on

---

* *L'Oeuvre de l'Abbé de Voisenon* (Paris: Bibliothèque des Curieux, 1913).

with my enterprise. At my very first attempt, the Princess said: "You're hurting me."

Cerasin immediately shouted: "Why don't you stop? Didn't you hear the Princess say you're hurting her?" In spite of this warning, I made a second attempt, slightly more vigorous than the first.

"Oh, I can't bear any more," said the Princess.

"Will you stop being so brutal, you damned little dwarf!" the high bonze shouted again.

In spite of this second remonstrance, I believe I was about to be victorious when suddenly my little finger, which at first had swollen to amazing proportions, suddenly shrank to its normal size. I stopped, greatly surprised at this transformation.

"Come now, the Princess is pining away, should such a one as she have to wait upon your convenience? What kind of a lazy little fellow is this?"

During this monologue, my little finger had returned to its state of a few minutes before. I took advantage of this development, the Princess uttered a cry of pain and then sighed, "Oh, my dear, you've killed me!" I was pleased to hear her call me dear; it seemed to prove that she had a good character; I made a few more attempts, but they were unnecessary.

The Princess gazed at me tenderly and said: "The spell is broken." The high bonze and all his hangers-on repeated in unison: "Glory be to Misapouf and his little finger, the spell is broken."

I was beside myself with joy; and I have to admit that ever since that happy moment, I have never been afraid of tall women, and am far more wary of short ones. Nature, in that respect, is almost as capricious as the Fairy of the Shadows, she likes to create what is contrary to reason.

I was intoxicated with my triumph, when that accursed Fairy of the Shadows came down from the clouds in her chariot. "Be quiet, foolish priests," she cried, "I'll teach you to sing hymns against me." So saying, she touched Cerasin and his high vicars with her wand; they fell over one another, and when they stood up again, oh surprise! oh frightening sight! I saw them and did not recognize them: their mouths were turned into rings! You cannot imagine how much this changed their faces, you would have had to see it to believe it.

Poor Cerasin said to me with a humiliated air: "Take pity on me!" All the priests repeated the same thing in unison; they made me so dizzy that I sent them away: they left with their bearded rings. They could easily have been mistaken for Capuchin friars.

Cerasin, who was very vain, looked in his mirror when he got home, and was horrified by what he saw. He could not understand how it was that a ring, which he had always regarded as a very pretty thing, could make him look so ugly. It just goes to prove that the chief virtue of anything consists in its being in its proper place. Finally he decided to send for his barber, who said to him as he came in: "I've come to find out what Your Lordship requires of me, for I had the honor of shaving him only this morning."

"Oh, really," answered Cerasin. "Look at me, am I not a pretty sight to behold?"

"Oh, great pagoda," exclaimed the barber taking three steps back, "what a mouth, what a beard! This is a miracle if ever I saw one, and I am not sure Your Lordship does well to have it chopped off. I could almost believe that our sacred monkey was trying to demonstrate his good will toward you by bestowing upon you the lower half of his face."

"Don't let that keep you from doing a good job of lathering me," answered Cerasin.

The barber obeyed and lathered His Lordship; however, when His Lordship was lathered and shaved, he was even uglier than before. He sank into gloom as he saw that he now had a perpetual pout. Furiously, he said, "Why, no one has ever seen a mouth like that before!"

"At least," the barber answered respectfully, "I may assure Your Lordship that no one has ever seen one like it under a nose."

"Oh, I don't need your remarks," Cerasin went on. "Here's your money, away with you."

"Ah, Your Lordship is surely too conscientious to pay for an ordinary shave," said the barber humbly. "This one was worth two. If Your Lordship will be kind enough to feel how tough his whiskers are! Why they cost me a razor!"

His Lordship was close to his money and dismissed the barber brutally; so the barber, in revenge, immediately spread the tale far and wide and the whole court made sport of it.

The Princess and I were still laughing over it that evening as we went to bed; however, our mirth was not long-lived, for no sooner had I put my little finger to the ring, than I was bitten good and hard. I let out a shrill scream and heard a burst of laughter; I was piqued and said to the Princess: "Madame, I don't know what there is to laugh about."

"But I am not laughing," she answered, "and have not the slightest desire to do so."

"It is all very well to say that," I said. "My word, it is witless enough; you are laughing out of vanity; you are delighted that I have been wounded." I made another attempt, but I was bitten even more cruelly: my shouts grew proportionately louder and so did the peals of laughter. Beside myself with rage, I thrust the Princess out of bed; she pulled every bell rope within reach and burst into tears. The women brought lights and were very astonished to find only two people in the room, one crying and the other scolding, and to hear, nevertheless, peals of hysterical laughter. Here was a case, if ever there was one, to suspect that there was more than met the eye; I was not one to fail to remark on this and even to give the matter a closer examination. What was my surprise to find, in lieu of a ring, a real mouth—unfortunately, equipped with all its teeth—and the mouth was laughing in my face! The Princess went into hysterics. "Madame," I said to her, "this is no time to lose our heads, we must simply send for His Majesty's tooth puller."

"Alas, sir," she answered, "he will have forgotten his trade by now, for my father lost his last tooth ten years ago."

This consideration notwithstanding, the man was sent for. Quite reasonably, he wished to examine the Princess's mouth: but I told him, "It's a bit lower down, sir."

"What do you mean, a bit lower down?" he asked. "Was I not brought here for the Princess?"

"Indubitably," I replied.

"Well, then," he went on, "what are you trying to tell me? Come, Madame, please get into position." The Princess stretched out on the sofa.

"Madame," said the surgeon, "this is not the usual position for someone who wants a tooth pulled."

"Sir," I began again, "this is the position which the Princess prefers."

"I cannot say I blame her," he answered, "but in the present case it simply will not do."

At length, I informed him of the circumstances, and he assumed that I was inventing. He called for a light and carried out his examination. "My! What a fine set of teeth!" was his first exclamation.

"Quite so," I said; "but they are quite out of place, no matter how beautiful. And those are the teeth which must be pulled one after the other."

"Pull those teeth!" he cried in anger. "Why, sir! That would be a crime. I see that you take me for one of those dentists who place no value on a tooth; but you are wrong! If it had been a mere matter of filling one, I'd have let it pass; it would come as no surprise that at least one of them should be hollow; but if you will be so kind as to glance at them yourself, you will see that all I can possibly agree to do is file them down."

"All right," I said, "let's try that." He immediately set to his task, asking me if I had heard any good jokes lately. Suddenly, he was amazed to see his file break in two. He took out another, which met the same fate, and he went on to break six in a row. "Zounds!" he exclaimed in anger. "You've given me diamond teeth to file." At this point, a voice spoke these words:

"This mouth will remain where it is, with all its teeth, until the Princess Nevertrustalady [Muchtoomuch's sister] shall be released from *her* spell."

Princess Muchtoomuch is very tall—six feet—while Prince Misapouf is but a boy and consequently much smaller than she. Nevertheless, it is the woman who has a small organ and the boy who has an organ so large that at first it cannot enter the woman's "ring." Later in the story a remark is made which indicates that it is better to believe large women have small vaginas and small women very large ones, an interesting play on the relative sizes of people and their sex organs.

The spell which the bad fairy had cast over Princess Muchtoomuch is reminiscent of a similar spell cast over Snow White, who must be awakened by a prince from her sleep (that is, whose dormant sexuality has to be awakened by her defloration, as in the case of Princess Muchtoomuch). No sooner is Princess Muchtoomuch made a woman than the bad fairy takes her vengeance by turning the mouths of the Princess's priests into rings (vaginas). We have several times come across this fantasy (together with its counterpart—the nose turned into a penis and the eyes into testicles) in erotic art, but never before in literature. In this case, the mouths of the priests, which have become vaginas, are even set in appropriate beards (pubic hair).

The bad fairy then turns Princess Muchtoomuch's vagina into a mouth, complete with a set of sharp teeth—the classical *vagina dentata* theme, though the Abbé de Voisenon is not likely to have had knowledge of it two centuries before Freud. The story reveals again the breakthrough of unconscious fantasies in literature and art, confirming many of the clinical findings and formulations of psychoanalysis.

LITTLE RED RIDING HOOD

Recently a modern erotic rewrite of the old story "Little Red Riding Hood" appeared. Written by Annakarin Svedberg, a Swedish woman writer, it was published in Volume I of *Kärlek*, a series of erotic short stories (Malmö, Sweden: Bengt Forsbergs Förlag, 1965). The original fairy tale may not carry exactly the same erotic meaning as the rewrite by Miss Svedberg, but no doubt the author has brought to light some of the latent erotic significance of the old version. Miss Svedberg has added the important element of social satire and political commentary, which is certainly neither overtly nor covertly present in the original.

Little Red Riding Hood, in the modern tale, is a swinging teen-age girl who is bored to death in the sticky bourgeois milieu of her parents' home and the village where she lives: "The young fellows in the village only talked about getting engaged, marriage, family life, and other boring things. They never talked about fucking."

The only other member of Little Red Riding Hood's family who felt the same was her Grandmother. Sick and tired of life in the village, she had moved into the woods where she felt freer to do what she liked, amusing herself with the animals and the hunters who regularly called on her when they were near her hut. Of course, Little Red Riding Hood never missed a chance to visit Grandmother, preferably alone, and these rare occasions were the happiest moments in the girl's life. She was therefore all the more pleased when, one day as she was sitting by the window bored to tears, her mother asked her to take some food and medicine to Grandmother, for she had heard that Granny was ill.

Little Red Riding Hood wasted no time in getting under way, and happily she sang and skipped along as she went. When she had gone some way into the woods a wolf suddenly appeared before her. The little girl looked delicious to him, not for eating but for sex, though like all hypocritical wolves, he did not dare admit that to her. Instead he said something to her about the weather and similar things, and bored Little Red Riding Hood just as though he were one of the polite young men in town.

Nevertheless, the Wolf learned from the girl that she was on her way to Grandmother, and that bit of information interested him very much. "What," he thought to himself, "if I could get there ahead of Little Red Riding Hood and screw the old lady first. That would make two wonderful numbers in the same day!"

The Wolf ran ahead to the old lady's house, knocked, and pretended to be Little Red Riding Hood. When Grandmother saw that it was not Little Red Riding Hood but the Wolf, she was delighted and cried, "How marvelous! Come right in, don't be bashful, and let's have some fun!"

The Wolf and Grandmother had a wonderful time several times in a row, until Grandmother, finally exhausted and satisfied, fell asleep. This was the moment the Wolf had been waiting for. Quickly he took off the old lady's nightshirt and put it on himself. Then he lay down in bed, complete with Grandmother's nightcap, waiting for Little Red Riding Hood to appear. He did not have long to wait.

When Little Red Riding Hood enters the house, there ensues the same kind of question and answer game as in the original fairy tale, until matters take a different turn:

"Have you got hair like that everywhere?" said Little Red Riding Hood and, moved by curiosity, lifted up the bedcovers.

"Why, Grandmother," she cried, "but you've got a cock!"

"So that I can fuck you with it!" replied the Wolf, suddenly grabbing Little Red Riding Hood, tearing the clothes off her, and sticking it into her.

"Why, Grandmother!" cried Little Red Riding Hood all confused as she opened her legs wide. "Grandmother! How wonderful it is! Oh! How beautifully you fuck. But w-what a st-strange k-kind of ill-illness! Ah!"

She sank completely into the bed and stared absently into the face above her. It was only then she noticed that it wasn't Grandmother's face at all, and yet somehow it seemed familiar to her. For a second or two she was confused, then, suddenly, she recognized him.

"Oh, it's you! I wouldn't have thought you had it in you. You acted so stupid before. Why didn't you tell me right off that you wanted to fuck me? In that case, we could have done it immediately out there among the anemones. I'm not playing hard to get. But what have you done with Grandmother? Where the hell is she? Aha! I am beginning to understand—you've killed her by fucking!"

"Not exactly," said the Wolf, much flattered. "She is lying in the kitchen, resting."

But that was not the case. Grandmother had heard the bed going in the next room, and suspecting that something interesting was going on, she had come in to watch (the old lady was, among other things, a great voyeur).

Now she stood in the door with a sweet smile on her lips. The blanket hung loosely from her shoulders so that one could see her breasts, belly, and cunt.

"That's what *you* thought," she said excitedly. "Welcome, Little Red Riding Hood! How sweet you look. Well, how do you like the Wolf? Isn't he fantastic?"

"He sure is," said Little Red Riding Hood.

There follows a lesbian scene between Grandmother and Little Red Riding Hood:

Little Red Riding Hood's hand slid deeper and deeper into Grandmother's vestibule, which was wide open and soft. The Wolf liked what he saw. In fact, he liked it so much that he got hard again.

"Look, he's getting ready again," said the young girl. . . .

The Grandmother opened her eyes and inspected the Wolf's member. "You're right," she said. "Not bad." . . .

Something was, indeed, stirring deep inside the Wolf. After all, what Wolf is able to lie between two women who are making love to each other without being affected by it, no matter how exhausted he may be? He gently bit into a shoulder, nibbled at an ear lobe. He slid his index finger between the cheeks of Little Red Riding Hood's behind, only to collide with that of Grandmother. Little Red Riding Hood sighed and opened her legs still wider to receive all the caresses, no matter where they came from. . . . Grandmother's grotto lay exposed, but not for him. As he tried to get into it, he was intercepted by Little Red Riding Hood's lips and tongue which licked and sucked.

The three continue in this vein, trying first this and then that combination, until they all fall into happy slumber. It is at that point that the Hunter appears. The Hunter has more than once enjoyed the favors of the gay old lady and proves not to be free of prejudice and jealousy.

Inside, a scene met his eyes that took away his breath and a lump of jealousy and passion lodged itself in his throat. It hurt. There they were, all three of them, sleeping it off, after all the feasting and fucking. They lay there so beautifully relaxed in each other's arms, their bodies so obviously in harmony with each other, that the picture would have moved anybody—anybody, that is, except the Hunter. He wasn't touched at all; he was furious.

With two quick, deliberate steps he went up to the bed. He raised the butt of the rifle to crash it on the Wolf's head. But he remained motionless, paralyzed by anger.

"Just look at that!" he hissed, and his fingers closed like a vice around the raised gun. "Just look at that!" . . .

A Wolf!

A Wolf had cheated him of his fuck. A Wolf had raped first Grandmother and then the young girl who was lying there with swelling breasts and upraised knees in all her nudity, so one could see the pink flesh of her cunt peeking out between her thighs.

The tensed fingers of the Hunter tightened for the deadly blow.

Just then Little Red Riding Hood woke up. Sleepily she blinked and stretched herself so that her breasts tightened and her ribs stood out. Somehow she had vaguely guessed in her sleep that something was wrong. But she had trouble orienting herself, being still midway between sleep and sensuous memories of what had so recently happened.

At that moment she noticed the Hunter.

She sat up and stared at him. Who the hell was this guy? Why was he there and what did he want? She noticed the gun, poised above the Wolf's head, ready to bash him.

No! She had to prevent it!

Little Red Riding Hood threw herself upon the Hunter's arm. "Are you crazy?" she whispered. "You must be nuts. What do you think you are up to?"

"Don't be afraid," gasped the Hunter. "Don't be afraid. I'm not going to do you any harm."

"No, you aren't going to do any harm to me," said Little Red Riding Hood, "but you were going to kill *him!*"

"Of course, I want to kill him. Stupid female! The way he's treated you and Grandma. He deserves to be killed!"

"No," pleaded Little Red Riding Hood. "No, no! He hasn't done us any harm. He was marvelous! Don't kill him. It would be terrible."

"What do you mean, he hasn't done you any harm? There you are, both of you, raped, the victims of his perfidy!"

"No," said Little Red Riding Hood, and the tears were running down her cheeks. "You are wrong. His perfidy fit just fine. We wanted it. It was marvelous."

"You wanted it yourselves!" gasped the Hunter, and hatred welled up in him again. "So, he's brought you to the point that you wanted it yourselves! For that he deserves to be killed all the more!"

While the Wolf and Grandmother are still asleep, the Hunter tries to have sex with Little Red Riding Hood. But she refuses him obstinately, although she is wet again with desire, as the Hunter notices. Still she keeps refusing.

"Why did you want to kill the Wolf?" she demanded by fits and starts.

"Would you have fucked me otherwise? I mean, if I hadn't gone after the Wolf?"

"Why, of course!" exclaimed Little Red Riding Hood, clinging with her whole body to his. "Of course! But do you think I'm going to let myself be fucked by a killer?"

"But I haven't killed him after all," said the Hunter hoarsely, pushing his hard-on against her cunt. "Look, he's alive."

"Sure. But if I hadn't awakened just in time . . ."

Little Red Riding Hood felt how it was swelling under the coarse fabric of his pants. She got goose pimples and her cunt hair bristled. He pushed a finger into her from behind.

"You are wild in there," he whispered. "You want to get fucked. And I haven't killed the Wolf!"

"Fucking is better than killing," whispered Little Red Riding Hood and made room for his searching hand.

"Yes, it is," he groaned.

"You mustn't kill him. I don't want to fuck somebody who wants to kill."

"I want to fuck. Fuck."

"You don't want to kill any more?"

"I don't want to kill any more."

"Only fuck?"

"Only fuck. Fuck! Fuck!"

Little Red Riding Hood and the Hunter go at it for some time; during their bouts Grandmother and the Wolf wake up, look around, and wonder who she is fucking. The Wolf goes outside to get some fresh air, comes back in, searches for wine, finds they have drunk it all, and eats some grapes instead. Then he sits down on the floor beside Little Red Riding Hood and the Hunter, who are lying intimately entwined after their love-making. Little Red Riding Hood is on top.

"Upon whom are you lying?" asked the Wolf.

For an answer Little Red Riding Hood only gurgled sensuously against the neck of the Hunter.

"Oh, I see," said the Wolf, stroking her gently on the back. "You are all fucked out."

Caressing the cheeks of her behind, he touched with his finger-tips the legs of the Hunter. He felt with his hand for Little Red Riding Hood's cunt, only to come upon the shaft of the Hunter, who was still embedded there.

But at that the Hunter got angry again.

"Take your paws off, you swine!" he said.

Puzzled, the Wolf pulled back his hand. He wasn't used to being treated like that by his fuck companions.

"I'm not a swine. I'm a Wolf," he said.

"What the hell are you doing?" Little Red Riding Hood asked the Hunter, feeling very hurt. "Are you nuts, chasing him away like that?"

"Only I am allowed to touch you now," hissed the Hunter and pressed her against him tightly.

"Nonsense!" replied Little Red Riding Hood. "Of course he can touch me. As much as he wants to. And Grandmother too. You too can touch Grandmother—it's all right. Just don't start getting jealous. That's ridiculous. Nobody's going to be the better for that."

"He's touched my cock!" complained the Hunter.

"Has he?" said Little Red Riding Hood. "Why, that's wonderful. Then you've got all the less reason to be jealous, for it shows that he likes you too."

"That's dirty!" replied the Hunter between his teeth.

"Nonsense! It's wonderful," said Little Red Riding Hood, and nonchalantly rolled off the Hunter.

Little Red Riding Hood now performs fellatio on the Wolf, much to the jealous disgust of the Hunter; but Grandmother invites the latter to come and have sex with her. The Hunter tries to subdue his newly rising passion, being excited by the idea of having been touched by the Wolf, but he can't admit it and tries hard to take offense. Grandmother keeps inviting him, but since he won't join the others, Grandmother accepts the Wolf, while Little Red Riding Hood squats over her head and lets Grandmother perform cunnilingus.

Finally, the Hunter cannot stand it any longer. He jumps up, rushes to the bed, throws himself upon it, and—before he knows how—is deeply imbedded in the Wolf's behind. He has to admit that he likes it, and so does the Wolf, who is happy about the unsolicited addition to his act with the Grandmother. But as soon as the Hunter has an orgasm, all his old prejudices and preconceived notions reassert themselves and he again threatens to shoot the Wolf. Again Little Red Riding Hood interferes at the last second.

"You goddam bastard! Now you've broken your word! You said you weren't going to kill him—only fuck. Now you've fucked him and still you want to kill him. Is that any way to thank somebody for one's pleasure?"

General chaos followed. Grandmother screamed. The Wolf, who saw with surprise that his life was threatened by the very person whose member he had just a moment before felt inside himself and whose spunk was still running down his thighs and legs, growled angrily and bared his teeth in defense. The Hunter lowered the gun and aimed. All the others threw themselves on him and wrestled with him. The Wolf took a bite at him. But when the Hunter felt for the second time the fur of the Wolf against his skin and at the same time the touch of women's breasts and stomachs, his cock stood up afresh.

"Don't kill me!" he whimpered in desperation. "Don't kill me! Just fuck."

The Wolf's biting on his shoulder had made him wild. "Come, bite me on the cock, Wolf," he cried, "bite me on the cock. Not on the shoulder—bite me on the cock. Let's fuck, only fuck! Wolf! Riding Hood! Grandma!"

But Little Red Riding Hood had lifted the gun and took aim at his heart.

"Please, don't kill me." he whimpered. "Let's fuck!"

"You goddam spoil-fuck!" cried Little Red Riding Hood. "One can't trust you!"

"Do with me as you like. As you like! Throw away my gun . . . throw it in the well! . . . Come, Wolf! Come! I've got a big cock. Come!"

Little Red Riding Hood lowered the gun.

"I shall do as you say," she said. "And do you know why? Because one can't trust you. One just can't trust you. As long as you've got the gun, you are liable to behave the same way again after the next number. I'm not going to take a chance on it, so I'm going to throw the gun in the well, just as you said. That's the only way we'll be safe."

Having said this, she went out and threw the gun in the well. The Hunter let out a sigh of relief, grabbed the head of the Wolf and pushed it between his thighs. The Wolf's mouth closed around the cock of the Hunter. It was big all right. That's how the bad Hunter was converted.

This modern fairy tale dramatizes the mechanism of denial in the face of attraction, whether to members of one's own sex (homosexuality) or to members of races thought to be inferior. And, in reality, as the newspapers testify daily, denial and repression are readily converted into violence and bloodshed.

ANDRÉA DE NERCIAT

Although this is not an anthology of erotic literature, but a selection of erotic fantasies, one cannot but give a special place to the Chevalier de Nerciat (1739–1800), whose writings set the tone of all subsequent French erotic literature. In this connection, we should point out that no consideration has been given in this volume to the writings of the Marquis de Sade, a contemporary of Nerciat, because Sade's writings—which all deal with his sexual fantasies—deserve a more exhaustive treatment in their own right. Sade's fantasies are primarily concerned with sadomasochism and other sexual deviations which are intimately related to his political philosophies and which must be discussed in that connection.

The erotic fantasies which Nerciat presents are fairly typical for those of French erotica and must therefore reflect a good deal of national sex psychology, though not necessarily of national French sex behavior, whether in the eighteenth century or at any time. For, as we have pointed out earlier, one must not equate fantasy with behavior, which is the error made by censors, who cannot conceive of a fantasy world apart from that of reality, and whose simplistic logic leads them to assume that fantasy must necessarily lead to action.

Relatively little is known about the life of Andréa de Nerciat. The only study devoted to his life and works is a short introduction which Guillaume Apollinaire wrote for a selection of Nerciat's writings published in the collection *Les Maîtres de l'Amour*. (All of Apollinaire's prefaces in this collection have recently been published by Gallimard.) From this we learn that Nerciat was born in Dijon of a well-to-do family (his father was a lawyer) and that he received a good education. His first vocation was the military, and he remained in the army until 1775. He had been writing in his spare time, but the bulk of his work dates from his retirement at the age of thirty-six. It would seem that this retirement was only apparent, for all the evidence points to his having been, like his contemporary Mirabeau, a secret agent for the various French governments until the end of his life. In 1780 he got a job as assistant librarian at the court of Frederick the Great, whose remarkable library he attempted to organize. Intrigues caused him to lose his job. His role during the French Revolution was extremely suspect. He acted as a spy for the Revolutionary government, but he hated the Revolution and was probably betraying it at the same time. He also worked for the Consulate's secret police, but his role in Naples, where Napoleon sent him, was again that of a double agent (he was a passionate Italophile). In 1798, he broke with the Republic and was imprisoned in the Castello San Angelo by the French occupants. Following the evacuation of 1800, he was set free and returned to Naples. However, he had fallen seriously ill in prison and died soon after his release. Apollinaire has little to say about the motives that may have driven him to write, and in a sense Nerciat's books speak for themselves: he was a pure hedonist, one of the purest that literary history has known.

MON NOVICIAT

Nerciat's well known work *Mon Noviciat* (*My Period of Probation*) consists, supposedly, of the confessions of a young woman: "Keep in mind that I am barely twenty-four, tall and slender, without being skinny, of light complexion, without looking sickly, blonde, without seeming colorless."

This young beauty is put into a monastery. There she shares a room with a twenty-year-old girl friend, Felicia. One night Felicia has a dream during which she makes such strong intercourse movements and talks about a certain "Jonas" (the gamekeeper of the author's father) that the other girl awakens. The first thing she hears is Felicia saying, "This time you have certainly made me a child, for I can feel your elixir of life in my innermost being."

When the author repeats the movements and words to Felicia, the latter confesses that she is having an affair with Jonas. In the wake of the confession, she starts fondling the other girl and masturbates her to orgasm. One thing leads to another—the two girls first rub their genitals together, after which Felicia performs cunnilingus on the other girl.

Afterward the girls talk, and Felicia tells her story, a story which is really a fantasy of the transsexual or sex-reversal type which, as we shall see, is fairly common in erotic literature.

Felicia tells that she lost her parents at an early age and was brought up by an uncle. However, her mother had raised her as a boy, so she started to work at an early age as a chimney sweep, then as a bootblack. As a manservent, she went to work for a high-class prostitute in Paris.

One day she walks in when that lady is making love to a client. When the man withdraws, she sees the open sex of the woman and the penis of the man. This is the first time she realizes that she is a girl and not a boy. Far from being ashamed or angry, Felicia's (or rather Felix's) employer embraces her and invites her to stay and watch the next bout from the beginning. When toward the end the woman pulls back, Felix sees how a man ejaculates. The prostitute scolds her lover for not having withdrawn sooner on his own accord, so as to prevent pregnancy.

"Thus I learned," says Felicia, "in one single lesson that I was not a male, that a man has what I had just seen, that a woman receives such a thing into the same kind of thing as I had, that she has pleasure in doing so, and that babies are made that way, if the woman lets the semen enter into her; but that one does not let this happen to avoid the danger. How many revelations in a single moment's time!"

Felix's employer washes afterward in her presence and makes a pass at her (she is only sixteen at that time). In that manner, the lady discovers Felix's true sex, and—in typical erotica fashion—offers to make a career for her. Felicia pretends to agree, but really plans to get away from the lady.

Having run away, Felix sleeps the first night with an eighteen-year-old boy who agrees to share his bed with her (he is one of a company of young fellows who sleep together in a kind of dormitory for young workingmen). Thinking of the events of the day and being unable to sleep, Felix wants to find out if this fellow has the same kind of thing as her former employer's friend. She feels the young man and finds only a flaccid penis. Soon, however, it starts to move, growing gradually to full erection. Delighted, Felix tries to insert it into her vagina, without awakening the young man. But he wakes up and, thinking he is being homosexually approached, hits Felix. The other men wake up and threaten to hand Felix over to the police, but desist from doing so when, during the ensuing scuffle, they discover Felicia's real sex.

They offer to let the girl stay with them, but she, having had enough of them, packs up and leaves. In the dark street, Felix runs into a former customer (when she was a bootblack), who offers her shelter for the night, then tries anal intercourse when he thinks Felix is asleep. Felix feigns sleep in order to find out what it's all about. At first, the man cannot penetrate, but finally succeeds. Felix, feeling pain, gives up her pretense of being asleep, and tries to get away. Her host, however, prevents her from doing so. Instead he lights some candles and proceeds to undress Felix. In doing so, he discovers the real sex of Felicia, who calms down when she realizes in the light that the liquid she felt running down her thighs is not blood but semen. However, this romance, too, comes to a premature end when, just as they want to commence regular intercourse, there is a rap at the door and Felicia's new protector is served a warrant for default of debts.

This takes place in some kind of tenement house, explaining why the arrival of the police attracts a number of other tenants, among them a certain man who simply takes Felicia by the hand as they lead her friend away, and escorts her to his own room in the same building. He tells her to "get into bed" and leaves her, but returns a few moments later with her clothes. Noticing that it is man's clothing, he asks her why she is wearing it, and Felicia tells him her story. Later that night this man deflowers her and has intercourse with her four times, during which Felicia experiences only a little pain and some pleasure.

One day, the girl who is narrating the story and who has taken Felicia to stay with her at her home, puts a sleeping drug in her mother's wine and lets a man, dressed as a nun, enter through the window by a ladder. The man undresses the two girls and himself, puts them on the bed, and starts with the girl telling the story.

Afterward, the man has intercourse with Felicia, ejaculating outside her, while her friend watches, reflecting on the scene as follows: "And now tell me frankly, you true lovers and connoisseurs of the art of love, can you imagine anything more marvelous and interesting than the sight of two perfectly beautiful bodies which, by the introduction of a male member, full of health and vigor, unite themselves into one ecstatic being? . . . Any real amorist who does not appreciate seeing that which he himself enjoys so much doing is indeed an ungrateful person."

It turns out that the man is unable to penetrate our raconteur who has had much less experience than Felicia. He therefore suggests that Felicia get on top of him, while the other girl straddle his face, so he can perform cunnilingus at the same time.

They do this with much delight and success, after which the never tiring Felicia suggests he have anal intercourse with her, so he can ejaculate without fear of consequences. (Nerciat is always didactic, eager to impart some new knowledge or bit of moral philosophy to the reader.)

Next night, the man returns with two blindfolded comrades of his. When he takes off their blindfolds, they are delighted to see two lovely young girls, rather than a couple of old nuns as their friend had made them expect.

It transpires that the storyteller is still a virgin. Felicia tells one of the men, who is particularly eager to have intercourse with the virgin, to take it easy and be gentle with her. He promises he will, and Felicia notices with relief that he has a smaller penis than the other two.

With the help of Felicia, the young man manages to deflower the girl, but in the excitement he forgets his promise to withdraw in time and would have ejaculated inside had not the ever watchful Felicia recognized the signs of the approaching climax and removed him just in time.

Instead of thanking her for her care, the ungrateful girl scolds Felicia for having robbed them of a still more perfect pleasure. Felicia takes it in good stride. "Aha!" she says, "you mean I should have let him make you a child. What I should do is give you a good spanking! . . . Remember this, little lady, don't ever, under any circumstances, allow a man to ejaculate inside of you during the first bout. The following rounds are, with most men, still a little dangerous, but much less so than the first, and with the majority of men, they are completely harmless." (Nerciat sincerely believed that the chances of conception were reduced if not altogether set aside by repeated intercourse; formerly a not too uncommon prejudice.)

Felicia now has intercourse with her partner, while the first girl watches, gets excited, and resumes intercourse with her own partner, who this time ejaculates in her while she is having orgasm. Then they watch the other couple.

Felicia's partner has done her four times, when the door opens and the narrator's mother enters.

The man who entered the house dressed in nun's costume turns out to be a certain Count who has known the girl's mother for many years. He reminds the mother that they were lovers long ago in Paris, that she is as passionate or more so than her daughter, and so on. Moreover, Felicia and the daughter have watched the mother read a licentious book and have seen her masturbate. Felicia now tells this to the mother. The Count tries to seduce her, she resists, and during the ensuing struggle she displays her "mature charms" to all. In the end, all three couples have intercourse together on the same bed.

The story goes on in this vein, but takes a more devious turn when the author relates a scene with two older men and four Italian musicians (two men and two women), during which one of the older men has a younger man perform anal intercourse with him, while the other older man performs anal intercourse with the second young man. (Here we see how easily Nerciat switches from the descriptions of heterosexual to homosexual activities; the strong bisexual interest of this author appeared also in the ambiguity of Felix-Felicia's sex identity.)

Bisexuality, transvestitism, and homosexuality become even more prominent as the story progresses. In a scene involving seven men and five women, the hostess suggests dressing one of the pretty young men as a woman and offers him to an aristocratic Englishman. The young man is somewhat less than enthusiastic about this proposal because he had his eyes on the pretty female narrator. But he has to obey the hostess's suggestion, as etiquette at such occasions demands.

It turns out, however, that one of the young Italian musicians, Silvio, looks very girlish. When, at one point, he returns to the party dressed as a girl and calling himself Silvia, the disguise is so perfect that the female narrator wants to make sure by manual examination whether he is really a girl. When she feels his half-erect penis under his skirts, she knows that he is Silvio.

When the narrator tries to fondle Silvia's behind, she meets with the Englishman's hand on the other side. The latter suggests she have Silvia first, then hand Silvia over to him. The

Englishman lies down next to the narrator and does everything
to her that she is doing to Silvia: "He felt me everywhere, kissed
my little slit, my behind, brought a pretty respectable spear into
play, and would, had I encouraged him in the least, given me
preference to Silvia." However, the narrator takes hold of
Silvia's penis and is about to put it into her vagina when the
Englishman offers to render this service to the two, which he
does, adding some ardent kisses to the place of their junction.

As soon as Silvio ejaculates, the Englishman enters him
from behind. The narrator quickly disentangles herself to become an observer: "I didn't find it either interesting, nor particularly strange, but rather ridiculous." She picks up a leather whip
and gives the Englishman a whack on his behind. Her victim, far
from complaining, encourages her to do more of the same since
it excites him.

Meanwhile, another man, a cousin of the Englishman, takes
another whip and flagellates the narrator. She rather likes the
mild flagellation, but feigns a struggle in which she is thrown on
the mattress "and thoroughly fucked."

Two men vie to have Felicia, who initially masturbates the
two as they sit on either side of her. She prefers one of the men,
but pretends to let fate decide which of the two is to have her
first. The men would have to guess, she explains, which of two
fingers she would wet, and the winner is to have her. She wets
both fingers, to make sure the man she prefers can win. However, the loser grabs her hand, finds both fingers wet, and
complains bitterly. At that, Felicia says, "All right, gentlemen, in
that case you shall both satisfy yourselves." And raising her
skirts to under her arms, she adds, "I believe that even the one
who is going to be least favored, will have no reason to complain." She throws the Englishman on the couch, puts him on his
back, and lodges herself on top of him, then invites the other
man to enter her from behind. The young man, unused to such
sport, hesitates and, instead, mounts a girl by the name of
Lauretta. The Englishman's uncle, on the other hand, who has
heard the invitation, and who has had anal intercourse with
Silvio, cannot resist it and enters Felicia from behind.

The story goes on in this way, adding incest and further bisexual scenes. One more quotation from the book will serve to call attention to Nerciat's constant moralizing or proselytizing:

You are still far from the knowledge of the true art of love, if your desire is immediately reduced by the presence of a third party and if the weak flame of your passions is easily squelched by others witnessing your pleasure. Stupidly and insensitively you are submitting yourselves to the simple dictates of that which is supposed to be "natural," thereby missing completely every refinement of sensuality and are satisfied with the simple satisfaction of your passion—something which we have in common with all the animals. As to myself, I would like to stage the choreography of a love ballet for eleven thousand people, if such were at all possible. For, the more witnesses to my pleasure I have, the more women I can see dying away under the forceful administration of male members, and the more men I can see pouring their souls into the deepest ground of the female conch shell, the more intense and deep would be my own pleasure.

LES APHRODITES

Nerciat's *Les Aphrodites ou Fragments thali-priapiques pour servir à l'histoire du plaisir* was published in 1793. The first episode below concerns a gentleman farmer from Gascony (almost all of Nerciat's male characters are members of the aristocracy or *haute bourgeoisie*), Monsieur Trattignac, and his initiation into the secret society of "Les Aphrodites," founded by a former madame for the erotic consolation of persecuted nobility (the book was published four years after the beginning of the Revolution).

After the required medical examination, the pretty maidservant, Célestine, prepares to put the newcomer to another test while his pants are still down:

CÉLESTINE: While we are at it, and in order to avoid putting you out again, I shall ask one more favor of you.
TRATTIGNAC: Your wish is my command, you lovely thing. I'd brave a fiery inferno for the likes of you!

What was required of him was not nearly so difficult. She signaled to the page who was standing by and obtained a wooden basket approximately one foot in diameter. An iron hoop running around the upper edge was attached to four symmetrically placed chains of equal length suspended from a thick ring, so that the basket hung down like a censer. The inside of the ring was lined with thick, soft padding. In order to measure the strength of a person's erection, he was required to slip the glans of his *boute-joie** through the ring and to support an increasing weight of cannon balls of various sizes as they were placed in the bushel one after the other. Trattignac was only too willing to comply with any instructions that might be forthcoming from a damsel whose good fortune it was to suit his fancy, and he lent himself to the ordeal all the more gladly as Célestine agreed to fit the ring into place herself. This ceremony could only add to the lewd applicant's capacities. At the outset, a hundredweight was placed in the basket, and he lifted it as though it were empty; twenty pounds more were child's play; ten pounds were added and still he supported them.

CÉLESTINE: I'll stop when you say "enough."

TRATTIGNAC: Keep on with it. . . .

CÉLESTINE (*adding ten more pounds*): Now you don't want to strain yourself, sir.

TRATTIGNAC: If I were allowed to . . . (*He lifted his hand to her tucker, but a severe, dignified glance arrested him; the bushel, however, still did not budge.*)

CÉLESTINE (*putting in two five-pound weights*): If you can hold this much more, you will be the equal of our strongest guests.

TRATTIGNAC: Put them all in at once. (*He supported them and even managed to give that tremendous weight a little jounce. Nor would he allow it to be removed immediately. Not until three minutes had gone by did he lower it to the floor.*)

CÉLESTINE: Wonderful, sir! We'll be glad to have you with us!

The next excerpt precedes the copulating contest which is the climax of the book. The contest itself, related by the man who is to judge it, is of mediocre interest, but this description of the special piece of equipment used by the contestants is a fine example of "apparatus" fantasies.

---

* This word, invented by Nerciat and found, to our knowledge, in his works alone, might be rendered as "batter-joy" or "battering-ram of fun" or some such.

Twenty minutes before the performance was to begin, several pages appeared and placed on the grassy embankment, facing the seven arcades opposite the exit, pieces of furniture the likes of which I had never seen. They were neither beds nor chairs; Monsieur du Bossage, their designer, told me he had dubbed them *avantageuses*.

An *avantageuse* is a kind of cradle designed to support both antagonists in a joust. The lady approaches it as she would an ordinary chair and, grasping two well-padded handles—whimsically carved in the shape of two vigorous pegos—she lets herself sink back. She is now supported, from the top of her head to within an inch and a half of the place where the furrow between the buttocks begins, by a fairly thick, satin-covered cushion or short mattress, which is firm rather than fluffy. The rest of the body is free of any encumbrance; the feet, however, slip into a pair of fixed, padded stirrups fastened at only a short distance, so that the knees are bent at a sharp angle. It is easy to imagine the freedom that this position cannot fail to afford the lady when it comes to doing the splits of working her hips, as she is no longer hindered by friction of any sort. Her rider's position on the *avantageuse* is no less cleverly contrived. While his knees are supported by a fairly broad and very soft crosspiece, his feet are braced against a kind of cantle. Leaning forward in this position, he finds himself within perfect range of the goal of his exercises.

He slips his arms under the lady's and grips two cylindrical hand rests on either side of the woodwork. Thus deployed, the lady and her rider are free to touch one another if they so desire only at the point where they are meant to join, telescoping themselves as deeply as they like: the rider can draw himself upward with his hands or else the lady, by bending her legs, can slide down against him.

I realized clearly that these arrangements allayed all the inconveniences of entwined arms which cause overheating and hinder the breathing apparatus, and of cumbersome legs and thighs which, when the lady crosses them behind her rider's back, tend to make the frictional process slower and more difficult. No doubt the situation with regard to the event about to take place on these *avantageuses* was similar to that of a horse race: the utmost ingenuity was brought to bear in order to achieve every possible advantage, no matter how slight. We all know that when there are no such imperatives, there is nothing so pleasant as holding one's lady fair close over or under oneself in bed, wrapping one's arms around her pretty bust, being squeezed against two divine titties, burying one's nose in them to one's heart's content, feeling oneself drawn in by two crossed silken legs, etc. However, such lazy dalliance as this is quite out of place when it comes to throwing seven vigorous fucks in the space of two hours, as was the objective of the forthcoming contest. The time had come for our seven couples to show us whether they were capable of attaining it.

LE DIABLE AU CORPS

This book, in three volumes—undoubtedly the most important one by Nerciat—bears in the original edition of 1788 the imprint: "*oeuvre posthume du très-recommendable Docteur Cassoné*," a pseudonym which the author assumed because of the strict censorship of his time.

Le Diable au Corps (*The Devil in the Flesh*) is a sequel to *Les Aphrodites*. While the plot is as slender as that of the earlier book, and the construction as loose, *Le Diable au Corps* is far richer and more varied in its inventions. Louis Perceau, the great bibliographer of French erotica, regarded it as the finest of all French erotic novels.

It would be pointless even to outline the many adventures of the Marchioness and her friends. We have, where necessary, simply indicated the point of departure for each scene.

A peddler named Bricon (Break-Cunt) is showing the Marchioness (who is in bed) his very special assortment of wares. She has already looked at and purchased a couple of conventional dildoes, as we pick up the following dialogue:

MARCHIONESS: Why . . . what is that? I frankly confess I cannot make head or tail of it. Two branches! And that plate covered with hair! It's terrifying, monstrous!

BRICON (*smiling*): Well said! Very amusing. Your Ladyship cannot fail to have read the "Story of Y"? You remember the *gaudeant bene nati?*

MARCHIONESS: Oh! How naïve of me! A peg for each hole, I suppose. What a delightful folly! But don't you think you're going a bit far with this one, Monsieur Bricon?

BRICON (*with less apprehension*): Fiddlesticks! Such prejudices are out of date.

MARCHIONESS (*with a knowing look*): Oh, yes indeed!

BRICON: Nowadays, even the most honorable persons may take any liberty they please.

MARCHIONESS (*putting on a dignified air again*): So long as it's not disgusting. Be that as it may, I want to know all about it.

BRICON: These two . . . uh . . .

MARCHIONESS: Those two cocks! Go on, speak up.

BRICON (*with a smile*): This is how they are worn. (*He holds the apparatus in front of his belt for a moment.*) The upper one, as you can see, addresses itself to the usual spot, of course.

MARCHIONESS: Splendid! And, as a result, the other is within range of its backdoor neighbor. I'm beginning to understand.

BRICON: Now, if Your Ladyship will be so good as to observe the lower cock. May I?

MARCHIONESS: There's nothing like the evidence of the senses.

BRICON: As I was saying, you will observe that the lower cock is longer and thinner.

MARCHIONESS: I was about to ask you why.

BRICON: It is longer because it must be inserted first—its channel of penetration is a bit difficult of access, and it must be given a head start, so to speak.

MARCHIONESS: Why, they've thought of everything! Now I see that it is thinner and sharper in order to avoid inflicting some injury.

BRICON: It is a sincere pleasure to exhibit one's wares to persons of experience . . . (*biting his tongue*) I mean persons with insight.

MARCHIONESS: That's better.

BRICON: When this one is in place, the other finds the right path of its own accord. As for this plate, you can see that it is a kind of mask representing the masculine attributes. The lady can tie it onto herself with ribbons. For, you see, this little plaything was originally designed for the amusement of two lady friends.

MARCHIONESS: And what if it took a lady's fancy to amuse herself with it in the company of one of her men friends?

BRICON: Then, as Your Ladyship can see, the upper branch may be removed (*he takes it off*) and replaced by the natural one, or, if the operator is tired and difficult to rouse, then the apparatus remains as it is and the disgraced member may be hidden away inside the hollow surrogate.

MARCHIONESS: I've never seen anything so indecent. And the price?

BRICON: For you, Madame, three louis will be my very last word.

The Marchioness next makes a bet with the Countess Motenfeu (Cunt-on-Fire)—bets are frequently taken as pretexts in Nerciat—concerning the propensity of donkeys for human females. The Countess maintains that a he-donkey, if approached by a woman, will perform quite readily, while the Marchioness denies this. The outcome of this bet appears in Chapter 10, in the section entitled "Animals."

The main event in the second volume is a huge orgy—it takes up several chapters—which is certainly one of Nerciat's finest *morceaux de bravoure*. We can cite only a brief excerpt here, but it does give an idea of the elaborate sentence structure and achronological narrative techniques which he uses to convey a vision as detailed as possible of such fantasies. At times his style foreshadows that of Pierre Klossowski.

For a clearer understanding of this passage, it should be pointed out that when it begins, the Negro, Zamor, is making love to the Marchioness, while the ambivalent "mine-owner" (also a prelate of sorts) is sodomizing him.

A fresh incident added zest and variety to the scene. Who was this pretty little freak who came forward to the strains of a spirited jig, displaying beneath a bosom worthy of Venus the proud attribute of the god Lump-Sac? Comical was the contrast between the adorable pink and white belly and the swarthy dildo made of Venetian leather. . . . However, let us give thanks to Mother Nature who, in her benevolence, refrains from fostering such charming creatures as Nicole fitted out with real *boute-joies* as estimable as the imitation of which the little maid had just tied on. For if we had such desirable androgynes for rivals, would any beauty deign to favor us? Where, however, did she get that handsome replica, adorned with its perfectly imitated appurtenances and a curly head of hair that looked just like the real thing? What was she intending to do with it?

"You little rascal!" exclaimed the "mine-owner" at the sight of her masquerade. "It wasn't for you that I kept that piece of furniture on hand; give me back my lieutenant, give it back right away!"

Nonsense! A girl didn't put on a thing like that and then not get any use out of it. Actually, it was with the gallant intention of skewering her friend Philippine that Nicole, whose tastes were well-known, had armed herself with that artificial weapon. For ever since her mistress had taken Zamor away from Philippine and was keeping him so thoroughly occupied, to the girl's bitter regret, she had had nothing better to do than prepare for further adventures. She performed her ablutions with ice and returned fresh as rose, wanting nothing better than to find a suitable partner; everyone, however, was either busy or unworthy in her eyes of becoming a successor to the illustrious Zamor. Adolph, however, fooled by the vivid crimson hue of a lively slot glimpsed from afar while it was being cleansed, thought he had found another arena suitable for the bloody exploits of which he was so fond,* and tried to . . . However, as soon as he touched her, his exceedingly nervous hands unfortunately caused some pain; the spark of desire died instantly in the breast of the oversensitive Philippine, and she tore herself away from the clumsy virtuoso.

It was at that very moment that Nicole, rummaging through the old clothes in the neglected package, lay hands on the splendid dildo. This was a fine opportunity for Nicole, who had given Philippine many sincere tokens of her affection in the past, to provide her friend with an agreeable pastime. If Nicole, then, had closed off the channel of true pleasure in herself, it was the better to provide someone else with the benefits of its artificial image. However, she was not to have her masculine fling exactly as she had planned it. Before her friend could reach her, Philippine had yielded to the "mine-owner's" pleas and agreed to lend him her adorable jewel for a few minutes of tonguing. The only way for her to accommodate his whim was to form a kind of arch with her arms over Zamor's back (for Zamor was still belaboring the Marchioness) and lift her thighs onto the prelate's shoulders, one on each side of his head, so that his mouth was in a convenient position with respect to the delightful little slot. The pleasure derived by Philippine from this privileged role was enhanced by the pleasure of her eyes, for in the mirror she could see, in foreshortened perspective, the bodies of Zamor and the Countess, whose point of junction and midsectional movements were displayed under the most favorable angle. Now that the group was formed, the enchanting features of her beloved Philippine became an additional source of pleasure for the Marchioness, and she smiled at the girl. Each time that Zamor raised his hips to deliver a blow with his formidable battering-ram, he could feel the gentle pressure of two elastic titties, as well as their warmth and that of the girl's burning breath.

It was while all this was being arranged and executed that Nicole, feeling idle and frustrated, noticed the affected writhing of the "mine-owner's" hips and the explanatory mimic of his hand. What was this? Was the man mad enough to want Nicole to skewer *him?* Indeed, this was precisely what he had in mind. Nicole guessed

---

* Adolph, we have already learned, is interested only in menstruating women.

as much and was, moreover, willing to grant him that rare favor. The extravagant creature, already somewhat the worse for having drunk of Dr. Bischoff's aphrodisiac, seized the unchaste prelate's hips and boldly drove the imitation *boute-joie* home. Now while this kind of specious intromission is worth only as much as the subject's imagination, this was not true of the very real pleasure which that lewdest of human beings derived from his double role—operator with Zamor, patient with Nicole—from tonguing a Hebe, and from the sight of the ravishing scene that lay over the horizon formed before his eyes by Philippine's divine rump; for, reflected in the mirror in front of which they were so weirdly grouped, were the perfect bust and features of the pseudohermaphrodite; and the mirror, at least, saw the frolicsome hand that reached under the inanimate engine, teased and kneaded the manly bulbs and, by tickling the root of the very animate engine that was crammed into Zamor, sent the genital balm boiling forth. As a general rule, whenever our prelate was in the process of satisfying an initial whim he thought to reserve for himself the possibility of enjoying another, thus multiplying the sources of pleasure at the disposal of an imagination that was far more active than his senses. This time, however, he was in no position to economize his substance in this way. Riveted to the spot by Nicole and driven outside the bounds of his system by the hand that was pawing his private parts, he could not prevent himself from coming to a very abundant conclusion. The clever Nicole could feel the sublime elixir bubbling past her finger tips, and so she deigned to accelerate her movements and to utter those tender little words that add so much zest to a man's pleasure; then triggering at last the plunger in her dildo (filled, as we know, with warm milk), she made the happy "mine-owner's" illusion as complete as possible.

Toward the end of the second volume, the Marchioness comes down with smallpox. Anxious that her friends should not witness the disfiguring progress of the terrible illness, she retires to the country. On her arrival she is observed by a middle-aged monk Hilarion, and a very young lay brother, Felix, both of whom are extremely attracted to the still beautiful woman. Soon the Marchioness is much worse; her beauty seems permanently destroyed, and in fact the doctor has given her up for lost.

Finally, one evening [it was the day after the departure of the doctor who had pronounced the death verdict], the friar was alone at the condemned woman's bedside, babbling prayers to his heart's content, quite convinced that he was performing for the last time a duty which could never more be sweetened by amatory dreams, when the most extraordinary occurrence took place! He was in the process of commending her soul to Heaven when the Marchioness, who had scarcely shown any sign of life for the past hour, suddenly began to sigh heavily.

Yawning horribly, she threw back the covers, reached out, sighed again, and said in a perfectly lucid tone of voice: "Yes. I feel sweetly touched . . . so deeply penetrated!"

The astounded Hilarion broke off the ritual and fell silent. While he was quite flattered, he was convinced that although the dying woman had seemed utterly prostrate, she had actually been meditating, savoring the exaltation of episcopal teachings, that she had been visited by the grace of God, *touched* by his eloquence, *penetrated* with contrition and divine love.

But she went on talking: "I confess that from the very first, I hoped that you would find me attractive."

This, it must be recorded, gave the Reverend Father an entirely different notion! "Well, well! Can it be that she has actually recognized me? Can I have been fortunate enough to . . . ?" The monk in the performance of his religious duties had vanished. In his stead stood *the man of flesh and blood*, who now turned his mind to lecherous reasoning: "What a pity," said he to himself, "that such a precious sentiment has been born in the heart of a noisome, disfigured woman about to breathe her last! She was so lovely when she made such an ineffable impression upon me."

MARCHIONESS: You may be sure that you are not indifferent to me . . . and that had I been able to prove it to you sooner that nasty cowl would not have stopped me."

HILARION (*aside, and in a state of rapture*): By Saint Francis! I am loved! (*His blood was starting to boil.*) Oh, My Lady! . . . (*He did not know what more to say.*)

MARCHIONESS (*interrupting him softly*): Shh! . . . No so loud. Remember that "they" are here!

HILARION: Who?

MARCHIONESS: Can't you see them? I see them quite distinctly.

HILARION (*looking around*): Whom do you mean?

MARCHIONESS: Nicole and Belamour.

HILARION: But they are not here! We are all alone!

MARCHIONESS: They're watching us, I tell you! Speak softly . . . If they heard us. Oh! What luck! Look . . . they won't bother about us now! Still, it is a bit thick! Everyday it's the same thing. And not a thought for me! That's the third time that little whore Nicole has been stuffed today.

What a strange fit! How could it fail to upset the Reverend's only too sensitive fibers! His imagination was already lewd enough without the need of such descriptions! Already his angelic forehead was glowing a deep crimson; already the arteries swollen with frothy blood could be seen pulsing feverishly at his temples.

"Actually," she added deliberately, "I'm amused at their little set-to, and I'm really surprised to find that we have not yet had the good sense to imitate them."

This time, the thrust struck home: could the Devil himself have dreamed of a more subtle way to pervert a monk? Beneath his heavy coat, Hilarion could feel the enemy of chastity rearing its indecent head and throwing back its cowl. In vain did our sinner obey the last anguished cry of reason and force himself to gaze upon the revolting deformities of that unspeakably horrible countenance: his inspection was not enough to smother the blaze which had been fanned by such vivid images. The demon of the flesh had seized the sceptre and was despotically driving the Reverend Father to commit the threefold crime of breach of trust, fornication, and sacrilege.

For a finishing stroke, the spirit of indecency prompted the delirious woman to utter these impassioned words: "Come, my boy, don't be so timid. Put it in me. I want you to do it. I order you to do it. It would have been more honorable of you and more flattering to me had the thought occurred to you without my having to ask . . . but at least I shall not have the humiliation of asking in vain. Come, dear Felix!"

"Felix!" shouted a hoarse baritone voice in a tone of surprise and indignation. Dismayed and deeply hurt, Hilarion was about to draw back.

"Shhh!" was the sick woman's candid retort, "don't answer, my dear. That ugly old goat, Hilarion, is calling to you; I recognize that foghorn voice of his. Forget him. Don't go. He won't dare come in here. Hide behind this curtain. Or better still, come hide under the sheets, my love. Come!"

Thus, with every word she merely added insult to injury! Every word proved how far his foolish pride had led him astray! His pride—yes, monks have their pride like anyone else—and his disappointment were about to put an end to that unwonted scene. However, by a stroke of luck, the delirious woman, whose words and gestures were still strangely coordinated, was clinging to the cord around the wicked man's waist, so that when he tried suddenly to back away the poor creature was just as suddenly jerked halfway out of bed. The blackcoat, however, reacted quickly enough to prevent her falling on the floor: bending his leg, he checked her fall with his knee. Now a charming foot, a still shapely though somewhat skinny leg, and the full length of a divinely shaped thigh . . . nay, more than that: all of that black target of love which, as we know, in the case of our beloved heroine, had been the object of so many bull's-eyes—all these treasures were unveiled by the brutal Hilarion's angry gesture. Heavens! What a sudden change of heart came over him at the sight of so many magical charms! Little did it matter that the slightly yellowed ivory was covered with ugly little spots, that danger was lurking in those inflamed heads in the form of subtle poisons: Hilarion was a man as well as a monk. Already, he had mentally worshiped these things without any precise idea of how perfect they really were; now that he had actually seen them, how could he possibly . . . ? The anguished voice of his wounded pride fell silent. The Reverend Father was in one of those states of frantic predisposition wherein every cunt is like a god demanding an immediate sacrifice upon its altar. To put it another way, nothing was left of the humiliated, revolted Hilarion save his *boute-joie*, and that instrument knew nothing of the insult which his heart had suffered, nothing of the repulsion that his eyes were vainly striving to communicate to his loins; there was nothing left but an abstract relationship between the overmagnetized *boute-joie* belonging to the hottest of all monks, and that dark jewel which held no less attraction for it than the magnetic pole. . . .

Already he had deposited matter for amusement in a hand which had also managed to make itself understood. Grasping that gigantic plaything, she herself was guiding it toward the proper objective. And oh! if it had not been for that, all might still have been undone, for ever obsessed with that brat Felix, upon coming in contact with the huge engine the Marchioness exclaimed: "My God! Such a big one at your age! What will it be like when you're twenty-five?"

However, as we have said, the Devil was a party to the scene; moreover, a monk's pride is the least noble pride there is, and it is no match for a monk's lechery. While she may have thought it was Felix upon whom she was bestowing her favors, it would be Hilarion who would be taking and giving pleasure.

Keeping this very sensible notion in mind, taking a firm resolve and commending his soul to the lovely creature who had inflamed his imagination on that first day, the Reverend Father removed his splendid *boute-joie* from the grip of a burning hand (and just in time, too, for she was toying with it in a way that threatened to spoil the main purpose) and, without wasting a second, drove it two-thirds of the way home in one fell swoop, like a real monk. The remainder of that force-pump was not even lodged when the bountiful unction of his thick soup squirted deep into the vagina. However, it would have been hard to say whether the few sharp sobs uttered by the passive victim of this monachal sacrifice were not in fact her last gasps. Little did it matter. The sacrificer, inspired to the point of frenzy, was too far along to stop. Now that his fiery *boute-joie* had taken the bit between its teeth, it was not going to pull up short when the race was just getting under way. For a blackcoat bursting with good health, the incident that had just occurred was a mere prelude. He therefore stood his ground, and immediately set about hugging, shaking, and belaboring . . . what? Was it a woman or a corpse? This is what we shall soon find out.

Naturally, it turns out to be a woman, very much alive. For it is in keeping with Nerciat's outlook that one good love-bout is enough to cure even smallpox. Hilarion, of course, is thrown out of the house by the outraged servants (who had indeed been making love, as the sick woman had imagined), but the Marchioness has been brought back from death's door. Soon she is well and beautiful again and ready for another volume of adventures.

A brief analysis of *Le Diable au Corps* shows a remarkable array of sexual fantasies: a double-dildo for simultaneous anal and vaginal intercourse, animal contact, homosexual anal intercourse, a man who likes only menstruating women, the dying Marchioness being cured by the power of sex.

Most interesting of all these sexual fantasies are, no doubt, the ones about the man who prefers menstruating women and the healing power of sex. In the first case, we would say that those few men who actually do prefer menstruating women are most likely expressing a psychological reaction-formation against menstruation. It has been clinically known for some time that the first observation or vague realization of the phenomenon of menstruation can be extremely traumatic to boys because of the implied castration threat. Some analysts have therefore been inclined, and probably rightly so, to believe that this sort of menstruation trauma may not only be highly significant for the psychosexual development of men, but also may be much more widespread than one might think—a notion which seems to be corroborated by the menstruation taboos and countless superstitious beliefs surrounding menstruation in almost all cultures.

Aside from the possibility of a reaction-formation against the menstruation trauma, a supposed preference of certain men for menstruating women, rare as it might be, might also signify a breakthrough of very primitive, infantile urges to "mess," which up to a certain point may still be quite healthy and within normal range, or even be therapeutic, but, if exaggerated into a decided preference, would mean a serious symptom of regression and ego breakdown.

Finally, the story about the Marchioness being rescued from certain death and brought back to life by sexual intercourse compares in the most striking manner to some of the folklore stories of Poggio and Aretino. It shows again how deeply rooted in the human psyche this particular notion is, an impression which is further strengthened by many related magical beliefs and superstitions; for example, an old man may be rejuvenated by sleeping with a very young girl, or, as in certain primitive cultures, the crops can be made to grow better by copulating in the fields.

In the following chapters the excerpts are grouped according to dominant theme or subject matter, rather than chronologically. As mentioned, there is often considerable overlap in such grouping—a story with a dominant lesbian theme may have sadomasochistic, transsexual, fetishistic, incestuous, or any number of subthemes. Furthermore, some stories that we consider important for the study of sexual fantasies do not seem to fit any of the main categories, and these are presented separately, after some of the more typical, though not less interesting or less important, fantasy categories.

4

Homosexuality

FEMALE HOMOSEXUALITY

Erotic literature abounds in descriptions of female homosexuality. However, most of it is not worth discussing because most so-called lesbian stories are written by and for men. Consequently they do not reflect the true feelings of female homosexuals, nor are they descriptive of lesbian attitudes or sexual practices. Out of a welter of such material, we have therefore selected only a few examples which, because of their literary merit or the unusual nature of the fantasies involved, deserve closer attention.

DEUX GOUGNOTTES

This story by Henry Monnier (1799–1875) appeared first in *L'Enfer de Joseph Prudhomme, c'est à savoir La Grisette et l'Etudiant, Deux Gougnottes* (Paris, *ca.* late 1860's).

Henriette Fremicourt and Louise Laveneur, the two "*gougnottes*," are spending the weekend in the castle of a mutual friend. Their husbands are away hunting, and for some reason the two women, who scarcely know one another, are obliged to spend the night in the same bed.

After discussing the inadequacies of their husbands and of men in general, they become more and more intimate, until their lovemaking reaches fever pitch. After several climaxes there is a pleasant lull, following which is a scene of special interest, because it involves the wishful fantasy of one of the women to make love to the other with a real penis, and secondly, because it dramatizes the effect of certain taboo words on the sexual imagination of some people.

LOUISE: Listen, pussycat, there is something I'd like . . .

HENRIETTE: What can you want that I can still give you? Go through all my possessions. What can you want that I haven't already given you?

LOUISE: I tell you there's something I'd like.

HENRIETTE: What?

LOUISE: I want us to say . . .

HENRIETTE: What do you want me to say?

LOUISE: Dirty words.

HENRIETTE: I don't know any.

LOUISE: Yes you do! Yes you do! Please! Pretty please!

HENRIETTE: They didn't say any dirty words in boarding school.

LOUISE: They did at mine . . .

HENRIETTE: Then you begin.

LOUISE: Pussycat, think of a way you'd like to caress me.

HENRIETTE: I've already caressed you every way there is.

LOUISE: Tell me the name of one. No, don't do it . . . tell me what it's called. Now what would you like to do to me?

HENRIETTE: I'd like to . . .

LOUISE: What, angel? What would you like to do that would make us both very happy. And even happier if I could hear you say it first. Say it, pet, say it!

HENRIETTE: I'm too embarrassed . . .

LOUISE: Pretty please. Say it out loud!

HENRIETTE: I'd like to suck you.

LOUISE: We already said that. Darling, say something we haven't said: what do you want to suck?

HENRIETTE: Your sweet little bottom.

LOUISE: My little bottom?

HENRIETTE: Yes, your little bottom.

LOUISE: But it's not my little bottom you're touching with your finger. What's the name of the thing you're touching?

HENRIETTE: I don't know.

LOUISE: Really and truly?

HENRIETTE: I give you my word.

LOUISE: It's my little cunt, pussycat, my little cunt. Say "my cunt," treasure, "my little cunt!"

HENRIETTE: Your little cunt.

LOUISE: Give your mouth so I can thank you; your sweet little mouth! Say that word again, it's so pretty coming out of your mouth: "my cunt." Say: "my cunt."

HENRIETTE: Your cunt, angel baby, your sweet little cunt!

LOUISE: Would you like to fuck me, little man?

HENRIETTE: Yes! Yes! I want to fuck you!

LOUISE: What would you put in my cunt to fuck me with?

HENRIETTE: My thingamajig.

LOUISE: What thingamajig? If I say the word, will you say it after me?

HENRIETTE: Right away.

LOUISE: My cock.

HENRIETTE: Your cock.

LOUISE: It's a cock, baby; with your cock, your cock in my cunt, your big fat cock!

HENRIETTE: Your lovely cock, your fat cock in my cunt.

LOUISE: Would you suck my cock?

HENRIETTE: I'd suck it, I'd take it all the way into my mouth, the way I put my tongue in your cunt. Spread your legs and let me do it some more.

LOUISE: There, there, there!

HENRIETTE: Oh, thank you, thank you! How I love to suck your pretty cunt!

LOUISE: Why shouldn't I suck yours? Wait until I get into position. There!

HENRIETTE: I've never wished I had a cock as much as this before!
LOUISE: Spread the lips with your fingers so you can get your tongue deep inside, the way I'm doing to you. Good! Good! Now faster, faster! Good! Good! You dirty little thing . . . I'm coming . . .
HENRIETTE: I'm coming, I'm coming . . .
LOUISE: We're coming.

Monnier expresses in this story a typically male fantasy, projected onto a lesbian situation. In real life, few women with homosexual preferences wish to have a penis (any more than most homosexual men would want to have a vagina). Implicit in this fantasy is the male overvaluation of the male sex organ, an emphasis which one encounters at every turn, especially in those cultures which are primarily male-oriented, such as the Near East or, to a lesser degree, the Latin civilizations of Europe and South America.

GAMIANI

Gamiani ou Deux Nuits d'excès [*Gamiani or Two Nights of Excess*] *par A.D.M.; Pour les Amateurs du Romantisme* (Paris, 1928), with a preface and footnotes by Gustave Colline, is one of the most famous erotic novels. Written in 1833, it is generally supposed to be the work of Alfred de Musset, at least in large part. According to legend, he took up a challenge at a dinner party to write an obscene book without using obscene words. *Gamiani* is supposed to have been written in the two days that followed.

It is also claimed by some that George Sand was the author of *Gamiani*, or at least of the second part of the book. Many critics, including Gustave Colline, see in the character of Gamiani a sexological portrait of George Sand.

Alcide, the narrator, attends a fancy-dress ball in the palatial home of the Countess Gamiani. Having learned that she is a lesbian, he becomes extremely excited and resolves to spy on the Countess in her private apartments. From his hiding place, he watches Gamiani virtually rape a young woman named Fanny. When he discloses himself, a wild threesome ensues. He and

Fanny are eventually sated, but Gamiani is still unsatisfied. She gets out of bed and goes into the next room. Peering through a window in the wall, Fanny and Alcide witness the Countess writhing about, like one demented, on a large catskin rug, frantically rubbing her breasts against it. (In a footnote we are told that "women of Lesbos always used them [catskin rugs] because of their static electricity.")

Gamiani calls for her maid Julie, who immediately ties up her mistress's hands and feet, then dances around excitedly (and, of course, in the nude) before the powerless Gamiani. This merely has the effect on the latter of "redoubling her furor." At this moment of erotic fever pitch, Gamiani calls for Fido, and "a huge dog came out of his hiding place, rushed over to the Countess, and began passionately licking the red, inflamed tip of her protruding clitoris." Next, she exhorts Julie to give her "the milk."

I was trying to understand the meaning of that exclamation, uttered with a scream of genuinely agonized suffering, when Julie appeared, brandishing a huge dildo filled with warm milk which could be squirted a good six feet by pressing on a spring. Using the two straps attached to it, she buckled the ingenious instrument onto herself in the proper place. The most generously endowed stallion at the height of his powers never showed himself off to better advantage, at least not in width. I could not believe that insertion was possible, but to my great surprise, five or six frantic onslaughts, accompanied with piercing, heart-rending screams, were enough to swallow up that enormous apparatus, completely hiding it from view. The Countess was suffering the pains of hell! Her motionless body was rigid as marble.

We read that Fido, finding himself deprived of his plaything, availed himself of "the swaying, parted thighs of the virile Julie," while she was serving the Countess, and that he did his work so well "that Julie suddenly stopped moving and went into flights of ecstasy." Adds the author, in the same dry, professorial tone of the numerous footnotes: "This form of pleasure must be particularly intense, for its outward manifestations in women are like nothing on earth."

Under the forceful reminders of the Countess, Julie regains control of herself and continues her ministrations to her: "Now her motions were stronger than before. A wild shudder ran through the Countess; her eyes were closed and her jaw hung loose; from these signs, Julie knew that the moment was near and she pressed the spring with her finger" (upon which Gamiani experiences orgasm).

At the end of this first part of the book, Alcide, wishing to keep Fanny out of the Countess's clutches, takes her away with him. In the second part of the book, however, Gamiani manages to enter Fanny's bedchamber in Alcide's home and seduce her once again. As before, Alcide is hidden in a closet, the eternal voyeur. The following short passage from that section of the book is particularly interesting from the psychological point of view, all the more so if all or at least part of the book is in fact by George Sand:

GAMIANI (*to Fanny*): Listen . . . what is a man, what is a lover compared with me? Two or three bouts are enough to lay him low; after the fourth, he lies moaning and impotent, his back is bowed in the spasm of pleasure. What a pitiful sight! Whereas I am still strong and quivering, my thirst is unslaked. Oh, yes, I embody the burning pleasures of the flesh; I'm lecherous and implacable, I provide endless pleasures, I am *l'amour qui tue*!

We shall leave aside for the moment the main body of this second night of debauch because it concerns another fantasy involving an animal (this time a huge orangutan) which we intend to discuss in another context.

After this, Gamiani tells the story of a lesbian orgy which is supposed to have taken place in a convent and during which a number of nuns are impaling one another in chain fashion with dildoes. This episode has a very strong anticlerical flavor and is rather offensive in parts.

Talking to Fanny, the Countess gets more and more frenzied in her lovemaking to her, so that in the end, Fanny is nearly exhausted. It is at this point that the demented Countess slyly decides to take Fanny with her in a mutual love-death:

"Here, take this!" shouted Gamiani, holding out a phial of which she had just drunk half the contents. "Drink it down, it's the elixir of long life. Your strength will return!"

Fanny was too weak to resist and swallowed the liquid that the other woman poured into her open mouth.

"Ha!" exclaimed Gamiani in a resounding tone of voice, "now you are all mine!"

There was a hellish gleam in her eye. Kneeling between Fanny's legs she fastened her fearful instrument onto herself and brandished it threateningly.

At the sight of it, Fanny went into even more violent raptures. She seemed to be wracked by some inner fire which drove her to a frenzied pitch. With an effort, her widespread thighs lent themselves to the onslaughts of the monstrous simulacrum. The mad fool! Scarcely had she begun that horrible torture when a strange convulsion caused her to writhe about in every direction.

FANNY: Ow! Ow! the elixir burns, ow! my stomach! It's eating into my bowels! Oh! I'm going to die! Damned wicked witch, I'm yours, all right! Oh!

Gamiani, heedless of these screams of suffering and torture, drove on even harder. She broke and tore the flesh, sinking through a sea of blood; but now her own eyes began to turn up. Her limbs writhed and the bones in her fingers snapped. There was no longer any doubt in my mind that she had swallowed and had given Fanny a deadly poison. Terrified, I rushed to her aid. Breaking down the doors in my frenzy, I dashed into the room. Alas, Fanny was no more. Her horribly contorted arms and legs clung to Gamiani's; the Countess was left alone to carry on her struggle with death. I tried to separate them.

"Can't you see," she said with a death rattle in her voice, "that the poison is gnawing my vitals. Every nerve is writhing. Go away. This woman belongs to me. Ow! Ow!"

"This is horrible!" I exclaimed, beside myself with anguish.

GAMIANI: Yes, but I had already experienced every form of sensual debauch. Can't you understand, you fool? The only thing left for me to discover was whether or not there was pleasure to be had by mingling a woman's death throes with my own. The answer is yes, and that pleasure is atrocious! Do you understand? I'm dying in a frenzy of pleasure and a frenzy of pain; I can't stand it any more! Euhhhh!

And with that protracted scream, which rose up from the hollow of her chest, the horrible fury fell dead over the corpse.

The last part of the story is the most interesting from the point of view of sexual psychology. It is expressive of very powerful jealous feelings on the part of Countess Gamiani. This is the main motivation in her wanting to poison Fanny together with herself. This jealousy also seems to reflect female homosexual psychology more than the descriptions of all the frenzied erotic activities, the writhings, pantings, and flights of imagination, such as the dog incident or the scene with the dildo, which appear to us more typical of male sex psychology. We are, therefore, not at all sure whether George Sand (or any woman alone) could have been the author of this French sex classic. We think, rather, that the mixture of male and female sex psychology indicates some kind of collaboration between a male and a female author, as seems to be the case also for *l'Histoire d'O*.

LES COUSINES DE LA COLONELLE

There is one French book with lesbianism as its dominant theme that is almost certainly written by a woman: *Les Cousines de la Colonelle*, by "Madame la Vicomtesse de Coeur-Brûlant" ("Lisbonne: Chez Antonio da Boa-Vista, 1880").

Both Apollinaire (*L'Enfer de la Bibliothèque Nationale*) and Perceau (*Bibliographie du Roman Erotique au XIXᵉ Siècle*) agree that the writer of this book is undeniably a woman, and cite a number of aristocratic bluestockings of the period as possible authors.

The first volume tells how two sisters, Julia and Florentine, obtain their sexual initiation: Florentine marries a man in his fifties, while Julia has an affair with a young man of twenty-five. The latter, however, must abandon his true love for a shotgun marriage, and Julia marries an old man, who dies at almost the same time as her sister's husband. At the beginning of the second volume, we find the two widows consoling one another:

"Forget everything that was not agreeable, my dear, forget it utterly and completely," replied Madame Vaudrez [Florentine] in an effort to divert her sister's thoughts from the treacherous slope of remembrance.

"Come close to me you silly thing." And suiting the action to the words, the young lady drew Madame De Corriero [Julia] to the sofa and made her sit down, smothering her with kisses on the eyes, the mouth, and the ears.

The swing mirror stood facing them.

"Julia, look how well your black hair goes with my golden locks," said Florentine.

"Indeed," answered Julia, gently removing the comb and pins from Florentine's hair, while Florentine undid her sister's long tresses and draped them about her shoulders. Those billowing, silky locks of contrasting shades mingled their balmy odor and created the prettiest, most sensual setting imaginable for those two delightful faces of women in love.

"And this little birthmark on your neck, Madame," said Florentine, unbuttoning her sister's bodice, presumably for a better look; "I've never seen it before, how pretty it is!" and the young woman kissed it.

"But I do believe it bears a strong resemblance to the mark that Madame Vaudrez has on one of these globes of hers that are trying so hard to burst their veil."

"I believe you're right; and the comparison is easy enough to make."

Briskly, Julia unhooked the black kid [cuirass] that her sister was wearing. This operation laid bare two white, firm, faultless breasts the sight of which drew cries of admiration from Julia.

"Little sister," she said, "I've never seen you in the role of the goddess of beauty before. You're blonde . . . and so, they say, was our mother Eve. Let me admire you in the simple apparel she wore the day she won the serpent's heart."

"Will the courtesy be returned in kind?"

"Of course, and we shall stand in front of the mirror and have a delightful time composing *tableaux vivants* in which the figures will be only a little less clad than those to be seen in Madame Rattazis's garden."

"We will also enjoy the advantage of being less exposed to the elements than the beauties who devote themselves to the plastic arts in the good lady's garden."

While chatting thus, the two young ladies had removed their clothes and their bodices lay on the carpet beside their petticoats. Soon their corsets were lying next to their shoes and stockings and after a moment's hesitation the misty curtains of cambric which were still in place slid over two pairs of pink and white feet, disclosing two splendid female bodies representing two ideal types of beauty: the one blonde, the other brunette.

"How lovely you are!"

"What a delightful creature!"

These were the exclamations that fell from the lips of Madame Vaudrez and Madame De Corriere.

For a moment, the two women gazed at each other like two girl gladiators about to grapple; then Julia, putting her left arm around her sister's waist, drew her gently to her and began kissing the nape of her neck so as faintly to excite the nerve centers. Then, with graceful gestures, she began to make a necklace of caresses for her sister. Gradually she worked her way down to the breasts, whose little heads were already reared up and eager for pleasure.

"Aren't they the little devils, though!" she said. "You're going to be taught a lesson you little rascals." And one after the other, Julia took the little sensualists in her mouth and rolled them gently back and forth, causing Florentine to sigh ecstatically.

After a few minutes of this exercise, Florentine was writhing in the arms of her new-style lover, and Julia propelled her towards the couch and toppled her onto it.

"I'll bet no one has ever done what I'm going to do to you," said Julia.

"What's that?"

"You'll know soon enough, and you'll even see it. Just look in the mirror."

As Florentine watched in the swing mirror, Julia, after skillfully magnetizing her body with dexterous fingers, took a firm grip on both her thighs and, kneeling on the bearskin at her feet, smothered in passion kisses the golden thicket around the grotto of love.

"Oh! What are you doing?"

"Nothing much . . . yet. But I'm going to make you swoon for joy." And, pursuing her manipulations, the young woman remembered and slid an ardent tongue over the pink hillock that was already swelling from her caresses, and began to tickle it. Then, moving downward with a rhythmic movement to and fro, she would now and again thrust her tongue in as far as the entrance to the vagina.

Florentine's response was no longer limited to little sighs of satisfaction; she had reached the stage of loud exclamations.

"Oh! My God! What is it? Go on. Why, I didn't know a thing . . . go on . . . faster. I had no idea what it was like to go wild, to be drunk. Oh, darling, don't ever stop!"

"Just you wait and see. This is only an appetizer," said Julia to herself, for she was only waiting for the physiological moment before dealing her master stroke.

She did not have long to wait. While caressing her sister, she had laid her out on the couch.

When the swollen state of the outer fortifications told her that it was time to touch off the final spasm, she went into action: without interrupting the motion of her tongue on the clitoris, she dug her finger sharply into the canyon of love and with quick, staccato thrusts she drew from Florentine's throat those inarticulate noises, throbbing and protracted, which last until the nervous energy is completely expended. Madame Vaudrez's head fell back on the cushion. She no longer responded to her sister's embrace, and Julia laughingly said: "Well, well! are you going to go to sleep now, you horrid little egotist!"

Admonish her as she would, however, Florentine did not move. Kneeling before her, Julia went on trying to revive her, deeply affected by the ardor of her recent actions and also by a faint sense of anxiety which had crept over her at the sight of her sister lying so pale and prostrate. Suddenly she gave a start and tried to stand, but two hands clamped themselves firmly to the small of her back to prevent her from doing so and she felt a loving tongue caress her as she had caressed her sister.

"Oh, my goodness! Who's there?"

"My lady mustn't move," answered a familiar voice, "it's me, Dorothée, the chambermaid. Oh, if only I had dared, long ago I would have . . ."

"You seem to have made up your mind at last; well, since you're off to such a good start, get on with it," said Julia, bending over Florentine's chest and thus giving her maid even better access to the two protuberances with which nature had endowed her.

Now that her mistress was perfectly submissive and no longer had to be held down, Dorothée set about artfully exciting her and this was not difficult to achieve. Her tongue wandered back and forth, nor did her fingers remain inactive.

These manipulations could not go on for long without producing some result; thus only a few minutes had gone by when Dorothée played her trump card: Florentine, now partially revived from her ecstasy and quietly watching the strange scene that was taking place before her, saw Dorothée whip up her skirts revealing a splendid masculine engine, perfectly shaped and respectably proportioned. Wielding it like one accustomed to such things, she steered it straight up the path of happiness, and her attitude drew from Julia a shout of voluptuous surprise, and it was immediately followed by others, for Dorothée was imparting to the instrument the natural movement peculiar to a sturdy virile member.

"Ah! Ah!" shouted Julia, who was aiding and abetting her partner to perfection, "I'm dying . . . I'm melting with pleasure. Heavenly joys! Who is lavishing that warm elixir of love on me like that? It's killing me! Ah! Ah!"

Dorothée, judging that her task was at an end, backed away and dropped her skirts again. Then, seizing her mistress around the waist, she lay her on the couch next to her sister.

MALE HOMOSEXUALITY

As one might expect, male homosexual fantasies in literature are much rarer than lesbian ones. As mentioned, the simple explanation of this fact is that the majority of lesbian fantasies happen to spring from men. In the case of these lesbian stories written by men, the male (heterosexual) author or reader projects himself through fantasy into the lesbian situation, seeing himself as one of the lesbian participants. This, incidentally, might explain the frequency of the use of dildoes in these stories, through which one of the lesbians is transformed into a male or, at least, into a phallic female.

Few heterosexual men ever have conscious male homosexual fantasies, since this would be too threatening to their self-esteem, male homosexuality being much more socially disapproved than female homosexuality.

There are some fascinating homosexual fantasies to be found in erotic literature, the most important of which are present here.

TELENY

Teleny, or the Reverse of the Medal, a Physiological Romance of Today (2 vols., "Cosmopolis, 1893"), a curious and well-written book, has been attributed to Oscar Wilde. This we consider to be most unlikely. Nevertheless it appears that Wilde had something to do with the book. He may have either written part of it or given editorial advice, for it seems certain that the author is to be found in the little circle of intellectuals and artists around him.

The setting of the story is supposedly Paris. Des Grieux, a young man of good family, becomes violently infatuated with Teleny, a famous pianist of twenty-four. Much is made of the effect of Teleny's marvelous playing upon the sensitive, romantically inclined, neurotic youth who does not miss a single one of his idol's concerts. When they are introduced, the attraction seems mutual.

The first volume is taken up mainly with the description of Des Grieux's feelings, dreams, and fantasies which sometimes border on hallucinations. There are also some subplots in this part of the book: a longish description of a trip to a brothel, an experience which only serves to nauseate the young, homosexually inclined esthete; a scene about one of his mother's young maids who gets raped by the groom and, as a result, commits suicide by throwing herself out the window—again, a typically homosexual if slightly exaggerated view of heterosexual relations.

Meanwhile, Des Grieux does not see much of Teleny, circumstances preventing them from getting more closely acquainted. However, they do meet a few times, which only serves to feed Des Grieux's fantasies about Teleny, to fixate on him all the more, and to develop a jealous possessiveness of him which drives him to despair. In one of these moments, as he is about to end his torments by jumping into the Seine, Teleny softly approaches and takes hold of him.

This is the beginning of their real relationship. Teleny takes Des Grieux home with him and all goes well for a while. However, dark clouds soon appear on the horizon. The two young men attend, for instance, a kind of orgy, during which the company is using a bottle on one of the guests. As bad luck would have it, the bottle breaks inside him, and the young man goes home and shoots himself.

But the worst problem is Des Grieux's insane jealousy. He imagines all the time that Teleny is having an affair with a woman. And, in the end, all his paranoid suspicions seem to be justified when he discovers that the woman in question is none other than Des Grieux's mother.

Under the shock of this discovery, Des Grieux rushes madly from the house, once more determined to take his life by throwing himself in the river. But again death is foiled: he wakes up to find himself in the morgue where he had been taken for dead.

It transpires that Teleny, deeply in debt, had engaged in the relationship with Des Grieux's mother only for financial reasons. Thinking that his friend has killed himself over this matter, he commits suicide by stabbing himself, and Des Grieux is just in time to be with him in his dying moments and assure him of his forgiveness.

Here are a few excerpts which throw a particularly revealing light on homosexual sex feeling and psychology:

How can I express all that I felt from the contact of Teleny's hand? It set me afire; and, strange to say, it soothed me at the same time. How sweeter, softer, it was than any woman's kiss. I felt his grasp steal slowly over my body, caressing my lips, my throat, my breast; my nerves quivered from head to foot with delight, then it sank downwards into my veins, and Priapus, re-awakened, uplifted his head. I actually felt I was being taken possession of, and I was happy to belong to him.

In another place, the author reports a meeting of the two young men in the street which shows that the intensity of feeling between two men, achieved just by touch or mere proximity, can parallel similarly intense feeling between man and woman.

For a moment I thought he would kiss me—nay, the crisp hair of his moustache was slightly tickling my lips, producing a most delightful sensation. However, he only looked deep into my eyes with a demoniac fascination.

I felt the fire of his glances sink deep into my breast, and far below my blood began to boil and bubble like a burning fluid, so that I felt my——(what the Italians call a burdie, and what they have portrayed as a winged cherub) struggle within its prison, lift up its head, open its tiny lips, and again spout one or two drops of that creamy, life-giving fluid.

But those few tears—far from being soothing balm—seemed to

be drops of caustic burning me, and producing a strong unbearable irritation. . . .

All the blood vessels of my member were still strongly extended and the nerves stiff, the spermatic ducts full to overflowing; therefore, the erection continuing, I felt a dull pain spread over and near all the organs of generation; whilst the remainder of my body was in a state of prostration and still—notwithstanding the pain and languor—it was a most pleasurable feeling to walk on quietly with our hands clasped, his head almost leaning on my shoulder.

Another passage illustrates the kind of conditioning and early sexual imprinting that is necessary to produce the sexual feeling for other men which is apparent in the previous excerpt. (To be sure, the feeling and events related in the following passage would have to be preceded by similar, though much earlier ones, or the young boy would not react in the manner here described.)

My first infatuation was for a young Hercules of a butcher, who came courting our maid. . . . I often used to sit and watch him unawares, noting every expression on his face whilst he was making love, almost feeling the lust he felt himself.

How I did wish he would speak to me instead of joking with my stupid maid. I felt jealous of her although I liked her very much. Sometimes he used to take me up and fondle me, but that was very seldom; one day, however, when—apparently excited—he had tried hard to kiss her, and had not succeeded, he took me up and greedily pressed his lips against mine, kissing me as if he were parched with thirst.

Although I was but a little child, still I think this act must have brought about an erection, for I remember every pulse of mine was fluttering. I still remember the pleasure I felt when—like a cat—I could rub myself against his legs, nestle between his thighs, sniff him like a dog, or pat and paddle him; but alas! he seldom heeded me.

My greatest delight in my boyhood was to see men bathing. I could hardly keep myself from rushing up to them; I should have liked to handle and kiss them all over. I was quite beyond myself when I saw one of them naked.

A phallus acted upon me as I suppose it does upon a very hot woman; my mouth actually watered at its sight, especially if it were a good-sized, full-blooded one, with an unhooded, thick and fleshy glans.

Withal, I never understood that I loved men and not women. What I felt was that convulsion of the brain that kindles the eyes with a fire full of madness, an eager bestial delight, a fierce sensual desire. Love, I thought, was a quiet drawing-room flirtation, something soft, maudlin and aesthetic, quite different from that passion full of rage and hatred which was burning within me. In a word, much more of a sedative than an aphrodisiac.

The next excerpt from *Teleny*, though not strictly related to the theme of sexual fantasies, is of the utmost importance from a sexological and psychological point of view—namely, a description of the male orgasm and its subjective, individual experience, related with great sensitivity and insight.

My own hand hesitatingly followed the lead his had given. Our fingers hardly moved the skin of the penis; but our nerves were so strained, our excitement had reached such a pitch, and the seminal ducts were so full, that we felt them overflowing. There was, for a moment, an intense pain, somewhere about the root of the penis—or rather, within the very core and centre of the veins, after which the sap of life began to move slowly, slowly, from within the seminal glands; it mounted up the bulb of the urethra and up the narrow column, somewhat like mercury within the tube of a thermometer —or rather, like the scalding and scathing lava within the crater of a volcano. It finally reached the apex; then the slot gaped, the tiny lips parted, and the pearly, creamy, viscous fluid oozed out—not all at once in gushing jets, but at intervals, and in huge, burning tears.

At every drop that escaped out of the body, a creepy, almost unbearable feeling started from the tips of the fingers, from the ends of the toes, especially from the innermost cells of the brain; the marrow in the spine and within all the bones seemed to melt, and when the different currents—either coursing within the blood or running rapidly up the nervous fibres—met with the phallus (that small instrument made out of muscles and blood vessels) a tremendous shock took place; a convulsion which annihilated both mind and matter, a quivering delight which everyone has felt, to a greater or less degree—often a thrill almost too intense to be pleasurable. . . .

Flashes of lightning seemed to be passing before my eyes, a torrent of fire was coursing through my body.

"Enough, stop, enough!" I groaned. My nerves were extended, a thrill came over me; the soles of my feet seemed to be drilled through; I writhed; I was convulsed. . . .

Still he went on quicker and quicker. I writhed in a delightful torture. I was melting away, but he never stopped till he had quite drained me of the last drop of life-giving fluid there was in me. My eyes were swimming in their sockets. I felt my heavy lids half close themselves, an unbearable voluptuousness of mingled pain and pleasure shattered my body and blasted my very soul, then everything waned in me.

While researching erotic literature, we came upon a rare French translation of *Teleny*, published in 1934, which included an introduction by *"un vieux Bibliopole"* ("an old Biblioprick") who signed his notes with the initials Ch. H. (i.e., the scholar and book dealer Charles Hirsch). These notes shed further light on the question of the authorship of *Teleny*, though they do not answer it entirely. More important, they contribute to our understanding of Oscar Wilde's personality and his way of life.

NOTES AND SOUVENIRS FROM AN
OLD BIBLIOPRICK

Among the customers of the *Librairie Parisienne* who assiduously frequented my little store on Coventry Street (even before I became its titular head), I had noticed, because of his very particular bearing, his physique, and his slightly eccentric dress, a gentleman about twenty years old, tall, rather podgy, a pale olive face without a trace of beard and slightly puffy, wearing a series of thin gold bracelets studded with colored stones on his wrist.

He hardly ever came alone. Young, distinguished men who seemed to be artists or writers always accompanied him and accorded him familiar deference. In a word, he cut the figure of a Master surrounded by his disciples.

At that time (1889) I had just arrived in London and was still very ignorant of contemporary English literature, and especially of society's outstanding personalities. I didn't know this gentleman's name nor his profession. He spoke fluent French and even affected to speak no other language the moment he entered the bookstore. Later I learned from some other client that he was a very well known poet and playwright whose plays at the Saint James Theatre were the talk of the town.

But I had to read T. Johnson's article in *Le Figaro* before I was able to learn the prominent place this writer occupied, not only in the world of letters of his day, but also in the eyes of the public.

Oscar Wilde was the man in vogue whose taste and innovations in art, in furniture and decorating styles were admired by all and imitated by snobs.

He was captivated by our literature which he knew quite thoroughly and bought all the novels by the best authors: Zola, Maupassant, Bourget, etc. It was only later, after he had placed his trust in me, that he ventured to order certain licentious works of a special genre, which he referred to by the euphemism "socratic." I had some difficulty in obtaining such books for him, the texts on that subject by ancient and modern authors being very rare. I did furnish him with the translation of the book by the Italian Pallavicini, "*Alcibiade enfant à l'école,* the *Lettres d'un Frère ignorantin à son élève;* then, in English, *The Sins of the Cities of the Plain* and some more recent brochures with ribald titles, printed in Amsterdam, whose vulgarity displeased him; he returned them so that I could disencumber him of them by throwing the lot into the fire.

One day towards the end of 1890 I believe, he brought me a thin notebook, with a commercial format, tied up and carefully stamped with a wax seal. He told me: "One of my friends will come round to fetch this manuscript. He will show you my calling card," and he mentioned a name which I have forgotten. And just as he had said, a few days later, one of the young gentlemen I had seen with him came to take possession of the package. He kept it for a while and then brought it back saying in turn: "Would you kindly give this to one of our friends who will come to fetch it in the same person's name."

The identical ceremony took place three more times. But the last time, the reader of the manuscript, less discreet and less conscientious than the others, brought me the package unsealed, tied with just a simple ribbon, barely closed. . . .

It was a very strong temptation. I confess that I succumbed to it. I opened the package and on the grayish paper cover which held the bundle of handwritten pages I read this simple title written in large capital letters: TELENY. However, since I wasn't yet familiar with English penmanship, I took the "T" for an "F" and read: FELENY.

That very night I satisfied my curiosity by deciphering the two hundred pages of the manuscript. What an odd mixture of different handwritings, of scratched out, omitted, corrected or added to passages by various hands! It was obvious to me that several unequally talented writers had collaborated on this anonymous but profoundly interesting work.

One detail struck me during my hasty reading of the manuscript, and that was the continual borrowings that the author made from the Holy Scriptures, the Bible, the Gospels. For every chapter, citations and passages from the Holy Books were adapted to the episodes of the novel. Was the writer a clergyman completely imbued with theology? Add to that the numerous reminiscences of Greek and Latin classical literature, the examples taken from mythology or ancient religions, finally, expressions borrowed from foreign languages, all that composed a completely different stew from what one was used to finding in modern erotic works (with perhaps the exception of Mirabeau's *Erotika Biblion*). In a word, great erudition, polished style, sustained dramatic interest all betrayed the stamp and craftsmanship of a professional writer. The only fault one could attribute to this bizarre assemblage issuing from various imaginations was the impropriety, the futility of certain details which needlessly drew out and weighed down the narrative.

Reading that extralicentious production I easily guessed why its propagator, who no doubt had a wife, children, and servants, had no desire to have that compromising manuscript being freely hawked about in his house.

Not long afterwards, I returned *Teleny* to its owner and heard nothing more about it until the day when Leonard Smithers, the publisher (who had given up his post of solicitor in Arundel Street to become associated with Nichols the bookseller), having obtained I don't know where the work in question, published it clandestinely in two volumes with a run of 200 numbered copies at the price of five guineas, bearing the mention: "Cosmopolis, 1893."

Copies of this edition obviously fell into my hands. I found that its general outline conformed to the original manuscript but that the details had been greatly changed. A subtitle had been added: *Or the Reverse of the Medal*. The prologue had been omitted, which meant that the dialogue began abruptly without the reader being acquainted with the characters. But the major difference was the following: whereas in the first version everything was essentially and fundamentally English—personalities, mores, place names, etc.—in the final text a clumsy editor had transferred the entire drama, including its décor, to the other side of the Channel, to Paris itself! The result was that its shocking anomalies caused those people who knew Paris and London and the difference in mentality, ideas, and ways of life in France and England, to shrug their shoulders.

As examples I will quote the following passages that I have translated literally from the Smithers edition. Read this description of the Latin Quarter:

"Our cabs took us through narrow streets, somber lanes, stinking passages where painted women appeared in gaudy dress at the filthy windows of their miserable lodgings. It was late. The stores were closing, except for those shops where fish, mussels, and chips are sold. An ill-assorted crowd filled these streets; bestial-faced drunkards, down-at-the-heel shrews, wan-faced children dressed in rags and hollering obscene songs."

This picturesque tableau is very exact, except for the fact that it does not represent the environs of the Boulevard Saint-Michel, but rather certain isolated corners of Soho Square or some areas in the East End.

In another situation, the hero of the novel is wandering, after midnight, along the banks of the Seine in the center of Paris. Standing on a bridge, he sees "on each side of the river enormous somber buildings, looming up through the mist, their domes caked with soot, gigantic stone needles lost in the fog," etc. This description, no less exact than the preceding one, admirably depicts the nocturnal aspect of the Thames' embankments, near Westminster.

Later I pointed out these unlikelinesses as well as others to Smithers whom I met at the 1900 Exposition. He told me then that he had touched up the text out of prudish scruples, "in order not to shock the national pride of the British subscribers." He added that a definitive version existed and that he was going to print a second edition as soon as the original 1893 one was out of print. He was unable to carry out this project and after his death the manuscript remained in the hands of our mutual friend Duringe, who let me have it with a view to a French translation—which will undoubtedly appear one of these days. . . .

To come back to my customer. Afterwards I saw him rather often at the bookstore and once I even went to his home on Tite Street where he was ill in bed, to deliver a small package of new titles. I had thus the occasion to glance at the completely original artistic disposition of his residence, where I found some of the bizarre furnishings, tapestries, and ornamentation which corresponded quite closely to the descriptions I had read in *Teleny*—further proof that his surroundings were relevant to the book.

Then in March, 1895, there was the trial and the horrible accusations brought against Oscar Wilde by the Marquis of Queensbury, followed by the appalling downfall, the shattering of the reputation of that celebrated man, up until that time adulated, admired, sought out by everyone. Personally I was heartbroken, but not very surprised. I had seen him in public, with the young Lord Alfred Douglas, be so bold as to act in such a way and with such a lack of restraint that their conduct was really too revealing. One night, among others, at the Empire Theatre, as both of them were seated in the row in front of me, he had his arm around the neck of the Ephebe who was pressed against him, in a gesture which would have been considered improper, even in a less strait-laced milieu, even in one less exacting about external appearances and "respectability."

I met him again in Paris in November, 1898, after he had left the Reading Gaol, using the pseudonym of Sebastian Melmoth, in that very modest hotel on the Rue des Beaux-Arts where, morally and physically annihilated, he vegetated. At that time I had the intention of publishing an English translation of Pierre Louÿs' masterpiece, *Aphrodite*, and I thought of asking him to do this work for which he was uniquely qualified. He accepted and quoted me a price. But my colleagues who saw a lot of him those days dissuaded me from concluding the affair. "At this point he is incapable of writing two lines," they told me. . . .

I saw him again at the Exposition's Vieux Paris, where he often came to dine at the Taverne du Près-aux-Clercs, surrounded as of old by a coterie of young friends, no doubt Englishmen come to Paris to visit the Exposition.

Not much later the end came. But not oblivion. His memory, cleared of the mud which had momentarily covered it, regains today a deserved upsurge of admiration and celebrity. For the younger generation, the name Oscar Wilde only evokes the memory of a sensitive poet, a perfect stylist, a charming and brilliant conversationalist.

Сн. H.
[Charles Hirsch]

ERNEST

After *Teleny*, the most important homosexual story we know is a German book, *Ernest*. It was privately printed (probably in the 1910's) by its author, the Berlin collector Werner von Bleichröder (with sixteen artistically valuable erotic illustrations by Professor R. Hegemann). The book is extremely rare and therefore practically unknown.

There is no real plot; it consists of a series of loosely connected episodes involving a boy named Ernest who becomes homosexually enslaved, first by his uncle and then by a Dutch restaurateur, whose establishment is a sort of cross between a respectable restaurant and a male bordello.

A summer day, full of sun, heat, and light. An improbable blue emanating from the sky, absorbed by the sea and reflected back. Yellow boasts the beach; the garden is dreaming in opulent, saturated green.

Gernand is lying nude on his bed, a light white blanket cuddling his muscular arms and legs which stretch and flex themselves in voluptuous lassitude after a three-hour ride. The body is still hot, the blood still boiling. He is dreaming with half-closed eyes in the twilight of the room. The green silk drapes are closed and are waving lightly in the mild summer breeze.

He had been lying like this yesterday, too, when suddenly his twelve-year-old nephew had jumped into the room. He had loved this smooth, tall boy for a long time, had kissed him many times, and undressed him equally often under one pretext or another. His nudity had intoxicated him and he knew then that some day this boy simply had to be his altogether.

Ernest, on his part, worshiped his tall, elegant uncle and had been admonished by his mother, who was still attached to Gernand by the memories of a youthful crush she had once had on him, to be especially well-behaved toward his uncle—an admonition which was quite superfluous, since the child was almost slavishly devoted to Gernand anyway.

It was yesterday that Gernand had made use of the opportunity! His desire had killed all scruples and he had spent an hour of the most incredible voluptuousness with the boy. The initial resistance, crying and fighting of Ernest, was soon broken by the older one's superior physical strength and will-power, and in the end, the child, half choked by shame and pain, had submitted to all his wishes. Finally, he had sent him home and told him to be back at ten o'clock today.

By now it was already half past ten, and he still was not holding the boy in his arms! He jumped up cursing, tore the drapes open, flooding the room with a bright sunlight that exploded all dreams. He put on his bathing costume and robe, stepped to the open window and, screaming with rage and desire, called out "Ernest! Ernest!" No answer. Only the rustling of the trees and the soft, distant roaring of the sea. His desire grew with every second. He had to have the boy; this very moment!

He tore down the steps, through the park, to the beach. Already from a distance he could see the one he was looking for, romping around in the sand with two other boys. No sooner had Ernest seen his uncle, when he came running up to him and wanted to fall on his neck.

Gernand caught the supple body, took him tightly by the arm, and said, "Why didn't you come as I told you to?" He held the narrow wrist of the boy as in an iron vice.

The boy blushed from ear to ear and stammered something about, "I had to go to the village and then Mummy wanted me to . . ."

Gernand interrupted him and let him loose at the same time: "Okay, young fellow, we shall see!"

Meanwhile, the other two boys had joined them. They too were in bathing suits and offered in their seminudity a highly attractive and seductive picture. Ernest was wearing a blue and white striped bathing suit, which left his slender, full-sculpted legs free to the hip. Only one of the shoulder straps was fastened, the other one was hanging down and the cut-out of the sleeve had apparently been torn while playing, for a gaping tear let one see half of the lissome body beneath.

Gernand was wild with excitement.

He now turned to Ernest who stood a little aside, as if embarrassed: "Oh, Ernest, I have completely forgotten to take along my typewriter. Come along and help me get it."

The boy winced a moment, then he obediently followed Gernand who had slowly gone ahead. The man stopped to let the victim catch up with him, then proceeded, his hand on the boy's bent neck, quickly into the dunes and out of view of the people on the beach. There he stopped still, looked the boy in the eyes and let his free hand slide down the child's body. He looked at it all and his hand tightly encircled the little member and testicles.

Ernest did not move: his small head felt as if it was burning.

"How can you run around with a torn bathing suit like that, kid; take it off right away! You'll walk home with me across the boardwalk completely naked so that people will see that you are my slave!" With these words, he had unfastened the other shoulder strap and the bathing suit lay on the ground. The boy stood before him completely nude. He grabbed him a few more times between the smooth thighs and on the little cock, then he pushed him ahead across the boardwalk, his hand tight in the boy's neck.

Once in the quiet park, he slowed his steps so he could play with the boy's body and still keep on walking. Inside the house, which stood quiet and sleepy in the heat of the sun, he stopped a moment in the vestibule and asked Ernest to choose one of the riding crops, hanging on the wall. Full of premonition of what was to come, the boy sobbed and only a strong blow on his little behind made him obey the command. He grabbed the nearest whip and meant to hand it to his uncle.

"Carry it yourself and hurry up!" said Gernand, taking hold of the boy by the hair and quickly mounting the stairs with him. "See, those who don't want to listen, will have to learn by experience," he added, brutally pulling the boy's silky hair.

The tears had started running down Ernest's face.

At last they had gotten to the top of the stairs. Gernand pushed the trembling boy into the room and locked the door. "Shut the window and pull the drapes!" Ernest did as he was told. "Come, and kneel down here!"

Meanwhile, Gernand had thrown off the bathrobe and in his bathing suit stepped up to the nude, kneeling boy. His cock was almost coming through the black, silky material. He grabbed the riding crop.

"You didn't come today, even though I had told you to do so. I am going to punish you, punish you severely so that you'll learn to obey my orders. You'll have to do everything that I demand of you!"

He gave the boy three resounding slaps on each cheek that made his head red like a beet. Ernest let out a yell and started to cry and whimper audibly. Gernand took hold of him by his cock and balls, pulled him around, and whipped him like mad, no matter where. The boy, writhing in pain, tried to get away, but the man's left hand held him like a vice so that every movement only increased his agony.

"I'm going to keep on beating you, till you stop crying and keep absolutely quiet, understand?"

Ernest sank on his knees and became quiet. He lay on the floor, broken. The tears kept running down his face, but he was quiet; his heart was beating wildly.

"Get up and take off my bathing suit. Hurry up!" A sharp blow got the boy to his feet. With trembling hands he opened the man's bathing suit and slid it off his beautiful, strong body. Gernand's big, rigid member stood up, brandishing its deep red tip; below, the testicles swelled like apples.

"Kiss my hands, the whip, my feet, and my cock, but long and tenderly, and keep kneeling down!"

Ernest did as he was told.

"Take my cock in your mouth and play with it with your tongue, lick it from top to bottom, and the same with my balls!"

The thick, stiff rod disappeared in the sweet childish mouth, while the little red tongue kept working. Suddenly, Gernand pulled out his cock and pulled it back and forth across the boy's face, whom he commanded to open his mouth and stick out his tongue. Gernand's cock, balls, and hair, as well as the whole burning face of the boy got covered with his saliva.

After this, Gernand placed the boy in all kinds of positions to study his body and enjoy its beauty. Doing so, he indulges in a strange sort of fantasy, comparing the young, supple body of Ernest with those of young circus acrobats, being thrown around by the older acrobats like balls, "and about whom one cannot help but imagine that they would be used by their elder colleagues outside the arena to all sorts of wild excesses."

When Ernest closes his eyes in shame at being exposed to Gernand's looks in these poses, he is told, "You are going to get used to the idea that your nudity and every part of your body belong to me—and perhaps to quite a few other people besides, if I so choose!"

The boy is told by his uncle that his time of apprenticeship in voluptuousness is about to begin:

He put the boy flat on his back, spread his legs wide apart, and began to masturbate him, holding his little balls tightly in one hand and boring his index finger from time to time deeply into the little hole. At the first time, Ernest uttered a suppressed cry of pain, but a sharp cut of the whip made him keep quiet instantly.

"So, now you are to do the same to yourself, while telling me clearly and distinctly: 'Many thanks, dear Uncle, for having taught me how to masturbate; I am going to practice diligently whenever and wherever I can.' Do you understand?"

The little boy worked away at a fast clip, some encouraging slaps helping him along. The tight little member stood up as though poured in bronze, the little purple head glistening from a wet film that had begun covering it. Obediently he pressed his little balls with his left hand, or stuck a couple of fingers deep into his tight little hole. He was told to assume a thousand different poses, doing it once lying down, another time kneeling, still another time with his legs high up over the headboard of the bed. Finally, he had to stand to attention, military fashion, and keep on masturbating without interruption.

After some more of this Gernand tells the boy to stop, but admonishes him to keep practicing, both at home and at school, where he is to become the willing tool and plaything of his comrades. The uncle warns him under threat of severe punishment not to default in these duties or to give anybody cause for complaints.

Gernand tells the boy that he will soon have to be "deflowered," that his little hole is far too small, but that a certain sailor Godin, who has a member three times that of Gernand's, will take care of that. He then teaches Ernest how to properly perform fellatio on a man, always accompanied by mild punishment and humiliation, which is really the dominant mood of this story: "These are the first lessons in the art of satisfying a man with your mouth. That will be henceforth your main job and therefore all the more reason why you should learn it thoroughly. Your face and mouth are made for it, and countless members will come to enjoy themselves in your little mouth, big ones and small ones, young ones and old ones, fat ones and skinny ones. And you will suck them all, till the hot stream of their passion is appeased by pouring down your throat!"

Gernand gives the boy another passionate and violent lesson in the art of fellatio, culminating in a wild orgasm, after which he first rubs the boy's body with his semen, then performs a frenzied act of urilangia on him.

The book, short as it is (only fifty-six pages), is full of highly erotic scenes, always told from a slightly, and sometimes not so slightly, sadistic, homosexual point of view. Below is a scene from the last part of the book in which Ernest is the main attraction in the establishment of the Dutch ex-sailor Godin to whom he has been lent by his uncle.

"Come here, Ernest!" somebody shouted from the corner table at which Gustav had been sitting.

It was the so-called table of honor, reserved for especially distinguished or high-paying guests. Today there sat the big, well-known Dutch antique dealer and his elegant, aristocratic friends. He was a man in his late thirties, whose puffed face with the black goatee still showed the mark of a once classical beauty that had been his.

Ernest obediently sat down on the Dutchman's lap, who loved the young fellow passionately and immediately proceeded to shower him with kisses, while his lascivious hands felt and poked his body everywhere. They gave the boy a full glass of champagne and clinked their glasses together in a resounding toast.

The fat Dutchman had already opened Ernest's pants and

gently masturbated him, paying no attention to the others who looked on curiously and amused. He pressed Ernest's right hand tightly into his lap, in which he could feel his hard cock. A young Count, who was sitting next to the Dutchman, suddenly bent down and substituted, to the accompaniment of general hilarity, his mouth for the hand of the fat one. Nobody thought anything of it; in fact, similar scenes were taking place at some of the other tables as well.

Now the pianist got up and waved Ernest over to him. He quickly freed himself from the embrace, excusing himself in so doing, closed one of the buttons of his rectangular fly—Godin had forbidden him to close both buttons while in the establishment—and went with a plate from table to table to collect for the band. It was a deal between the bandleader and the host, for when the beautiful boy took up the collection, the contributions increased tenfold. At every table Ernest was being fondled and kissed, hands slid into his open shirt or into the wide pants, feeling the soft, tempting skin of the most secret parts of his childlike body. It also happened quite often that one or the other of the gentlemen would unbutton the boy's fly and play with his little hard-on, a privilege which, according to the rules of the house, was worth twenty marks extra. Not infrequently, too, Gustav took Ernest from the table and disappeared with one or the other of the guests into the toilet.

The story goes on in this vein, coming at the end to the description of a particular evening during which the usual goings-on finally developed into a veritable orgy.

Those of the beautiful boys who had remained were lying in the laps of the older men, were being kissed eagerly, and played with inside their pants. Everybody had taken off their coats, because the air in the rather low room had become stifling hot.

Ernest was again the main target of the general passion, a passion which was raised to the nth potential that night. They had pulled off his pants completely, and had put him, completely naked, diagonally across the lap of the Dutchman and his neighbors. Hands did not stop playing with him; again and again, one or the other of the heated faces would bend down to suck and lick with wine-scented tongue the beautiful spots of his body.

Suddenly Godin jumped up and went to fetch from his bedroom a strange kind of object. Carrying it high above his head, he put it in the center of the Dutchman's table: It was a faithful replica of his famous huge member, made of wax.

It turns out that one can drink from this contraption, if it is filled with wine, and thus it makes the rounds of the guests. When it comes to Ernest's turn, the thing is empty. Immediately, it is filled again. At that point, the owner announces that he will demonstrate how his cock can be at the same time in the mouth and the behind of someone. The Dutchman doubts it, and a bet is concluded.

Gustav now pushed one of the small, empty tables into a corner and called Ernest away from the lap of the fat one where he had been lying. Frightened, the boy stepped up to him. Immediately, Gustav pulled his shirt over his head and took his sandals off his feet. Thus, the beautiful, slim boy stood completely naked in the midst of the circle which the wildly excited guests had formed around them.

Gustav grabbed the boy tightly between the legs, lifted him high into the air, and put him on his stomach across the table, so that his head was sticking out over one side of it. Quickly he pressed the filled wax cock into the hand of another boy and told him to get up on the table and kneel down between Ernest's spread legs. . . . Then Gustav carefully greased Ernest's little hole and narrow crack with some butter and ordered his assistant to push the big wax replica slowly into it. At the same time, Gustav stepped over to the side of the table where the boy's head was placed. With a single movement of his hand, he tore open his fly and out sprung the throbbing, iron-hard member which was, if anything, still larger than its reproduction. He now pressed Ernest's face tightly over it, and at once the boy started obediently to lick it and the balls below with his tongue. Finally, the mighty rod forced itself between the wide open lips, while the boy's legs were held open by the spectators, so that the other boy could push the wax phallus all the way up. With the other hand, a second boy reached underneath Ernest's belly and pressed his little cock so hard, all the while masturbating him briskly, that Ernest was writhing in pain.

"Now, I am about to come, watch out!" whispered Gustav haughtily, winding himself in the hips and pulling his victim by the hair so close that Ernest thought he was going to suffocate and desperately hung on with his hands to the giant's balls.

At that moment, the hot jet of aroused male strength shot into his throat and gurgling and groaning he swallowed the inexhaustible stream of semen. At the same time, the wax phallus was being shoved all the way up his small behind and the full load squirted into his belly. The pain was indescribable, he felt he was being suffocated and torn apart simultaneously under the impact of the double discharge and he fainted dead away.

The guests who were surrounding them, were seized by an erotic delirium. They bit blindly into the tender flesh of the victim lying before them, satisfied themselves on one another in every conceivable way, without the slightest restraint. . . .

Ernest, who had remained on the table as though dead, was brought to with some cold water, and left, swaying on the arm of his insatiable lover, together with one of Gustav's friends and two other boys, for the latter's bedroom.

We have seen that while the dominant theme of the cited story is homosexual, the prevailing mood is one of dominance/ submission. There is an all-pervasive undertone of brutality—a brutality, one suspects, which also plays an important role in homosexually toned excesses of the police, the military, certain "male" sports, etc. In all these instances one may find latent homosexual impulses which are repressed or denied but which return disguised in hypermale forms of aggression (hitting, stabbing, clubbing, shooting, etc., taking the place of the more direct, but rejected, homosexual sex contact). At the same time, there is a sadomasochistic variant to homosexuality, just as is the case in heterosexuality. *Ernest* is typical of this kind of sadistic deviation within a basically homosexual context.

If one is tempted to say that a story like *Ernest* shows the latent roots of Nazism and fascism, one must keep in mind that this is, unfortunately, a phenomenon which is not limited to certain nationalities, but which lies dormant in any culture. It is true that a male-oriented or militaristic culture, like that of pre–World War II Germany, would be more prone to this sort of mentality than a more pacifistic society. (The little boy Ernest being ordered to masturbate while "standing at attention" would not make much sense in a non-militaristic culture, just as the concept of, say, a Black Mass would not have much meaning to people not raised in a certain religious environment.)

While thinking of the stormtroopers in Nazi Germany (who were of Ernest's generation), one cannot help but think of parallels we have been witnessing more recently both in Europe and in the United States. One is reminded, for instance, of the sadism in Kenneth Brown's play *The Brig*, a documentary of the happenings in a U.S. Marine Corps jail, where humiliation and the breaking of the human spirit seem to be the main object of the sadistic guards. Images of police brutality in the uprisings of the French workers and students in Paris and the students in Mexico City, the brutal beating down of student revolts in Berkeley, New York, and elsewhere, flash before one's mind, together with the events surrounding the 1968 elections, and similar sad instances. In all these cases it seems obvious that latent homosexual and sadistic impulses play an important role, and it is clear that they are not absent from ordinary warfare as well.

In order to minimize violence and foster a more peaceful coexistence of people it is of paramount importance that these impulses find some sort of harmless, substitute expression. Art and literature offer one such possibility. It behooves us for that reason alone to be tolerant—and tolerant to a fault if need be— in permitting the free and unhindered expression of these and other antisocial tendencies in the arts and literature, that is, in fantasy productions, rather than invite their acting out on a personal or group level in real life.

It seems as if homosexuality in men is somehow related to sadomasochism, though this is no more than a clinical impression of ours, reinforced by the marked sadism in almost all homosexual writings that have come to our attention. It is a dominant feature of the next story, though it also does not lack a strange kind of tenderness, possible—as if by contradiction—only in men who have accepted their homosexual preference.

L'APPRENTI SORCIER

Though inexplicably unsigned, we find on the back cover of *L'Apprenti Sorcier* a statement that it is "by the author of *Le Vieillard et l'Enfant*." *L'Apprenti Sorcier* is a recent book (Paris: René Juillard, 1964).

The narrator, a boy of sixteen, is spending the summer in the care of a thirty-five-year-old, heretic, homosexual priest.

Strangely exalted sadomasochistic scenes, such as the one that follows, alternate with very chastely described love scenes between the narrator and a thirteen-year-old boy from the nearby village. It is striking that homosexuality seems to be taken for granted by these three characters, as if the setting were the Middle East rather than the Perigord region of France.

We went upstairs to his bedroom and there, with the door closed and the light out, he tied me tightly to a chair as usual, so that I would be entirely at his disposal. For this purpose, he kept a drawer full of ropes.

Whip in hand, he sat beside me on another chair. Sitting with my clothes around my ankles, I had the feeling whenever he thrashed me that I was being literally eaten alive, that my flesh was peeling off in strips, that I was being roasted . . . that he was eating me for supper. He laid the whip across my legs; in the dark, I could feel his hands on my bare flesh. He touched me as one might caress a woman, with broad, slow strokes along the inside of my thighs. For some time already I had been in the process of becoming his maidservant, behaving as I thought priests' maidservants did, although in point of fact they may not behave that way at all and I may have been giving my priest more and better satisfaction than if I had really been his maid. Besides preparing our frugal meals, I had to clean the house and on certain evenings not only did I get a taste of the whip, but also had perforce to play the affectionate wife. This change in my situation was agreeable to me, not because of any anomaly in my nature or of any sexual debility, for I was as virile as could be and took pride in my virility; no, it was because I thought that in this way I could acquire power. Before he beat me, he would put his arms around my waist and whisper in my ear, and I felt the woman in me rising to the surface; of course, when I was alone there were times when I was my own wife, but without too much conviction; in the arms of my priest, on the other hand, I was exceedingly happy to find someone who under cover of darkness possessed to some extent the conviction of my dreams and who managed to make me share it with him. On those occasions, I did not so much feel that I was yielding my body to him, as that I was discovering another part of myself, the wife of myself that dwelt within me. My reasoning went something like this: I had my whole life to play the man's role; at sixteen I had to find out what a charming, sturdy little maidservant I would have made for some priest. She would be incomparable in that role, a cunning purveyor of pleasure, both strong and gentle; when she was beaten, I pitied her and loved her all the more; when she was coddled, I marveled at her and admired the stamina with which she bore up under all that pleasure; this dialogue with my other self raised me to a pitch of perfect happiness.

There follows an explicit description of a whipping administered by the priest, after which he prepares some tea and rum for the two. At this point, the narrator resumes the strange and psychologically revealing dialogue with himself.

He leaned against me once more and we waited. What time of night was it? I had no idea. I felt an irresistible tenderness for the man and I gave his hand a squeeze; he was holding mine so tightly that I thought the bones would break. I kissed his hand. The garden had been taken over by the rain. Quickly flipping the lid back on the teapot, he quenched the burning rum; he found some glasses under the blankets, blew out the spirit lamp, and in the darkness that followed raised the sweet, steaming brew to my lips. I immediately experienced a sense of utter well-being and began to play the charming tender wife. This campsite with its disorderly blankets took me back to man's first nights on earth, to a state of nature, to all the primeval confusions. Pressing my face against my priest's fur-collared jacket as though it were the skin of a beast, I became intoxicated with pleasure. I was warm. I liked this cavelike kind of a room.

He caressed me with an exact understanding of my flesh, with the skilled fingers of a masseur, saying not a word, for fear of breaking the spell of my drunkenness. His long hands seemed to know my body perfectly; from head to foot there wasn't a bone or muscle that he failed to sculpt with a subtlety that entranced me. He was curing me of my loneliness as one resets a sprain. What made me happiest of all was that knowledge he had of my body; it was as though he wished to give me infinite pleasure, infinite unto the sublime, until I sank on my knees in his arms; it was as though he had known me since the beginning of time.

Perhaps more directly and dramatically than any clinical test could do, this passage illustrates the latent passive-female sex feeling in a young man, his need to submit to the dominant older man (as in Ernest's case), and the happiness he finds in this role.

But the story also makes explicit the hidden point or core of all masochistic submission, namely the power that is gained over the even more dependent sadistic partner.

HYACINTHE, OU LES MILLES PLAISIRS

The first part of this "novel," one of the more remarkable examples of primitive pornography, deals with a young Parisian, Hyacinthe, who is about to get out of the army and who lives with his widowed aunt. Hyacinthe has become infatuated with a young painter named Maxime after a single night of love. Hyacinthe, however, is tragically prevented from keeping their second appointment.

He settled down in the dining room to read the evening paper. Suddenly, he caught his breath, cast a glance about him to see if he wasn't dreaming, and finally decided to re-read the little paragraph which had so upset him. It was a banal news item: "The half-naked body of twenty-five-year-old Maxime P. was found in his studio this morning. The young man had hanged himself with his belt. Maxime P. had changed a great deal. He suffered from constant melancholy, probably due to a sorrow of the heart."

For a moment, Hyacinthe did not move. Maxime had committed suicide with the belt he had given him. He thought that he wouldn't come back, that he wouldn't keep his promise. He got up, locked himself in his room and threw himself on the bed. He didn't stir when his aunt came to tell him that dinner was ready; he told her he was sick.

He let darkness steal into the room. As the hour when he should have been in Maxime's arms drew near, he felt himself succumb to a strange fever, as though Maxime were laying a thousand hands on his body. He turned on the light. His fever rose even higher. He could see Maxime's half-naked body with a hard-on like those only hanged men get. As a symbol of his unquenched desire, Hyacinthe felt his cock grow as stiff as Maxime's. He unbuttoned his fly and freed it from his drawers. It slapped against his stomach. He began to masturbate. Then he stood up, reached for a bowl and took from it an eggplant which he had brought along on an impulse. He had noticed that it was the same size as his cock, and Maxime's cock was just like his own. He took off his trousers, and knelt on his bed. He spit into his hand, smeared the eggplant with saliva and, on all fours, rammed it up his ass and gave himself rhythmical pleasure while he jerked off. Another moan seemed to mingle with his own as though Maxime were really poking him. He made sport with death to keep his pledge, unconsciously re-enacting the Greek myth of Bacchus and Prosymnus.

Hyacinthe's stomach grew taut, a shudder ran through his body, then a second and a third. His buttocks drew back, the egg-plant slid further into his anus which pressed around it even harder as he spurted on the blanket.

Relaxed now, he lay flat on the bed. He hoped that Maxime's spirit would be appeased the way his body would have been. Then he fell asleep, exhausted.

Hyacinthe, of course, goes on to meet other young men, among them the wealthy Paul, who arranges for him to get a well-paying job in South America. The second part of the story, in which Hyacinthe plays almost no role, concerns one of his friends, Albert, another member of Paul's entourage. In the course of an orgy, they have playfully "martyrized" one of their guests, a sailor, by tying him up and pretending to thrash him.

Following this timid attempt at a torture session, Albert acquired a taste for it. Milo knew a very beautiful young workman of nineteen. He only went out with girls and was horrified by any other form of pleasure, even though his type of beauty predisposed him to it.

They decided to kidnap him.

Albert had stopped the car on a highway in the suburbs. He got out and left the motor running, pretending to examine a front tire. The radio was softly playing jazz, the spot was almost deserted. A young worker in overalls passed by. Albert called to him: "Hi there! How about giving me a hand?"

The boy came over. He was blinded by the headlights and couldn't see the man who had called to him, for he was standing in the shadows. He leaned over for a better look. A dull thud and the young man slid into his arms. Milo, who was sitting inside, helped get the body in, while he took a little gold bottle out of his pocket and poured a few drops into the young worker's mouth. It had all happened very fast and no one had seen a thing.

Albert, in spite of the danger involved, drove very fast. The worker was sitting in the back of the car. He was asleep, with his head resting on Milo's shoulder, lulled by the sound of the radio.

The car sped through the night with complete assurance. They were silent. They had the feeling that they were acting in an American movie. He pressed even harder on the accelerator.

What particularly excited Albert was to explore for the first time the body of a really handsome boy. His hands trembled as he undid the trousers of the still unconscious boy.

He took him to a room in the basement of the manor. He had an adolescent body. Milo helped him undress the boy completely. When he was stark naked, they dressed him in the clothes of Paul's maid.

Paul stood slightly to one side, watching them. The sailor was standing by his side. He had allowed him to attend this session in order to make up for the mild torture that had been inflicted on him.

Now the young man's sex was stiff, raising the dress. The liquid in the little gold bottle that Paul had brought back from India had the power, first, to put the body and the mind to sleep, then to arouse the senses down to their deepest fibers.

At this point, the young worker came to. He cast an astonished glance at his costume and his surroundings, unable to believe his eyes.

He could feel Albert's hand holding his wrist. So it wasn't a dream! He tried to break free. The hand tightened its grip. He started to struggle and as he was about to cry out, Albert put a hand over his mouth. They struggled in silence for a moment, the young worker with the energy of despair. He was strong and managed to break loose. He ran up the stairs. Once he was in the park he started running again, but each time he met with hands ready to seize him. He panted and staggered, completely out of breath.

He retraced his steps and almost ran into the Negro. He heard his laughter ring through the night.

Albert had let him go on purpose. It was part of the show.

Then he collapsed on the grass, panting. Several hands pinned him to the ground, with his face pressed against the earth. His dress was ripped up the back and lying thus, half-naked, he felt pain plough into him. He was being raped. The liquid from the little bottle was doing its work, filling his body with a vast unknown pleasure. He lost track of time and the men screwing him had become a single lover, the purveyor of infinite, ever fresh pleasures.

He came several times in his dress. Then he felt something like a bee sting on his thigh, a great sensation of well-being overcame him and all his pain vanished. He was floating. Then he lost consciousness.

When the young worker opened his eyes, it was daylight. He began to struggle, then he realized that he was alone, lying on the grass, wearing his clothes again as if by magic, not far from the spot where he had been stopped by the car. Had that car really existed? Perhaps he had dreamed the whole thing. He had a sensation of well-being, although his body was sore the way it is when one has spent the night sleeping outdoors.

The young man thought he must have lain down and gone to sleep. He tried to remember his dream. Confused images crowded into his mind. Unconsciously, he unbuttoned his trousers and inserted a finger between his buttocks. It slid in easily. It hurt a bit, but he left it in and moved it around. This suggested very precise images and his cock began to swell. So it hadn't been a dream.

He sat up. He had just remembered his wallet. Had they taken his money? But it was still there, with some twenty thousand francs added. He counted them dreamily. He ought to go to the police station and tell them how he'd been kidnaped.

The young worker looked at his watch. He didn't have time. He had to get to work. He stood up. He felt a slight dizziness, but otherwise his body felt light. The sensation of well-being was still with him.

With a surge of joy, he remembered that this was Saturday and that he had two full days ahead of him to rest up. He started walking in the morning light. He said to himself that there was no hurry about going to the police station.

In this homosexual fantasy we have seen again the ever present sadistic trend, coupled with the masochistic collusion of the victim, whose pleasure in being victimized is here made perfectly overt.

PÉDÉRASTIE ACTIVE (ACTIVE PEDERASTY)

This novel, by "P. D. Rast" (London and Paris: Société des Bibliophiles, 1907; mentioned under item 265 in Perceau's catalogue, *Bibliographie du Roman Erotique au XIXᵉ Siècle*), is extremely rare and well written. (Note the pronunciation of the author's full name, "pederast.")

The story concerns the goings-on between the narrator, who is an older man, and Albert, a young boy, and, later, his younger brother Philippe. In a subplot we also hear of two other boys, Just and Thomas, and of the latter's seduction by his mother (a feature which is of special interest because of the homosexual context).

In the beginning we learn that the narrator had always had his eyes on young Albert, a particularly handsome and charming boy in the village in which the action takes place.

Consequently, my wandering imagination had, in the course of its lascivious dreams, taken pleasure in completely undressing this gamin, going into raptures beholding his adorable nakedness, sucking his two little pink tits, delicately manipulating his nice little balls, sucking his pecker, plunging as far as possible my tongue into his asshole. Very often during the day—and especially at night—had I sweetened the enjoyment of solitary masturbation by imagining—sweet illusion!—that it was Albert, my darling Bertie, who with his hand, as expert as it was lewd, rhythmically agitated my long stalk. And when at last the final spasm shook me convulsively, it was again Albert whom I crushed against me, covering him with fiery, passionate kisses and it was against him that, annihilated, I fell back.

When fantasy becomes reality and young Albert spends an evening in the narrator's home, the latter first quizzes him lasciviously about his masturbation habits, making the boy show him how he does it and use "naughty" words. (It is strange how dated such scenes read today when these naughty words have become commonplace and thereby lost their former erotic supercharge.) One of the oddities in this connection is that the author sometimes uses the name Jesus for the male genitals, which we have not encountered in other erotic writings. He uses a number of other religious references throughout the book for the obvious reason of providing additional erotic tension by the use of sacrilegious terms.

The narrator, having quizzed Albert about his "secret vices" (masturbation), opens his fly, takes out the boy's penis and exclaims, "A delicious average-sized stalk of spring asparagus. I'm mad about that vegetable, especially when it is served with white sauce" (a broad allusion to semen). "So without wasting any time," he goes on, "I began to devour that delicious asparagus. However, since it was rather unyielding, it took me a good five or six minutes before I got the better of it. But by God, was it good! . . . Have you ever tasted it? A virgin boy's jissom is incomparably delicious. I savored it once more that evening. But what a sexual state it puts the gourmet in! Only you who have tasted it, you blessed mortals, can know it!"

At the next meeting with the boy, the narrator interrogates him again about how many times he "has been doing it" either alone or with someone else. The boy confesses to seven or eight times (for the past few days), alone and in company with two other boys. Then, undressing his young lover, the narrator muses: "Never has a woman had for me the attraction of one or another of the males I've had, of the males before whom I've prostituted myself during the long course of my sodomistic existence. . . . There is no thorough exercise in pederasty that does not include the maneuver of buggering. There is nothing, in fact, more lewd, more luscious, more satiating than to per-forate the anus of an attractive little boy, to search his bowels, to flood them with scalding jissom and, finally, to expire from lust, while the two interpenetrating bodies soldered to one another form only one!"

From there he goes on to his theory of "69" from the homosexual point of view, always with reference to Albert. Then he decides to enhance the situation by getting Albert's younger brother Philippe into the game. He first has anal inter-course with Albert, while his brother is masturbating him to orgasm. For the next round he places the two boys so that Albert, lying on his back, can perform fellatio on Philippe, while the narrator is able to have anal intercourse with him at the same time: "Getting into a slow swing, the trio went on," he relates not without a weird sense of humor, "the amorous task being carried out on both sides: sucked by his brother, buggered by me, the lad wriggled like an eel in a frying pan and expressed his happiness by monosyllables which left no doubt as to the inten-sity of his sensations. Alas! Everything here below must come to an end; blissful eternity is not for this world."

At Christmas time young Thomas arrives in soldier's uni-form and saber—both of which he soon sheds to get into bed with the narrator and "bugger" him. "Besides, in no time at all, his shirt had joined his other military effects and Thomas, just as much of a blackguard as I, was in the raw. God! Was he lovable! Especially his huge plunger. Ah, reader, pity my poor little asshole, because this terrifying machine is going to burrow inside it so deeply that its blond fur will caress my orifice."

Not without interest for its inherent humor and insights into homosexual psychology is the verbal exchange between the two during anal intercourse.

While with my arms and legs I was tightening my grip on my male, all I could hear was: "Oh, my darling! My little blondie! Oh! My adored sweet thing! My woman . . ." to which I responded with: "My big wolf! My enormous pet! My Thomas! Deeper, harder . . ." and I felt myself being vigorously searched, our tongues, mouths, and breathing were merging. The final spasm wasn't long in arriving. The morsel of Thomas that I had absorbed got even bigger, dilating my anus; his eyes were convulsed, mine were swimming; his fingers drilled into my flesh and I remember stabbing him furiously with mine; his lips were about to make my lips bleed, our sighs intermingled, and we spent. At the precise moment when his jissom was burning my insides, my cock, pressed between our two bellies, ejaculated copiously.

After this, we have Thomas' confession. It starts with an aside about the other boy, Just, who was so eager to experience intercourse with a woman that he paid forty pennies to an old beggar hag, derisively nicknamed "The Trunk of India," to "devirginize" him in a hayloft.

When Thomas hears this, he envies Just the experience but apparently knows no available female to do the same with him. However, his problems are solved when his mother takes it into her depraved mind to initiate the boy herself.

His mother was right next to him, rubbing her body in heat against his, taking enormous pleasure in his rousing tales, making him elaborate at certain points in the story and repeat the crude words the Parisian had used. She kept filling his glass the moment Thomas, his gullet burned by alcohol, had emptied it. It wasn't long before the lewd conversation took a more personal and confidential turn. Skillfully questioned by his mother who had put her arm around his neck, Thomas admitted that he adored to make love and that he would be perfectly happy the night he would be able to sleep with his own little wife in his arms. . . .

The hour of the crime, of incest had struck. . . .

"Thomas!"

"What?"

"You're going to go to bed with me. We're going to sleep together."

"Oh! No! After all!"

"Why not?"

"Because . . . because you're my mother. Oh, no! Not with you!"

"Imbecile, anybody could see that you're drunk!" (She poured him another glass for good measure.) "You're going to sleep with me not for what you think, obviously, but because the mattress of your bed is being redone."

Presented under this deceitful form, the prospect of sleeping with the person who had brought him into the world wasn't so shocking. Half an hour later Thomas was stretched out in bed next to her in the place usually taken by his father. The bitch had taken a peculiar pleasure in watching him take off his clothes, one article after the other, staring at his feet, his legs, his thighs, relishing the idea that in a few seconds she would finally be able to realize the abominably lewd dream she had cherished for so long: to grab the amorous tool of her Thomas and to be impaled by it in such a fashion that the two of them would make one body! Thomas undressed without looking at his mother. She, on the other hand, was anything but embarrassed in her nightly washing-up.

In spite of the drunkenness that was overtaking him more and more, he was vaguely aware that it wasn't really very normal for a young man twenty years old to be sleeping with his mother. But there they were, lying next to each other. In a few minutes the odious crime, the dreadful incest was about to be consummated! Thomas' mother had already entwined her legs around those of her son, and while with her left arm and hand she clasped his waist to bring their bodies together, with her right, in spite of the protests of the poor boy, "Oh, no! Really!" repeated over and over again, she quickly had lifted his shirt up and was caressing his tool. But she had hardly begun her obscene, incestuous roamings, when Thomas, so erect a few minutes before, began to wilt. In vain his mother, now lying on her back, had forcefully made her son lie upon her in the prescribed position; in vain did she cross her legs over his loins and

kiss him enough and to spare; in vain did she make efforts to introduce the filial penis into the maternal cunt. Thomas' prick got
smaller and smaller.

"Oh, no! Mommy! You can see that I can't!"

"You must!"

And she started telling him numerous dirty stories, while at the
same time masturbating him ferociously. He still wasn't close to an
erection. The rigidness achieved by his mother's vigorous rubbing
disappeared as soon as she had ceased the masturbating movement to
attempt penetration. She begged him, beseeched him, entreated him:
"My Thomas, fuck me!" She also insulted him: "Good for nothing!
At twenty you can't even shoot your wad! And to think that this
thing is going to be a soldier! Oh, la la!"

Ashamed in spite of himself, more ashamed of his impotency
than of the undignified duty his mother demanded of him, Thomas
silenced his scruples about filial decency. Seriously, ardently, he
tried to prove his manhood. Recalling his amorous memories, he
called upon his imagination to buck up his dormant senses. In vain!
His wilted, flaccid prick only managed to drag along the lower belly
of the female in rut, his mother! Then he remembered that the same
thing had happened to him the first time he had crossed the threshold of the county whorehouse. The chosen prostitute, when he
began to despair of being able to consummate the sacrifice, told him
gently; "Wait a little, you big, handsome boy, you'll get there." And
she began to suck him. The effect had been irresistible. A few
minutes later he had reached the paroxysm of enjoyment. Thomas
had hardly finished telling this lewd episode of his youth than his
mother, infuriated because she hadn't thought of such a method
herself, put the silent clarinet to her lips. Before too long the
musical instrument, nibbled, sucked, and delicately manipulated,
began to swell, stiffened, and became a beautiful hard penis.

The female, when she thought that it had attained the summit
of its length and thickness, planted it brutally into her uterus. No
less brutally, Thomas clasped her to him with his skittish arms, gave
four or five thrusts with his ass in order to make it penetrate even
further and only had time to exclaim: "Oh, God, fucking God,
good sweet Jesus of shit . . . Shit!" And so saying, all congested
and suffocating, at the same instant as he felt himself ejaculate
copiously he also felt his mother's juices burning his prick. The
bitch had come at last! Her son had impregnated her! However, she
wasn't satisfied yet.

Thomas had barely regained his strength when he felt his
mother, with whom he had remained coupled together, start again

the rhythm of the lustful movements of copulation, and while she was kissing him on the mouth, her hands moved in the most libertine way over his back, his buttocks and thighs, without neglecting the crack in his ass. The incestuous son's penis, which had not left its hot prison, ramrodded again, so much so that within ten minutes the second emission of prolific liqueur had mixed with the first. Receiving it in her vagina, the indecent creature sighed: "Oh, Thomas, you've given me a child!" Her maternal instinct hadn't deceived her.

Thomas didn't hear her. Completely fagged out, he had finally been able to get out of his mother's clutches and, turning his backend on her, was already sleeping the sleep of the satisfied brute. As for his accomplice, she placed a thankful kiss on the neck of the man who had made her so happy, then went to sleep herself, chuckling: "If he has really made me pregnant, it won't be all that funny." You bitch, you're pregnant and it was your son who did it, because his genital seed met one of your ovaries just at the right time to fertilize it!

After six or seven hours of heavy sleep, Thomas woke up first, feeling an enormous desire to piss. He struck a match, got out of bed, took the chamber pot and urinated copiously.

His movements woke up his companion who immediately felt all her lewd instincts reviving in her by just looking at Thomas relieving his bladder. Feeling the need to do the same thing, she squatted down on the pot as soon as Thomas had finished, purposely lifting up her shift way above her tits, the breasts which had in the past nursed the man to whom she was prostituting herself today! Since there was only one hour left before they had to get up, she didn't have too much trouble in getting Thomas to devote that hour to making love again, that criminal love of mother and son.

The two infamous lovers had barely taken their respective places in the conjugal bed transformed into a sanctuary of their incestuous adultery than the profligate female began to masturbate her boy with all the skill of a shameless ghoul. True, this detestable operation was absolutely necessary because now that Thomas' drunkenness had abated, he was beginning to reflect on the horror of the situation. Little by little he began to feel overwhelmed by an intense feeling of remorse and disgust. But what male can resist his penis being caressed, especially when it's a mother masturbating her son? Thomas plucked up enough courage to masturbate his mother, massaging her clitoris. And when both felt the prodromes of genetic enjoyment, for the third time they copulated, for the third time in the same night mother and son fornicated, mixing their seed and consummating their sacrilege.

Thomas got up painfully to go to work. His loins were broken, his legs like rubber, eyes sunken. He had some breakfast and left. Seeing him arrive in such condition, exhaustion showing all over his face, his comrades kidded him without suspecting the incredible truth: "Hey! Is it possible! Your Blondie mustn't have bored you last night! How many times did you come, to be so beat!" So that they would leave him alone, Thomas replied that he had fucked three times, but he carefully avoided mention that it was his mother he had straddled.

In the psychogenesis of homosexuality, the fear of the seductive mother's incestuous intentions toward the male child is apparent (the old beggar woman is a thinly disguised mother figure). Out of this apprehension there can develop a revulsion against women in general and a flight toward the person's own sex. Of course, there are many other psychological factors which combine to produce a homosexual preference. But the threat arising from an incestuous interest of the parent of the opposite sex can be and often is one of these factors.

In the following chapters we will review sexual fantasies which are deeper than these sterile recitals of pseudohomosexual scenes, in particular, transsexualism, bondage, and sadomasochism.

5

Transsexualism and Bondage

Among the strangest phenomena in erotic literature are those sexual fantasies in which the sex roles of the characters are reversed. We have already had a glimpse of this in the work of the Chevalier de Nerciat, where characters dressed as men are really women, or vice versa. In the following examples of cross-dressing and the reversal of sex roles, the dominance-submission theme becomes increasingly important, and cross-dressing is often only the outward expression or symbol. In the eighteenth century, cross-dressing, or the reversal of sex roles, though frequently connected with flagellation, was not yet part of the later dominance-submission theme. Instead, it was simply, and one is almost tempted to add innocently, used as a literary gimmick to heighten the element of suspense and surprise, to enrich the plot, and to stimulate bisexual fantasies which frequently succeeded in increasing the erotic tension of the story without being at the moral expense of either sex.

TABLEAUX DES MOEURS

One such instance is a curious scene of cross-dressing in *Tableaux des Moeurs de ce Temps dans les différents ages de la vie,* by Crébillon *fils* (Amsterdam [actually, Paris], 1760). Crébillon *fils* was a contemporary of Nerciat and ranks with him as a writer of erotica. *Tableaux des Moeurs* is a series of witty dialogues which contain a great variety of material, all intended as social satire.

The passage below concerns a character named Auguste whose escapades, especially lesbian ones in a convent school, the reader has already come to know in the first part of the book. Having made a marriage of convenience as was then the style, we encounter her here as Madame de Rastard, though she does not seem any more interested in men than before.

Having heard that one of her acquaintances, Madame Copen, is a lesbian and that her greatest thrill is being thrashed by another woman dressed up as a man, Madame de Rastard arranges to take the place of the prostitute who ordinarily plays opposite the eccentric lady. To complicate matters, Madame Copen's son-in-law, having learned that his wife's mother had a rendezvous with a "man," dresses up in Madame Copen's clothes, presumably to play a joke on "him."

MADAME DE RASTARD: Is that you, Madame Copen?
SON-IN-LAW: Indeed yes! This is she!
MADAME DE RASTARD: So you are the lady who claims to be in love
  with me and yet you let me chill my bones out here on the
  grass for hours on end? Do you think I am the sort of fellow
  who puts up with that? Come here quickly and get down on

your knees! I am going to give you the punishment that you deserve! Come now, lie down here next to me. Turn over. Now just you wait, my little heart, just wait until I've bundled all that up to suit my fancy.

SON-IN-LAW: Why what do you mean, my little man? Have we not got something very different to do? Now my behind is quite bare. Ouch! . . . Ow! . . . You're thrashing me, and with a switch! Do you know that that *hurts*, and that I am going to pay you back!

MADAME DE RASTARD: I don't care a fig, you cheeky little creature. You've got more than that coming to you.

SON-IN-LAW: Ow! Ouch! More? Aren't you ever going to stop? Ah! Now that feels good, stroke my behind nicely, that's more like it!

MADAME DE RASTARD: Is this that famous behind I've heard so much about? Why, it's no bigger than a thimble! 'Tis a sorry sight indeed!

SON-IN-LAW: Why you little rascal! Bundling up my skirts without so much as a by-your-leave! Now let's see what's under the seat of those breeches of yours. Just wait till I get this unbuttoned . . . we'll have a look at your pego afterwards. Now hold still, and let's have a good look at your little arse, that's a sight I always enjoy. What the devil! It's twice as big as mine! You were right! Like two pumpkins! What a pity I can't see more of it!

MADAME DE RASTARD: Go ahead and whack them, you insolent female! I'll see that you're repaid in kind!

SON-IN-LAW: I've never seen a boy with a behind so beautifully plump and firm. Just hold still, you little rascal, while I take a closer look. This is the arse of a gelding or eunuch if ever I saw one. I've got to find out what the front side is like.

MADAME DE RASTARD: Here, you little scamp, now I'm on my back. You can have the front after all. I've no secrets from you.

SON-IN-LAW: Aha! Aha! Aha! 'Twas all a hoax, you little knave, or rather you little hussy! You're just a little hussy in disguise. And you've got the sweetest little cunt in the world! But how do you expect a girl like me to make a shift with that?

MADAME DE RASTARD: Well, you silly creature, you can have my little cunt to play with to your heart's content. Lie down on top of me, belly to belly. There. Now let me pull your gown all the way up, it's in the way. Now I'll just slide my breeches down and pull up my shirt. 'Tis the least I can do by you! Press close to me now so we can play with each other. Ah! That's fine! Kiss me! Good! Put your arms around me. Hug me tight. Why, what's that thing I feel! What are you trying to stick into me? Speak up, you impudent hussy! Hi there! You're hurting me! Ow! Ouch! Ouch!

SON-IN-LAW: 'Tis only a little pego.

MADAME DE RASTARD: Oh! Oh! what's happening? And what are these? Balls? Ow! Ow! Is that you, Madame Copen? Ow! Ow! It's not possible. Ah! ah! ah! Fuck! Fuck! I'm undone!

SON-IN-LAW: No, my pretty, you're only fucked, and well-fucked at that!

"FRANK" AND I

Simple cross-dressing and flagellation are also the chief characteristics of the English sex classic *"Frank" and I*, published in 1902. The book deals with the life and adventures of a wealthy young Englishman who accidentally meets a runaway boy, invites him to stay with him at his home, then discovers that the boy is really a girl. Here, the dominance-submission theme is absent, or at least remains in the background, though flagellation sets the mood of the story.

When the narrator first meets "Frank," he describes him as follows:

He was apparently about thirteen years old; a slenderly built, good-looking lad, with small hands and feet; short, curly hair, and blue eyes. He was dressed in a Norfolk jacket and trousers of dark tweed; neat, laced boots, and a white straw hat, but I noticed that his clothes, though almost new, were dusty and travel-stained. His manner was quiet and self-possessed, he expressed himself well, speaking with an educated accent; and he appeared to be in every respect a little gentleman.

At the first infraction of the house rules by "Frank," his new protector is, of course, eager to give him a birching, but the boy seems strangely resistant:

"Oh! Oh! Oh!" he cried. "I know I deserve to be punished, but please don't birch me. Punish me in any other way but that."

"I will not punish you in any other way. Let down your trousers at once. I did not think you were a coward."

"I am not a coward. I am not afraid of the pain. I can bear it. But I am ashamed to let down my trousers before you," he sobbed out.

"Don't be silly! When the lady spanked you, you had to let down your trousers; and it is more shameful for a boy to let down his trousers before a woman, than to let them down before a man. Now unbutton! Look sharp!"

"Oh! don't make me let down my trousers," he again said, beseechingly. I lost patience. "If you don't at once obey me, I will send for Wilson and get him to take down your trousers, and then hold you on his back while I flog you," I said, in a loud voice.

"Oh! don't do that. Don't do that!" he cried out, in terrified accents, with a look of horror on his face. "I will let down my trousers."

On this occasion, Frank's secret is still preserved. But when he is again to be punished for some misbehavior, the disclosure of his true sex becomes imminent:

"I am ashamed, and very sorry for what I have done. I expect to be punished," he said in a low voice, his eyes filling with tears, and his lips trembling. Then, without another word, he let down his trousers, and placed himself in position across the end of the sofa.

I tucked his shirt up and began to apply the rod, and as I was angry with him, I laid on the cuts smartly, raising long, red weals all over the surface of his white bottom. He wriggled, writhed, and cried as the stinging strokes of the birch fell with a swishing sound on his plump, firm flesh, striping the skin in all directions; but I went on flogging him, till at last he could no longer suppress his cries, and he began to scream in a shrill tone, at the same time putting both his hands over his bottom. I seized his wrists and held them with my left hand, while I continued to apply the rod with a little more force, extorting from him louder screams.

"Frank" is not an instance of real sex-inversion. Though dressed in the attire of the opposite sex, she remains essentially female with female sex feelings.

MONSIEUR VENUS

However, *Monsieur Venus*, by "Rachilde" (Paris: Flammarion, 1888), contains a fantasy in which there is a true reversal of sex roles and sex feelings, similar to those expressed in some of the homosexual fantasies.

Raoule de Vénérande, a wealthy young woman-about-town, takes as her lover Jacques Silvert, a beautiful young man employed in an artificial-flower factory, an effeminate occupation of socially inferior status. Through the complicated wandering of the novel, in the course of which it becomes clear that Jacques has homosexual tendencies, they gradually reverse roles. The following scenes take place near the end of the book. Raoule has married Jacques, and this scene begins just after the wedding supper, as Raoule prepares to join her groom. He has retired earlier in the evening, as brides will often do after "normal" weddings.

Having bolted the dressing-room door, Raoule stripped off her clothes with angry pride.

"At last," she said, when the dress made of chaste, shimmering damask had fallen about her impatient feet. She picked up a tiny brass key, opened a closet hidden behind a drape, and took out a black dress suit, complete with patent leather ankle boots and embroidered shirt. As she stood in front of the mirror, which reflected back to her the image of a young man as handsome as any hero in a novel idolized by teen-age girls, she ran the hand that wore the gleaming ring through her short, curly hair. A bitter grin twisted her lips that were blurred by a faint brown fuzz.

"Happiness, my dear aunt," she declaimed in a cold voice, "is all the more real as it is more wild; if Jacques does not awake from the sensual drowsiness that I have instilled into his docile body, I'll be happy in spite of your curse."

She went over to a velvet door curtain, jerked it aside, and paused, her breast throbbing.

Seen from the threshold, the setting was magical. That pagan sanctuary, built in the midst of modern splendors, gave off a subtle, incomprehensible vertigo which would have intoxicated any human sensibility. Raoule was right: love can be born in whatever cradle is prepared for it.

Mademoiselle de Vénérande's former bedchamber, rounded at the corners and with a cupola ceiling, was hung with blue velvet and paneled with white satin, which had gold highlights, and marble fluting.

A carpet, designed after Raoule's instructions, covered the floor with all the delights of oriental flora. This thick woolen carpet had such bright colors and vivid relief effects that one might have been walking on an enchanted flower bed.

In the middle, beneath the night light that hung from four silver chains, the bridal bed was in the shape of the primitive vessel that carried Venus to Cytherea. A group of naked cupids, kneeling at the head of the bed, were lifting with all the strength in their little fists the conch padded with blue satin. The statue of Eros, with his bow across his back, stood on the top of a marble column; with his looped arms he was supporting lavish curtains of oriental brocade which fell in voluptuous folds around another conch. Beside the bed a bronze tripod held an incense burner studded with precious gems in which a flame was dying with a vague, pungent odor.

The bust of Antinoüs with enamel eyeballs sat facing the tripod. The windows of pastel stained glass had been rebuilt in ogival form and fitted with bars like the windows of a harem.

The only furniture in the room was the bed. Raoule's portrait by Bonnet was attached to the hangings and surrounded by blazoned draperies. It showed her wearing a Louis Quinze hunting costume, while a red greyhound licked the stock of the whip in her splendidly rendered hand.

Jacques was lying on the bed; with the coquettishness of a courtesan expecting her lover, he had pushed back the quilts and the eiderdown. The temperature in that sealed room was warm and invigorating.

Raoule approached the altar of her god with dilated pupils and eager mouth. "Beauty, you alone exist; I no longer believe in anything but you," she whispered ecstatically.

Jacques was not asleep; he sat up slowly without forsaking his indolent pose. Against the azure-blue background of the bedcurtains, his supple, wonderfully shaped torso stood out, as pink as the flame in the incense burner.

"Then why did you once try to destroy this beauty that you love?" he answered in a loving whisper.

Raoule sat down on the edge of the bed and seized the flesh of his arched torso in both hands.

"I was punishing an unwitting betrayal that night; just imagine what I would do if you ever really betrayed me."

"Listen to me, dear master of my body, I forbid you to recall the shadow of suspicion that came between our twin passions, it frightens me too much. Not that I'm afraid for myself!" he added, laughing his adorable, childlike laugh. "I'm afraid for you."

He laid his submissive head across Raoule's knees. "It really is lovely here," he whispered with a grateful glance. "We're going to be very happy here."

With the tip of one finger, Raoule was stroking his regular features, outlining the graceful arch of his eyebrows.

"Yes, we will be happy here, and we mustn't leave this temple for a long time so that all these hangings may be steeped in the perfume of our love. We had decided to go on a trip, but now we shan't. I do not wish to flee this merciless society who hate us even more each day; I can sense it. We must show them that we are tougher than they, because we love each other."

She was thinking of her aunt; he thought of his sister.

"All right," he said resolutely, "we shall stay! That way I can complete my education as a serious husband. As soon as I learn to duel, I'll try to kill your most wicked enemy."

"Well, what do you know! Is Madame de Vénérande talking about killing someone?"

He leaned over backwards with a graceful movement until he could reach her ear: "Well, I have to want to kill someone since I'll never be able to give birth to anyone!"

They couldn't help laughing uproariously; and in their merriment, which was at once cynical and philosophical, they forgot the merciless society which had abandoned the De Vénérande townhouse claiming that they were abandoning a tomb.

Their insolent merriment gradually subsided. Their lips as they met were no longer grinning. Raoule drew the curtain to her, plunging the bed into a delightful semidarkness, in which Jacques's body glistened like a star.

"You know what I wish?" he said in a very low voice.

"This is the time for wishes to come true," answered Raoule, putting one knee on the carpet.

"I wish you'd really woo me as a husband would at a time like this, a husband of your class." And he writhed coaxingly in Raoule's arms, which were twined about his bare waist.

"Oho!" she said, withdrawing her arms. "Then I must be very proper?"

"Very! Look, I'm hiding! I'm a virgin." And quick as a boarding school girl who has just said something saucy, Jacques burrowed under the sheets. A cloud of lace fell across his forehead so that only his round shoulder appeared; veiled in this way, it resembled the broad shoulder of a working-class girl who had accidentally found her way into the bed of a rich man-about-town.

"How cruel* you are," said Raoule, parting the curtains.

"I am not," said Jacques, not realizing that she had already begun the conceit. "No, no I'm not cruel! I just want to have a little fun, that's all. My heart is full of happiness, I feel drunk all over, drunk with love and full of wild desires. I want to get some use out of my royal standing. I want to make you scream with rage and bite my wounds again the way you did when you were jealous. I want to be ferocious too, but in my own way."

"Haven't I been waiting night after night, begging my dreams to provide the pleasure you deny me?" Raoule went on, standing and staring at him with that somber gaze whose power had already added another monstrosity to the rosters of humanity.

"That's just too bad," Jacques countered, the tip of his moist tongue protruding past his purple lips. "I don't give a hang about your dreams, reality will seem all the better afterward. Now please begin right away or I'm going to get angry."

"Why, this is the most awful torture you could inflict upon me," Raoule went on in a quavering voice, pitched low, like a man's. "Wait? When ultimate happiness is within my grasp? Wait? When I've sacrificed everything for the right to keep you near me, night and day? Wait? When my greatest joy would be to hear you say: 'It feels so good to lay my forehead on your breast, I want to sleep there.' No, no, you can't do a thing like that!"

"Yes I will," Jacques declared, frankly disappointed to see that she wouldn't indulge in the masquerade without getting the benefit of her own pleasure. "I tell you it's a whim!"

Raoule dropped to her knees and clasped her hands, delighted to see that he himself was fooled, *out of habit,* by the masquerade he was begging for, unaware that it had been the object of her impassioned speech for the last twenty minutes.

"Oh! you're so mean! I think you're simply hateful!" said Jacques in an annoyed tone of voice.

Raoule had thrown her head back and moved away.

"I can't set eyes on you without going mad," said Raoule, involuntarily using the masculine form of the adjective; "your divine beauty makes me forget who I am and sends me into a lover's raptures; I go out of my mind contemplating your ideal nudity . . . so what does the sex of our caresses matter to this wild passion? What does it matter what tokens of attachment our bodies ex-

---

* From this point on, Raoule uses the feminine forms of adjectives when referring to Jacques. The fact that most of these in French are phonetically very close or even identical to the masculine forms accounts for Jacques's misconstruction of her words.

change? What do we care for the memories of love of centuries past, for the reprobation of mankind everywhere? You're beautiful. I'm a man. I worship you and you love me!"

Jacques had finally realized that she was complying with his wishes. He propped himself up on one elbow, his eyes brimming with a mysterious joy.

"Come here!" he said with a dreadful shiver. "But don't take off that suit. Your lovely hands alone are enough to keep your slave in bondage. Come here."

Raoule hurled herself upon the satin bed, uncovering once again the white, supple limbs of that enamored Proteus whose virginal modesty was now thrown to the winds. For an hour the only sounds to be heard in that modern temple of paganism were their long, panting sighs and rhythmic kisses; then suddenly a heart-rending cry split the air, like the scream of a vanquished demon.

"Raoule!" cried Jacques, his features contorted, his teeth biting his lip and his arms outstretched as though he had just been crucified in a spasm of pleasure. "Raoule, aren't you a man? Can't you be a man?"

And his dashed illusions, dead and buried once and for all, rose from his loins to his throat in the form of a sob. For Raoule had opened her white silk vest and, the better to feel Jacques's heartbeat, had laid one of her naked breasts against his skin; a round, cup-shaped breast with a closed nipple that would never bloom in the sublime pleasure of nursing. Jacques had been roused from his torpor by a sudden revulsion of his whole passion. He pushed Raoule away with clenched fists: "No! no! don't take off that suit!" he screamed, in a fever pitch of madness.

Only this once did they play out their masquerade sincerely; they had sinned against their love, a love which, in order to thrive, needed to face reality, while combating it at the same time with its own innate strength.

AMOURS INVERTIS

True inversion of sex feelings is present in *Monsieur Venus*, at least on the part of Jacques (dominance-submission overtones being present, but playing only a minor role). In a similar vein, though much more complicated as far as the main plot and the several subplots are concerned, is the story *Amours Invertis* (*Perverted Love*) by "Doct. J. de Cherveix" (Paris: Librairie Artistique & Editions Parisiennes Réunis, 66 Blvd. Magentha [all obviously fictitious]; no date, but around the turn of the century).

This book is divided into two parts with entirely different plots and no direct connection between them, except that they both deal with inverted sex. The setting at the opening of the first part is Italy. Tonio, a poor, effeminate Italian boy, has an affair with the wife of his employer, is caught, and is forced to submit to anal intercourse with the offended husband. To his surprise, the experience turns out to be not as disagreeable as he had anticipated.

Afraid of further abuse by his employer, Tonio runs away to Marseilles. As bad luck would have it, one day he runs into his boss there and is obliged to flee again—this time to Barcelona. Here he meets a young woman with whom he falls very much in love and who seems to have enough money to support the two of them. It never occurs to him that she might be a prostitute. But one evening he catches her accidentally with a young customer.

Mad with rage, he took out his knife, took a couple of backward steps on the landing and with a fantastic shove, broke through the door. Pepa was in the arms of a man! He could have killed both of them, but wanting to know who his rival was, he seized him by the hair and violently dragged him out of the bed and threw him on the floor. It was a young boy, fifteen years old at the most. He was completely naked. A terrible idea came to Tonio: brutally grabbing the poor boy's organs, he cut them off neatly with his knife, threw the horrible scraps of flesh in Pepa's face (who had fainted), and fled out the door.

This fantasy is a very clear indication of castration anxiety, which underlies Tonio's problems of sex inversion. In the end, he becomes virtually impotent and breaks down in tears when another woman, after having vainly tried to seduce him, derisively tells him that "he cannot do anything."

Tonio, now a fugitive from the law, flees to Montevideo and assumes the name of Antoine. He meets a general's daughter who invites him to her home. In the course of that meeting (during which, again, nothing happens), she entrusts some diamond earrings to him, which he is to take to a jeweler to be cleaned and repaired. But Antoine is a true loser. He no sooner puts the earrings into his pocket than the girl's father is heard approaching. Afraid to be found with a lover in the house, the girl hides Antoine in a closet, but he is found, the earrings are discovered, and he is arrested, jailed, and convicted—because the hypocritical girl won't admit that she had invited the young man to her room.

However, Antoine escapes while working in a chain gang by jumping into the river. A sailing ship is becalmed at the mouth of the river, and he swims to it, climbs on board, and sets off for New York as a sailor. When they arrive there, the goodhearted captain gives him clothes and money as he leaves the ship to try his luck in the New World.

Meanwhile, Antoine has become more and more of a sexual invert. He tries from time to time to have an affair with a woman, but each time he fails at the last moment, sadly convincing himself that he is just "not like the others."

At length, he joins a group of men going West to seek their fortune. One day while hunting, Antoine is captured by a party of Indians. Brought to their encampment to be tortured and killed, an Indian squaw takes a fancy to him and escorts him to her hut to have him as her husband. But try as she may to seduce him, Antoine remains unresponsive. The Indian girl tells the elders of the tribe that the curious pale face seems to have no desire for women and appears to be a sexual neuter. Surely, he must be a messenger of the gods. The elders agree, and the Indians now accept him as a member of their tribe, making him a medicine man, as is their custom.

GYNECOCRACY

We turn now to fantasies in which the dominance-submission theme is paramount, while sex-role reversal is used as the symbol of ultimate humiliation for the male. The classical case for this sort of fantasy is the three-volume novel *Gynecocracy:*

A narrative of the adventures and psychological experiences of Julian Robinson (afterwards Viscount-Ladywood) under petticoat-rule, written by himself (Paris and Rotterdam [i.e., London], 1893).

Julian, an adolescent boy, is sent to an uncle's estate in the country for having caused somewhat of a scandal at home by turning up a maid's skirts while she was carrying a tea tray up the stairs. It turns out that the uncle's three young daughters, assisted by a bevy of maidservants, are running the place. Julian is subjected to strict discipline, is dressed as a girl, and is treated as such. Nevertheless, he seduces and deflowers one of his girl cousins, an unpardonable offense for which he is all the more severely disciplined. At this point the prospect of physical castration is added to the almost-accomplished mental emasculation. However, he is let off with a mere operation for phimosis.

Following this, he adjusts more and more to his role as a girl. At last he is so conditioned that he likes nothing better than being a "girl," wearing women's dresses and underwear. He even considers himself a hermaphrodite.

He is initiated into homosexuality by Lord Ridlington, which does not prevent him from getting married in the end. Nevertheless, he maintains even in marriage his inverted sex preference.

On page one of the book, the narrator succinctly states the thesis of submission under female domination:

From my own experience, I have reason to respect the petticoat and chemise, the drawers and long stockings, the high-heeled boots and tight corsets—and what they contain—and to believe that good may accrue to a young man by being disciplined by a smart girl. This may be thought a very peculiar view.

The country estate where the narrator (Julian) is brought to be cured of his obnoxious (male) comportment is lorded over by a young woman who is referred to as Mademoiselle. It is she who makes all the rules and decisions, lending Julian, as it were, to the other females for further humiliations and discipline whenever it pleases her whims.

Julian's first lesson in subjection to "petticoat-rule" reveals much about this strange perversion.

. . . at that moment, Mademoiselle entered, very determined looking. She spoke a few words to each of the girls about their work, and then sat down in her low chair, very elegantly and gracefully.

"Now, Master Julian," she said, "you have to realize that I am your governess and that you are my absolute slave. Don't interrupt! From you I shall expect and shall exact the most implicit obedience and the most abject submission. You will tremble hereafter at the mere rustle of a petticoat; by it you are to be governed. If you are sufficiently foolish to continue your insubordination and the ridiculous temper you displayed this morning, it will be the worse for you."

"Mademoiselle," I broke in, "I do not understand you; my father sent me here, because I am too delicate for school."

"And too unruly for home. Too indecent!" (At which I blushed.) "Too inquisitive! Too anxious to know what young ladies have under their petticoats." (I was dumbfounded, and furtively glanced at the girls who were eagerly listening.) "Yes! I know all about it. The petticoat will have its revenge now, and you will be under it in more senses than one for some time. Kneel down there at my feet." (I hesitated, especially seeing the girls highly amused.) "Kneel down at once," she repeated, settling herself in her chair, and assuming a more erect attitude, "and put your hands behind you."

This was not very bad after all, and I felt so abashed and ashamed, and had so little to say for myself, that I complied somehow. Then Mademoiselle rang a handbell.

"Elise," she said, "strap this boy's elbows behind his back as tightly as you can."

Elise grasped me firmly by the upper part of the arm. I was surprised to feel her strength. The little resistance I made was soon overcome. I cannot describe the mixture of sensations I experienced with her standing over me, my head level with her waist, and her pulling me about roughly as she delighted executing Mademoiselle's orders.

I noticed what Zola describes as "a powerful feminine perfume"—the *odor di femina*.

Having tied Julian up, the dominant young woman lectures the hapless fellow as follows:

"Now, Master Julian, you are in a fit state for punishment, and you shall have it. You were rude to me." Smack, smack, in my face, one on each cheek; one with the left, the other with the right hand. How those soft, lovely, dimpled hands stung! How my cheeks tingled! How I struggled in absolute helplessness to get free! "You object to a governess, to feminine domination, to petticoat-rule"— giving me two smacks at each enumeration. "I think I shall convert you. You see"—smack, smack—"you must endure it. . . .

"And now, Julian, you shall be deprived of your trousers. Take a long leave of them. When you will see them again, I do not know; they teach you all sorts of resistance and naughtiness, and make you assume airs of ridiculous superiority which you do not possess. We must make a girl of you. Elise, make him stand up and take them off."

Here the male clothing is the symbol of male superiority, which is precisely the reason the young man has to be divested of it in order to learn submission. Female attire is thus the symbol of submission and inferior status, and consequently Julian is not only stripped of the male status symbols, but made to wear the mark of the inferior or "second" sex: he must stand in a corner with a petticoat over his head; he is forced to wear a pair of women's drawers as a shirt, his arms stuck ridiculously through the leggings; and so forth.

In like manner he is obliged to perform cunnilingus on Mademoiselle:

She was seated on a low and long-seated armchair. Placing her knees against its left elbow, she directed me to seat myself on the floor, with my legs underneath the chair, and with my face close to the front of the seat.

I found this no easy matter, and went to work rather clumsily, receiving one or two playful but sharp slaps, "for not carrying out a lady's wishes with more alacrity." When at last I had succeeded, she unfastened and took off the drawers from my arms and the body of the dress I was wearing, leaving my arms, neck, and shoulders bare. I was much incommoded by the corset, a very ill-fitting one, and felt exceedingly awkward in my unfamiliar attire, and indeed hurt myself with the busks of the longwaisted thing as I assumed the required posture. My long legs, uncovered by the petticoats (which my efforts to seat myself as bidden had gradually worked quite up to my knees), were disposed in a very ungraceful and clumsy heap beneath the chair. I sincerely trusted Mademoiselle, martinet and stickler for elegance as I knew her to be, would not notice this, dreading the consequences if she did. Perhaps, however, she considered the irksomeness and the discomfort of the badly arranged drapery beneficial, for, although she must have noticed the bundle and my immodestly uncovered legs, when she had got me close enough she gave me no further directions. By a dexterous movement and half-turn, accomplished before I had time to guess what she meant, she whisked her petticoats over my head and lodged her right leg across my left shoulder. The result was that I found my head again between her soft and warm thighs, each voluptuously pressing one of my cheeks. Her legs were enveloped in exquisitely fine linen undergarments; and there was wafted to me a fresher and stronger prevalence of that strange intoxicating perfume that I had noticed about the red flannel petticoat. My natural impulse was to retreat, an effort promptly prevented by a tight grip of Mademoiselle; stooping over, she lifted up her skirts and looking at me with a strange fierce light in her eyes, but with a rosy smile upon her face, said, "Now, Julian, if in the course of your incursions underneath my petticoats you should encounter a mouth with a moustache you may kiss it; and, in fact, when I press my heel against your back, like this, you are to kiss it, you understand, and to continue doing so as long as I press you."

She then again dropped her voluminous garments over me, and threw herself well back in the chair. My head, already well above her knees, came to the open part of her drawers, where I felt her satin-like skin and soft warm flesh, this time naked, against my cheeks. To my astonishment, my nose, mouth, and chin were tickled by some hairs. This must be the moustache, thought I, and before I had time to determine what to do, Mademoiselle gave a wriggle, and holding me close with her legs, rubbed something very hairy and moist all over my face, my eyes, my nose and my mouth, in a very lingering manner. In the midst of the hair I found what seemed like a mouth set length-wise instead of across, and felt a little protuberance near it, too, which was pressed forcibly against my own shoulders, and I gave it a kiss; it was instantly pushed into my lips and my mouth was forced wide open; unable to kiss it, I tickled it with my tongue.

Mademoiselle's movements, as I did so, became more and more vigorous, her hold on me grew tighter and tighter, and she pressed me still more closely. Feeling her foot heavily against my shoulders, I continued to play with what I concluded was her raw flesh, to bite it gently with my teeth, and to lick it with my tongue, especially that little protuberance, as soon I discovered the transports which that gave her. To my wonder, the aperture grew larger and larger, until I actually seemed to lose my face in it. It had wet me, and appeared to cover me all over in it. I felt as if I was some distance inside her body, and I grew furious with a strange excitement, which increased with her own, Mademoiselle's throbs became more and more convulsive, indeed as violent as mine had been on the ottoman.

At last, centering herself upon my mouth, there came a series of violent spasmodic throbs lasting for some seconds, then becoming gradually slower and slower. . . . I could hear Mademoiselle's exclamations, although her garments partly smothered the sound. At last her efforts ceased, her grasp relaxed, and she seemed to repose as she let my head rest against one of her knees.

What an experience! There was no longer any need to describe to me how a man differed from a woman. How delightful that she should be so formed and possess an organ so receptive, so responsive, so capable of appreciating and returning the passions of my own.

Julian's bliss was not to last long. Now called "Julia," instead of Julian, he is finally put nude into a bathtub, tied up so that he is unable to move.

I had . . . to lie flat on my back in a long, narrow shallow bath, in which she fastened me by means of a strap over my breast which prevented my rising. The bath was slightly tilted up at the foot.

She then took off a slipper and struck seven or eight times what I was so anxious to put into her, hurting me greatly, observing that it deserved punishment and not further kind treatment.

Julian next finds himself in grave danger of being treated to the "golden shower":

I was not reassured by what took place next. She stood across me in the bath ravishing me with a sight of her pretty figure overhead, her legs bared to her frilled drawers; and coquettishly lifting up her petticoats with both hands to her middle, she carefully drew the drawers well apart, disclosing to my full view what I had been kissing that afternoon, with entrancing glimpses of lovely pink flesh.

Great heavens! There can be no doubt what she intends to do to me! I shall die of disgust!

"Mademoiselle," I cried. "Don't! Don't . . ."

She looked at me with an amused and satisfied smile.

"Why should I not? It would serve you right!"

When Mademoiselle is done with him, she hands him over to the equally, if not more, sadistic maid Elise for further petticoat discipline.

She roughly jerked me out of the cupboard [where he had been made to stand after the bath] by the arm, administering with the other hand, as she did so, a succession of sound, stinging slaps on various parts of my body, and expressing much curiosity as to what I had done to get myself made water upon by a young lady, and especially how I liked it. I indignantly denied it.

"None of your lies to me, you nasty dirty boy. I know very well what she did. I ought not to touch you with tongs. I know where that water came from; don't tell me! Come off to the bathroom at once. Quick! We have not time to fool about!" Elise ordered.

A hot bath and a big sponge were very welcome. It was curious being washed by a maid. And when she soaped the flannel and washed me like a baby between the legs, I squirmed and blushed and felt utterly foolish. The skin of my bottom was quite sore from the birching and kicking. Elise heeded this very little, in fact not at all, and rapidly dried me with warm rough towels; then taking me to my room, as rapidly dressed me. Silken vest, *chemise en coeur* (I had a plump breast and well-rounded arms), drawers, a corset which fitted much better than the first, stockings, and the rest; in short, a young lady's evening toilette. Even my hair was done up like a girl's, with a broad ribbon around my head after the Grecian mode, it was not long enough for any other style.

I must not omit one particular article she added to my attire that gave me a peculiar inconvenience as the evening wore on. At the end of my longwaisted corset in front, about four inches apart, were two hooks. As soon as she had tightly and severely laced that horrid instrument of torture, she proceeded to adjust a square piece of linen, to two corners of which were attached two tape loops. These she slipped over the hooks; and through the loops she inserted a folded napkin, and drawing it between my legs, tied its ends together, after putting one through a broad steel eye, which was sewn into my corset at the back. It was pulled quite tight, and the effect, of course, was to drag down the square piece of linen in front and envelop in it what I had down there, so that that thing was kept straight down and, the napkin being mercilessly tight, well between my legs. It was a most uncomfortable affair and incommoded me dreadfully.

But my protestations were altogether unheeded. Elise remarked that some contrivance was imperative to prevent any indications on the surface of my petticoats that would belie my sex, and if I had the privilege of being dressed and looking like a girl, I must put up with some punishment for being in reality a boy!

It is perfectly clear that this sort of fantasy could germinate only in a male-oriented culture where maleness means superiority and femaleness equals inferiority. Under any other conditions this fantasy would not only be unlikely to arise, but would be devoid of any erotic stimulation. The narrator muses on this while soliloquizing about the meaning or philosophy of petticoat-rule.

I do not believe that equality of the sexes will ever be established until the seat of a woman's womanhood is transferred from between her legs to her head. A man exists for something else than for procreation. But it is the beginning and the end for a woman.

"Love," says the poet, "is a woman's whole existence." It is all that she seeks, whatever she may affect; and if you can tickle her clitoris, either with your fingers or by way of her imagination, she will obey you as exactly as a vessel with steerage obeys the helm.

Noting the inconsistency of the latter part of the statement in the light of his experiences, the narrator makes allowance for exceptions. But it cannot change his basic attitude and conviction: woman is an inferior social being who can only dominate through the power of her sex appeal, and in that respect she has to rely on the same female attire that is the mark of her social inferiority. But, since the ultimate or, at any rate, the most intimate power rests with woman on account of her sex appeal, then it is worthwhile, indeed, to undergo, like her, social humiliation. For it is she, the weaker vessel, the socially underprivileged, the dependent one, who is destined in the end to conquer the superior strength, intelligence, and social position of the male with her all-powerful sex.

MISS HIGH-HEELS

The peculiar psychology of female sex feeling in the male and the consequent desire to be treated as a woman, even to the extent of enduring mental and physical cruelty at the hand of women, is further illustrated in *Miss High-Heels* (the title page of the original edition states that it was "Privately Printed, Paris, 1931").

In this novel a young heir named Denis is brought under the domination of two female relatives. Gradually he is made to give up the privileges of birth and social position, while his female sex identification and the pleasure he derives from victimization become stronger and stronger.

"Bah! I do not trouble my head about your position [says the leading female character to our hero], you are in your own house it is true, but you are under the control of your beautiful stepsister who very properly stripped you of your foolish trousers two years ago to punish you for your impertinence. You are over eighteen years old—I admit it, but for two years you have been mincing in petticoats in a girls' school. You are a young gentleman, are you? Nobody would believe it. Your hair reaches down below your waist. You have the figure, the face, the soft limbs, the hands and feet and the breasts of a girl." I was dreadfully ashamed at Phoebe's outburst. I could not deny a word of it.

"You are a very important person, I suppose," she went on jeering at me, "with a great career in Parliament! Heavens how you used to plague my ears with your boastfulness! It may all be true. What I am concerned with is that you should be beautifully dressed for the dinner party which your stepsister, Miss Deverel, is giving on her twenty-third birthday. Stand up at once, or I will lace you into a corset one inch tighter than the one you are wearing now."

"Oh Phoebe," I cried, "I can hardly breathe in this one."

I was alarmed. Her tone was so menacing. She was much stronger than I was. She could carry out her threat if she chose. I stood up. I had a special reason for being obedient tonight.

"That's better, Miss Denise," she said.

I was dressed in an exquisite décolleté frock of white transparent chiffon glittering with silver embroideries over an underdress of soft white satin. The corsage was cut very low, the sleeves being merely shoulder straps of flashing silver bugles, and my tight unwrinkled white kid gloves reached up to my shoulders. A sash of white satin encircled my slim waist and was tied in an enormous bow looped through a huge diamond buckle on my left hip, whence the broad streamers fringed with silver floated down to my feet. A bunch of pink roses was pinned on the right of my corsage at the waist. The sheath skirt molded my hips in its gleaming satin and chiffon, outlining the girlish curves of my figure and was caught tightly in at the ankles by a scarf of tulle passed through a big sparkling diamond buckle in front of the dress and tied in a great bow behind. My legs were quite bound by these dainty fetters of satin and tulle. The skirt was hemmed with tulle and was bordered with a festoon of tiny pink roses, and on the left side a row of flat diamond buttons sparkled up to the knee. The skirt had a long train of white satin, lined with pleats of tulle which rustled deliciously at each movement. Phoebe arranged the train in a gleaming swirl about my feet, and stood up.

"Now Miss Denise, those smartly gloved hands behind your back!"

"Behind my back! Like a child!"

"Don't argue. Behind your back with them at once, palm to palm, the fingers pointing down."

A little further on, we come upon passages that help explain the strange masochistic attitude necessary to make the bondage situation really operative and rewarding to the victim.

I had dreamed, in a word, of a world in which ladies, to punish me, dressed me as a girl in the most exquisite of frocks and high-heeled shoes, gloves and corsets, and then laughing at my pretensions to a career, kept me in bondage and subjection as a toy for their amusement. I had fought against these fancies because I felt them to be enervating, effeminatizing, and likely to sap my will. I had ridiculed them as preposterous. Yet they seemed part of my nature, they returned and now—they were translated into fact, and being translated into fact fascinated and obsessed me with a force a thousand times stronger than ever. If it had thrilled me with strange delightful emotions to imagine myself dressed in the luxurious gowns of a fashionable girl, undergoing punishments and humiliations and dainty tortures at the hands of a laughing beautiful woman deaf to my prayers, how much more was I of necessity thrilled and excited when the dream became true as it was true now!

I tried however to struggle against the strange sweet pleasure which invaded me. . . .

Meanwhile the pleasure mastered the fear as it had done before. For it was the enervating pleasure of a dream fulfilled which had made me offer so miserable a resistance to my first corset and my banishment to a girls' school. There! The truth is out.

Similar to the napkin-like contraption Julian had to wear over his penis in *Gynecocracy*, Miss Denise is forced to wear a buttoned kid glove over his male member as the ultimate symbol of his humiliation.

Miss Priscilla had one more question to ask of me as I stood there before the mirror with my ivory ankles together and the big buckles flashing on my glistening slippers.

"There was a third, tight, white kid glove I arranged for you to wear. Have you it on?" I went scarlet. But if I did not answer I should be punished. I hung my head.

"Yes, Phoebe buttoned it on," I replied in a whisper of confusion. Miss Priscilla was content.

"It will teach you to be modest in the presence of women, Denise, and to remember that you are under their authority. You will wear it always."

There are many more passages in *Miss High-Heels* which leave no doubt about the hidden attraction for certain masochistic males in this sort of humiliation and sadism at the hands of women.

But what made the spectacle so piquant and seductive to me was the knowledge that the pretty girl was myself, an effeminate youth in corsets with his kid-gloved hands quite free. He could have torn the gag from his lips in a second. There were only two ladies to prevent him. But he did not dare. He was undergoing discipline in girls' frocks and pearl-embroidered satin slippers at their hands. He was being punished by them. He was in subjection.

One of the most outstanding features in this psychology is the pronounced narcissism of the effeminate male, a narcissism so strong that it is able to endure the most severe pain and humiliation. At first glance, this may seem to be a contradiction in terms. And yet, passages like the following point out very well why it is worth while to men of this particular psychological predisposition.

There were mirrors let into the wall panels and I could see myself in my glistening white frock, which delightfully reflected the light from the buckles and pearls gleaming on my satin slippers to the curls of my exquisitely coiffured head as I stood in this humiliating position of subjection. Yet how the spectacle aroused my passions! I felt dreadfully excited.

Or, again, as in these excerpts which show the pleasure principle operating even in the presence of severe physical and emotional discomfort.

"Lock and chain together those satin slippered feet at once, Helen," cried Lady Hartley.

"I will indeed," answered Helen. "Come Violet, Miss Hartley, help me please." With the assistance of the two young ladies she absolutely carried me from the corner, lifted me on to a chair, and held me standing on it.

"Support her please," said Helen. I was quite helpless, with my satin train swathed round my legs and my hands and arms tied behind me. Helen opened the leather case and took out a pair of bright fetters of thin polished steel.

"Oh, they are too small," I cried. "They will never go round my ankles." "Hold your tongue," said Helen and she stooped over my little buckled feet. Oh, wonderful blissful moment! I felt the cold cruel bands close about my ankles. Click, click, sounded sharply through the rooms. It was done now, past recall. I was chained. Thrills of voluptuous exquisite delight tingled warmly through me from my high heels to my curls. I looked down—oh bizarre and entrancing spectacle! I saw the bright bands of steel glistening on my filmy silk stockings, fettering my ankles. I saw the small feet in gleaming white satin pearl-embroidered slippers, made doubly dainty with quivering butterfly bows and blazing diamond buckles—slippers for a beautiful girl to dance in at a Court Ball, chained together unable to move. Oh what waves of sensuous pleasure swept over me! . . .

It was I, Denis Beryl, the youth with the great fortune and the lofty ambitions who was speaking. But her kid-gloved hands caressed me. I could give no other answer. I gave up my will, my life to her and to Helen. I leaned towards her as far as my handcuffs and my bonds would allow. I was in an ecstasy. To live satin-slippered and corseted with handcuffed gloved-hands and strapped ankles in beautiful décolleté frocks—yes, I learned that night from Miss Priscilla's hands that this was the supreme joy life held out to me.

The effeminate hero literally revels in his sensuous identification with women—he feels with their senses, he admires his female beauty in the mirror, he feels desirable as a woman; now it is he who is the object of men's desires, no longer is he dependent on woman's beauty and on her sexual favors for his sexual happiness. Having become a woman by total identification, now he is really in control. Consequently, he is willing to suffer, for the gains far outweigh the discomfort, all the more so as the very humiliation and pains he is made to suffer make him even more a woman by feeling her humiliation by the male, as well as her ultimate triumph and dominance over him through the granting or withholding of her sexual favors.

Miss High-Heels also contains descriptions of unusual forms of erotic torture or punishment which shed light on the psychology of sadomasochism. In the first of these instances, the victim Denise is helplessly exposed to insects and worms on her bare skin, an experience which, though not exactly pleasurable, would not be too uncomfortable or anxiety-arousing to a real man, or even to a non-neurotic, modern girl. However, for Denise, who has become thoroughly identified with woman, and not just woman, but with the special kind of hyperfeminine, neurotic, turn-of-the-century or Victorian woman, this experience turns out to be truly harrowing.

Of the destination of the room at a first glance no one would have guessed. At a second, one would have noticed some sinister particulars. Across the ceiling a grooved gilt wheel ran on a strong rail and from the groove of the wheel, a thick strong gold rope depended. The wheel was worked by a small lever in the wall and at this moment was in a corner of the ceiling with the rope tied to a hook. On the ottomans and chairs I noticed a gleam of steel rings and bars, and one long flat sofa was furnished at the end with a pair of sticks. There were cases with glass doors fixed against the walls and glancing into one, I saw a stand of bamboo canes, into another a stand of birches daintily tied with blue and pink satin ribbons, and into a third, handcuffs and fetters and irons of all kinds in polished steel. I was afraid. But what most terrified me was a mahogany chair raised an inch or two from the ground on a solid frame. It was luxuriously padded and cushioned in white satin. Yet its aspect appalled me.

"Sit down dear," said Helen pushing me towards it. I advanced timidly in my satin slippers, mounted the frame, and sat down in the chair. Helen fixed a strong satin strap round my waist, buckling it tightly behind the chair. To the back other straps were attached, and these she fastened over my shoulders, drawing them tight under each arm. My body and bust were thus securely imprisoned. The chair was furnished with short arms thickly padded in white satin and an inch or two beyond the extremities of the arms two strange square boxes of glass were supported on steel pedestals fixed into the frame of the chair. On the sides of these boxes facing the arms of the chair were holes thickly padded with white satin for the wrists, the upper part of the glass sliding upwards in grooves to admit the hands. The other sides and the bottoms of the boxes were covered with looking glass and little bulbs of electric light placed at the corners flung a strong light upon the interior. The top surfaces of the boxes like the sides facing the chair were of glass. Helen lifted up the sliding portions of the glass.

"Lay your arms flat upon the arms of the chair, Denise darling, so that your hands are in the boxes, and your wrists rest in the glass grooves," she said in her most honeyed accents. "The palms of your gloved hands uppermost, dear."

I obeyed her in dreadful alarm. Lady Hartley looked on in delighted curiosity, while Miss Priscilla strapped down my elbows and forearms with satin straps to the arms and rested in the glass holes of the boxes, my hands being quite inside the boxes. Helen then slid down the upper pieces of glass, and made them fast by locking a steel bar along the tops. My wrists were now hermetically imprisoned in these glass pillories. I could twitch my kid-glove fingers inside the boxes, and I did so, making the brilliant light play upon the smooth shining white kid gloves. But I could do no more.

In front of me at the end of the frame, supported also upon steel pedestals, was a bigger box of the same make as the boxes for the hands. Only in this bigger box there were holes for the ankles a little apart from each other and raised so that with my feet in the boxes they would be in a straight line with my knees as I sat in the chair.

"Raise your legs, dear, and insert your dainty feet," said Helen.

She flung back my skirt exposing my silk-stockinged legs, my garters, and the frills even which decorated my knees. Timidly I raised my legs and inserted my feet into the box, letting my legs rest in the grooves made for them, while Helen held up the upper slide of glass. As soon as my legs were in position she slid down and secured the glass, tightly fitting me into this strange pair of glass stocks.

My legs fitted very tightly into the holes just where the calves began to swell, so that my ankles as well as my feet were enclosed in glass boxes. Helen turned on the lights in each of the boxes and at once a flood of bright illumination sparkled on slippers and buckles, stockings and gloves, and flung up the dazzling reflections of the dainty things in the most fascinating way. Then Helen by means of a little silver knob on the outside of each box drew out for an inch or two the mirrors which formed the bottoms, and disclosed shallow cavities underneath. At once, from these cavities a brown dust whirled out and flew about the boxes as if driven by a wind. The brown dust settled on my shining white gloves, my smart glistening slippers, my gleaming stockings of silk. I could move my fingers. I could also work my toes and insteps up and down though I could not twist my feet from side to side. I worked both hands and feet to shake the dust off in vain and then I felt two or three sharp pricks on my insteps and others on the palms of my hands at the small opening of the gloves. I shook my hands and feet more violently and then I began to feel the pricks all over my ankles and feet wherever my stockings were openworked and all over my hands too. Meanwhile the little clouds of brown dust spun about the boxes.

A suspicion of the truth dawned upon me. I was seized with a dreadful irritation wherever the dust touched my flesh. I could not lean forward, for I was strapped firmly back in my chair. But I fixed my eyes upon my twisting fingers, my twitching feet; and I discovered the truth.

"Oh, oh!" I cried. "Helen, the specks of brown dust are fleas. You are punishing me in my new kid gloves, my satin slippers, my dainty stockings with fleas! Oh! They torture me. It's horrible."

And in a frenzy I worked my feet, I twisted and clenched my fingers. It was of course all in vain. My ankles, my insteps, my hands were at the mercy of these obscene insects and they simply devoured me.

Lady Hartley was in raptures.

"What a delightful punishment for a pretty girl!" she cried. "To tie her into a chair in her lovely evening frock and then to give her satin-slippered feet and slender little ankles in their exquisite stockings to fleas to devour and punish! I think you are wonderfully clever, Miss Deverel."

Helen smiled in acknowledgment of the praise.

"It is at all events an appropriate punishment," she answered modestly. "Denise is being punished for her vanity in making a coquettish display of her little buckled slippers and dainty feet. To hand them over in their finery to fleas seemed to me the best way of teaching her humility."

They stood and complacently watched me as I writhed and twisted in my bonds. The fleas were driving me mad. They got inside my stockings, down under my slippers, round my ankles and bit me terribly. They were ravenous. My hands too were helpless. The fleas were inside my gloves, between my fingers, everywhere. My feet and hands twisted in their glass prisons. The mirrors reflected back to me with irony my flashing buckles, my dainty bows and heels, and the tightly fitting elegant long gloves.

"Oh, oh! the torture is excruciating," I cried. "Oh Helen, you are cruel! I am being eaten up. The irritation is driving me out of my senses." I burst into tears, I tugged at my legs and arms to break the glass and free myself. I felt the blood rush to my face. I was growing delirious.

"It's a disgusting punishment," I moaned.

Helen laughed.

"Is it indeed, Denise? I don't allow young ladies to use such language about my punishment which I feel it my duty to inflict upon them. If the fleas are disgusting to your delicate sensibilities, what I wonder will you say to this?"

Into the tops of the glass boxes little silver boxes were let in, one over each gloved hand, one over each satin-slippered foot. Helen touched a spring in each of these boxes and the bottom which in each case was inside the glass box fell down upon a hinge. And to my inexpressible loathing from each box there dropped a horrible fat, big, slimy worm. There were four of them. One dropped on to the kid-gloved palm of each hand, one on to the pearl-embroidered toe of each of my slippers. I uttered a piercing scream of horror. I suppose that it was very feminine of me, but I couldn't help it. The sight of those loathsome fat worms on my pretty gloves and shoes filled me with nausea. I shuddered. I felt that I was going to be sick.

"Oh take them off! Take them off," I screamed. I shook my hands and feet in a panic. Then the worms began to crawl! Oh it was revolting. They crawled over my toes leaving a disgusting brown trail of slime on the dazzling sheen of my white satin shoes.

They mounted on to the buckles and bows. They were crawling towards my open-worked stockings. Oh I should feel them on my flesh. Perhaps they were poisonous too, I thought in my panic. They were crawling about my fingers as well. I touched one with the tips of my fingers as I closed one hand spasmodically and the soft feel of it as it moved and wriggled caused me to shriek again.

"Oh Helen! Please set me free!" I moaned. "It's a horrible punishment."

The tears poured down my face. My slipper buckles flashed and flashed in a thousand many-colored rays as I arched and bent my feet to shake them off.

"That's a wonderful punishment," said Lady Hartley. "It appeals to the imagination as well as to the body. Ugh! The slime on the dainty slippers and the shining tight white kid gloves! How ashamed of herself Denise ought to be!"

I interrupted her with a yell. One of the worms had crawled inside my left glove and I felt it wriggling on the flesh of my palm. It was unendurable. Then I felt something wet and soft crawling over my insteps. The worms were on my stockings feeding on the silk and lace. My screams redoubled. The chair shook with my frantic struggles. All the while too the fleas were biting and torturing me!

Helen watched me complacently. She was delighted with the success of her bizarre experiment. She listened to my sobs and screams, she watched my tear-stained face, reveling in my abasement and sufferings. Then, with her hypocritical kindness, she said: "The lesson, darling, you have to learn is this. If you were wearing high boots and thick stockings you would not mind the worms. Therefore the more daintily you are dressed, the more careful you must be to be obedient and modest."

I interrupted her sermon with a scream. One of the worms had crawled through the open-worked pattern and was inside my stocking clinging to my flesh. It was the last straw. I went off into a fit of hysterics. I screamed, and laughed, and sobbed all at once. My face flushed red and was convulsed. I was going mad. Even Lady Hartley was terrified by my appearance.

"She has been sufficiently punished, Helen," she said.

Helen took a little tube with an indiarubber ball at the end. She pressed the tube through a tiny hole in the glass closed by indiarubber and only opening from pressure from without. Squeezing the ball at the end of the tube, she discharged into the boxes one after the other a strong insecticide powder which at once killed the fleas and worms. Then Phoebe stripped my stockings down my legs.

Helen released me from the stocks, my gloves, shoes, and stockings were taken off and left in the glass boxes to be destroyed. I was still sobbing, bitterly shaken with convulsions and shivering fits and tortured by the irritation of the flea bites.

Lady Hartley said good-night and went away with her daughter, while Phoebe brought a basin of warm water in which some herbs had been soaked and bathed my inflamed and swollen hands, ankles, and feet.

"There's no reason for you to go into hysterics, Miss Denise," she said with a rough kindness as she knelt at my feet, bathing me. "This infusion will soon cool your legs, and remove the irritation, and tomorrow morning there won't be a mark on your pretty white skin."

We note that the ladies who are punishing Denise remark especially the "slime on the dainty slippers"—a reference to seminal fluid. The hysterical fits on the part of the victimized boy-girl Denise have all the earmarks of a true hysterical orgasm-equivalent ("I screamed, and laughed, and sobbed all at once. My face flushed red and was convulsed").

Another unusual punishment Denise undergoes bears definite signs of foot fetishism. Already we have seen references to Denise's "pretty little feet," "satin slippers," etc. In this scene, foot fetishism is expressed in the form of sadism, a fact which clearly shows the subterranean connection between the two phenomena.

In the corner by the fire with its back to the wall stood a chair upholstered in white satin and gold, a solid chair with arms. To it was attached a pair of stocks for the legs. She placed me in the chair, turned back my skirt and opened the stocks.

"Put your legs in the grooves."

The stocks were of polished mahogany with the holes lined and padded with satin, so that they could hold the legs in a vice and yet not tear the most delicate silk stockings. I put my legs in the grooves. She shut down and locked the upper plank of the stocks and wheeled one of the big three-sided mirrors in front of me. I could see my ankles and feet sticking out from the stocks in their dazzling finery of high heels and diamond buckles and lace, and satin and silk. There was not a mark on the new white soles. They were the slippers of a wealthy debutante and I was going to be punished in them.

Miss Priscilla kneeled and took my right foot in her hand and in an instant piercing shrieks from my lips rang through the room. She bent down my instep until I was sure that the bones must snap. Then she twisted it to the right until I was certain my ankle must break, then again to the left.

"Oh please, Miss Priscilla, this is dreadful. It's torture! Oh, oh, my foot! You have lamed me for life."

But she was a doctor. She knew exactly how far she could punish me without breaking bones or spraining sinews.

The last portion above expresses exactly the kind of conditioning process which must go on during a person's formative years in order to predispose him toward any of the more pronounced sexual deviations. But it also shows that "knowing all about it," i.e., having insight into it, does not necessarily mean "cure" or freedom, a theoretical error which accounts for much disappointment in mere insight (or uncovering) therapy. For it is obvious that a habit pattern and emotional tendency that has been conditioned over many years needs to be subjected to a systematic unconditioning process, together with insight therapy, if the results are to be genuine and lasting.

6

The Bondage Problem

In the previous chapter we have considered only that source material which combined the bondage theme with the primary transsexual one. Bondage appeared only to supplement female sex feeling in men, and was simply a necessary and logical consequence or condition.

Bondage, however, does not always appear in literature in connection with a dominant transsexual or homosexual theme, though the latter may well be at the heart of bondage psychology in general.

AUX PIEDS D'OMPHALE

The first novel to be considered in this enlarged context is *Aux Pieds d'Omphale* (*At the Feet of Omphale*) by Henri Raynal (Paris: J. J. Pauvert, 1957). The story deals at some length with the erotic qualities of some of the new sleek and transparent plastic materials in modern women's apparel. It is a useful description of the development of a new cultural clothes fetish such as existed, prior to World War I and even into the 1920's, with regard to satin, velvet, kid leather, ostrich feathers, lace, etc.

Against the background of this modern fetish, one understands better the scene below. Luc, the hero, has been thoroughly subjugated by his cousin Mathilda and her husky maid, Lina.

Another time, Luc dreamed that Lina had decided it was too good for him even to enjoy the benefits of air and light, that there was no reason why his face should receive them in all innocence, why he should share them freely with everyone else. It was too good for him to retain a human appearance, to wear a bald human face. Quite the contrary, it would be a good idea if his very appearance were to show the mark and the mask of his condition, a good idea if daylight were to reach him only through the thickness of an appropriate livery, filtered, rationed, and clouded. "Get in there!"

Suiting the action to the words, she made him slip his legs and body into a strange piece of clothing, a kind of skintight, one-piece suit made of a plastic which was as transparent as a grapeskin. When half his body was covered, Lina made him put his arms into the sleeves. "Now the head."

The elastic membrane fitted perfectly around his skull, encasing and imprisoning it, spreading over his face and clinging to it like a moist hand.

Only his feet and hands emerged. "Upsadaisy!" With a satisfied air, Lina zipped up the back of this new kind of suit which could be ripped open in a single movement like a banana skin. Another, horizontal zipper allowed her to seal up his mouth at will. "Zip your lip! There now. Isn't he sweet? Made to order. A perfect fit!"

And when he saw himself? A living mummy. A silent buffoon,

locked in his own confusion. A scaly lizard. A tadpole. A white worm. A stunted larva. An inferior creature driven back into the nether world to go through its novitiate, after covering its head with the operculum, donning the tegument, swathing itself in the chrysalis and the sack of slavery. A metamorphosis in reverse.

Not so much a trained bear that lacks only the studded collar and the bell, as a side-show cockroach. A domesticated cockroach.

"At any rate, your face will no longer offend our gazes and you will no longer be tempted to imagine that you are still like other men. Air and light are not for you. Now you are in suspended animation, a prisoner right down to the five senses and all over the surface of your body. Now you are entangled in your slavery, coated with it, not an inch of it goes to waste. Let it enfold you. Let it stick to your skin like pitch, like glue.

"Not *beyond* life, but *short* of it.

"And now, get to work!"

Sexual pleasure is here derived from being completely enclosed in some kind of skin or covering (which replaces the female clothing in the previous chapter). There are, to our knowledge, no statistics on how many people may possibly be involved in this sexual peculiarity. A public scandal occurred not long ago in England when a man was arrested for having sold such outfits by mail; he had also published a kind of illustrated newsletter and how-to guide on tying up, immobilizing, and enclosing people in the fashion of this story.

What strikes us most in the above excerpt is the emphasis on prebirth or embryonic symbols ("tadpole," "white worm," "stunted larva") which are made even more explicit by the deprecatory tirade against the helpless, enclosed male in which he is "an inferior creature, driven back into the nether world to go through its novitiate, after covering its head with the operculum [cover, lid], donning the tegument [natural covering], swathing itself in the chrysalis [the final stage through which certain insects and butterflies pass before reaching their winged state], and the sack of slavery [an allusion to the amnion, or thin, innermost membrane surrounding the fetus]."

In other words, the victim is reduced to a prehuman, embryonic existence. Although degraded, the embryo-victim is striving for an "ideal," intrauterine existence in which all his wishes and wants are automatically supplied without toil or labor—a state toward which all regressive human tendencies are directed like the needle of the compass to the North Pole. In other passages, the author dwells at length on the tactile pleasure of the material which he describes as the despised and despicable covering of his hero-victim, Luc. One should not ask for consistency in such matters, but perhaps man or maleness is supposed to represent the intellect or mind. Reducing him to a pre-intelligent state of development would be equivalent to mental castration. And castration, mental or otherwise, enforced or voluntary, is always the ultimate aim of all bondage psychology, no matter how subtly disguised and embellished this sinister aspect of it may be.

Masochistic needs in women are differently motivated from those of the male. Her identification with the male aggressor and the false sense of feeling more of a woman through humiliation and pain seem to be closer to the core of the matter. At the same time, the acceptance of humiliation from the male also degrades the aggressor and so automatically evens the score.

In both male and female masochism, other motivations enter the picture, primarily the eroticization of pain and of the feeling of being humiliated which, of course, derive from childhood conditioning and early (sexually toned) experiences. For a fuller discussion of the psychology of sadomasochism, the interested reader might consult Theodor Reik's excellent study *Masochism in Modern Man* (reissued in paperback as *Masochism in Sex and Society* [New York: Grove Press, 1962]), a good starting point for further study of this highly complex problem.

In many stories the bondage fantasy is so predominant that all other features, such as cross-dressing, restraint, and flagellation, recede into the background. If, for instance, in a typical bondage fantasy the male victim is dressed up as a woman, this is merely a symbol of his humiliation and servitude, but not necessarily a recognition of his female sex feeling, as in some of the previously examined stories (e.g., *Miss High-Heels, Gynecocracy*). In *Aux Pieds d'Omphale*, the fact that the hero is finally made to get into a tight-fitting plastic suit is simply, as we have seen, a device to emphasize his utter helplessness and ultimate degradation to some sort of primitive subhuman or prehuman form of life; it is not primarily an instance of sex inversion or latent homosexual tendencies. Still, homosexual attitudes certainly do play a role here. In fact, examining hundreds of such fantasies and comparing them with our own clinical experience has led us to the growing conviction that latent homosexuality is at the core of all bondage psychology, if not of sadomasochism itself.

FORT FREDERICK

Fantasies in which the male becomes the more or less willing slave of a dominant female abound in *Fort Frederick*, by "Françoise des Ligneris" (Paris: Grasset, 1957). The real name of the author is unknown, but there is little doubt that the book was written by a woman, a fact which makes it psychologically even more important.

The gist of the story is that a young woman called Anne lives a solitary life in her ancestral mansion, Fort Frederick. A fugitive from justice—a simple man who has become a rapist—has taken refuge in the large house without her knowledge. She discovers him and decides to shelter him, first out of pity, but soon out of a growing fascination with the power she exerts over him. Soon he is doing domestic chores for her and is fast becoming her slave and plaything.

"Listen carefully, Jean Gédéon," said Anne. "You are going to stay here in my house. I'll make you work quite hard at any job I choose, anything at all. And, pardon me for this detail, but I won't pay you. Well, get on with your dishwashing! You're not making any progress!"

The man obeyed. His hands were now obviously trembling.

Still leaning against the wall behind him, she asked: "Do you agree to stay?"

He kept on working. After a moment's silence, he answered, "Yes," in a tone of voice that was almost quiet.

"As long as I wish . . ." said Anne. "Repeat after me."

"As long as you wish."

"And if I wish, it will be forever. Repeat that."

The man repeated her words: "It will be forever."

Suddenly he seemed to awake from a dream. "People will see me in your house. They'll find out. I'll be arrested again."

"That is my concern," said Anne. "I shall take the necessary precautions. And then, if one day I decide that you must give yourself up, then you shall do so."

The man gave a start.

"Repeat after me," said Anne. She was breathing a little harder. She had to test her power, see just how far she could go.

Gédéon abandoned his dishes. "I can't promise that," he whispered.

She moved closer to him and lay her hands familiarly on his bare shoulders. "Not today," she said. "Not today. That's a promise you'll make me another day."

She stroked his cheek and the base of his neck with the same familiar gestures which she used to caress Fleur-de-Mai when her horse had properly jumped a hedge or a stream. Gédéon did not move a muscle, his head hung down and his hands were motionless.

"I'll stay," he whispered, "because . . . you're beautiful!" Timidly he tried to press his mouth to Anne's hand, turning his head and raising it towards that hand.

"Oh no!" she said. She backed away and leaned against the wall. "Not my hand," she went on. "What are you thinking of, Jean Gédéon! Your mouth is fit only for my sandal, which is not very new and probably smells of the stable. My sandal. Well, do you understand?"

And when he was kneeling under the sink, in the puddles of dishwater:

"Now swear," she said. "Swear to the things you've only promised me."

Anne acquires a greater and greater ascendancy over the man, whom she now dresses as a woman and calls by the name of the little girl he raped, Jacqueline, while she herself is donning more masculine attire.

She heard Gédéon come in but did not look up immediately. "Go get my skirt," she said, pointing to the closet.

She noticed that his hands were still wet, either because he wanted to show that he had carried out Anne's orders or because he had washed too hastily in his desire to return to her side.

He came with an old flowered gray skirt, bought at a rummage sale and which she wore around the house from time to time.

"Take off my slacks."

Gédéon's hands, suddenly awkward and clumsy, wrestled with the buttons. In the mirror she saw her white cotton panties appear, then her long firm thighs. The man's breathing grew harsh.

"Brush them now and put them away." She sat down on the bed, half-naked, wearing only her white panties and a faded poplin bodice cut like a man's shirt, which she wore with the sleeves rolled up past the elbows.

The sound of the brush on the corduroy slacks grew fainter and then the brush fell, hitting the wooden bedstead. The man had forgotten that he was holding the slacks, and the cuffs were dragging on the floor. He was pale, almost unaware of what he was doing as he moved closer to the bed.

"Now, that's better, Jacqueline," said Anne in a soft, sarcastic tone of voice. "You're breathing just like anyone else now. Put my skirt on me."

He didn't seem to hear. He stood motionless before her, very close, panting.

Two loud slaps rang out.

"Haven't you got it into your head yet," said Anne slowly, as he knelt behind her a moment later, hooking up the skirt with its dull, gray flowers.

She turned around and took his head in both hands; the gesture had a familiar, possessive quality. Gédéon's arms went around her dress without squeezing, without so much as touching Anne's body. For a few moments she stroked his hair with absent-minded gentleness.

Then, bending over him: "Listen to me," she said. "You're going to put on a pair of trousers that I will give you. You're going to go across the park by the back way and up the road to the Piquette farm. You'll tell the woman that you work in the forest, that you're here for the summer, that you're thirsty, and that she's very pretty."

There was a moment's silence. Gédéon's arms fell back to his sides. He bowed his head very low.

"Do you understand?" she asked, "or must I have you repeat what I just said?"

She tried to make him look up. He resisted, so she grabbed him firmly by the hair and forced his head back so that she could see his face. Two tears were rolling down his cheeks but the eyes that stared up at her were as devoted as those of Fleur-de-Mai.

"May I ask you something?" Gédéon asked. This was the first time he had been so bold as to make a request.

"Yes," said Anne. "You're going to ask me not to call you Jacqueline any more. Isn't that right?"

He nodded.

"Jacqueline is a pretty name," said Anne dreamily. "She must have been a pretty little girl. Blonde? Answer me. No? Not blonde? Then she was a brunette, with a hair ribbon? What color was the ribbon?"

Gédéon stood up. He backed away a few steps, as though he'd lost his bearings. "Do you hate me?" he asked.

"Do I hate you?" She was silent a moment, then shook her head. "Why, no," she said.

This scene had already lasted too long as it was. She concluded in a dry, cold, distinct tone of voice: "I won't call you Jacqueline any more. Now go look for Germaine, Jean Gédéon."

Anne begins to feel that she should abandon the perverse joys of her mansion and her slave, move to Paris, and marry a nice young man. At the last minute she revolts against a bourgeois marriage. In a state of indecision, she strolls about Paris. For once, she is "all dolled up," an attractive, seductive female, complete with a little dog on a leash, and the inevitable happens—a man follows her.

When Anne realizes that she cannot discourage him, she decides on another course of action—she engages the man in a conversation during which she becomes the aggressor and gains control, while the man loses ground steadily. In the end, he is made first to tie her shoe laces (which are perfectly well tied) and then to kiss her dog's ear.

Anne felt herself beginning to glow. She felt wonderful. The man was going to obey. Her eyes as they stared at him and her triumphant smile conveyed that feeling of certainty. Suddenly life acquired color and depth. She was no longer the anonymous passer-by of a moment ago, trundling her share of relatively painful problems. She was leaving common destinies behind her. She was in harmony with herself. At that moment, the street belonged to her. Paris belonged to her. And so did this man.

The man shook his head. "This never happened to me before," he said.

His lips brushed Figaro's upraised ear and this unusual treatment drew forth a chorus of outraged barking.

"You obtain strange things from me," said the stranger.

Without a word, Anne turned aside and started on her way again. As her victim protested, she turned and said over her shoulder: "Now, now, let me go home, sir. Don't make me call a policeman."

"You'll never call a policeman," said the man behind her. "You can see that you don't need a policeman to be obeyed. Here is my card. Go on, take it. I know that some day, some time, it will amuse you to see just how far your power will go."

Later, Anne looked at the card lying on her bedside table. Daniel Henricot. The address, the phone number, it was all there. Anne imagined herself alone with the man in this room.

"Find out how far my power can go? Why, quite far, farther than you think, Daniel Henricot. Were you perhaps expecting some diversion from me? An hour of libertinage? Rather should you speak of ceremonies and sacrifices in which you won't feel a bit like smiling, of lands without signboards and without frontiers in which your very fondness for abjection will be left far behind. And when your body—yours or that of someone like you—is no longer anything but the anonymous flesh of a slave, then I'll have found once more . . ." Anne's gaze fell on the ring. She clenched her hand. She stared in front of her and saw her grandmother in her black riding habit looking back to her. [The next day, Anne returns to Fort Frederick and Jean Gédéon.]

In the last sentence there is a hint that the heroine's need to dominate and enslave men may have had its origin in her relationship with the "grandmother in her black riding habit." It would seem that the grandmother was a domineering woman with whom the heroine identified in her childhood. One may also guess that the men in her family circle were rather weak and ineffectual, so that the little girl could not possibly learn to respect them. (We shall later come to know the reaction against the domineering female in the writings of Pierre Klossowski and in Pieyre de Mandiargues's story "Le Pont.")

ARÈNES OLYMPIQUES

The fantasy of man's domination by the strong woman may also be expressed in more directly physical terms, as in the story "Arènes Olympiques" by Louis Chauvet (in *La Petite Acrobate de l'Hélvetia* [Paris: Flammarion, 1954]). The scene is a boxing and wrestling stand in a traveling carnival.

"And now ladies and gentlemen, our extraordinary, incredible star attraction, Mademoiselle Ida! This little girl, though barely sixteen years of age, is endowed with truly Herculean strength! You don't believe me? Show 'em, baby."

At these words, Ida stripped in a trice. Removing slacks and sweater, she appeared in shorts and gym shirt, displaying the physique of a hardened young gladiator and shapely, powerful thighs. The crowd gasped in admiration as Ida took up the classical athlete's stance and, raising her fist to her forehead, displayed unexpectedly bulging biceps and flexed them mysteriously back and forth. Then she turned around to exhibit her back muscles, making them stand out and ripple as well.

Another quarter turn brought into view her feminine curves, perfect bosom and almost childlike profile. The pony tail made her look like an infant empress. . . .

"She'll take on any male adversary in boxing or wrestling. She offers a prize of 5,000 francs to any amateur who can pin her, but here again we cannot insure her opponents against broken arms or other minor accidents. Step right up all you budding athletes, all you brave young men! Who'll volunteer? Who has the guts to tackle our lovely little amazon?"

"Me!" said the boy who had just climbed onto the platform. . . .

At each show, while the young men were hesitating to accept her challenge and while Pop Leonard went on with his taunting spiel, Ida peered into the crowd, looking for a boy she'd like to fight. It was never long before she found the one whose gaze was the most flattering. She would stare back at him in provocative amusement. Sometimes she would find him attractive. When the outside show was over and the crowd broke up, she would have misgivings as she watched him leave; but they would be tempered by the thought that perhaps he had misgivings, too. . . .

When Pop Leonard had finished his ballyhoo vaunting her athletic prowess and some young man from the crowd had finally volunteered to take her on, Ida always put on a good show. No matter how big the challenger was, she nodded her head vigorously, wagging the short pony tail and childish profile. She would stamp her right foot on the floor as if to show her confidence, raise her right hand and wave it courteously toward the ring in a gesture of invitation.

"You really aren't scared?" she would finally ask the upstart, leaning out over the crowd with her hands on her knees.

She herself never knew fear. Blows scarcely hurt her, and those she dealt out herself rarely missed their marks. As she had won bout after bout, she had gradually acquired a sense of supreme self-confidence and come to regard these young men as harmless little creatures whom she could handle easily if she ever felt like treating them the way she had often seen them treat other girls.

"Why shouldn't I take one of them if I want? He couldn't stand up against me!" The thought made her smile. . . .

"Let's go girl, are you asleep?" she heard Pop Leonard say.

It was her turn. She leaped into the ring and clasped her hands over her head in greeting as she had been taught to do.

"And now ladies and gentlemen . . ." the old barker began.

She took off her sweater and again flexed her steely muscles with an angelic smile on her face. She picked up the chest expander and stretched it several different ways with startling speed, threw one of the big thirty-pound balls into the air and caught it easily on the nape of her neck, and finally carried the five other wrestlers hanging from her arms like a bunch of grapes, jumping and spinning about to show she wasn't straining.

"Your turn, young man!" the proprietor shouted, turning to François. "Have you said your prayers? If you've changed your mind, it's still not too late to leave! A good-looking boy like you wouldn't want to have his pretty profile spoiled, especially by a girl!"

François made no reply. He had stripped down to his T-shirt. They had lent him a pair of regulation shorts. He stepped over the ropes and went into his corner.

"You'd better take off that T-shirt. We don't pay for torn underwear."

When the gong sounded and they faced each other in the center of the ring, the girl feinted quickly, then seized her opponent's wrist in a twisting grip that made him wince. Taking advantage of the opening, she clamped a bear hug on him and made ready to throw him to the mat. François felt the extraordinary strength of those muscles encircling his abdomen. He strained to the utmost, but could not break the hold. The more he tried, putting all his energy into his attempt to break the hug, the more it felt as though he were caught in an iron corset. He lost contact with the floor and immediately she threw him with a quick movement of her hip. He crashed to the mat on his back. From then on he was helpless. His young opponent had him solidly pinned and he couldn't move a muscle. He squirmed furiously, bucking about in the hope of changing their respective positions, trying to free some small part of his body, slip out, slither under, cheat her domination in some way. But at each attempt he fell back again. Now Ida took a new initiative, leaning forward and shifting her weight suddenly . . . and Francois had lost the first bout. His shoulders touched the mat.

In the second bout, he got a chance to put on a neck lock and it was Ida's turn to wince with pain. In a few seconds she had realized that this boy was no softy, and that his muscles weren't made of soft taffy. Still, he lacked her experience, and she was able to make use of her edge in the nick of time. Stooping down, she managed to grasp her opponent's leg, jerked him off balance and forced him to release his hold. She still hadn't caught her breath after his partly successful stranglehold.

The crowd was going wild, shouting encouragement to the amateur challenger.

François took the initiative again, trying to lift his opponent, grab her shoulders, and throw her. He muffed it and they both rolled on the mat. He had missed his last chance. Ida knew all the secrets of groundwork and, moreover, the threat of defeat had made her furious. She wrapped up her opponent in nothing flat. Francois felt such a sharp pain that he slapped the mat with the flat of his hand.

When he climbed to his feet in a thunder of applause that was not for him, he was shamefaced and his whole body ached.

We have come across several cases of this masochistic attitude on the part of males in the course of our own clinical experience. Usually, these men cannot be sexually aroused unless they are physically assaulted, or manhandled, as one of them put it (with more than a hint at the hidden homosexual derivation). They enjoy the company of women who are expert in the art of judo or karate, and are sexually stimulated by the idea of a woman abusing them physically.

UNPUBLISHED MASOCHISTIC STORY

This unpublished and untitled sadomasochistic story was given to us by a young man who wrote it as an erotic fantasy for himself.

The ad was in French: *"Fille d'appel chêrche bon à tout faire. GUL 88.10."*

"Now what in the world," thought David, whose French was better than that. "Fille d'appel, fille d'appel . . . girl . . . appeal . . . appealing girl? Ridiculous. Call . . . girl call. Call-girl! That's it, call-girl! Now, what's she looking for, a maid? That might be a misprint, and then again, supposing it wasn't? Supposing she really wanted a *'bon' à tout faire* . . . a male maid. That's right up my alley," thought he. For David had long been a conscious disciple of Leopold von Sacher Masoch. Until now, however, his experiences along these lines had been strictly platonic and tacit. And while he had always dreamed there must be women in the world consciously desirous of such a relationship as Wanda may have had with Leopold, he had always doubted it. Doubted it very much indeed. And yet here was this ad! How else could it be interpreted?

And with trembling hand, David dialed GUL 88.10.

"Hello" said a noncommittal female voice.

"I . . . I read your ad," said David hoarsely.

"You sure you read it right?" was the somewhat coarse reply.

"I . . . think so."

"Translate it!" There was a shade of warm anticipation behind the knife-edged, commanding voice.

"C . . . Call-girl seeks man-of-all-work . . . or manservant."

"Aha! Alors voo pahrlay frahnsay!" she chortled triumphantly with an atrocious accent. So she wasn't French after all, David thought.

"You're the first one who's gotten it, dearie," she went on. "You must come for your interview this evening at ten sharp—35 Tottenham Road, Flat 15, got that?"

"But I . . . I've got . . ."

"Now look, honey, if you're going to work for me, you've got to jump when I say the word, understand?"

"Yes . . . ma'am."

"Call me Blackie. It's short for . . . well, you'll see." She chortled again in that weird way and hung up.

There was something irritating about the woman's manner, thought David. Something exciting, too, he felt as his hand strayed to his trousers. Very definitely exciting. What about his date with Shirley? What about that concert they hadn't wanted to miss (or rather he hadn't wanted to miss it—Shirley didn't care much for music one way or another, all she was interested in was looking at women's clothes and showing off her own). That clinched it. To

ell with the concert. He had the records anyway. This was a
hance of a lifetime.

At ten o'clock sharp, David was ringing the doorbell of flat
umber fifteen. His heart was in his throat and it hung there a long
ime while no sound came from within. Then, when he was almost
eady to sneak away, the door opened silently and he was faced
vith a sight he had never expected to see in his life. For the woman
ramed in the doorway was dressed like the girls in those little books
hat David sometimes bought from the stationer in Warder Street,
vith the difference that *her* clothes fit, and then some! To begin
vith, it was all black leather! Not the cheap, shiny kind that is all
hat most specialized whores can usually afford, but the expensive
upple variety with a dull, subtle sheen that makes it look alive. The
alf-high, spiked-heel boots were cut like the finest opera pumps and
nust have laced up the back, for their trim, smooth tops were
nbroken by even a seam. The trousers that were tucked into them
lung like tights to movie-star legs and thighs, while the sleeveless
unic was cut higher in the front than in the back, producing a cape-
ike effect. It was cut high around the throat and fell loosely—but
ot too loosely—over a full, aggressive bosom. The shapely arms
hat protruded from the slits in the tunic were bare only to the
lbows; the rest of the marble flesh was sheathed in close-fitting
gloves which matched the rest of the outfit and emphasized the
eauty of the tapering fingers. Her hair was ash blonde, cut fairly
hort and held in place by a thin headband, also of black leather.
Her make-up was heavy, but skillful, with lurid eye-shadow and
rtificially protracted eyebrows.

"Hello," she said and her professional smile was full of
romise. David wondered whether he was really supposed to be
pplying for a job. Without another word she gripped him by the
houlder and steered him down a darkened hallway, shutting the
ront door with an easy swing of her booted foot. Though she was
ot squeezing very hard, David felt the strength of those long
ingers through the wool of his jacket.

The room which they entered was better lit than the hallway.
And tastefully furnished, thought David as he glanced around at the
omfortable settee, the armchairs, the . . . Oh oh, thought David.
What's up? For there was already another man in the room. He was
vell dressed but a good deal older than David, in his middle forties,
robably. He stood up politely as David caught sight of him. An-
ther applicant? wondered David. Or?

Blackie introduced them perfunctorily after asking David his
ame. David didn't catch the other man's, and he had the feeling

that the latter made no special effort to catch his. The woma
motioned David to a chair beneath a lamp and sat down across from
him. He could no longer see her face very well, but as she crosse
her legs, the leather grew even tauter on that long, tapered thigh
The effect was heightened by a beam from under a nearby lamp
shade, and David wondered whether it hadn't been adjusted o
purpose. The woman said nothing and suddenly David realized tha
she was letting him "get an eyeful." Blushing a little, he looked up a
her shadowy face and she flashed him a mocking smile.

"Of course, you would have to take care of my wardrobe, kee
everything neat and pressed. But I see you'll like that," she sai
without warning. David heard the man titter a bit. "You'll also hav
to clean house and do a bit of cooking. Do you know how to cook
You'll learn," she went on, before David could even open his mouth
"Of course, you'll have to sleep in. I may need you at any time, yo
know," and the man tittered again. He was getting on David'
nerves. This wasn't exactly what he had expected.

"But that's the easy part. Now we come to the hard part. Stan
up!" As she gave this order, she swung easily to her feet and steppe
into the middle of the room. Hesitantly, David stood up. What di
she want of him? As he stood in front of his chair, she looked hir
up and down with an appraising eye, seemed satisfied with what sh
saw and said: "Now come here." He took a step towards her, the
another. She stood looking at him with a faint smile on her face, he
boots planted slightly apart and her arms dangling loosely at he
sides. David felt a strange, unnamable fear creeping over him and a
the same time a secret delight. He took another step forward.

That was when she hit him. She clenched her fist in a funn
way—one gloved knuckle seemed to be sticking out and David eve
had time to think: what a sissy way to make a fist—and she hit hin
around the bottom of the ribs. She didn't really hit him hard, i
shouldn't have hurt very much—but David felt as though she'
stuck a knife in him. With a gasp of pain he doubled up, but in th
very moment of his doubling up and before the breath had gon
completely out of him, he felt a sharp tug at his hair and a knee o
leather and steel flashed in front of his eyes, catching him square o
the bridge of the nose. As a thousand needles dug into his brair
David was again confusedly aware that she had pulled her punch
But he also knew that his nose was starting to bleed. As his hea
snapped back he felt an excruciating pain in the ankle and after tha
he lost count: each blow struck home on a different part of his bod
and each touched off a reaction which immediately left him ope
for the next. An elbow in the solar plexus would be followed by

chop on the back of the neck when he bent double, a finger jab in the throat would hurl him backwards and a knee in the groin would double him up again. He pawed at the sleek leather-clad fighting machine that was putting him through this humiliating torture, he tried to cling to her to keep from falling, but his arms would be ruthlessly chopped away or an unbearable electric pressure on his spinal column would make him gasp for breath and break the clinch.

Then, as suddenly as it had begun, it stopped. He felt himself sagging to the floor, but even the respite of collapse was to be denied him. Those leather-clad hands of steel grasped his lapels and heaved him erect. He stood there gasping, his face only inches from hers, and through his dazed brain only one thought could race: she isn't even out of breath! She held him there for several long seconds, gazing into his face with an almost gentle smile.

"Rough, isn't it, baby," she said inexplicably.

"Why . . ." David began.

"Shhh . . ." she said, almost gently.

While they stood thus motionless, David did hear someone panting, however. He realized that during the massacre he had completely forgotten that there was a witness, and his shame increased tenfold! He tried to turn around and look at the other man, but now those gloved hands began tugging at his lapels as though to tease him. The gentle movements seemed incongruous with the brutality that had proceeded, but suddenly he felt the sharp blow of a boot against the side of his ankle and his feet flew out from under him as if by magic. He landed square on his rump and had the wind knocked out of him once again. Before he had recovered it, he was smothered by the black leather mass of her bosom. He tried to struggle but the weight of her hip on his floating rib was so painful that he soon subsided. Now he felt his wrist being caught in a steel pincer and twisted, twisted so deftly and surely that again the image of the fighting machine came to his mind, a leather-clad robot in the form of a beautiful woman. He screamed, but just as he felt his wrist was about to break her weight slid from him and he was able to scramble onto his stomach to ease momentarily the inhuman pressure. But this, he immediately realized, was just what his torturer wanted for suddenly he felt his hand whipped toward the back of his neck as she applied the most cunning, vicious hammerlock he had ever experienced. He gasped with pain but this did not prevent him from hearing another, louder gasp from the audience. Again that feeling of humiliation rose hot within him, crept into his loins.

Behind him he could feel the woman moving about, doing

something, but the hold on his wrist was not relaxed one iota. Then there was a metallic rattle, click . . . and he felt cold steel—real steel—close about his imprisoned wrist. Handcuffs! He had the incongruous, fleeting impression that she was a policewoman and that this had all been some sort of trap to arrest him for . . . for what? He thought of Kafka. Suddenly he felt a cruel tug at his hair and his head was jerked off the carpet. For a moment he thought his neck was broken.

"Now be a nice boy and give me the other hand," she whispered. He hesitated a moment and she increased the double pressure ever so slightly, but it was quite enough. Performing a veritable acrobatic feat, he managed to twist his other arm around behind him and far up his back. There was another click and his face flopped back onto the carpet. The leather vice was removed from his wrist leaving only the steel one. He sensed her standing up, got a whiff of polished shoe leather and felt the toe of her boot prod his jaw.

"On your back, honey," she said with that same surprising gentleness he had noticed before.

Painfully, he rolled over and sat up. Not four feet away from him their audience was still in his chair playing with himself. As David caught his eye, he seemed somewhat discomfited, but was obviously too excited to stop. David felt a certain loathing come over him. His leather-clad nemesis was behind him now, and he felt a tug at the hand-cuffs. He struggled to his feet, felt himself being drawn backwards quickly—he almost fell again—and his foot touched the wall behind him. Then there was one last upward jerk on the handcuffs, so painful that he half-screamed, and as she stepped away from him, the pressure remained constant, unbearable. He realized that she must have hooked the cuffs onto the wall somehow. By standing on tiptoes, he quickly discovered, the pain could be eased considerably, but how long, he wondered, could he keep that up. My God! It occurred to him this is regular torture! Just like the Gestapo! Only it was all being done by a beautiful woman in tight leather pants. For the first time since he had been assaulted so brutally, David realized that this was his secret dream! Never had he dared imagine undergoing physical violence at the hands of a woman! His dreams had always involved only moral humiliation, such as being a woman's servant. But now that the actual pain had stopped, the past five minutes seemed, in retrospect, the most beautiful he had ever known!

In the meantime, Blackie was standing before him, gazing at her handiwork. There was a tiny, insinuating smile on her face. Suddenly her hand went out and down, and David flinched involuntarily. But what was his amazement when he realized that she had merely zipped open his fly, and how much greater it was when his swollen member flopped out almost of its own accord! She chortled frankly when she saw it and gave it a few deft manipulations. He was already dribbling when she withdrew her hand, backed away and went over to the man whom David had come to regard as her customer. A wave of frustration ran through David's body. She wasn't going to finish him off, the bitch! That had just been part of the torture! Never had he wanted the use of his hands more than at this moment!

In the meantime, the black-clad figure had gone down on the man in the chair. The leather stretched tight and gleaming over her firm buttocks, the high heels were pointing back at him as though warning him to stay put. He longed to bridge the gap between his throbbing, exacerbated member and those voluptuous leather curves. Even with his hands bound, he fancied, he could rub against that supple armor, insert himself between those shapely legs of steel. He tried to thrust himself upward and off the hook or whatever it was, but to no avail. The device was cleverly designed. I'll just have to wait, he thought. Perhaps when she's finished. Just then the man began to wail, threw himself forward, and pawed at the leather tunic. A gloved hand rose from the shadows and thrust him gently back into the chair. David could tell that she was giving a few, final pulls as the man moaned contentedly, lying back with his eyes closed. She stood up and without another glance at him whirled about and came over to David.

"OK, honey, time's up!" she said cheerfully. She reached behind him and he felt the pressure ease. He could move away from the wall. "Hold still a minute!" she said playfully, and he could feel her unlocking the handcuffs. Despite the stiffness in his arms, his hands flew almost instinctively to that neglected member.

"No, no, I'll take care of it . . . just this once!" she said softly, and led him from the room. Her customer seemed to have gone to sleep in his chair.

The room she led him into was dark until she switched on the light. With a gentle shove in which he again sensed her uncanny skill at handling the human body, she sent him sprawling on the bed. Squatting comfortably beside him, she took his wrist between gloved hands and began to massage it gently.

"How . . . how did you learn to do all those things?" he asked as his pain-wracked body began to relax. She smiled enigmatically: "The army . . . military intelligence!" He must have looked surprised. "But that was some time ago," she added almost wistfully.

"But what is it?" he asked as she began to massage his neck and shoulders. "I've never seen anything like it. My God," he thrilled, "when you dug your finger into my back, I thought you had some kind of electro-shock machine in your glove!"

She laughed outright for the first time that evening. "Just a nerve center . . . there are lots of them," and he felt a shooting pain in his shoulder. "See what I mean? It's karate and judo and some other things. Blackie is short for black-belt; you know what that is, don't you?"

David marveled: "Sure . . . but I never thought a girl could get to be one . . . I mean . . ."

She smiled. "Well, now you know different. How do you feel?"

"OK . . . but . . ."

"I know," she said with another smile, and her hand slid to his groin. David sucked in his breath as her thumb and forefinger closed about his bulging penis and began a subtle manipulation.

"Tell me," he began faintly, "was that a real interview or what?"

"Of course," she said. "If you come to work for me, that will be your job. That's my specialty. The fellow in the next room paid fifteen quid to see that!" David's eyes bulged.

"How did you get into it?" He was beginning to breathe hard now, but he felt that such a tale would not distract from his pleasure . . . quite the contrary! She smiled almost as if she realized this.

"Well, when I got out of the army, I didn't really know what to do with myself. I used to hang around this bar in Soho and men used to try to pick me up, but I wasn't having any. I was waiting for a sugar-daddy at the very least. Then one night there was this gorilla who tried to do it the tough way and I gave him what you got. Only I didn't pull my punches; he was six months in hospital." David sucked in his breath sharply and asked timidly:

"Tell me what you did to him . . . please!"

"Well . . ." she gave him a knowing smile and her fingers closed around the full length of his penis as she began a rhythmic up-and-down movement. "Well, there isn't much to it. He grabbed me around the neck and tried to kiss me. I figured a little judo would discourage him, so I gave him a hip throw. He was plenty surprised but he came right back for more and I guess I got a little mad. I clasped hands the way they taught us and swung up to knock his arms away and then down on the bridge of his nose. That hurts like hell and can do a lot of damage. He bent over with his face in his hands and it wasn't very hard to chop him on the tail-bone. That's a real finisher . . . you can kill a man. He went down for the count." David was panting now, as the scene swam before his eyes. "After that," she concluded, "well, it wasn't long before I-was getting very interesting propositions from some of the men who'd watched, and since my precious twot wasn't in danger, and since I've always gotten a bit of a secret kick from giving guys a licking . . ."

David let out a loud wail as his sperm spurted almost to the ceiling. The girl was obviously quite impressed and drew out the orgasm as long as she could.

JOSIANE ET SON ESCLAVE

This is the place to consider another extremely rare and perhaps more bizarre story in this vein, namely, *Josiane et Son Esclave* (no author, place, or date, but known to have been originally published in 1911, and reprinted in 1928 with the subtitle, *A story of masochism, of a woman, and a youth of nineteen*).

Josiane is a twenty-nine-year-old widow who, bored with her existence, wants to amuse herself with a human being whom she can treat literally like a dog. In her mind she runs through the entire register of her male acquaintances, but none seems to really fit the role. Suddenly the nineteen-year-old Hubert, an old friend of the family, occurs to her. She has already had a few brushes with him as he was growing up over the years, and she knows he will do anything she wants. She immediately sets to work on Hubert, her main pastime being to have him perform cunnilingus not only on her but also on her lady friends for hours at a time, until the young man is ready to collapse. Then she thinks of more extravagant pleasures for her and tortures for Hubert.

"Hubert, come here! . . . Now you're going to read to me."

She installed herself on top of him and after having given him a book, placed her feet on two tall stools, leaning against the back of a chair. She seemed absorbed in the story. She remained this way for three-quarters of an hour, completely immobile. As the day before, the cushions had given way and Josiane was practically sitting on Hubert's mouth. His voice became raucous and hissing, sweat dripped off his forehead. Josiane recognized this symptom and seemed to wait for it. Leaning forward in order to look at him she said with a voice that seemed to be trembling:

"You're tired, you're thirsty, aren't you?" Without waiting for a reply, she continued: "Never mind, on the contrary, carry on and listen to me carefully: No matter what happens, don't interrupt your reading under any circumstances."

Then she added in a harsh voice: "If you do, I assure you that you'll rue the day!" and she lay back on the cushions. . . .

She had been dominating a strong desire to urinate for the last few minutes. She wanted to accumulate a lot, and was already savoring the joy of pissing, sharpened by Hubert's torment. All of a sudden she flushed and, holding her breath, she let herself go.

Hubert, surprised at first by this hot jet, had interrupted his reading, instinctively closing his mouth. But, coming out of her torpor, Josiane leaned over him, hollering hoarsely, her mouth strained with wrath: "Read! Speak! Open your mouth! I want to hear you all the time!" Horrified, his eyes wild, he repeated the last phrase, then read it over again while Josiane once more lay back supinely, let the hot liquid run, sometimes holding it back to prolong her pleasure, saying softly, her voice harmonious and sweet: "Ah! My good, my little Hubert, drink. Drink your Josiane! You see, I promised you a surprise." Then there was no more liquid left. Hubert was half suffocated. She leaned over him again and with an arch smile said: "It's all over. You can breathe now." Then, as he opened his mouth wide in order to take a deep breath, she spurted a jet of urine she still held and let out a peal of laughter, just like a schoolgirl's. "You shouldn't be thirsty any more, should you! How do you like my gingerbread? Hah! Hah!"

Then, eyes shining, she frowned at him: "Enough of this joking!" And throwing the cushions that supported her and falling upon the already exhausted, miserable boy, she shouted: "Hurry up! Caress me! Lick me! I want it . . . like tonight. You know . . . ah! Yes. Like that . . . more! Don't stop! Ah! I'm coming. God it's wonderful! Here, here! Eat! So eat!"

L'AVEU

Arthur Adamov has given eloquent expression to the male masochistic attitude in his book *L'Aveu* (*Confession*) (Paris: Editions du Sagittaire, 1946). "As far back as I can remember," he writes, "I have always had the same temptation, the same cruel need to suffer, to grovel in the lowest depths."

The narrator tells of deriving, at the age when boys like to take bicycle trips, "a strange, disturbing pleasure" from taking off his shoes and allowing the pedals to dig so deeply into his feet that they drew blood and gave him "a bitter sensual gratification." He gives a lucid description of the masochistic male's need to be abused and humiliated by woman: "I want to be humbled by woman, and by woman alone, because she is 'the other' *par excellence*, the outsider, the opposite of myself. Woman is the image of everything which rises up from the depths and possesses the lure of the abyss. The lower one sinks, the lower one wants to sink. Having fallen to the bottom of the world, I seek an even deeper nether world in the thrall of woman. I want to be lower than the lowest."

He then goes on to say that for that reason woman is to him "the eternal prostitute, with her painted face and her bewildered gaze." He has the fantasy of seeing himself kneeling "at the feet of some poor creature on a dusty dungeon floor"; he sees himself "on some insane journey, in a sordid, lower-class railway carriage in midsummer, and I see a girl dressed in rags sprawling on the seat, letting a crowd of anonymous men kiss her feet"; and he sums it up in a grand fantasy which contains the key to male masochism, as well as to the strange sort of inverted bondage psychology that we have been considering in the preceding pages.

I am lying naked in a public square, in the midst of other naked men. In the center of this quarantine camp of love, a provocatively beautiful woman, clothed in tawdry theatrical finery, is standing on an absurd scaffolding of beams and girders, like a target riddled by a thousand feverish gazes. Slowly she lifts her skirts until her belly is bare and then, with a negligent hand, she caresses the most secret recesses of her body; her face freezes in a mask of indifference; and her vague, inexpressible smile sends me spinning into an abyss.

The sex feeling in male masochism, associated with humiliation, must be established in a person's childhood experiences. "I know of no greater sensual pleasure," states the writer, "than that of openly being the object of the contemptuous insults of a woman for whom I myself have nothing but contempt, while at the same time I am a slave to the giddy desire which she arouses in me." He talks of the "haughty indifference" in the woman's looks, "the mocking curl of her swollen lips," all indications that we are dealing with early childhood impressions which are repressed, "forgotten," inaccessible to the conscious mind, but which continue to govern sexual orientation because they have never become associated with the original situations in which they arose, nor therapeutically "worked through" until they lose their compelling strength.

But *L'Aveu* also calls attention to another feature which is indispensable to the operation of male masochism (and which was only thinly disguised in the bondage fantasies of *Gynecocracy* and *Miss High-Heels*), namely, the masochist must suffer insult and injury at the hand of someone for whom the victim has, in turn, "nothing but contempt."

This feeling of contempt for the person who acts as a sexual stimulus also has its roots in childhood experience. "That woman," the narrator says, and one can almost picture the crucial woman in his childhood environment, "with her endless, throaty laughter, the self-satisfaction that oozes from every pore of her face, her idolization of herself, her aimless pride and her habit of screwing up the corners of her mouth in what is meant to be a superior smile—that woman represents everything that fascinates me, and everything I despise."

In another place, the narrator speaks of his disgust and loathing for anything that boasts of virility in a man. He could not bear to hear that someone had said, "He's a real man." This is a typical way women speak of certain men, and it is clear that such praise must be at the expense of someone else (not a "real" man). It would seem reasonable to assume that a young boy hearing such remarks in a certain emotional setting might well consider himself or an important father figure slighted by them. He could understandably develop a sort of "loathing" for anything virile. In other words, the boy would pick up the hidden castration-threat in such remarks (directed against other men) and find it safer to identify with the aggressor and "castrate" himself, that is, make himself non-virile or present himself as such to mislead the castrating female—a feature which is clearly present in all the bondage stories with female sex feeling on the part of the hero.

LE CLUB DES MONTEURS HUMAINES

There are fantasies of bondage and humiliation in which male masochism is *not* a salient feature. In these fantasies, the erotic charge derives from the idea of servitude, of humiliation, of enslavement itself. Around the turn of the century, there flourished a whole literature about humans serving each other as riding horses in which one cannot say that the humiliation of one sex or the other is central, since both are subjected to the same treatment.

A fantasy of this type is the story *Le Club des Monteurs Humaines* (*The Club of Fanciers of Human Riding Horses*), by "Bernard Valonnes" (Aceaux, Seine: Select Bibliothèque, 1924). The scene is alleged to be tsarist Russia, but what plot there is to this curious story and others like it is insignificant.

Madame Weinberg got up and stood in front of the sofa. Using both hands, she grasped her heavy velvet gown, richly trimmed with lace, and raised it to reveal the swimming reflections in her patent leather boots and, with a triumphant smile, she waited. The young man knelt behind her, lowered his head and gazed intently at the shiny leather.

He hesitated a moment and then, in a voice which quavered with emotion, asked with his Caucasian accent, "Madame, before I have the honor of feeling your weight upon me, will you allow me to pay homage to the lovely feet which I will soon have the good fortune to hold in my hands?"

"Of course. Not only will I allow you, but I will remind you that it is the duty of every gallant steed to pay homage to its rider. Only don't forget that your kiss must be full of respect and that your lips must touch nothing but boot leather." Madame Weinberg's tone was quiet but imperious; it made a deep inpression on the young man as he bent over, kissed the boots, and put his head between the two shining shafts of leather. Slowly he raised himself, hiding his head under the jumble of lace that trimmed the elegant Jewess's luxurious lingerie. Gradually he vanished beneath the velvet gown which she lifted as he did so. From the way the skirt filled out, we could tell that his head was already above the thighs. With her feet planted wide apart, Madame Weinberg leaned slightly backward and shifted her round bottom in order to get a good purchase on the saddle.

Finally the saddle was in place; for a few more seconds the rounded behind slid from side to side, feeling for a stable position; then, the portly amazon lifted one foot off the floor, keeping her balance with the tip of her other foot. Finally she lost all contact with the floor and wrapped her legs around her steed. The prince took the elegant feet of his imposing rider in his hands and slowly stood up. We could see the tension of the muscles in his slender feet; he lifted his heavy rider gradually and without swaying. Finally he was standing up. We applauded. . . .

"Now," Madame Weinberg explained, still addressing Madame Savinov, "I can assure you that my steed cannot hear a thing: my thighs are pressing hard against his ears."

And skillfully, with a dexterity that one would never have suspected in a woman who was over forty and quite plump, she drove her steed around the room, guiding him solely by authoritative little digs of her heels, by the pressure of her dominating feet and the swaying of her body. The young man obeyed her commands quite docilely.

Finally, Mademoiselle Bobrow appeared, wearing a short black dress, very low cut to reveal her pretty bosom, and with a tiny, yellow leather saddle strapped on her back.

"Excuse me for being a little late," she said, a bit out of breath, "would you like to mount me right away?"

"Of course, it's time."

I stood up and climbed on a stool.

"Oh, that won't be necessary," protested Mademoiselle Bobrow. "If you don't mind, I'd like to lift you off the ground."

She knelt behind me and put her head between my thighs. . . .

We took part in the dancing with the other couples; then came all the other forms of entertainment in vogue at the Club, as well as all the exercises that are practiced there; male and female riders used and abused their steeds, demanding of them all the tokens of submission and servitude which it was their right to expect.

On the way back to the boudoir, Madame Weinberg took my arm, and this embarrassed me a little because I could feel that it was increasing the weight which my charming steed had to carry; then, too, when one is straddling the shoulders of a human steed, it is not easy to give a similarly mounted lady one's arm; this takes a good deal of practice for both rider and steed, and Mademoiselle Bobrow must have been much stronger than she looked, for she acquitted herself well of this difficult task.

It was in this formation that we joined Madame Savinov with the intention of resting on the sofa on which we had left her. It was conveniently designed so that the saddles could rest on the top edge of the back, making it possible to give our steeds a moment's rest without having to dismount. While we were still riding, however, Madame Weinberg leaned heavily on my arm and readjusted herself on her saddle, pressing her thighs together.

"How warm it is," she said, "this gown is too heavy for dancing. And," she added with a lascivious smile, "I expect my young prince is not feeling any too cool, either. As it happens, I'm not wearing my gymnastic tights, but only my silken lingerie. My stockings aren't long enough to reach the part of my thighs which are pressed against the prince's cheeks, and since my undergarments have ridden up a bit (unless that sweet little boy has pushed them up himself) his cheeks are pressed against my bare flesh. Can't you just imagine how, if I press my thighs together, his cheeks are practically glued to my skin. It's strange, isn't it, Prince?"

She looked down at the young man who, now that his rider had loosened her thighs, could hear our conversation. "It feels as though we formed a single body," she went on; "I really feel as if my steed were part of my own body, that his feet, which are carrying me, are simply my own feet, and that mine are merely an ornament, a fetish meant to be worshiped. And at times they become an instrument of punishment," she added, giving her exhausted steed a hard kick with her heel.

She wore a diabolical smile and these details excited me greatly.

Mademoiselle Bobrow then explains her domestic functions in the home of the Petroffs, where she serves as a kind of *au pair* girl:

"Officially, I'm a student at the women's college and I live with the Petroffs as a *dame de compagnie;* actually, however, the only studies to which I apply myself seriously are my physical culture classes at Mr. Beck's school, which have made me an excellent steed."

"Do you have any duties as a slave in the Petroff home?"

"Of course. I am Mr. Petroff's Club steed."

"Isn't his wife jealous? She is ugly and looks much older than her husband."

"On the contrary, she is very fond of this sport and she often uses me herself; it gives her great pleasure to ride in front of her husband and he enjoys such scenes."

"In other words, you perform the function of champagne: you stimulate the husband's desire for his ugly wife?"

"Exactly."

"Isn't Madame Petroff afraid that you might become a threat to her?" asked Madame Savinov. "She must be jealous of you."

"Madame Petroff is not at all jealous of me and has no reason to be. On the contrary, she ought to be quite grateful to me. When I entered the Petroffs' service, she was completely neglected by her husband, who sought his distractions away from home; however, when his wife first appeared to him riding on my shoulders, when he saw me stroke her feet and do my best to please her in every way, he began to find fancy boots and luxurious undergarments more and more attractive, and it was while sitting on my shoulders that his wife saw her husband at her feet, for the very first time, perhaps, since they were married."

The sadistic and masochistic roles here are reversible, while in previous stories the male always played the masochistic-submissive role and the female the dominant-sadistic role. Thus we are dealing here with an entirely different psychology, distinct from the true bondage fantasy but similar to specific deviations and fetishes with humiliation as the prominent feature. The humiliation is mitigated by the fact that it is mutual and not at the exclusive expense of one sex over the other.

7

Sadomasochism

Having examined a variety of fantasies dealing with male masochism (told either from the viewpoint of the male masochist or, less often, from that of the female sadist), we turn now to the reverse of the medal—sadistic (male) fantasies in which the woman is the victim to be humiliated, or "put in her place."

We have in our files a story similar to the last one cited in the previous chapter, in that it also deals with the riding of human horses, but only female ones and with a decided sadistic twist which was much less pronounced in the first case.

THE PASSIONATE LASH

The story is entitled *The Passionate Lash, or the Revenge of Sir Hilary Garner*, by "Alan McClyde" (Paris: Pall Mall Press, n.d.). This excerpt is from the second part of the book.

Both girls were magnificently accoutered. On the back of each, just below the shoulders, was fixed a special human saddle of black glacé leather. The saddle was fixed to the pony by two steel runners that swept up their backs and hooked over their shoulders. From the lower part of the saddle two girth straps swept around to the front and fastened with shiny buckles at the navels of the girls. The bottom of the saddle itself swept out and upwards to form the seat for the rider.

The problem of the girls' arms was solved bizarrely and satisfactorily by encasing them beneath the saddle in a sort of straitjacket-cum-girdle which was tight about their waists and had long arms that were stitched to the main body of the girdle, ensuring that they had no freedom of the arms. The whole was in black leather with crimson lacing crisscrossed down the front.

The lower part of the corset ended in a curved steel bar, integral with the corset, that followed the sweep of the spine and heavily accentuated it to throw the buttocks outward in an exaggerated curve.

The buttocks were bare and their whiteness in the case of Terresa, accentuated the black severity of the corset and saddle. The base of the curved spine rod was pierced to allow the insertion of a plume—red in the case of Terresa, white in the case of Natia.

The pube in front was shielded from sight by a patch of gleaming glacé leather secured by a red thong around the waist and another that dipped between the legs, deep into their soft gashes, between the buttock cheeks and up to join the waist encircling thong.

The legs of the ponies were bare to the knees. From there their legs were encased in leather boots of black kid, laced up in front, again with crimson thongs. The heels were high—almost six inches—and from past experience all the watchers knew that this was one of the delights of the training period, teaching the pony not to stumble and suitably correcting it when it did!

All this finery was surmounted in each case with the girl's head bearing a golden helmet with a plume. Terresa's plume was black and Natia's white.

The helmets were secured below the chin by soft red leather buckles and the sides of the helmets swept down over the ears to the extreme base of the jawbone so that all of the face that could be seen was the lower forehead, the eyes, and the mouth.

But it was in the bridle that the exquisite art of the human saddler had come into its glorious own!

The bits—of stainless steel, smooth and shiny where they showed, rough and repressive where they bit into the soft mouths they were designed to torment—were fully four inches long. At each end was a brass ring to which was affixed the rein, and this was of the "bearing" variety.

That is to say the bit ran between the girls' mouths and the reins swept upward to pass through rings that were fixed in the shoulder harnesses so that by the slightest pull on the reins the head could be held back and the neck arched to give a proud, defiant, and spirited appearance to the pony.

The reins were short and again in soft crimson leather. The use of crimson to show off the severe black of the rest of the leather was the touch of a master!

The helpless hands of the fillies, hard at their sides, were encased in crimson gloves and this completed the bizarre ensemble as nothing else possibly could have done. . . .

Hilary strode among this exciting mêlée to where the bridles and other accessories hung. He selected a black bridle with silver rein rings and a curious piece of equipment composed of what looked like steel rods and much black leather. From the thousand and one bits on a table he chose one, a cruel looking thing in stainless steel with a harsh angle at each end to correct the mouth of a straying mount. For spurs he chose two with tiny golden wheels and needle sharp protuberances around their circumferences.

Molly Andrews shrank back in wonder and horror as he approached her with his selection.

He put all but the curiously designed jacket-affair aside.

He grabbed her and turned her and began to attire her unprotesting body in the strange apparatus.

It fitted in the manner of a corset but with differences that make the analogy far from perfect. The front of the thing reached from her chin to her pube. At the pube it swept out, steel-strutted, in a peak of glacé leather that looked something like a Turkish slipper in shape. As this peak came lower than her pube it hid her triangle of fanny-fur from view and gave that region of her body a queer, unreal appearance. From there the corset swept up—still in black glacé leather—to her breasts.

Here the fiendish ingenuity of the designer was well evidenced.

The cups that covered the breasts might be called a brassière inasmuch as they shielded the breasts, but they were made of woven wire, the ends of which turned inwards making the brassière a veritable hell of stinging pain as the thousand wire barbs pricked and tormented the titties encased in them.

Molly screamed as Hilary roughly pulled this up her chest and put his hands over her shoulders to cram her scintillating breasts into them.

"Oh, it hurts . . . it hurts!" she moaned.

"It's meant to hurt!" snarled Hilary. "It must have cost a hundred pounds. People don't spend a hundred pounds buying garb for sluts unless they themselves get some amusement out of it!"

The corset above the breasts was just as ingeniously contrived. It swept up to the throat, where it was secured by a buckle and then a leather-covered sunken plate came out to support the chin and therefore the head, in an unnatural, thrown back attitude, similar in appearance to the supports put into spinal jackets to support a broken neck. But in this case, of course, the purpose of the plate was not so much support as oppression! The head of the wearer was thrown back giving a wild yet proud appearance to the mount, much as the bearing rein gives this appearance to the real horse.

Hilary, seemingly unaware of the delicious pandemonium that now raged around him as the other riders went ahead with their harnessing, finished buckling the corset to Molly.

Her head now unnaturally thrown back and her tits heaving under the pricking clasp of the wire-shod cups, Molly was now stiff with the excitement of her torment.

He next fixed the saddle to her back.

She looked a proud, efficient hack with the saddle high on her shoulders, the stirrups dangling almost to her hips. The bottom of the saddle below the pommel was designed in two flaring arches that swept down to two pointed peaks wide on the lower part of the buttocks, almost to the thighs. This gave the effect of a frame to the vaulted domes of her bottom-cheeks as they thrust hugely from the frame and also made allowance for the fact that the whip or crop might need a completely open, unshielded target!

At each side of the chin-supporting plate were tiny eyelets. Through these Hilary threaded the ties for the helmet, a gorgeous affair in black lacquered steel with a crimson plume surmounting it.

The helmet fixed, he turned his attention to her feet. Natia had had boots made that finished just below the knee but the foot of which was made in the semblance of a pony's hoof.

In order to crush the foot into this unnatural shape, what was in effect a high heel had been incorporated, this also helped to achieve the highly desirable prancing effect. He laced these boots up her peerless calf and surveyed the result with satisfaction.

"Quite the pony!" he sneered.

He next selected a tail plume for her. Again he chose crimson. This plume fixed into a tiny silver thimble below the saddle pommel and the tail hung almost to her ankles.

Black gloves that buttoned to her elbows was the next part of the accouterment and when these were upon her lovely arms she was almost complete.

The reins were run through the rings at the shoulders of the corset and affixed to the vicious little bit. This was crammed without ceremony into her soft mouth.

He stood back and looked at her.

What a picture of loveliness under complete domination!

Here we have the exact opposite of the masochistic male bondage fantasies, for it is now the woman who is brought into bondage and who has to suffer humiliations. In short, heterosexual male sadism is expressed at the expense of the woman.

Sometimes, the woman toward whom the male sadism is directed has exactly the same characteristics as the domineering female in the masochistic fantasies. She is the emancipated, almost tough woman who has to be emasculated and put in her place by the dominant, revenge-seeking male.

THE REVOCATION OF THE EDICT OF NANTES

This psychology is especially pronounced in the writings of Pierre Klossowski. In Klossowski's *La Révocation de l'Edit de Nantes* (Paris: Editions de Minuit, 1959),* for example, we have two incidents which can serve as illustrations. The first concerns a fantasy of Octave, Roberte's husband. F. and X. are two boys of sixteen, friends of Roberte's nephew. They have made a bet that they will strip Roberte of her gloves (symbol of her feminine power).

---

* *Roberte Ce Soir & The Revocation of the Edict of Nantes*, trans. Austryn Wainhouse (New York: Grove Press, 1969).

What happened then? F. and X. had bribed the little shoeshine
boys and taken their place at the propitious moment, having got the
signal from the son of the building superintendent, whose collaboration had been previously secured.

Roberte was about to go through the exit door when a bellboy,
carrying some greasy liquid or other in a pot, seems to have dumped
it on her shoes as he whisked past, and the two little shoeshiners
promptly spring into action, whip the box into position, etc., etc.
But I'm dubious about this detail which looks a little to me as if it
had been invented afterward to explain Roberte's amazing gesture. . . . However, on with the story: Roberte was on the verge
of going through this final door when the two pseudo shoeshine
boys saw her pause before a mirror. Our conspirators do not seem
to have been very clever in their choice of the moment, for if
Roberte had arrived at the club with dirt on her shoes she would
have had them cleaned an hour earlier; now, she was making ready
to leave the establishment—that is why the bellboy incident isn't
altogether implausible—but the two little shiners or rubbers saw her
pause in front of a mirror. And it was while bending toward the
mirror, amorously no doubt, that, mechanically, there's no milder
way of putting it, she planted a foot on the box. The two little
rubbers got busy and she, leaving them to do their stuff was at the
stage of applying some lipstick when the lights went out. Roles
were shifted in a trice. X. had grabbed Roberte's foot, posed on the
box, while F., stationed behind her, reaching his arm around in
front, caught hold of the skirt, lifted it and the bottom half of the
coat and, sliding them along Roberte's raised knee, hoisted them
waist-high; with one hand X. had immobilized Roberte's jutting leg
at the ankle and with the other he received the pocket flashlight
which F. had snapped on underneath Roberte's thigh. X. played the
beam along the smooth contours of the calf and on up to the knee,
then shot it between the garters and the bare flesh and had got as far
as the point where thigh enlarged into buttocks poured into panties
when Roberte's long and gloved fingers settled on the bulb of the
flashlight. At that moment, Roberte, making a first effort to remove
her foot from the box, must have felt it, since she twisted around,
drawing back her hand with the intention of slapping. F., lifting the
hem of her coat and skirt up to the small of her back, had started by
caressing her, his fingers gliding to the crotchpiece of the panties
which were stretched taut in the wide angle between thigh and
thigh, since she had one foot on the ground and the other on the
box. She was probably planning to remove it from there by an
about-face movement with a view, if not to stop F.'s hand, already

venturing into the furthermost nooks and crannies, then at least to push away his head which he was leaning hard against Roberte's flank, but in front of her X. had presently taken a two-handed grip on her calf, which forestalled this movement, F., from the rear, seconding his companion by blocking her other, impatiently tensed leg, with his foot. For when Roberte's gloved hand had closed over the bulb, X. had quickly snatched the flashlight away and passed it to F. who now from below directed the beam upward toward the apex where the widely separated thighs converged, offering X. the rare sight of the crotchpiece that Roberte's nature was filling out like a sail. Time enough to see that triangular yoke billow into form and Roberte's hand grope and cover the light a second time when, having thrust it aside, that hand suddenly rose, Roberte then catching the beam of light squarely in the face. While she remained thus, motionless except for her heaving bosom, helpless under the influence of emotion, an emotion less of surprise than of embarrassment, gasping and therefore unable to emit a sound, able only to try to clap her gloved hand over everything F. was illuminating, X. noticed the curve of her brow as it bent forward, her knit eyebrows, the glint in her eyes. Maintaining the severity of her regular features, her nostrils fluttering, her chin set firm, she was battling with both hands on the lapels of her fur coat which F.'s adolescent fists were pulling open, tearing her blouse, bringing the swollen brassiere out of hiding. The very next instant, brushing past the fur, her breasts popped forth, as if blinking in surprise to measure themselves against unresisting, unlimited space under the concentrated ray of electric light; the rosy, scarcely awakened but already jaunty nipples disappeared again behind Roberte's gloved fingers, turned up next between the schoolboy's bare fingers—and as X., suddenly envious, clicked off the flashlight and snapped it back on in the zone delegated to him, yet again did Roberte's hand sweep down, fingers outstretched, and X. had got a whiff of the scented skin in the palmopening of the glove. Just when was it that Roberte thus reached her still gloved hand toward the treasure bulging inside the yoke of her panties? At the very moment they were awaiting her at the Chamber for an important resolution bearing on the State education issue. But all notion of time and place had faded away at feeling juvenile fingers slither purposefully under her loosened blouse, into her armpits, over the flesh of her shoulders, toward the straps of her brassiere, the while, lower down, her palm had made light contact with an exceedingly youthful face, in the darkness. Seeking a landmark, a last something real about herself to hold onto, she placed her gloved hand upon her groin. Actually, the young aggressor was

worrying her with an irresistible clumsiness fitting in a boy from a
middle-class family and barely in his teens, but everything the
petulance of this very lack of experience suggested of the view then
being taken of her, split her final strugglings into two contradictory
solicitations: a mixture of curiosity and attentiveness containing an
undeniable fervor which she had been far from suspecting the
moment before, and a more and more dizzying uncertainty as to
herself. To be sure, the awkwardness of such untaught fingers were
more crudely felt than the hoarier articulations to whose impor-
tunings she had been known to yield, after a show of resistance, and
this crudity, felt to the very tips of her breasts that had got away
from her own gloved fingers, strained to the snapping point every
one of the seams still holding her in between shoulders and crotch.
What was her hand doing in its glove, with this boy she sensed
behind her, squeezing her calf and pressing his cheek to Roberte's
knee so that she felt his hot breath upon her thigh? X. indeed was
breathing with ever greater difficulty from staring, dumbstruck, at
the back of that gloved hand of Roberte's whose thumb was stiffen-
ing, index and middle fingers lost in the folds of the yoke, ring
finger and little finger gradually separating as the middle finger,
the outline of whose nail showed through the leather of the glove, bore
into the material of the. undergarment, pushing ocher flesh out
underneath the lace—when suddenly cloth tore, seams gave, gloved
fingers made direct contact with the apparent bush while index and
middle fingers curled inside warm darkness, the back of the gloved
hand hiding the rest. And X., his heart beating wildly, was yet
hunting for the courage to touch that glove when, still clutching the
faultless curves of Roberte's long leg, he felt the knee suddenly
buckle against his shoulder. Roberte's foot had slipped off the box
and knocked away the flashlight. A pool of light gleamed on the
enameled molding, its reflected glow shone on Roberte's braided
hair. Her eyes shut, her lips compressed but arched by a contained
laugh which was dimpling her cheeks, with her other gloved hand
she was still fending off F.'s bare and impetuous ones teasing
Roberte's nipples inside her fur coat. Upon those naïve fingers,
naked and stubby, hers, long and supple and gloved, were proving
unable to find a sure grip—when at last, having caught her wrist, F.
drew their sheath off those fingers. Denuded, the long hand fell
slack, its palm luminous. Seeing the first point tallied by the adversary, X. could have evened the score had he not just been smitten
by that hot and rich-smelling exhalation from Roberte's penumbra.
There lay the other hand, still gloved in that glove which ought to
have reverted to X., that hand which, all its fingers joined close, lay

over the thicket. But F. was brandishing the empty glove, with this glove was lightly slapping the ungloved one's breasts: such was the force of that first tremor, so prolonged that shudder that X. thought he saw everything run out which the still gloved hand was retaining. The leather was still glistening under the light when Roberte felt her nature overflow her palm in a rush. Whereupon that hand of Roberte's he hadn't dared to unglove himself, nor even touch, turned over stretching its long fingers toward X. He, brought upright by an impulse that took him unawares, had moved only a little nearer; that gloved hand freed him slowly and surely, cleared the way for him so slowly and surely that X. could work the glove up Roberte's palm and pull in his turn: the root of the thumb appeared, and the whole of the palm's satin-smooth skin, and finally the long supple fingers which after that folded back over the boy's startled audacity, covering it with their sparkling nails. And when the root of Roberte's thumb grazed it—was it the blinding flash of the pearly nails?—X. lost sight of the reason for his pleasure while Roberte, her thighs and behind dripping with the impertinence of our two neophytes, surrendered to the last of her spasms, panting hoarsely and letting all her legislative obligations go straight to the devil, from parliamentary lawmaker turning whore between Condorcet and St. Lazare. . . .

In the following passage from the same book, the narrator is Roberte, socialist member of parliament, Klossowski's symbol for the modern liberated woman who would contest the traditional notion of the supposedly "eternal feminine" and who, consequently, has to be punished and humiliated for having, in the author's view, usurped man's role and place in the affairs of human life.

. . . After I came out of the manicurist's in the rue Scribe, Justin, who was waiting for me, couldn't get the Buick started. This didn't really inconvenience me, I had time to kill before returning to the Palais Bourbon and, having scheduled no appointment that would interfere, I decided to take advantage of this mild and wonderfully sunny afternoon. I hopped on the rear platform of a bus, the first that came along, and was leaning against the railing, dreamily watching the shops go by, when some peculiar touching obliged me to go and take a seat inside the bus. . . . As he persisted in staring at me, I stood up and got off at Théâtre Français. Walking through the Palais Royal gateway I entered the Galérie de Montpensier. Beneath the arcades, practically deserted at that hour, footsteps echoed mine, drew nearer; as can happen any day to a Member of Parliament, I was being followed. The fellow in question, a very big man, tall, beefy, smooth-faced, a good sample of the sort that does a littly spying on the side for the police, keeps two or three steps away from me and stops each time I pause to glance into a display window. Where on earth is this new lingerie shop Gilberte told me I ought to visit? I turn and start down under the Galérie de Beaujolais: there it is, on the right. But now the fellow overtakes and passes me. I push a plate-glass door, find I'm in the wrong shop—this one is just in the process of being converted—the fellow enters too. Even though the people who are strolling outside or standing in front of the bookstore across the way have only to look hard through the partially smudged windows to detect anything abnormal that might be transpiring in this empty shop, nobody thinks to for one instant. His back to the glass door, the giant blocks my path when I attempt to leave, reaching my hand to the doorknob. Then, through a door in the back of the shop, appears another man, of less than medium height, thickset, in his shirtsleeves. They give each other the eye. The second retreats behind the counter and leaves the inner door ajar. . . .

. . . Less than an hour later I sit down at a table on the terrace of the Régence, the blood throbbing in my veins. My hands are probably shaking and the waiter asks me at once if everything is all right. I smile, get up to go to the washroom, peer at myself in the mirror: no point taking out my compact, I look fine. When you come right down to it, what exactly is there to blame them for? If it gave them some deplorable pleasure . . . For me, it's now that the pleasure begins. I return to the terrace and I go through it all again. When on the platform of the bus I'd been leaning back against the railing, my forearm and hand resting on the edge of it, the giant, who had been talking to the conductor at first, had taken hold of my fingers. I'd gone inside and chosen an unoccupied seat; but he, who had come in and sat down opposite me, had started that rude scrutinizing. I was sitting with my hands spread flat on the leather seat-covering, my legs separated perhaps, and a smile was straying over my lips while the warm breeze blew in at me through the lowered window. Had I kept that smile, my lips parted, while his stare was becoming more insistent? I at least crossed my knees immediately and folded my hands on my lap. After all, I had my Légion d'Honneur rosette in the buttonhole of my jacket. That was the moment when I decided to get off the bus and, I remember, I pulled the rosette loose and dropped it inside my handbag. I nonchalantly crossed the Place du Théâtre Français, I entered the Palais Royal, and so on until I was under the Galérie de Beaujolais vaulting. . . . And then I try to retrace the fellow's itinerary, stage by stage. He liked me. It was too much for him, he had to touch my fingers and from then on there was no stopping all the way down to the cellar. Beginning with that furtive but irrepressible touch he gave me, what must have been the scenario, rapid but also minutely detailed, that unfolded in his brain? Or else had there only been a vision of those parallel bars the whole length of the route, and the fear lest the day end with them remaining unused and put in readiness for nothing? When afterward he found himself sunk to the floor in front of me, reduced to impotence, the two images, that of the fair stranger wearing the rosette in her lapel and that of the same woman, suspended at last and tied, did the one substitute itself for the other to the point of coinciding, or was the contrast between them such as to have been the cause of that excitement which swelled his sad face? Once off the bus, after having trailed me from a short enough distance to be able to see me strolling ahead of him under the Palais arcades, having already "contacted" the epidermis of my fingers, he must have elaborated this initial sensation, extended it to the whole of my body he was concentrating upon, studied the sway of my hips, my eventual poses in the imminent situation which he knew would be entirely new to me, inconceivable and therefore, for him, all the more imperative . . . until the moment when he had no choice but to nab me inside that empty shop. How he looked, almost dazed, at my hand on the knob of the door he was preventing me from opening while the thickset one was materializing through the door in the back, that fatal door left ajar and on the other side of which the secluded staircase wound underground. Noticing an exit on the landing above and which probably gives out on to the rue Beaujolais, I turn to make a dash for it. But the shorter man, who was waiting for me on the steps, aims a blow of his hand at my fingers clutching the railing; and I, still thinking escape is possible, I pull them quickly away, redescend and—almost in reach of the door leading back into the shop, just as I, still determined to put up a fight, hit the giant in the face with my handbag, I see him go down, really, he nearly crumpled . . . when that same instant his hand slips between my garters and my flesh, takes a firm hold on my thigh, his arm wraps around my legs, he lifts me, tilts me forward over his shoulder, this happening so unexpectedly and so swiftly that I had to hang on to his neck with both hands—and then that fantastic trip down the spiral staircase to the basement. The other one, who had preceded him, was by now opening the heavy steel door beyond which lay the big room, lit by neon and with dazzling white walls. The floor was gleaming lino-leum; enormous ventilation fans started turning overhead; and in the middle of an assortment of physical training apparatuses there were some parallel bars, straps attached to them. . . . Just to think that a short while ago I was sauntering idly between the Opéra and the Théâtre Français while these bars were awaiting me here all the time! So then, fastened by the wrists, my moist hands diffusing the scent of their lotion in the air, stifling despite the ventilators, my fingernails faultless and useless . . . Without concerning them-selves in the least about my bust or bothering to take off the jacket of my gray suit, they unhook my skirt and remove it along with the rest underneath. I'm still prancing my feet, they bind each of my ankles to the uprights—and all this in silence, a silence composed of my own muteness almost attuned to the two men's, as if our pant-ings were replacing whatever words we might have exchanged here. The giant's mouth approaches one of my bound hands and I have doubled it up into a fist, he pries open my fingers, passes their ends between his lips and lingeringly tastes each of my fingernails. Then, after a pause to catch his breath, reeling on his feet, sweating, hold-ing on to the bar, he sticks out his tongue whose tip curls up in a miserable effort and only manages to slowly brush my wide-open palm. Finally though his tongue stiffens and begins its ever more rapid titillations. I still have my head turned aside. . . . Soon it is too much for me to contain myself any longer, in vain I try to raise a knee, to hide the irresistible effects with my thigh. "Then get rid of those lights!" I say in a voice that isn't mine anymore while the smaller one, planted opposite me, ostentatiously displays a visiting card and slips it into my bag. But the lights stay on and, my eyes shut, under the whirring of the fans, I abandon myself in front of these two strangers. . . . The assuagement I then feel from opening myself at last, from unpenting myself before their stares in this impossible position . . . A dull thud at my feet. I open my eyes. The giant has collapsed. The short fellow hoists him up by the shoulders and holding his sagging frame erect, leads him away. For more than a minute I remain there, bound, alone—doubtless the least pleasant moment in what I can't even call a nightmare. And it's almost with relief I see the second one reappear, slowly, hands in his pockets—a blond lad, with a crew cut, with prominent eyes, an intelligent gaze. His shirt was neat, spotless, and his hands, which he now took out of his pockets to detach me, carefully groomed; he had a silver bracelet on his left wrist. He looks the other way while I readjust my skirt, goes to fetch my handbag and bringing it to me also offers me a glass of cognac. But I slap him. Whereupon, with a single gesture, he snatches off my skirt again, stands a foot on it, puts his hands back in his pockets and, without flinching, receives another slap; and here I am, and I lose consciousness before I am able to stop. . . . What could a woman be expected to do in such a situation . . . ? Scream, obviously, bring the whole building running—in such a busy section of the city—but we, the women who rode in the Red Cross vans, on "the front lines of charity," we, the women who are now at the helm of the nation, we women who "have been around" and through too much—if ever we be fair, if ever we have retained our beauty—we can do but one thing, and that is say nothing. Make an investigation? Because of this card which reproduces . . . my fingerprints? Get to the "bottom" of it all? Just the sort of job that bungling C. at the rue des Saussaies is cut out to handle? Nonsense. But, one of these days, to revisit the scene, to stroke those parallel bars with my hands, those bars where my hands were so firmly bound . . . that's another story. This special occasion for feeling my own self from the instant I jumped aboard that bus until the one, in the basement, when I woke up to find myself spread-eagled and shaken, this occasion is now neither more nor less than the bow which sends my thoughts soaring high above this lazy afternoon. What delicious croissants they serve here! How soothing, those fountains splashing under the sycamores! How exquisite this city is as it glides gently downhill!

LE PONT

If Klossowski humiliates the modern, "masculine" woman to bring her back to what he feels is her own traditional femininity, André Pieyre de Mandiargues goes much farther in debasing the dominant type of woman. In his story "Le Pont," in *Le Musée Noir* (Paris: Robert Laffont, 1946), he presents a fantasy concerning a restaurant-like establishment in which a number of young women play billiards against the male clients. They are so skilled in this "man's game" that they beat the men almost without exception. If, however, a man succeeds in beating one of them, the girl is his for an hour to do with as he pleases.

Polished wood, shiny brass, and green draperies—the interiors of the women's billiards parlors are almost always identical. The spotless appearance of these places, similar to that found aboard warships, affords a surprising contrast with their exteriors, but then these taverns are rigorously closed and appearances are kept up only within. At the back of the main room, under a staircase leading to the first floor, is a counter where drinks are served. The bargemen and lock keepers are very fond of automatons, and to amuse them there is a cuckoo clock to go with the cheap billiards tables, while for the more luxurious ones there is a player piano with mechanical figurines. It stands glittering near the counter like a rack of gilded rifles on which costumed mice run back and forth. The customary tables—from four to ten of them, according to the standing of the establishment—are surrounded by benches of rough oak which isolate them from each other, yet leave enough space so that the players will not be hindered by the feet of the men who sit waiting their turns or merely watching. The raw surface is strongly lit by drop lamps in the shape of many-turreted castles—in the shape of dreams—and these also shed their light on the heavy, theatrical wasps whom the house provides as adversaries: girls of the tallest variety, whose buskins make them seem even taller, and who wear a skin-tight costume circled with alternating red and yellow stripes like those on the sign outside. The color of their hair ranges from wood-shavings blonde to bleached brown, and they wear it in a tight knot coiled high up on the back of the neck. The balls carom merrily about, for while the men are in search of prey, the girls defend their freedom skillfully. Indeed, the law of the billiards parlor is that if a man can beat one of the girls, she shall have her hands fettered behind her back and be delivered to him to do as he wishes for one hour. However, these creatures are so skilled at a game to which they devote every minute of their lives, that there is little hope of beating one unless you manage to catch her fancy or get her drunk. As regards this last point, children frivolously gotten up as carnival butterflies attend to the customers' orders, and there are always three or four of them to be seen panting back and forth between the tables and the counters, beating their taffeta wings as if to fluff up the head of foam on the sweet beer that squirts out from under the lids on the huge mugs which they set down on a table corner, within reach of some overly skillful girl.

Damien would not soon forget the only game he ever won, nor his opponent's faintly piglike face, her broad nose which was turned up slightly, as though from a punch, her little, sunken eyes, the corners of her mouth, wet with spittle, or the down on her upper lip, always moist with foam. As she watched him, her tights betrayed the coarse, greedy laughter which her features were holding back, and time after time she missed easy opportunities to chalk up points. When he finally won the game, the commotion was all the louder as the house had not witnessed a male victory in nearly a month. They put a special roll on the piano—the factory hymn—and the defiant chorus of ventriloquial lock keepers joined in immediately. Then, bowed beneath the strains of this incongruous song, the manager of the billiards parlor came forth: a frail, pious-looking man whom one would expect to have seen quailing before those massive nymphs rather than seizing hold of the defeated girl as he did, whipping her wrists behind her back and shackling them with a pair of ash-covered handcuffs which he took from a peg over the hearth where ham was hung to smoke. When the victor's hand closed around the key to that iron paraphernalia, the girl was thrust ahead of him and she staggered with laughter as she climbed the stairs, while everyone tried to dash the contents of their mugs between the banisters and onto her calves. The rest took place in an attic room, with a ceiling so low that our hero could have written on it with a wet finger if he had felt the urge, and a bed so low that it resembled a big cushion flung on the floor in front of a fireplace disgraced with decrepit dolls under crystal bell jars. The best part of that tasty idyll was that despite all his companion's promises, Damien could not be persuaded to unlock the handcuffs. Entreat, insult him, as she would, he solemnly lay the key on the dome covering the most gnarled little imp of wax and dusty silk, then sat calmly down beside the girl and gazed earnestly at the figure lying in the hollow of the eiderdown, at the full curves which threatened, here and there, to burst the beer-soaked tights, and at the sickly pallor of the throat beneath a face which expressed first disappointment, then hate, and finally crumpled up with sobs.

The woman is totally destroyed by the man's refusal to take advantage of the rules of the house and possess the girl he has beaten in the game. He refuses to touch her, but simply sits and looks at her with disdain, watching the destruction of her self-esteem as a woman. It is important to keep in mind that in these stories the humiliation and degradation of one or the other principal figures in the fantasy is what matters. Any physical punishment inflicted upon the victim is only incidental to the primary bondage or humiliation theme.

Quite different is the situation with regard to the typical flagellation fantasy. Here the erotic charge derives directly from the mental images conjured up by the physical punishment, and the humiliation theme recedes into the background, although it may provide an added element of erotic attraction.

Flagellation fantasies abound in the erotic literature of almost all nations but are rare in Chinese and still rarer in Indian erotica. The reason for this is, undoubtedly, that at the peak production of erotic literature in Europe (the eighteenth and nineteenth century), physical punishment in the school and in the home was generally accepted. Frequently, these punishment situations were associated with sexual arousal, both in the child and in the adult, so that entire generations became conditioned to corporal punishment as an erotic event. Today, as corporal punishment is virtually unknown in America and Scandinavia and is rapidly going out of fashion in the rest of Europe as well, flagellation has become less of a factor in contemporary sexual behavior. The recent erotic literature produced in Sweden and Denmark is almost totally devoid of flagellation scenes (unless it is written for export).

ANONYMOUS FLAGELLATION FANTASY

Still it is well to understand the special attraction which flagellation fantasies can have for individuals with that conditioning. We have, therefore, chosen a flagellation episode from a hitherto untranslated German typescript from the 1910's which is, perhaps, less gory than most flagellation fantasies, of which there are all too many in literature.

The episode below deals with the punishment of a maid, Emma, by her employer, Madame Marga, in the presence of the latter's lover. The scene takes place in the bathroom.

"Emma, pull up your bathrobe to the hips, spread your legs, and bend forward."

The girl flushed deeply, but did not dare oppose Madame Marga's clear instructions. There now appeared before the eyes of the already excited man a pair of tight, nude legs, smooth round thighs, and—growing out of them—two beautiful bouncing lobes of the behind, all of this framed by the bathrobe which was raised to the midriff at one end and by dainty little leather houseshoes at the other, out of which rose a pair of slender ankles, supporting the fuller structure above. Karl Gerhard had not expected such exquisite treasures beneath the unassuming dresses of the maid. His fingers were already itching at the thought of letting the cane dance upon the nude female flesh before him.

The girl stood as she was told, spreading her legs and bending forward. That way, the thighs which had up to then been kept together, appeared in all their fleshy splendor and the two firm globes of the round behind stood out as if they were asking for the cane.

After the girl has received some caning in this position, Madame Marga has another idea:

"So, now bend over the edge of the tub. It may be a bit uncomfortable, but that doesn't matter."

The girl obeyed. She lay down on the edge of the tub with her tummy, supported herself with her hands on the floor of the tub, and stretched her legs backward so that the tips of her toes were touching the floor.

Madame Marga now reached underneath the girl's bathrobe and pulled it up so far that the whole lower part of the girl lay bare. Then she stepped up close to her and pushed down with both hands on the small of her back, giving her friend a signal to continue the chastisement.

Again the blows fell smack, smack, smack on the girl's stout behind, again Emma cried out in desperation, again she tried to raise herself up in order to get away from her tormentors, but it was all in vain—Madame Marga's firm grasp on her back kept her down.

In her desperation she was kicking her legs, lifting them alternately high up, while spreading them far apart at the same time because of the pain, so that Karl Gerhard had ample opportunity to continuously enjoy the unhampered view of her most intimate parts . . . well into the cleft between her ample thighs.

No sooner is the chastisement ended and the girl sent to her room than the two lovers get together and express their excitement with one another.

There is no point going further into flagellation fantasies, since they are all more or less variations on the same theme. However, we have come across some sadomasochistic fantasies which may shed some new light on these little understood aspects of sadomasochism. Certain anal-sadistic fantasies are of special psychological and sexological interest: *violent* anal intercourse or the *painful* introduction of objects (or animals) into the anus, the forced administration of enemas, etc.

HELENA

The first such story, an anonymous work entitled *Helena* ("Poitiers: Éditions R.S.U.," n.d.), concerns a young woman who, after World War I, has fallen into the hands of a Chinese erotomane. In the scene which follows, her anus has been found too small and is about to be enlarged "in the usual manner."

A servant untied the woman. She freed her numb arms and gazed in horror at her monstrously elongated nipples; already other servants were laying her out on a dark-green hemp carpet. Next they slipped a little velvet cushion of the same color under her buttocks. Soon the woman's arms were stretched out and fastened to the floor with pieces of rope, her ankles were again clamped into the manacles hanging from the ends of the straps and these were hoisted up, spreading her legs apart as far as possible and raising them almost vertically off the floor; thus, the rump was once again distended, with the cunt and the asshole thrusting forth from amber flesh.

A servant came forward, carrying a little crystal vase filled with warm milk and ending in a rubber tube with a nozzle, which she thrust into the anus; it sank in all the way up to the ivory neck. The servant raised the vase and gradually the milk flowed into the warm bowels. A few moments later she extracted the nozzle, making sure that a few drops of milk ran down the folds of the little rose, and then she withdrew.

A young Annamese boy came forward, carrying a long, fat snake coiled around his arm. Helena shuddered with repulsion at the sight of the shiny and sticky reptile as it stirred slightly on the boy's arm.

"Don't be frightened, darling, it can't hurt you. Its mouth is sewn shut and in any case it isn't poisonous. You'll see how pretty it is!"

One could sense that Tai was quivering with a strange excitement; the lights were dimmed in the room and only a pale green glow lit up the woman's intimate parts.

With a precise gesture, the servant thrust a little ivory spindle all the way into Helena's sex so that the labia closed over it leaving only a white disk visible at the mouth of the little pink cunt.

The Annamese boy lay the reptile on the carpet with its head toward the woman's ass, and he knelt down behind it; every gaze in the room was focused on the reptile who raised its head, looked around, and saw in the pool of light the orifice in the white flesh; it slithered forward until its head touched the drop of milk which had fallen on the green cushion and tried to lap it up with its sealed mouth. Failing this, it darted forward and lay its head on the anus dripping with warm milk; it lolled there for a moment, and the woman let out a scream, bucking and struggling against her bonds.

"Richard! Richard! No! No more! I don't want to . . . Richard! Richard!"

All in vain. The silent man sat clutching a sachet of opium and staring at his wife's naked belly, not lifting a finger, not uttering a word.

She gave a helpless sob and began to moan continually.

For a moment the snake was panic-stricken and raised its head, peering into the shadows; but the Annamese boy drew a flute from his loincloth and began to play. The snake looked at him and was calmed. Its head returned to the orifice, attracted by the odor of the milk. The first contact sent Helena into horrible convulsions, but soon she fell back in a state of collapse.

Now the snake was really enticed. Drawing itself up, it gave a thrust, and its pointed head slid into the elastic anus, which spread apart and admitted an inch of the sticky reptile. The snake stopped a moment, then drove forward again and its head could be seen to slip into the bowels and disappear altogether. The Annamese boy stopped playing, took a needle, and pricked the reptile's tail, making it writhe. With its tail whipping about, the snake gathered itself up and once again its body slid farther into the anus, which dilated as it yielded to the snake's frantic efforts. Now, however, the fattest part of the snake's head was trying to force its way in and the hole seemed incapable of further expansion.

The Annamite pricked the snake again. There was a writhing movement, the body began to swell, and the audience saw the opening enlarge still further as the animal made its way inward. Thus, four times in succession, the audience, their eyes filled with sadistic joy, saw the reptile stretch the narrow mouth and slip several inches into the muscular sheath of bowels which by now formed a circle over three inches in diameter.

The woman was writhing from the horrible friction and the painful stretching of her anus; the boy pricked the snake one last time, but it no longer seemed to react. Presumably it was strangling, but still it writhed inside: the woman and her convulsions and her heaving stomach testified to the struggle of the slowly asphyxiating snake in the contracted stomach.

The boy glanced at Hang-tou who nodded, and pulled on the snake's body, which was dripping with slime and milk. The head popped out of the bowels. The anus closed again and the woman stopped moaning.

This fantasy illustrates well the theory of anal fixation as Freud and the early analysts formulated it. Such individuals fail to make the transition from the normal anal-erotic stage of psychosexual development in childhood to the final genital stage. They remain, consequently, more interested in anal activities and anal intercourse than in genital eroticism. Too early or too severe toilet training is very much involved in the origin of such fixations.

SELMA

Certain specific childhood experiences may also lead to anal fixations—for instance, the trauma of forced enemas, the insertion of suppositories, the treatment for intestinal parasites (which can be accompanied by considerable anal irritation and itching), or any number of similar causes. It is therefore to be expected that anal fantasies should have found expression in erotic literature, and, indeed, entire underground novels, running into several hundred pages each, have been devoted to them. We shall reproduce here only a portion of one of these, which concerns the sadistic administration of a forced enema, with the attending humiliation of the victim, together with the strange secondary fantasy of the enema producing in the woman a false pregnancy. The anonymous book is entitled *Selma* ("Tours: Editions S.U.D.A.," n.d.), and it contains anticlerical elements, for the setting is a convent and some of the characters are monks.

Brother Sebastian drew near holding a container of water to which a faucet and a red rubber hose were attached. Brother Laurent held out a case containing an assortment of hard rubber nozzles, and the

Superior selected a huge one, one as big as any penis. It was composed first of an egg-shaped section two inches long by an inch and a half thick, then a narrow neck, followed by another egg four and one-half inches long by two inches thick, another narrow neck, and a ball two inches in diameter which ended in a cylinder an inch in diameter and two and one-half inches long: a valve was incorporated to this tube. The monk fitted the hose to the nozzle.

Brother Sebastian made Monique stand up again, so that once more she was bending forward, with her thighs and buttocks spread wide apart, and her hands gripping the ends of the great crucifix.

The Superior stepped close to Monique and, turning to the monks, said to them: "Brothers, your sister has performed all the sacraments of penance; now may your psalms accompany the purification by water of her entrails!"

He bent over the rump, which was still red from the violent flagellation, and lay the tip of the nozzle against the oft-violated anus. He gave a thrust. Obediently, the flesh gave way and admitted the first egg, then closed around the first neck; Monique whimpered softly as this contact awakened her senses. However, the Superior gave another thrust, and the huge egg that followed stretched the anus more brutally. Monique began to moan and writhe with pain. The two monks held her down. The rest slid in slowly, the pink edges of the little mouth licked at the hard rubber crawling up the smooth surface, climbing that steep slope. The flesh stretched, reached the top of the rise, seemed to coast inch by inch over the top of the huge, hard shape, then slid together again, swallowing the rubber monster until it reached the second neck. Panting and full of anguish, Monique felt the huge contraption slide into her stomach. She moaned softly, and her temples throbbed.

The Superior gazed upon the lascivious picture before his eyes, admiring the suppleness of the bottom-hole; then he gave the nozzle another push and, once again, watched the anus stretch to allow the narrower ball to enter the entrails and disappear, while the mouth closed again, thrusting the nozzle deep into the belly. The flesh pressed tightly around the hard rubber, of which only an inch or so protruded now from the buttocks.

The Superior stood up, shivering from the effort. The light fell on the lewd picture of that naked rump and the protruding tube; the bright red rubber afforded a striking contrast with the white flesh and the silky gray film of the stockings ringed round with delicate garters.

Monique breathed deeply and the horrible pain in her anus gradually subsided.

The Superior opened the valve halfway. The monks' voices rose in a psalm, and they sat back in their stalls to watch the girl squirm as the cool, purifying water gushed into the depths of her stomach. Slowly, the water level dropped in the container and all could easily imagine the cool liquid spouting forth inside the sticky entrails, swelling the stomach.

Monique's rump began to writhe. Her stomach grew heavy and swollen with the pressure of the water; she squeezed her buttocks, tensed her muscles in an attempt to stop the flow of liquid: all in vain. Her spasmodic contractions failed to compress the nozzle and the water inexorably swelled her entrails.

At times, Monique would strain her bowels in an attempt to drive the water back: all in vain. The tubular end of the nozzle was so thick that it prevented the water from seeping out around the sides. Then, under the pressure of the water distending her stomach, a throbbing pain rose up inside Monique and she moaned louder and began to writhe. She pressed her legs together, spread them apart, and shook her rump in an effort to dislodge the nozzle, but her efforts were wasted. Firmly lodged in the narrow orifice, it kept pouring the liquid into the stomach, and the stomach swelled and swelled. Now her moans grew increasingly raucous. At a signal from the Superior, Brother Sebastian shut the faucet. Brother Laurent brought forth a polished ivory egg three inches long and two and one-half inches wide at the base: attached to it was a little cord made of strong hemp.

Both of them leaned over the rump and spread the buttocks, and while Brother Laurent jiggled the nozzle slightly and then withdrew it quickly, Brother Sebastian pressed the egg against the anus and, before a single drop of liquid could escape, thrust it sharply into the rectum which swallowed it up completely, so that only the little cord was left dangling out of the narrow orifice.

Brother Laurent untied Monique's hands and raised her up, then spun her around to face his brothers, revealing, in all its splendid nudity the protuberant belly swollen by the water. It jutted out over the blonde pubis so that the navel seemed to have stretched.

Selma pushed her toward the little lamp facing the astonished monks and said to her, "Your belly! Your belly! See how lovely it is! You look like you were pregnant. Show it to us . . . show it to us better than that! Show us that it's alive! Dance! Dance! Dance!"

She lashed the buttocks viciously. Monique gave a start and the water sloshed about in her bowels with a muffled sound. Selma belabored the buttocks with three more lashes, as she raged: "Dance! Dance! I want you to dance!"

With a moan, the cowed Monique complied. Raising her arms over her head, thrusting her massive bosom even farther forward, she began slowly to sway, shaking her belly like an Arab dancing girl.

It was a choice spectacle to see those plump, fleshy forms glistening in the soft lamplight, forms that stood out even more vividly against the shadowy background. You could hear Monique's sighs, and the sound of the water inside her flesh.

The eroticization of enemas is understandable as a form of sexual conditioning. The anal sphincter is equipped with sensitive nerve endings, and the introduction of an enema nozzle could be experienced as pleasurably sexual. The water pressure in the bowels, as well as its release, can also be accompanied by pleasurable sensations. However, the additional element needed to produce the kind of fixation on anal eroticism illustrated in the above story must be the association of bowel evacuation, anal hygiene, etc., with other sexual elements. If, for instance, the adults in the child's environment create a sexually-toned atmosphere surrounding bowel evacuation, such sexual connotation is readily established in the child's mind. But the association between anal and genital stimuli can also be purely accidental, and if re-enforced through frequent repetition, it can likewise lead to anal-erotic fixations. At the same time, strong sadomasochistic elements are never lacking in anal eroticism, since the anal-erotic phase in the child's development is, as Freud has pointed out, sadomasochistic by nature. In the adult, such fixation therefore represents a fixation on or regression to a pre-genital phase of psychosexual development. This does not mean, of course, that anal-erotic and sadomasochistic elements ought to be ideally absent in normal adult sexuality. On the contrary, they form an essential and necessary element in all sexuality, on the human as on the animal level. However, in normal sexuality, anal and sadomasochistic elements are properly integrated and assimilated into the total psychosexual structure of the individual, rather than being an absolute pre-condition for his erotic response or the predominant feature of his sexuality.

8

Incest Fantasies

One of the best books for the study of incest fantasies (which abound in erotic literature) is a little late-Victorian tome *The Loves of Venus: or The Young Wife's Confession, a true tale from real life* (London, 1881). The title page states that it was "privately printed for the use of the Irish Land Leaguers."

The book consists of several interlocking stories written in the form of letters, all with incest as the dominant theme and some homosexual and flagellation fantasies thrown in for good measure. The book contains a curious apology for incest, giving all kinds of philosophical and historical reasons why incest should be permitted and even encouraged. Of course, the treatise does not face any of the revelant social and psychological problems, and is a typical one-sided rationalization such as one finds frequently in pornographic writings.

A young man, Fred, marries and writes of it to his sister, with whom he has had a long incestuous relationship. It transpires that Fred's bride was no virgin, but had been seduced first by her brother and then by her uncle with whom the two orphaned children had been living. The husband, himself much addicted to the joys of incest with his sister, readily forgives his bride, who promises to give him, in turn, all the freedom he wants, without getting jealous. As proof, she herself prepares the chambermaid, Sophy, to have an affair with Fred, and joins them as a third parity. (She has had previous experience along these lines, for in her uncle's home she and her brother and uncle had often had sex together.) Now the young wife, Ada, introduces her brother, Ferdie, to her husband, and the three, joined by Sophy as a fourth party, have heterosexual and homosexual experiences together.

The story opens with Fred's letter to his sister Frederica (note the similarity of the names Fred, Frederica, and Ferdie, which are almost interchangeable, as are, indeed, the sex roles of all concerned):

No apology is needed from me for getting married, and deserting a sister I always loved more than my life, a sister who sacrificed her honor, and everything we hold sacred to satisfy my incestuous lust, a sister whose loving wantonness would have always kept me with her, only being an elder son in a family of position it was absolutely necessary for me to keep up the succession for fear that some day our hated relatives might reap the benefits of the fortune left by our ancestors.

You, too, my dearest pet sister, being engaged to a special pal of mine, will soon be solaced for the loss of your dear Fred. Still we may confidently live in hope that some day Frederica and Fred will again have a chance of feeling all the joys of love, which an incestuous connection imparts to an exceptional degree. Forbidden fruit is always so sweet.

Fred reminds his sister of their parting night on the eve of his wedding: "As we sat in the library of the old home at Cunnusburg, how with tears in your eyes you kissed me in such an impassioned manner that I had to fuck you a fourth time, to the imminent risk of not being able to do my duty to Ada the next evening. How even then you would take a parting suck of my enervated pego, and again raised him in all his pride of life, till I spent even a fifth time, and you swallowed every drop, as you said, that the very essence of my being might go down to your heart."

Following a poetic insert about another wedding night, which Fred uses to prepare his own bride, we get to Ada's confession.

"You know I'm an orphan," she began, "and that I and my brother Ferdie have lived with our guardian, Uncle Harry, since our parents were lost on the City of Boston steamer, which was never heard of after leaving America, and you know uncle is still quite a young man, a year or two under forty; but, darling Fred, you must promise, before I go further with my tale, to forgive everyone I may mention, and remember too, dearest, that Uncle Harry is so rich, and besides when he handed you my dowery, did he not promise you another £20,000" (and perhaps may get it out of her uncle before the stipulated five years of kindness to Ada).

"It is hardly four years since I went to live at uncle's place in Hertforshire . . . Ferdie used to come into my bedroom (which was next to his) every night to kiss me before going to bed, and I soon began to notice that his embraces and kisses were getting more impassioned every day. One evening in particular he seemed as if he would never take his departure, so that when I had removed my dress, modesty prevented me continuing to disrobe until he was gone, 'Now Ferdie, one more kiss and be off, I want to go to bed!'

"He was sitting by my side on the edge of the bed, and suddenly clasping me to his bosom, glued his lips to mine in such a warm sucking kiss, that I blushed and tried to get away from him. 'For shame, sir! You shan't come into my room again!' I gasped, almost choked by his kissing, as I found one of his daring hands on my thigh under my skirts.

" 'I must, I will. Never mind me, Ada, I want to see if you are like a picture I have seen; would you like to look at it, darling?'

"He spoke excitedly, and I was too astonished to answer, my skirts were thrown up, and he put his fingers in my little crack, which made me feel so funny, and then forcing my thighs apart, began to kiss me there in such a way, tickling the little button you know of with the tip of his tongue so lasciviously, that I was lost at once, and quite gave myself up to the delicious sensations aroused in me for the first time."

One favor deserving another, Ada performs fellatio on her brother (which she had quickly learned by looking at the pictures that Ferdie was talking about), after which the brother invites her to choose any of the positions he had shown her in the album that he had meanwhile gone to fetch.

No sooner have they finished than Ada hears a suspicious noise, as if someone was sighing or breathing hard, and she immediately suspects that it might be Uncle Harry. It turns out that she is correct, for the uncle has indeed been spying on the two, but far from reproaching her, as she had feared, he shows himself as the classical permissive father figure in pornographic works, and is ready to forgive all, if she and Ferdie are willing to include him henceforth in their nightgames.

"While he was speaking his hand wandered under my clothes, and already got possession of my slightly fledged crack.

" 'What a beautiful little plump thing you have, Ada, how it excited me to see you and Ferdie kissing each other's affairs, I felt quite overcome, and had to frig myself, which made me sigh when I came, that was what you heard, darling!'

" 'What is frigging, uncle?' I asked in my simplicity.

" 'Rubbing my cock up and down with my hand, till I make the seed spurt, will my little love do it for her uncle?' he asked.

" 'Anything to give you pleasure, you love us so I know, shall I put my hand into your trousers and find him?'

" 'Yes darling,' he replied, kissing me ardently, 'you couldn't please me better.'

"I slipped down on my knees, and with trembling hands unbuttoned his trousers; there was a great hard thing under his shirt, and I soon exposed a fine manly weapon about nine inches long and thick in proportion.

"How proudly it stood, as I measured its length by grasping it one hand over the other, drawing the skin downwards, till the fiery red head was fully exposed, projecting quite two inches beyond what my little hands could hold of its length.

"My first impulse was to imprint a gentle kiss on its beautiful top, my tongue shot out instinctively to tickle and give him pleasure.

"He gave a deep, long-drawn sigh, as he murmured, 'Go on, Ada, my little love, kiss and rub me both at once, you will soon give me most exquisite pleasure! Ah—oh—go on—suck me—rub me quick—take it all in your mouth—don't be afraid, darling! Ah—that's grand—what a love—oh, oh, oh—there!' he ejaculated as I went on, and at the last I felt the same sudden spasm shoot along the shaft as I was handling him, and my mouth was flooded with his warm creamy emission, which would have choked me if I had not greedily swallowed it all, yes, and enjoyed it too, dearie!"

There follows another story within a story, this time about a certain Monsieur St. Roque and his wife (who was cold and unresponsive until Mademoiselle Sappho joined their sex life). All of this serves as an introduction to having the maid Sophy participate with Fred and Ada. Fred also has Ada invite her brother Ferdie to join the trio, thus making a quartet.

I loved Ferdie soon quite as much as his sister, and almost every night our first program would be for him to have his sister, they are both small but so beautifully proportioned, and seemed so thoroughly to enjoy fucking each other, that it was the greatest treat I could have to see them in the act. I would sit with Sophy on my knee, as I tickled her clitoris with my fingers, making her spend over and over again, as I would talk to her thus:

"Isn't it lovely, dear, to see such a pretty pair in action? Look at Ferdie's beautiful prick as it slips in and out of his sister! Don't you wish you had a brother to fuck you, Sophy? Now they're coming; look, look, how they strain, and shove to get in even another quarter of an inch. It's over, my God, how they must have spent, look at it oozing and dripping on the bed. Frig me quick, I'm coming now. Ah, you darling, how delightfully your hand does it; kiss me, give me your tongue quick!"

My favorite plan was to get Ferdie's bottom well spitted on my prick, as he sat on my lap, whilst his sister and Sophy gamahuched him by turns, till we both came again at the same time. Another way was to lay both the girls on the bed, on their sides, face to face, then I would straddle over them so that my prick could be kissed by both of them at once, whilst I also had my head buried between their bellies, with a cunt on each side of my nose, then Ferdie would get into me behind, and altogether we carried out such a voluptuous fancy that on more than one occasion the excess of excitement was greater than I could bear, and I fairly fainted in the act of emission.

Following this, we have the amusing story of an old Scottish brother-and-sister pair, Mr. and Miss McLachlan.

They had two communicating bedrooms, as Mr. McLachlan said his sister was liable to frights in the night, and could not sleep unless she was close at hand to him, and able to run into his room when a sudden fright came.

She was curiously excited to find out more about them, especially as one or other of the beds always seemed unusually tumbled, and once she found several spots and smears of blood on the lower sheet.

The weather was very warm, and Mr. McLachlan used to have his bedroom window partially open, although the blind was always drawn down, so as their rooms were on the first floor, it occurred to Sophy that the gardener's light ladder, which he used for trimming the grape vines, etc., would just enable her to see all that was going on. Bob, the gardener, being her sweetheart, she easily persuaded him to place the ladder for her, and mind it while she went up to peep at the old people. To further her purpose she had fixed the blind so that when pulled down it would just leave about half an inch of space at the bottom, and so afford every facility for both seeing and hearing everything from the outside.

It was rather a dark night when she and Bob put their plan in operation, and this is her description of the scene.

Mr. McLachlan is seated in an easy chair, apparently absorbed in reading several letters, which the old gentleman would kiss as he finished reading each of them.

Enter his sister on tiptoe, till she stood behind the chair glaring at the letters he was so taken up with, grinding her teeth, and shaking a birch rod over his head.

At last she snatches a letter, "Ha, ha! Caught you again, sir, reading that minx's letters, have you not promised me over and over again that you will give her up, you faithless wretch! I'll teach you to love any one but your sister! Eh—you're frightened, are you? Take down your breeches, sir, this moment."

The brother looks awfully frightened, but she takes him by the wrist, and leads him to the bed, and I could see the old girl had only her chemise and drawers on under her dressing gown. She tied both hands by the wrists, with a piece of cord which depended from the top frame of the four-poster, then one ankle to the right and the other to the left leg of the bed, so that he was most comfortably fixed up, indeed to judge by his looks he really dreaded her, I heard him frequently appeal for mercy.

"Oh, Maria, you won't now, pray don't, I can't stand it, you cut me up so the night before last, do forgive me, and I'll burn all the letters."

"You would, would you, sir; how often, James, have I caught you reading them, after the same broken promises? Do you still correspond with that designing girl? You know she only wants your money. I'll birch you out of that fancy, my boy, till you again love poor Maria. You shall never marry while I can hold a rod, sir, I only wish I had the girl here, her bum should smart, I'll warrant!"

She now pulled his breeches down, and tucked up his shirt so as to expose a fairly plump rump, which she patted admiringly, then her face seemed to get stern, and reaching the rod off the dressing table she again began to lecture him as she applied the twigs vigorously, so much so that he fairly screamed for mercy, "I'll never think of her again, Maria, indeed I won't, you know I love you so! You have such a sweet gray-haired cunt."

"What insult! How dare you say that to your sister. You shall get me at once Mrs. Allen's Hair Restore, Rowland's Kalydor, Breidenbach's Macassarine, and Ross's Extract of Cantharides. Ha, ha, you shall pay to make my hair its natural color, sir! But now I think of it, I'll get a Ross's Nose Machine for your poor old cock, it's awfully down in the world, and will only stand for little featherless chits, such as you correspond with."

All the while her cuts were something painful to see. . . . His bottom was all over deep red, fiery looking weals and scratches, and I could even see drops of blood oozing from the lacerations here and there; he seemed to writhe and twist about in a peculiar manner, as if he wanted to attract her attention, so much so that I soon caught glimpses of all he possessed.

"Look," whispered Bob in my ear, "did you ever see such a teaser as the old fellow's got, and as gray as a badger, by Jove!"

I nudged him with my elbow to keep quiet.

"You're showing me your impudence, are you, sir? It doesn't want a nose machine now, have I brought it to love its Maria, then?" said the old woman, as she first threw away her worn out rod, then quickly untying one ankle she turned him round, and knelt down and caressed his tremendous affair.

"How I love you now, darling!" she said, handling and kissing his prick, till I expected he would spend in her eye, but she was too clever to go too far, so loosening his other ankle and hands, she slipped off her dressing gown and sprang on the bed, whilst he threw off everything but his shirt, and was onto her in a moment.

"My James, my love, come to my arms, you do love me now," she said excitedly, opening her legs at the same time, and giving us a fair glance at a fat pair of thighs, at the top of which we could see a lovely pouting cunny, but as gray as possible. One of her hands directed his rampant prick to the longing receptacle, whilst her other arm thrown round his neck, drew his face to hers, and they indulged in a most loving kiss at the same moment, as he was fairly sheathed to the hilt, and she threw a fine pair of legs over his buttocks.

The story ends with an apologia for the practice of incest.

Adam's children must have married brothers and sisters, and their parent himself must have been something more than incestuous if the Bible is to be believed, for Eve was even part of himself, bone of his bone, and flesh of his flesh; did not Abraham have his own sister Sarah for wife, from whom descended God's own special people, and even the Messiah of the Christian World, in fact we are all the offspring of incest, or the globe would never have been peopled.

The ancient Egyptian Ptolemys always had their sisters for wives.

The wickedness of incest is a manufactured article made a sin, not by God, but by the restlessness of mankind, ever on the move to make fresh offenses, out of harmless things, and continually piling up the burden of our government which the growing instinct of liberty in the present generation will soon, I hope, sweep away. . . .

There are many who consider incest such a dreadful crime, but I would just ask such persons what can be more natural than for brothers and sisters to love each other, and allow all those freedoms which only strangers who may happen to marry them are supposed to have a right to.

How could I help loving you to distraction, my darling Frederica, it always seemed to me the most natural thing in the world that I should possess all those charms of my beautiful sister, which had ripened under my very eyes as it were. You always seemed my property, and why should I have left for a stranger the fruit which had, as it were, grown under my own eyes?

As with many other socially disapproved forms of sexual behavior, incest is not as infrequent as some people might think it to be, nor necessarily harmful from a mental health point of view. However, because in Western society the community and the family generally disapprove of all forms of incestuous relations, the attendant guilt feelings and social consequences can be highly destructive.

As the Kinsey studies have shown, incest in our society seems to be most frequent among siblings or between father and daughter, and least frequent between mother and son. It is also known from crosscultural studies that in those societies which allow for certain forms of incest, there are no visible ill effects from it, physically or mentally. In other words, the effect on the individual and the family depends largely on the social attitudes surrounding these incidents, rather than on the incidents themselves.

THE MODERN EVELINE

Another novel which revolves almost entirely around the theme of incest is *The Modern Eveline* (our text is from an edition published in London, 1904, in three volumes). The core of the story is the incestuous love between Eveline and her father, into which enters at times also her brother, but only tangentially.

Leaving aside the plot and the many subplots of the novel (some of which are interesting), we will deal with the incestuous fantasies involved. During a carriage ride, Eveline and her father speak openly for the first time of their erotic attraction for each other.

On this occasion it was nearly dark before we returned. We had enjoyed a very snug and confidential drive. His arm was passed round my waist and his right hand toyed as usual with mine. I leaned my head on his shoulder. My warm breath fanned his cheek. His eyes looked into mine. They were fine eyes on ordinary occasions. I fancied now they were full of passion. He kissed me hotly on the lips.

"My darling Eveline, you are cold. Your neck is uncovered."

He essayed to clasp my seal jacket closer. His hand wandered to my bosom. There it stopped.

"Poor little girl, she is too good, too beautiful to be cold when I am by to warm her. I will not drive to the club. I will return with you."

He tightened his grasp of my figure. He renewed his caresses.

"Dearest papa! If you knew all that your little Eveline thinks of you! How she values your love, and your kisses. She has never known much affection before. Now you are with me, all is changed —all is happy."

He turned still more. His breast beat upon mine. Our lips met in a long delicious kiss. He was half beside himself with passionate desire. I was fully as much entranced. The utmost disorder reigned in our embrace—in our posture. His hand trembled violently as he thrust it within my dress and grasped my bosom.

"Oh, my child! How beautiful are you! How magnificent already is your development! What a lovely bust!"

Our faces would have betrayed us had anyone suddenly appeared. They were scarlet with the wildest desire. I dare not give it another name. I noticed we were nearing home. I cautioned Sir Edward. He recovered himself with precipitancy.

We understood each other now. A silent confidence had been sown which would bear its fruits hereafter.

At the beginning of Volume III (Volume II is taken up with other matters), father and daughter are discussing her impending marriage, a prospect which understandably does not overjoy Eveline: "I do not anticipate any pleasure from my married state—not in the sense my darling papa can bestow it. I look forward to it with disgust rather than with satisfaction. I feel very dejected on the subject." To which her father replies, "Listen to me, Eveline. Your nature requires sexual excitement. You know it as well as I do. It is medicine to you."

In keeping with this prescription, the father promises to arrange meanwhile "something especially nice" for her—"something large and solid—stiff and strong!" And it turns out that the surprise is a date with a particularly well-endowed deaf-mute, which will reduce the danger of gossip. At this point the father's identification with the daughter is made plain—he wishes to experience vicariously her sexual pleasures: "To see you experience the height of sensual pleasure will be to me also a supreme excitement. We will roll in ecstasy. Our senses shall float in a world of pleasure."

There are, indeed, quite a few men who are able to identify so intensely with women's sex feelings that they depend for their own sexual happiness almost entirely on the response of their female partners. These men are frequently regarded by women as the best lovers, since they intuitively understand the female sex response and know how to evoke it effectively. They also take vicarious pleasure in those erotic affairs of the women in their lives in which they are not directly involved and are consequently relatively free of jealousy. They are stimulated by the fantasy of the woman's emotions, thoughts, and physical sensations not only with regard to themselves, but also with regard to other men. The focus of the fantasy and identification in these cases is with the *woman* and not the other man. Therefore, to speak as some clinicians have done, of "latent homosexuality" to explain this kind of eroticism, seems to miss the point.

The psychology involved in this sex identification applies to women as well. In another episode from the same volume, the father has set up a date for the daughter with three young men. "Tonight, Eveline," says her father, "in accordance with your wish, I have arranged our little *divertissement*. We start at nine precisely. You are still determined on the attempt? Not afraid, eh? little woman, of this double encounter?" To which Eveline replies, "I am ready, dear papa. Indeed, I long for the fun. We will do all we talked of. You will be near. You will look on and enjoy it too, will you not? Oh, it will be delicious if I only know you are enjoying yourself through me! That our ideas are so mixed and interchanged."

When Eveline marries, her brother comes to her after the ceremony just as she is fixing herself to join the wedding reception.

I was still before the glass. Five minutes had not yet gone since my entry. Already there was a tap at the door. I rose and opened it. My brother Percy pushed his way in. He immediately closed and locked the door again.

"Now I shall have at least a private view."

"What do you mean, you naughty boy?"

"Oh, it's no use riding the high horse with me, little countess! Your ladyship will please descend to the level of ordinary life."

He had seized me by the wrist; his other arm was round my waist in an instant.

"Oh, Percy! please leave me alone! Someone may come."

"I'm going to give the new Countess of Endover her first lesson in—Why! you have no drawers on! Fancy a countess without drawers!"

"You really must not tumble my skirt! Percy!—for shame!"

He had put me before the large armchair. Before I could prevent him I was made to kneel in it. He began raising my skirts from behind. All protestations were in vain. I was in horrible fear someone would want to come in. Still nothing was more natural than that my brother should come to offer me his private congratulations. He had only seen me before that day in the church. We had scarcely exchanged a word.

"Oh Eve! dear Eve! I've sworn to have you first after your marriage. I will not be denied. You looked so divinely beautiful at the altar—like an innocent angel of light. I declare I could hardly keep the buttons on my trousers. Turn your head, dear Eve, and look!"

I did as I was bidden—all power of resistance seemed to pass away. What I saw fired my hot blood.

"Oh Percy! you wicked boy! It is bigger and bigger! Make haste then! I shall have to go downstairs in a few minutes."

He pressed his belly to my bottom. My wedding dress and underskirts were thrown over my back. In another instant he was into me, up to the balls. There was no time to lose. He knew it. He worked fast to arrive at his climax. My own arrived. With a low groan I sank my head on the cushioned back. His weapon straightened—hardened, and with a sigh of lustful frenzy Percy discharged.

THE POWER OF MESMERISM

The Power of Mesmerism, "printed for the Nihilists, Moscow" (London, 1891), deals with the sexual exploits of a young man, Frank Etheridge, who has learned the art of hypnosis (or mesmerism, as it was then called). Frank had learned the art at his college in Germany when he accidentally came upon one of his professors in the act of mesmerizing a student in order to have homosexual relations with him. Frank tries his new power first on his sister, then on his mother and father, as well as on some other people, including their rector and two virgin nieces of his, all for the purposes of seducing and debauching them.

If the central fantasy of using hypnosis as a means for

sexual conquest is unusual, some of the details are even more bizarre. In his first hypnotic experiment with his sister, he proceeds as follows:

Frank could no longer resist, but holding her thumbs he commenced the magnetic passes, and she speedily fell into his arms, apparently in a deep slumber. He now sought to see if he was entirely successful in his attempt to produce the effect he desired, and therefore taking her in his arms, and laying her on the couch, he said, "Ethel, do you know where you are?"

"With my darling brother," she replied.

"Do you love him?"

"Madly," was the reply.

"What would you like to do to prove that love?"

"Anything he desires."

"Stand up."

She did so.

"Unfasten your dress; take it off."

She complied immediately.

"Loosen your petticoats, and take them off; now your slippers and your stockings."

The dear girl did exactly as requested, still in the same dreamy, languid manner. She now stood in her chemise and drawers only, and Frank felt as if he would faint. . . .

"Now, my darling," said he, "remove your drawers."

She did so, and he snatched them up and covered them with kisses.

"Now the chemise."

That also was taken off with alacrity, and she was before him perfectly naked.

He then ordered her to lie down on her back, raising her knees, and place her heels against her buttocks, then insert her finger in that divine cunt, and frig herself.

She did so.

"How do you feel, darling? Are you going to spend? I will that you spend at once."

Her whole body stiffened.

"Keep your thighs widely extended," he said, "so that I can see every throb that convulses your cunt."

The girl has an orgasm, but Frank is far from satisfied. He commands her to kneel in front of him, opens his trousers, takes out his penis, and has her perform fellatio on him. He then tells her to get up and kneel on the couch, in which position he examines her intimate parts and has oral contact with her anus. He longs to have intercourse with her, but does not dare. Instead, he orders her to dress and then awakens her from the hypnotic trance, content that she does not remember anything of what has taken place.

That same night, Frank enters his sister's bedroom and, seeing that the girl is asleep, induces a deeper hypnotic trance. Probing with his finger, he finds that the girl has apparently lost her hymen. "Thank God," he mutters, "she has been frigged, possibly fucked, and I shall not hurt her." He immediately proceeds to have intercourse with her, during which "they both spent simultaneously." He then commands her to get back into her nightdress and chemise, while he returns to his own room.

Sometime later, during his father's absence, he decides to try his hypnotic power on his still young and attractive mother. He manages at dinner to get her to drink more wine than usual, then suggests they send the servants to bed.

She assented, and after the order had been given, Frank looking triumphantly towards his sister, seriously commenced his attempt to mesmerize his own mother.

At first she involuntarily resisted his efforts, but at length she succumbed, and as her head fell on her shoulder, he openly made the necessary passes, and she speedily became entirely at his mercy.

"Now, Ethel," said he, "I will gratify my passion."

He approached his mother, she was in evening dress, and her lovely bubbies were half visible, while from the semirecumbent position in which she lay, every outline of her form could be clearly seen.

Her son first carefully raised those deliciously firm bubbies completely above her dress, then sucking one motioned to his sister to do the same with the other.

Mrs. Etheridge sighed slightly, and slid further down in her chair.

Frank then knelt in front of her, and his sister helping him, they gradually raised their Mamma's dress in front, till they had a full view of the splendid legs and thighs of their maternal parent, the former cased in pink silk stockings, with the swelling thighs filling out her drawers, and making them look deliciously tight. Placing his hand within the slit in front, he pulled aside the chemise, and gently extending her legs to their widest extent, he placed her feet on two chairs, and they now had a full view of the glorious cunt from which they both came.

The young man masturbates the mother, first manually and then with a dildo ("which he had previously charged"). His sister, having lain down on the floor below them, is ready to receive her brother's semen when the hot milk in the dildo is released into the mother at the moment of mutual orgasm.

When Mr. Etheridge returns home a few days later, Frank is ready to go to work on him as well. During dinner, Frank "seemed strangely excited, and occasionally pressed his sister's bubbies behind his parents' back. He also took every opportunity of pressing against his father." This is the first homosexual incest fantasy we have cited, which we take to mean that such fantasies are quite rare, as is the incidence of such contacts in real life.

Frank puts his father under hypnosis, then says to his sister, "My darling, Papa is now entirely unconscious of what he does, and entirely under my control; we will secure the door, and then shall suck the author of our being till his noble prick spends in your mouth." Ethel, the sister, performs fellatio on her father, while the brother has vaginal intercourse with her from behind. Father and son ejaculate simultaneously, after which, in a delirium of sexual excitement, brother and sister kiss to share their father's semen.

The incredible incestuous debauch continues as Frank rubs his father's "limp affair," which is still "moist and glistening," with his own penis until the father has a fresh erection. Frank directs Ethel to straddle the father and helps insert his penis into her. The boy then places himself behind his sister so that he can assist her by lifting her buttocks up and down with his hands. When he sees the father's new ejaculation approaching, he stimulates both of them orally, while masturbating himself to orgasm at the same time. Frank once more has intercourse with his sister, simultaneously masturbating his father to orgasm.

Then they "remove all traces of what had happened. Frank then willed his father to awake, which he did, and looking round vacantly, said, 'Dear children, I fear I have been to sleep, the fresh air does tire me so.' "

Frank, sure now of his power over both parents and the willing assistance of his sister, lays plans for a complete family orgy.

They were sitting after dinner when Frank quietly mesmerized both father and mother, and then asked Ethel to dismiss the servants for the night.

They then amused themselves by playing with their parents' private parts for awhile, and then Frank willed them to go to their bedroom. This they immediately did.

Brother and sister left them for a short time, retiring to their own rooms, and then returned quite naked.

Their parents now mechanically divested themselves also of every article of clothing, in obedience to the will of their son, while Frank also willed the housemaid Maud to come into the room naked.

The ending of the episode takes an unexpected turn.

As they were all four approaching the divine climax, Frank dissolved the mesmeric charm, and allowed both father and mother to realize the situation at a moment when it would be impossible for them to resist the impulses of their carnal nature. . . .

It would be impossible to describe the sense of shame, which overcame the poor parents; they seemed to think they were still under the influence of some horrible dream, an idea which their children did their best to foster.

Soon Mr. and Mrs. Etheridge need no longer be hypnotized and participate willingly in their children's sexual adventures.

As much as *The Power of Mesmerism* is in the realm of pure sexual fantasy, situations not too far different from what was here described—minus the hypnosis part—are not as unlikely to happen in real life as one might think. We know of a family situation in America where brother and sister, father and daughter, and son and mother, all had regular sexual relations with one another. This went on for some time until the teen-age son one day asked his father for fifty dollars to help him buy his first car. When the father refused, the son became very angry, went into town, had a few drinks, and in drunken anger walked into a police station and told the astonished policemen about the goings-on in his home. At first they did not want to believe the boy, but when he insisted, they took him home, questioned the parents and the daughter, and obtained a complete confession.

As for "mesmerism," it is, of course, impossible to hypnotize an unprepared subject simply by "making passes" at him with one's hands. However, the fact that everyone in *The Power of Mesmerism* seems to be pretty much prepared to be seduced makes it more believable that they would carry out the morally objectionable hypnotic suggestions without much resistance. But scientific accuracy is hardly an issue in this book, for we are dealing here with a fantasy in which the laws of logic and science do not apply.

MORE FORBIDDEN FRUIT

More Forbidden Fruit (a sequel to *Forbidden Fruit*), dated *ca.* 1890, tells of a mother-son relationship which culminates in the following passage:

"You've done it again, Percy, I shall have twins, and if they are girls you shall fuck them as soon as they are old enough," she said with a laugh. "But really, my darling, I should like my own boy to make me a baby—you would be both father and brother to it. Now we must get up for luncheon or Aunt Gert will be after us, she always knew I would have you, and now you may have her some day."

"You lovely mother," I said, clinging to her for another kiss. "I shall fuck you all in this house. I know I shall, now I think of nothing else. There's you, auntie, Mary, and Patty. I must have her too. May I, Mamma?"

"What a boy it is: but you must always love Mamma best, Percy, won't you?"

Because of our clinical practice and research, an incredible episode like the one above has a familiar ring. Not long ago we interviewed a young artist in his thirties who told us that he had been seduced by his mother when he was about fourteen years old. She had one day come into the bathroom while he was taking his bath, wearing only a bathrobe herself. Sitting on a low chair, she had opened the robe, explained to him the anatomy of the female genitals, and shown him how to caress a woman. Thus she had gradually, over several days, led him to perform complete sexual intercourse with her. Later she had helped prepare a girl of about his own age to have sexual relations with him, but mother and son had kept up their incestuous relationship until the mother's death a few years later.

INITIATIONS VOLUPTUEUSES

Initiations Voluptueuses (*Voluptuous Initiations*) by "Gladys de Rosemont," a very rare book, was published under the strictest secrecy ("A l'Alcove de Vénus," no date or place, but known to be Paris, 1939).

In this book a mother initiates her eighteen-year-old daughter Irene and sixteen-year-old son Dany into the mysteries of uninhibited sex. The mother is advised in this undertaking by her brother, Dr. Riman, with whom she has had a long-standing incestuous relationship. Lending a helping hand, too, is gay divorcée, Lucienne, twenty-six years old, whom the mother has engaged as governess for the children and lesbian companion to herself.

Mama starts with a practical lesson in sex education for her daughter by asking her to help with the administration of a vaginal douche.

"Well, you're going to help me, my darling, even though I suppose you don't know much about this. After all, you've got to know what to do on your wedding night. Here, fill up this tube. Yes, that's right, now take the nozzle. Put it in. Push my curlies aside first."

"Oh, Mommy! You've got so much and it's so thick! And so beautiful."

"Yes, dear. It's one of the beautiful parts of a woman, one of the things gentlemen value the most. Let me see yours."

"Oh, I don't have very much. Just a tiny bit of fluff."

Lifting her dressing gown and her nightgown, she showed me her cute little pussy. My fingers grasped the silky down.

"Goodness, what do you expect? I think that you're very well endowed for your age! Now put your two fingers on either side of my slit. Spread them wide. Good! Now insert the nozzle. No, not there. Lay it aside for a minute. Explore with your finger first so you can understand better. That's right. With your index finger. Ah! You found it. Do you feel the orifice?"

"Oh! The cute little hole!"

"Yes, isn't it? And to think that you and your brother came through there when you were born!"

A little later, Mama gives both her offspring a full initiation.

Was that really my darling daughter there, Mademoiselle Irene Dilas, who was considered by everyone the most reserved girl in our little town? Or was it a young, intoxicated bacchante? A bacchante who, with one perverse hand, forced her buttocks apart in order to let my eyes behold a young, sweet rosebud, who urged me to pay homage to it?

"Oh! Darling Mommy, your mouth, your lips, your tongue! Oh! I'm going to kiss you in the same way! I'm going to give you the same sort of kiss! Oh, it's exquisite!"

I allowed her to do it. She was all excited when I presented my backside for her to caress, all excited that I let my buttocks be covered with kisses. And when I placed myself in such a way that she could spread them apart for her mouth to penetrate, it was pure delirium!

The next afternoon I sent her off with Lucienne, back from Lyon, to visit some friends. I now knew enough about her temperament to be sure that the form of education I intended to give her would be well understood. I wanted to make a similar test with Daniel.

"Tell me, Dany," I asked when we were alone in my boudoir, "the other day you were peeking through the keyhole into the bathroom. Lucienne was massaging me at the time, as a matter of fact. She went out for a minute and caught you. I would like to know what your hand was doing in your fly."

He turned beet red and remained silent. I made him sit next to me on the couch, drawing his head onto my shoulder. As I was wearing a dress with quite a plunging neckline, I was thus offering him a generous look at my bosom in its nest of lace. I knew that he often stole glances in that direction anyway, especially at night when I kissed him good night in his bed, and with his arms wrapped around my neck he held me tight, leaning over him, treating himself to a charming view.

I repeated my brutal question.

"Tell me, darling, tell me what you were doing with your hand in your trousers."

"I had an itch, Mother."

"Don't lie to me, you rascal. Or if it's really true, that means that there's some reason for it! Let's have a look."

I must admit, a perverse thrill ran through me as the buttons flew. It has always been a singular pleasure for me to undo a man's fly—when I think of the number of them that I've undone! But in this case my joy was doubled because I knew I was doing something forbidden, depraved, more immoral than usual. And that excited me enormously! . . .

He remained silent all the while. I encouraged him with kind words. I did better than that. I opened my décolleté wider and bent his head between my breasts.

"There, there, my little one. Hide yourself there and speak to me, tell me!"

All at once he admitted it!

"It's like this, Mommy. An adult told me that when you touched yourself there it did a lot of good, it was nice. So I tried it, but I didn't feel a thing, except that it sure is nice to touch yourself there."

"And the way I'm touching you now, does that feel nice, my Dany?"

"Oh, yes, Mommy, that's even better!"

He was as stiff as a rod, the darling! I was terribly tempted to tumble him over on the couch the way I had done a few days before with the young virgin Albert, Lawyer H.'s office boy to try his pecker for size.

But I remembered my brother Marcel's advice. Yesterday, as he was gently working on me, making me come—for the second time—in my easy chair, he gave me certain "guiding rules" (if I may use such a presumptuous expression) which I had to follow during the double education system I had in mind.

"You see, my darling Simone, you come too quickly, you're not patient enough! When you feel like coming, for you it has to arrive quickly, all in a rush, in order to start right over again afterwards! Well, you'll have to restrain yourself if you want to be a good tutor for your children." . . .

"Mother, mother," panted Irene, "it would be so lovely if you could put your finger on my little cherry, like you did yesterday."

"No, my darling, I'm going to show you something else. Lift up your dress, tuck it up high! Here, straddle my naked thigh. Wait until I spread open the lips of your pretty pussy. Now settle down on my leg. Do you feel your rosy vulva all afire against my skin? Now rub—the way you used to do when you were little and you played horsey on my knees."

"Oh, it's so good! It's good to rub myself like this, Mommy!"

"Don't go too quickly, you greedy thing, or you'll come before I do. Keep on rubbing my clitoris above Dany's tongue. Here, Irene, suck my nipple. Aah, that's exquisite! There, my Dany, keep up see-sawing my backend. Don't stop working your tongue either! Ooh, my dear little ones, I'm going to come! I feel it, it's coming, I'm going to overflow, I'm going to burst! I'm going to release everything in your mouth, my darling big boy, and you're going to drink every drop I give you! Here, here it comes! It's coming! It's coming! Rub, Irene, rub! Faster! Faster! And you, Dany, go faster too! Aah, what divine pleasure! I'm coming, I'm coming! Aaaaaah!"

I was the first one to come back to my senses, and I felt my tender Irene lying, exhausted, on top of me. She still had my nipple in her pink mouth and on my thigh I tasted the great amount of milky froth she had discharged from her dainty little cunt. As for Daniel, he was still, eyes closed, licking up everything that had run from my vulva. He made a face when I lifted his naughty finger from my bunghole. But he stopped sulking when in low tones, so as not to wake up his sister, I told him:

"Stand up on the couch, my darling, so I can reward you."

I unbuttoned him with only one hand. His trousers and shorts dropped to his feet. I put my head under his shirt and my lips caught his pretty, nicely taut prick. How the odor of young flesh drives me wild!

"Oh, Mommy," he said, laughing, "your upper mouth is also greedy! Oh, what are you doing?"

It would have been very difficult to answer him, because I had my mouth full of his adorable pecker. Simultaneously, my hand, going around to his rear end, was pawing at his buttocks, his chubby, satin-skinned cheeks. My fingers crept along his crack and one of them, after having tickled his little hole, entered and sodomized him as he had done to me a few minutes earlier! His little club immediately got even stiffer and all at once I received the honey of his jissom, as he groaned with pleasure!

There follows at this point a digression about a certain lady who specialized in "deflowering" young virgin boys, a fantasy which we shall consider later. After that, Irene titillates her mother with the promise of a "new pleasure" she and her brother are going to give her. It turns out that they intend to put whipped cream into her vagina, to be licked out by Dany: "Sitting on my blonde fleece, the cream looked like a beautiful meringue. My son came over to satisfy his sweet tooth."

Another time, Lucienne, the governess, attaches an enormous dildo around Irene's waist and has her treat Mama anally with it, while Dany performs cunnilingus on her. He is rewarded afterward by the mother performing fellatio on him, and, in the end, by having vaginal intercourse with her: "And what a sensation! I couldn't think of anything else until I came a second time!"

Since Irene is engaged to be married, the family decides it is time she be deflowered: "It will be two months before you are married. Dany will have plenty of time to get your pink sheath in shape!" Later, at bedtime the same day, the defloration ceremony takes place in the mother's "fucking chair," with Lucienne on hand to help out and the mother herself guiding the son's penis into the daughter's virgin sex.

It turns out that Dany is such a good lover ("for weeks he's been alternately screwing Lucienne and me, and he had turned into an excellent fucker!" says Mama) that his sister afterward pleads with him, "Oh, Dany, after I'm married, you'll still fuck me, won't you? Promise me, even if we have to hide from my husband!"

In this chapter we have called attention to the fact that, rare as cases of incest may be in real life, they nevertheless exist. Having become acquainted with the incest fantasies of literature, it is of interest to consider the facts of incest behavior as it is actually known to exist in Western communities.

In the monumental study *Sex Offenders*, by the staff of the Kinsey Institute,* we find incest behavior broken down into the same main categories which they apply to the other types of sex

---

* Paul H. Gebhard, John H. Gagnon, Wardell B. Pomeroy, Cornelia V. Christenson, *Sex Offenders: An Analysis of Types* (New York: Harper and Row, and Paul B. Hoeber, Inc., 1965).

offenders: (1) incestuous relations of adults (fathers) with children (to twelve years); (2) with minors (twelve to fifteen years); and (3) with adults (fifteen years and over). The distinction suggested itself because the law regards incest offenses against children differently from those against minors and adults. But it turned out that this breakdown may be psychologically significant as well.

The Kinsey researchers note that the father-daughter incest taboo is, and has been, almost world-wide. Notable exceptions concern socially sanctioned brother-sister and father-daughter marriages in ancient Egypt, to which we may add similar customs in other ancient civilizations (e.g., pre-Christian Ireland). Such incestuous marriages were, however, usually condoned only for members of the highest religious or political strata of society, such as kings, priests, or the upper rungs of nobility, while strictly prohibited to the common citizenry.

This almost universal taboo on incest, particularly father-daughter incest, is understandable from a psychological and sociological point of view: it may threaten family cohesion through sexual jealousies between mother and daughter, lead to rivalries between daughters for the father's sexual favors, and complicate the inheritance of property, as well as the passing on of certain rights and obligations in the event these relations should result in offspring. Aside from this, a strong incestuous tie between father and daughter (regardless whether consummated in actual incest behavior or not, we may add) would make it considerably more difficult fot the girl to form relationships with men outside the family and to get married.

The Kinsey researchers point out that there is no natural or biological factor to hinder or discourage incest, either among humans or animals. In animals, incest behavior depends almost solely on availability and the opportunities of place and time. Although this is not spelled out in *Sex Offenders*, there is no biological harm from inbreeding as such; biological traits are simply passed on normally, though this would, of course, include any deficient as well as any superior characteristics that might be present. In short, the incest taboo among humans is solely cultural, and, as the Kinsey researchers state, "not a bio-logical necessity." It is our impression that the extremely strong case which the Kinsey researchers make in favor of the cultural causes of the incest taboo is somewhat overdrawn. Many of the psychological and sociological problems cited as justification for the taboo are not essentially different from those inherent in family patterns involving plural wives (or husbands) and certain systems of concubinage, as they still exist in some primitive societies. We do not wish to minimize these problems in the least; in fact, they would be multiplied and intensified if applied to a complex civilization such as ours. On the other hand, if the only real factors militating against incest behavior on the human level are culturally conditioned or of a psychological nature (complications of the Oedipal situation, sexual jealousy, intra-familial competition, etc.), they are subject to social change and dependent on personal attitudes, rather than on fixed and un-alterable conditions. We agree with the general idea that incest behavior in our society under present social conditions is, of necessity, beset with problems of many kinds and therefore highly inadvisable, but we cannot, without the above-mentioned qualifications, subscribe to the categorical judgment of the Kinsey group that "no known human society could tolerate much incest without ruinous disruption." It is rather our impres-sion that in this case even the Kinsey group, who are usually exceptionally free of cultural prejudice, have not remained un-affected by it.

In any case, the Kinsey researchers have made the most comprehensive survey, if not of incest behavior as such, then of incest offenders in the United States. And what they have come to know about this group of men and their families (no mother-son or mother-daughter or intersibling incest seems to have been included in their study) is very enlightening. In the first place, all three categories of incest offenders against children, minors, and adults are "the most guilt-ridden of any group" of sex offenders. They also have in common that they usually come from a lower social and educational environment, including a high percentage of cases from backward rural areas and city slums, which brings to mind images of poverty-stricken families in a Tobacco Road atmosphere, often with alcoholic overtones, on whom little of the cultural pattern of American middle-class life has had a chance to rub off. However, some of the incest offenders are of average or even superior intelligence and come from a more privileged socioeconomic background.

Incest offenders against children seem to differ markedly in several significant respects from the other two types of offenders. They appear to be really highly sexed in contrast to the other two groups of incest offenders, whose sex drive seems to be from low-average to definitely suppressed. (The Kinsey researchers speak of the former's "hypersexuality," a term which we would prefer to avoid, since it is based on the already suppressed cultural norm of contemporary American society.)

In support of their impression about the higher sex drive of incest offenders against children, the Kinsey group list several factors, such as these offenders' high sexual response to "thinking of or seeing females," their higher response to other erotic stimuli (pornography), their favoritism to prolonged sexual foreplay and mouth-genital activities (with their wives), their openness to experimentation with other sex techniques (26 per cent had had anal coitus with their wives), their greater tendency to dream to orgasm, their greater ability to indulge in conscious masturbation fantasies (frequently involving fantasies of prepubescent girls), as well as the fact that over half of that group began masturbating before reaching puberty and have a high incidence of prepuberty sex play.

The Kinsey researchers found no evidence in this group of any marked preference for extremely young girls at the time of their first sex contact that could indicate their later tendency in that direction. However, the report states elsewhere, "more of these offenders than those of any other group reported that their *initial coitus* was *unpleasant*" (emphasis ours). Taken together, these two statements might be interpreted to mean that at least one of the motivating factors in determining this group's later tendency to seek out very young incestuous sex objects might have been the unpleasantness of their first heterosexual experi-

ence with an older female outside the family. Together with
other predisposing characteristics, this could well be the determining factor in this particular deviation. The fact that
offenders against minors (ages twelve to fifteen) in the over-
whelming majority (81 per cent) enjoyed their first heterosexual intercourse does not, in our view, militate against this
interpretation. One must keep in mind that in these cases the
daughters were often sexually quite mature and that the preference in this group is not so much for very young girls as for sex
partners who are familiar and available (some of these men
found great difficulty in making contacts). Moreover, in the case
of minors, the girls not infrequently conspired actively or pas-
sively with the offender in committing the offense.

In contrast to the incest offenders against children, those
against minors were found to be *not* particularly interested in
sex. They did not respond readily to psychological sex stimuli,
were not particularly prone to sex dreams, had fewer masturbation fantasies than any other type of sex offender, and low
frequencies in every category of sexual activities. As the Kinsey
researchers state, "The typical case seems to be a run-of-the-mill
lower socioeconomic level husband who, for reasons *neither he
nor we clearly see,* has an incestuous relationship, and having
once begun continues it despite his fears and guilt feelings"
(emphasis ours). It would seem to us that the absence of any
specific reasons for the incestuous relationship is also its explanation. As the Kinsey group point out themselves, men from these
subcultural environments "regard any postpubertal female as a
suitable sex object." And that may be enough for those who
have not been imbued too deeply with the cultural taboos of a
social order to which they only marginally belong.

The last group of incest offenders—those against adults
(daughters fifteen years and older)—differed from incest
offenders against minors mainly in that they were found out
later than the second group (most of them had had their fi.st
incestuous contact with the daughter when she was between
twelve and fifteen years old).

Erotic literature glamorizes incest offenders as an intelligent, sophisticated, upper- or upper-middle-class group, endowed with much imagination and a rich fantasy life. In fact, most of the incest fantasies from the literature we have considered concerns relations with young adults, only a few with minors below fifteen, and practically none with children much below that age. It is remarkable to what an extent the actual facts of real life differ from those of sexual fantasy. As regards incest offenders against adults in real life, the truth is that they come from the very opposite of a glamorous environment. "The over-all impression," as the Kinsey researchers note, "is of a group of impoverished uneducated farmers or ranchers of less than average intelligence." Here we have again the Tobacco Road milieu which characterized the other two categories of incest offenders, if perhaps to a less dramatic degree.

Most of these men, the Kinsey staff report, were highly religious, moralistic, intolerant, prejudiced, conservative, rigid, and sexually inhibited individuals. They are the kind of people who call the loudest for the maintenance of "law and order," who are belligerent by temperament and racists at heart, who believe in violence, distrust democratic processes, and are highly suspicious of "new-fangled" ideas, who opposed the New Deal in the 1930's and derided the W.P.A. program, while deriving, of all groups, the most benefit from it, and who clamor for, among other things, censorship and the suppression of minority opinion at every given opportunity.

Psychologically, these are people who are able to deny reality in the face of all evidence to the contrary, and are the group most prone to deny their guilt with regard to the incestuous relationships of which they had been accused and convicted (full 42 per cent denied their guilt to the authorities and 25 per cent even to the essentially friendly and sympathetic researchers). As the Kinsey staff point out, this group of people have an unusual ability to completely deny or rationalize their behavior to bring it more in line with what they profess as their own moral code of conduct.

They were also found to be the group least responsive to visual and fantasy stimuli and the one with the least sexual activity, either before or after marriage (they also had the highest percentage of anorgastic wives). On the other hand, they were extremely fertile, producing more than the average number of offspring.

As a group, they are socially so inbred and inept in making human contacts that it is not surprising they later turned to their daughters for sexual gratification (their childhood family environment seems to have been too moralistic to provide opportunities for sibling incest). Remarkable too is the fact that they were found to be extremely heterosexual. These are the men who have virtually no homosexual contacts, not even homosexual sex play in adolescence or pre-adolescence, who have no conscious homosexual fantasies and are unable to recall dreams with homosexual content, and who are, we may add, often among the most rabid persecutors of homosexuals, if given the opportunity. On the other hand, they were found to have a relatively high percentage of animal contacts, a fact for which their rural environment and social isolation seems to account.

Thus we see how wide the gap is between fantasy and reality, if we compare the glamorous or at times extremely witty accounts of incest in erotic literature with the lives and background of actual incest offenders as described as a group by the Kinsey study. While it is impossible to make similar comparisons for every type of sexual deviation occurring in sexual fantasy, we shall do so where particularly relevant, as in the next chapter, which deals with those who offend society with regard to the young age of their nonincestuous sex partners.

9

Juveniles

As in the case of incest, fantasies concerning children and juveniles are extremely frequent in erotic writings. For the most part, they, too, are banal and unconvincing, having been obviously thrown in for good measure, to give every type of reader something for his money. Still, there are a few erotic books in which sexual activity with children, or rather minors, is the main fantasy, and it is these writings that we will examine now.

THE NEW EPICUREAN

No doubt the most famous book in this genre is *The New Epicurean,* by Edward Sellon. The book is subtitled in the style of the time: *The Delights of Sex, Facetiously and Philosophically Considered, in Graphic Letters Addressed to Young Ladies of Quality* (*1740*) (London, 1865). Sellon's tastes seem to have run in that direction and he writes about sexual activities with young girls with a definite ring of authenticity. Nevertheless, his writing is embellished and exaggerated to such an extent that the episodes of his book are undoubtedly sexual fantasies and not autobiography.

The plot of *The New Epicurean* is actually more of a setting than a real plot. Sir Charles, an English gentleman, establishes in the countryside an estate on which he can live entirely to his tastes.

The grounds I had laid out in the true English style, with umbrageous walks, alcoves, grottoes, fountains, and every adjunct that could add to their rustic beauty. In the open space facing the secret apartment before alluded to was spread out a fine lawn, embossed with beds of the choicest flowers, and in the center, from a bouquet of maiden's blush roses, appeared a statue of Venus in white marble; and at the end of every shady valley was a terminal figure of the god of gardens in his various forms; either bearded like the antique head of the Indian Bacchus; or soft and feminine, as we see the lovely Antinoüs; or Hermaphroditic—the form of a lovely girl with puerile attributes.

Even in the physical setting and decor of the place, the fancy for young girls finds clear enough expression. Interesting too is the reference to the "hermaphroditic" statue, which provides a significant clue to the hidden motivation or background of this sex psychology.

Having installed in his idyllic establishment a "discreet old housekeeper," "a bouncing, blooming cook," and a "sprightly trim housemaid," Sir Charles is ready to indulge in his debaucheries with the young girls. True, he is married, but Lady Cecilia, his wife, is most understanding and, far from interfering, joins at times in his orgies. (This was perhaps a wish-fulfilling fantasy on Sellon's part, for in real life his wife showed herself extremely jealous.)

The book is written in the form of letters to various imaginary young ladies, and both the setting and the style of writing purport to be that of the century before, as the false publication date is meant to indicate (Sellon died in 1866).

Sir Charles's enthusiasm for young girls is evident from the outset of the book. Receiving a contingent of new little girls from a handy procuress, he invites them into his mansion.

"Come, my little darlings," said I, to two delicious young creatures who, coquettishly dressed, with the most charming little hats in the world and full petticoats that barely reached their rose-colored garters, sprang, nothing loth, into my arms. . . . They were charming children, and when I tell you that their limbs were moulded in the most perfect symmetry, and that their manners were cultivated, elegant, and gay, I think you will agree with me that Madame R. had catered well.

"Now my little loves," said I, giving each a kiss, "what shall we do first; are you hungry, will you eat?"

This proposal seemed to give great satisfaction, so taking each by the hand I led them to my room; and patties, strawberries and cream, apricots, and champagne disappeared with incredible rapidity. While they were eating, I was exploring; now patting the firm dimpled peachlike bottom of the pretty brunette, now inserting a finger into the pouting hairless cleft of the lovely blonde. The latter was called Blanche and the former Cerise. I was beside myself with rapture, and turning first to one and then to the other, covered them with kisses.

The collation finished at last, we all went onto the grounds, and having walked them round and shown them everything curious, not forgetting the statue of Priapus, at whose grotesque appearance with his great prick sticking out, they laughed heartily, I proposed to give them a swing. Of course in putting them in, I took care that their lovely little posteriors should bulge out beyond the velvet seat, and as their clothes were short, every time they swung high in the air, I had a full expansive view of those white globes, and the tempting rose colored slits that pouted between them; then, oh! the dear little feet, the fucktious shoes, the racy, delectable legs; nothing could be finer.

But the sight was too tantalizing. We were all heated; I with the exertion of swinging them, they with the wine, so they readily agreed to my proposal to proceed to a retired spot, where was a little lake lined with marble, not more than four feet deep. We were soon naked, and sporting in the water; then only was it that I could take in all their loveliness at a glance. The budding small pointed breasts, just beginning to grow; the polished ivory shoulders, the exquisite fall in the back, the tiny waists, the bulging voluptuous hips, the dimpled bottoms, blushing and fresh, the plump thighs, and smooth white bellies. In a moment my truncheon stood up hard and firm as a constable's staff. I put it in their hands, I frigged and kissed their fragrant cunnies, I gamahuched them, and then the saucy Cerise taking my ruby tipped ferrule in her little rosy mouth, began rolling her tongue round it in such a way, that I nearly fainted with bliss.

At that moment our position was this. I lay stretched on my back on the grass; Blanche sat over me, a leg on either side, with my tongue glued to her rose. Cerise knelt astride of me also, with her posteriors well jutted out towards me, and one of my fingers was inserted in her rosebud. Nor were the hands of the delicious brunette idle; with her right she played with my balls, and with the forefinger of her left hand she exquisitely titillated the regions beneath.

But human nature could not stand this long; so changing our positions I placed Blanche on her hands and knees, while Cerise inserted my arrow, covered with saliva from her mouth, into the pretty Blanche. She was tight, but not a virgin, so after a thrust or two, I fairly went in up to the hilt. All this while Cerise was tickling me, and rubbing her beautiful body against me. Soon Blanche began to spend, and to sigh out: "Oh! oh! dear sir, give it me now! Shoot it into me! Ah! I faint! I die!" and as the warm fluid gushed into her, she fell prone on the ground.

When Blanche had a little recovered herself, we again plunged into the lake, to wash off the dew of love, with which we were drenched.

Thus sporting in the water, toying with each other, we wiled away the hot hours of the afternoon, till tired, at length, we left the lake and dressed ourselves.

Afterward, Sir Charles muses: "I was astonished that so young a creature [speaking of Cerise] could be so precocious, but I learnt from Madame R., who had brought her up, that every pain had been taken to excite these passions in this girl, since she was seven years of age; first with boys, and subsequently with grown-up persons. Blanche I had thought most delicious, but there was a furore in Cerise's fucking which carried you away, as it were, out of yourself."

One of Sir Charles's favorite tricks with young girls is to

take them to the chicken yard and show them "how the cock
treads the hen," or to the stables to witness the stallion mounting
the mare. The sight of the copulating animals never fails (as it
shouldn't in an erotic fairy tale) to instill lustful thoughts and
desires in the girls.

Typical of Sellon's writing, as of the psychology involved,
is the following passage in which a ten-year-old girl is brought
to Sir Charles.

She told me that her little girl [Chloe] was a sweet pretty creature,
ten years of age, and as she knew that I liked to amuse myself with
children sometimes, poor innocent soul, she thought I might like to
have her.

I at once consented, and in a few days arrived one of the
sweetest flowers that ever blushed unseen in the woods of Hamp-
shire. I was charmed, and lost no time in providing suitable clothes
for the little pet and, with the aid of Phoebe, her frocks were so
contrived that they only reached her knees. This, you will readily
understand, was for the purpose of giving me facilities for seeing
her young beauties, without doing anything that might alarm her
young innocence. . . .

In the course of a few days, our young rustic had quite rubbed
off her first shyness, would run in and out of my room, sit on my
knee, hide my snuff box, kiss me of her own accord, and play all
sorts of innocent tricks, like other children, in swinging, climbing
up trees, and tumbling about on the grass; the little puss not merely
showing her legs, but everything else besides. . . .

One evening, after the usual performance of washing, skipping
about, etc., the little saucebox came and jumped on my knees,
putting a leg on either side of them, and began courting a romp.
Had I been a saint, whereas you know I am but a sinner, I could not
have resisted such an attack on my virtue as this.

Only imagine . . . this graceful lovely creature in all the
bloom of early girlhood, stark naked, except her stockings, her
beautiful brown hair flowing over her exquisite shoulders, imagine
her position, and how near she had placed herself to the fire and
then, say, can you blame me?

Following this, Sir Charles and the older Phoebe give little
Chloe a practical lesson in sex education, Sir Charles showing her
his erect penis and Phoebe telling her about the cock and the

hens. Sir Charles proceeds to give Chloe a demonstration of human intercourse by engaging in it with Phoebe. When it is over, he sends Phoebe out of the room for some refreshments, using her absence first to masturbate little Chloe, then to perform cunnilingus on her, and finally, his energy having returned, to teach her to perform fellatio on him.

Another time, Sir Charles and his wife are playing hide-and-seek on the grounds of their wooded estate with a bevy of their young girl cousins. They have just shown them the stallion mounting the mare, so the idea occurs to Sir Charles to place his wife, while the two of them are "it" and have to hide, in the position of the mare and have intercourse with her from behind. He then calls out to the children that they are ready to be found.

Into the wood they all came shouting and laughing, but could not for a long time find us: at length Agnes and Augusta, taking an opposite vista to their companions, came suddenly upon us, just as my climax came. I immediately drew out, and thus gave them a complete view of that red-headed staff, at the sight of which, and of their cousin's ivory posterior, shining in the sun, they stopped, turned round, and bounded off to their companions, crying out:

"Oh! Miss Jennings; oh, Miss Bellew, here's Sir Charles doing to cousin Cecilia just what the horse did to the mare!"

Then we heard a whispering; and presently I became aware, by the rustling of the branches, that the girls were placing themselves in ambush, to see all they could.

The idea of such beauteous spectators, brought me up to the mark again in a moment, and at it we went in good style. Every now and then, a little eager face would peep out from among the leaves, and then be withdrawn in great trepidation; which caused such a thrill to run through my veins, that I brought that second embrace to a conclusion much sooner than I had a mind to.

A little further along in the story, Lady Cecilia seduces a young boy.

A few days afterwards, as I lay on the banks of the lake, listlessly feeding the carp, Phoebe came running to me, and having seated herself, quite out of breath, by my side, she told me that Cecilia and

her brother were amusing themselves in the grotto, in the grove of
beeches, and if I would make haste, I might see something that
would amuse me. So, throwing my arm round Phoebe's waist, I
accompanied her, going round to the opposite side to the entrance.
We looked through a chink in the rockwork, and could both see
and hear all that passed.

First I observed Cecilia seated on the mossy bank, and holding
the boy, whose breeches were down, between her naked thighs; his
hands were toying with her bubbies.

While she, having tucked up his fine cambric shirt, with her
right hand, caressed his little stiff thing, and with her left patted his
pretty dimpled soft and girlish bottom.

"Oh, you dear little fellow," she said, "what a beautiful figure
you have got, your waist is so small, your bottom so plump,
dimpled, and rounded, and your skin so soft; you have such a lovely
face, your hair is so silky, luxuriant, and beautiful, and you have
such little hands and feet, surely nature quite intended you for a
girl, only she gave you this little saucy cock instead of something
else, which, however, I am very glad of, as you will be able to play
with me. Dear boy, do you like me to tickle it?"

"Oh, yes, my lady," cried the lad, "very much indeed, and I do
love these little breasts so, do let me kiss them."

And pulling her bubbies out, he buried his face between them.

"But," she exclaimed, "you have not looked at this other little
secret place—but perhaps, you have seen girls before?"

"Why, my lady, to say the truth, I have, but only little ones. I
should like to see Your Ladyship's beautiful cunt very much."

"Oh, fie, naughty boy, do not use such naughty words. But
look, here it is."

And she straddled open her legs.

"Feel it with your pretty little hand. Oh, you dear fellow, that
is nice, now lie down upon me, and I will show you what love is."

And grasping his beautiful buttocks, she drew him to her, and
he slipped in with ease.

"Now, dear boy, move up and down, that's it, my little stallion [he too has had a practical lesson in sex education by way of the
stallion and mare demonstration]. You are, I see, an apt pupil."

Then holding open those white hemispheres, she inserted her
delicate finger into his little rosy orifice behind, and entwining her
lovely limbs round his loins, they were presently bounding and
heaving with delight.

Naturally, the sight proves too much for Sir Charles, and he
and young Phoebe follow the example of Lady Cecilia and the

boy. In this passage, note should be made of the author's comment that the boy looked almost like a girl. Prepubertal girls, whose secondary sex characteristics are not yet well developed, also can be seen as beautiful, effeminate boys. We suggest that the attraction of young children for some adults lies probably to a large extent in this ambiguity or indistinctness of sex identity. The adult in these relationships can, in real life or in fantasy, imagine the prepubescent boy or girl to be of the same sex as the adult, or at least he need not identify his partner definitely as a member of the opposite sex. In this manner, men can avoid anxieties connected with the female genitalia (menstruation trauma, vagina dentata, etc.), while women may be able to ward off corresponding anxieties about the fully matured male sex organ (penetration, impregnation fears, etc.). Moreover, the sex hostilities which are latent in almost all adults do not apply to the same degree to younger persons, thus making them less threatening as sex partners.

CHILD LOVE

Child Love, or Private Letter from Phyllis to Marie (London, 1898), a Victorian novel also in the form of letters, deals exclusively with the imaginary sex activities of adults with minors or between minors themselves. The Dedication reads: "I, Phyllis Norroy, dedicate this book to pretty little girls who, while satisfying their own desires and those of their lovers, be they new women or children like themselves, have retained their virginity and have 'never told tales out of school.' "

In the Preface, the anonymous author states the point of view from which the book was written.

. . . the seduction of very little girls [inducing them to have coitus], be they ever so pretty, ever so loving and ever so reciprocal to their lovers' desires, is an *enormity* and species of physical barbarism.

Pretty little girls are often but too ready to excite passions in others, which lead to the gratification of their own; but it is a cruel return to exhaust by acts of violence the physical health of those who are so willing to resort to every pleasure-giving action, and whose virginity alone gives extra force and enjoyment to those with whom they shared their love. . . .

I have naught to say against the indulgence of men's strongest passions with little maidens . . . but regardless of everything else, it is for physical reasons wrong and in itself destructive of the intense pleasure which men so much desire to resort to the act of seduction [coitus] till about a year after their little victim has first suffered from the illness peculiar to her sex.

But after that time the pretty child will, if as a virgin she has felt the pleasures of love, be able to receive and enjoy a closer intercourse, giving out the essence of her charms to meet and combine with those of her lover.

The Preface, like the Dedication, is signed Phyllis Norroy and is followed by this ditty:

> My pretty little Jane
> It would only give you pain
> If I fucked your little "Fanny" when so young,
> So lie down on your bed
> And I'll "bugger" you instead
> And I think you'll find the process rather fun.

In the first letter, we hear that Marie intends "to provide the public of Europe with 'naughty photographs' of little girls" and is asking the writer (Phyllis) for advice. Phyllis expresses the view that it is, in her opinion, "a mistake to show the children in an entirely nude state, for example, black or dark-colored stockings always seem to improve the curves of the legs, and it is often the case, that a complete disarrangement of the clothes so as to expose to the full extent that part of the child's body from which she desires and gives most pleasure, will make the best picture."

To break down the false modesty of young girls' having their nude or seminude photos taken, the writer suggests showing them nude pictures of other girls of the same age. She goes on to say what one may reasonably expect of even a very young girl whose passions have been sufficiently stimulated, either mentally by reading, pictures, etc., or by physical caresses and kisses.

Hardly any little girl, after her first modesty has been overcome, and her passions have been aroused to their full extent . . . will refuse to use her lips in such a way that she not only satisfies but exhausts—as no woman could do—his burning desires.

It is true that the first time she may shrink from the flow into her mouth, which her lips and tongue have drawn from her lover, but afterwards, she will cease to have any repugnance to the action, for she will share the joy she is proud of being able to excite at so young an age.

Little girls like having grown-up lovers and think they are almost women if they are able to share and satisfy their most intense passions and this a pretty child can always do if she will but try.

Phyllis then describes to her old friend Marie her first sexual experience with a grown man, a wealthy baronet, Sir Harry Norton. She had known this gentleman, a neighbor, for some time and was already fond of him before the incident which marked the beginning of their sexual relationship. One day, after she had been bathing as usual at a secluded spot on the beach, she ran into Sir Harry, opera glasses in hand, who had been watching her from a distance. He coaxed her into going with him to a "grassy bank, hidden by some trees," played with her sexual parts, showed her his erection, and asked her to masturbate him. When she at first refused, he gave her a sound spanking, after which she was more amenable: "I never really wanted to resist him, but to a little girl of twelve, it was all so new that it was not till he had whipped me that I lost my feeling of shyness and gave myself to gratifying his desires."

Sir Harry now rubbed his penis between her labia and inserted the tip slightly into the vagina before he had an orgasm, the first one little Phyllis had witnessed: "Of course my legs were dripping wet with what my childish attractions had drawn from my lover, but oh! it was so nice to know that, as I lay on my back once more, he was gently drying my naked limbs with his handkerchief, and then to feel that he was kissing me between the legs and making my little slit quiver again by the action of his lips and tongue, as if repaying his child love for the help she had given him in the accomplishment of his desires."

Before they part, Sir Harry gave Phyllis a sovereign "to

buy chocolates," and a heart-shaped gold locket with little
diamonds and pearls, and a pretty golden chain—"and after
many kisses and a loving good-bye, I went home to my dear old
aunt, who found me so flushed and happy that she said the sea
air and bathing was making quite a little woman of me."

The chapter ends with another rhyme.

> I love Phyllis, and Phyllis loves me.
> And Phyllis's cunt is fair to see,
> So I sucked it once, and I sucked it twice
> And oh! it was juicy, and soft, and nice
> As a schoolgirl's slit should be.

Next day, Sir Harry went on a trip, but before leaving he
introduced Phyllis to his wife, Lady Norton, who, the following
day, had a confidential chat with her. Instead of scolding her
for what had happened between her and Sir Harry, she assured
the young girl that she was not jealous or angry in the least. She
proceeded to tell Phyllis the story of her own childhood and
seduction by the same Sir Harry when she was fifteen years old.
The story is retold by Phyllis.

Although Eva [the later Lady Norton] lay quietly asleep and unconscious of all pertaining to the outer world, the hour in which she
should give up her virginity had arrived.

The front of her nightdress was fastened along the deep line of
frilling and this Harry gently undid as low as her waist and laying
the sides back fully exposed her girlish breasts. His next action was to
undress himself and when naked he raised the lower part of her
nightgown above her hips, and thus—as her legs lay wide apart—the
very center of her girlish charms was fully exposed to his view.
Then he bent forward to kiss the little tuft of hair which failed to
hide from his passionate gaze the V-shaped point where the rounded
lips of her little cunt met and joined her body. But Eva's time had
come. Harry quietly crept into the bed where she lay, and half-
kneeling, half-lying between her outstretched legs he grasped and
held her firmly in his naked arms. Then Eva awoke.

There is no doubt that young girls, who have from childhood
been accustomed to practice little acts of love upon themselves in
private, and have as they passed into girlhood given full play and
indulgence to hotter and fiercer passions, suffer much less pain

during their seduction than those of a colder nature who are innocent of former pleasures, and who submit to give up their maidenheads perhaps for money or through force. To a fifteen-year-old
school girl, unacquainted with the art of satisfying the passions
which naughty thoughts or books have aroused, the act of seduction
causes the intensest pain; and it may be that her lover has to enter
into her five or six times, and at each freely emit his fluid into her
body, before she herself becomes capable of feeling the delight she
creates in him.

Eva was not that sort of girl, as we have seen, and finding her
lover bent on accomplishing his wishes, which was the climax of her
own desires also, she gave him every help by bending her knees, and
keeping her legs apart, and even with her hand she held the point of
his prick where she knew it must force her maidenhead and enter
her virgin slit. Then pain, bravely borne, without a greater cry than
"Oh! Harry it hurts" and that only whispered, and then came to her
that indescribable sensation when a young girl's vagina is for the
first time distended by the fully grown organ of a man many years
older than herself.

Eva was now almost writhing with a pleasure the intensity of
which she had never dreamed of before; then Harry pressed her
closer and she could feel his prick was convulsively rising and
falling as it moved, and she knew it was the end, and then it came,
and as they exchanged their burning kisses, she could feel that her
lover was pouring into her girlish and quivering body the very
essence of his manhood.

And thus ended Lady Norton's story which with her gentle
voice and manner had fascinated me. Lying on the grass she had
caressed me freely as she told the tale of her seduction, and at the
most passionate parts her fingers found their way between my legs
and this and her own sweetness made me love her even more, I
think, than had she been a man.

Soon, not only was Sir Harry having a full-fledged affair
with young Phyllis (though still abstaining from coitus) but
Lady Norton (who was not really Sir Harry's wedded wife,
because she was heiress to a large fortune which she would
jeopardize by marrying) also was having a lesbian relationship
with her. (At one point, she taught Phyllis how to use the dildo
on her, while administering a birching at the same time.)

Finally, Phyllis met Algy, a friend of the Nortons. The first
of their more intimate encounters took place outdoors. Algy tied

down her wrists to forked sticks he had set in the ground, lifted up her clothes, put a new pair of silk stockings on her legs, then brought her to orgasm twice with manual and oral stimulation, before having anal intercourse with her.

At their next meeting, the occasion of Phyllis's birthday, Algy first performed cunnilingus on her, brought her to orgasm, then had her fellate him—she doing it for the first time and being so good at it (inserting a wetted finger into his anus and not pulling away at the moment of his ejaculation) that Algy is full of surprise and praise.

Phyllis the same day introduced a young girl, Helen, to Algy and helped him perform anal intercourse with her, after which the two girls went "down to the seashore and I told her how I loved him, and how he had that morning spent into my mouth, and all the other things he had done to me, and we talked till our naughty feelings came back again as we got home. So we first went up to my bedroom and satisfied each other's longings once more; then we made my bed and spent a quiet evening together till the servants returned home."

There follows the description of how Sir Harry, with the assistance of both Eva and Phyllis, deflowered the fifteen-year-old cousin of Phyllis. Again, tying-up plays an important role in this scene—the legs of the girl being tied to a silk band which was stretched from wall to wall across the lower end of the bed.

In another curious scene Phyllis teaches Helen how to fellate a man by demonstrating it to her with the aid of a dildo which is filled with warm and slightly salted milk. While Phyllis masturbates the girl, she is to suck the dildo and learn to swallow the milk when it is released into her mouth at the moment of her own orgasm.

The last chapter, or twelfth letter to Marie, tells how the narrator (Phyllis) "is seduced at the age of thirteen, and the result!" Having, as usual, brought the girl to orgasm several times by other means, Algy now takes her maidenhead. There is only slight pain when he actually ruptures the hymen, but the second intercourse only a short while after proves extremely painful and traumatic to the girl. She faints, or rather goes into shock, and is slowly nursed back to health by the Nortons and Algy. This, then, serves as the explanation for the missionary passion with which the author advocates that young girls should be introduced to all the arts of love except vaginal intercourse, and that not until they are old enough for it (which is, according to the author, about a year after onset of menstruation, or about age fifteen). So fanatically is this point made and the traumatic defloration experience is so realistically described that one is tempted to speculate whether *Child Love* might not have been written by a woman rather than a man. However, it is also possible that a male writer might have simply used this device hypocritically to provide some excuse for the description of the highly salacious scenes.

FLOSSIE

Another late-Victorian novel, *Flossie*, is likewise devoted to fantasies about the sex life of minors, or rather of a particular minor—Flossie, "A Venus of Fifteen," as the book's subtitle explains. Anonymously written "by one who knew this charming goddess and worshipped at her shrine," it is the story of Captain Archer's affair with this fifteen-year-old, as told—in contrast to *Child Love*—from the man's point of view.

The story appears to be partly autobiographical, at least it would seem highly improbable that anyone would invent out of whole cloth so individualistic and imaginative a young girl as Flossie. That is to say, the sexual fantasies of the heroine are truly remarkable and bear the mark of being basically those of a woman, though undoubtedly embellished and reinterpreted by a man's mind.

Flossie, it appears, likes to play-act and impersonate other people. She seems to be living most of the time in some sort of dream or fantasy world of her own into which she fits the "real" persons she meets, such as Captain Archer, and makes them play certain roles opposite her. No sooner has the twenty-seven-year-old Captain been introduced to her by a former mistress of his, than she starts her first scene with him, in which she pretends to be the "Great White Queen of the Gama Huchi Islands."

. . . she wore my "billycock" hat and a pair of blue pince-nez, and carrying a crutch-handled stick, she advanced upon me with a defiant air, and glaring down over the top of her glasses she said in a deep masculine voice:

"Now, sir, if you're ready for Ibsen, *I* am. Or if your tastes are so *low* that you can't care about a play, I'll give you a skirt-dance."

As she said this she tore off the long dress, threw my hat onto a sofa, let down her hair with a turn of the wrist, and motioning me to the piano picked up her skirts and began to dance.

Enchanted as I was by the humor of her quick change to the "Ibsen woman," words are vain to describe my feelings as I feebly tinkled a few bars on the piano and watched the dancer.

Every motion was the perfection of grace and yet no Indian nautch girl could have more skillfully expressed the idea of sexual allurement. Gazing at her in speechless admiration, I saw the violent eyes glow with passion, the full red lips part, the filmy petticoats were lifted higher and higher; the loose frilled drawers gleamed white. At last breathless and panting, she fell back upon a chair, her eyes closed, her legs parted, her breasts heaving. A mingled perfume came to my nostrils—half *odor di femina*, half the scent of white roses from her hair and clothes.

I flung myself upon her.

"Tell me, Flossie darling, what shall I do *first?*"

The answer came, quick and short.

"Kiss me—*between my legs!*"

In an instant I was kneeling before her. Her legs fell widely apart. Sinking to a sitting posture, I plunged my head between her thighs. The petticoats incommoded me a little, but I soon managed to arrive at the desired spot. Somewhat to my surprise instead of finding the lips closed and barricaded as is usual in the case of young girls, they were ripe, red, and pouting, and as my mouth closed eagerly upon the delicious orifice and my tongue found and pressed upon the trembling clitoris I knew that my qualms of conscience had been vain.

Shading her eyes with her hand she gazed in my direction:

"Aha! a stranger; and, unless these royal eyes deceive us, a man! He shall see what it is to defy our laws! What ho! within there! Take this person and remove his p—"

"Great Queen!" I said, in a voice of deep humility, "if you will but grant me two minutes, I will make haste to comply with your laws."

"And we, good fellow, will help you." (*Aside.*) "Methinks he is somewhat comely."* (*Aloud.*) "But first let us away with these leg garments, which are more than aught else a violation of our Gama Huchian Rules. Good! now the shirt. And what, pray, is *this*? We thank you, sir, but we are not requiring any *tent-poles* just now."

"Then if your Majesty will deign to remove your royal fingers I will do my humble best to cause the offending pole to disappear. At present, with your Majesty's hand upon it—"

"Silence, sir! Your time is nearly up, and if the last garment be not removed in twenty seconds—so! you obey. 'Tis well! You shall see how we reward a faithful subject of our laws."

And thrusting my yard between her lips the Great White Queen of the Gama Huchi Islands sucked in the whole column to the very root, and by dint of working her royal mouth up and down, and applying her royal fingers to the neighboring appendages, soon drew into her throat a tribute to her greatness, which from its volume and the time it took in the act of payment, plainly caused her Majesty the most exquisite enjoyment. Of my own pleasure I will only say that it was delirious, while in this as in all other love sports in which we indulged an added zest was given by the humor and fancy with which this adorable child-woman designed and carried out our amusements.

---

* Don't believe I ever said anything of the sort, but if I did, "methinks" I'd better take this opportunity of withdrawing the statement.—Flossie.

There is a curious similarity between this book and *Child Love* in that both authors stress that it is proper to initiate girls into amatory experiences very early in life, but that it is utterly wrong and criminal to "seduce" them, that is, to have vaginal intercourse with them before they have reached physical maturity.

In *Flossie*, Captain Archer spares the young girl with regard to defloration, engaging instead in mouth-genital relations, in which Flossie shows herself already unusually well versed from the outset. Realizing that Captain Archer may wonder about this, she anticipates any questions on his part by saying:

"I know you must be wondering all the time how a person of my age can have come to be so . . . what shall we say, Jack?"

"Larky," I suggested.

"Yes, 'larky' will do. Of course I have always been 'older than my age' as the saying goes, and my friendship with Ylette and all the lovely things she used to do to me made me 'come on' much faster than most girls. I ought to tell you that I got to be rather a favorite at school, and after it came to be known that Ylette and I were on gamahuching terms, I used to get little notes from almost every girl in the school over twelve, imploring me to sleep with her. One dear little thing even went so far as to give me the measurements of her tongue, which she had taken with a piece of string."

"Oh, I say, Flossie, *come now*—I can swallow a good deal but—"

"You can indeed, Jack, as I have good reason to know! But all the same it's absolutely true."

The metaphorical language frequently employed in this story reminds one of *A Description of Merryland, Arbor Vitae*, and similar older writings. In this style, the writer deliberately uses synonyms rather than direct terms, alluding to sexual matters, rather than speaking of them plainly. A self-imposed language taboo is thereby set up which calls attention to the forbidden or taboo subject matter in the same manner as fashion may call attention to the eroticism of the female form by deliberate covering up.

Flossie advocates that, since girls will have mouth-genital contact with each other anyway, it would be much better if they had it with boys, but only if one could be sure that nothing else was going to happen.

"Don't laugh, Jack. I am very serious about it. I don't care how much a girl of (say) my age longs for a boy to be naughty with—it's perfectly right and natural. What I think is bad is that she should *begin* by having a liking for a girl's tongue inculcated into her. I should like to see boys and girls turned loose upon one another once a week or so at authorized gamahuching parties, which should be attended by masters and governesses (who would have to see that the *other* thing was not indulged in, of course). Then the girls would grow up with a good healthy taste for the other sex, and even if they did do a little gamahuching among themselves between whiles, it would only be to keep themselves going till the next party. By my plan a boy's prick would be the central object of their desires, as it ought to be. Now *I* think that's a very fine scheme, Jack, and as soon as I am a little older, I shall go to Paris and put it before the Minister of Education!"

"But why wait, Flossie? Why not go now?"

"Well, you see, if the old gentleman (I suppose he *is* old, isn't he, or he wouldn't be a minister?)—if he saw a girl in short frocks, he would think she had got some private object to serve in regard to the gamahuching parties. Whereas a grown-up person who had plainly left school might be supposed to be doing it unselfishly for the good of the rising generation."

"Yes, I understand that. But when you *do* go, Flossie, please take me or some other respectable person with you, because I don't altogether trust that Minister of Education, and whatever the length of your frocks might happen to be at the time, I feel certain that, old or young, the moment you had explained your noble scheme, he would be wanting some practical illustrations on the office arm-chair!"

"How dare you suggest such a thing, Jack! You are to understand, sir, that from henceforth my mouth is reserved for three purposes, to eat with, to talk with, and to kiss you with on whatever part of your person I may happen to fancy at the moment. By the way you won't mind my making just one exception in favor of Eva, will you? She loves me to make her nipples stand with my tongue; occasionally, too, we perform the *'soixante-neuf.'*"

"When the next performance takes place, may I be there to see?" I ejaculated fervently.

"Oh, Jack, how shocking!"

"Does it shock you, Flossie? Very well then I withdraw it, and apologize."

"You cannot withdraw it now. You have distinctly stated that you would like to be there when Eva and I have our next gamahuche."

"Well, I suppose I *did* say . . ."

"Silence, sir," said Flossie in a voice of thunder, and shaking her brown head at me with inexpressible ferocity. "You have made a proposal of the most indecent character, and the sentence of the Court is that at the first possible opportunity you shall be *held to that proposal.* Meanwhile the Court condemns you to receive 250 kisses on various parts of your body, which it will at once proceed to administer. Now, sir, off with your clothes!"

"Mayn't I keep my . . ."

"No, sir, you may *not!*"

The sentence of the Court was accordingly carried out to the letter, somewhere about three-fourths of the kisses being applied upon one and the same part of the prisoner to which the Court attached its mouth with extraordinary gusto.

In the above passage, we have another instance of Flossie's theatrical flights of imagination, setting up a court scene, in which she, as the judge, metes out the punishment of two hundred and fifty kisses to be administered to Captain Archer's body.

In the next scene, it is not she but the Captain who is to be the judge, and not in a court scene, but in a most unusual contest. He is to measure the sexual parts of Flossie (Eversley) and the older girl Eva (Letchford) to determine which of them is superior to the other.

"There's one other measurement I *should* like to have taken," said Eva, "because in spite of my ten years '*de plus*' and the fact that my cunt is not altogether a stranger to the joys of being fucked, I believe that Flossie would win *that* race, and I should like her to have one out of three!"

"*Lovely!*" cried Flossie. "But Jack must be the judge. Here's the tape, Jack: fire away. Now, Evie, come and lie beside me on the edge of the bed, open your legs, and swear, to abide by the verdict!"

After a few minutes fumbling with the tape and close inspection of the parts in dispute, I retired to a table and wrote down the following, which I pinned against the window curtain.

LETCHFORD *v.* EVERSLEY.

Mesdames,

In compliance with your instructions I have this day surveyed the private premises belonging to the above parties, and have now the honor to submit the following report, plan, and measurements.

As will be seen from the plan, Miss Letchford's cunt is exactly $3\frac{1}{16}$ inches from the underside of clitoris to the base of vulva. Miss Eversley's cunt, adopting the same line of measurement, gives $3\frac{5}{8}$ inches.

I may add that the premises appear to me to be thoroughly desirable in both cases, and to a good, upright and painstaking tenant would afford equally pleasant accommodation in spring, summer, autumn, or winter.

A small but well-wooded covert is attached to each, while an admirable dairy is in convenient proximity.

With reference to the Eversley property I am informed that it has not yet been occupied, but in view of its size and beauty, and the undoubted charms of the surrounding country I confidently anticipate that a permanent and satisfactory tenant (such as I have ventured to describe above) will very shortly be found for it. My opinion of its advantages as a place of residence may, indeed, be gathered from the fact that I am greatly disposed to make an offer in my own person.

> *Yours faithfully,*
> J. ARCHER.
> (*Captain 174th Regt.*)

The humorous scene of measuring the sex organs of the two girls reminds one of certain passages in *My Secret Life,* in which Walter tries to find out how many shillings a girl could hold in her vagina without losing them, and another in which he wants to determine the maximum volume of a vagina by inserting a balloon inside, with a mouthpiece to blow it up (in the first case, he succeeded, in the second he failed).

DÉBAUCHÉES PRÉCOCES

A very unusual French novel, *Débauchées Précoces* (*Precocious Wantons*), dating from the turn of the century, deals with the adventures of a most seductive and experienced nymphet, Agatha. An orphan, Agatha has been living with her uncle who is responsible for having introduced her to a variety of sexual activities, short of coitus. At one point, a friend of the uncle, a man named Célestin, takes the girl to Paris where she is to attend a boarding school.

What was going through Célestin's mind? He wouldn't have been able to say. This child astride his knees aroused his sensual appetite. He was getting a bigger and bigger erection, wondering if he wasn't going to rush her to appease the furious passion that had taken hold of him.

The decision was his alone to make! Nobody would intervene. At that time train compartments had not yet been fitted out with protective glass panels designed to impose good behavior upon the amateurs of railroad lechery.

One of his arms had slipped around Agatha's waist. She smiled at him and suddenly, childlike, she pinched his chin and exclaimed, "You look at me just the way my uncle does!"

This exclamation restored his composure; he released slightly his tight grasp on her and replied, "But my eyes aren't the same as your uncle's."

"No, not at all! Yours are black and his are blue. But they both have the same expression. Isn't that funny?"

She put her hand on the one he had on her waist, and he said, "What's so funny?"

"Oh, I don't know. It's not up to me to explain!"

She shook her head in the manner of a level-headed adult expecting to be understood, and he went on: "And if I kissed you, my little friend, would you explain to me what you find so funny about my eyes!"

"Kiss me. We'll find out."

She leaned against his chest. He kissed her on the forehead. She didn't move. He lowered the kiss to her nose. She closed her eyes. His lips reached hers. She opened her eyes and said:

"Oh! You think just the way my uncle does!"

She got down from his knees and he let her go. He felt his ears turning red and began to be frightened by the adventure he could see coming.

As they continue the journey, Célestin asks the girl:

"Would you like to play house and be my little baby?"

Play house! He breathed in the odor of the girl's young flesh. A mutual warmth enveloped them. He said, "Do you play house with your Uncle?"

"Sometimes."

His head moved up to lean against Agatha's chest. She let it rest there. She felt she was inured to it. She felt his head next to her shoulders, next to her face. She patted his cheeks with her hands. When Célestin's fingers, having opened her drawers, touched her flesh, she quite naturally spread open her thighs, and she closed her eyes when very gently he tickled her button.

This forty-odd-year-old man, up until this moment master of his passions, was being overpowered by rapture. He had always loved women and he had not lacked occasions to satisfy his desires. He had traveled to the four corners of the earth, availing himself of pleasures like a man whose fortune afforded him every conceivable folly. He could practically consider himself blasé. And yet this gamine, this precocious *débauchée* infused an unknown effervescence into his veins.

His barely closed hand was placed between her thighs and gave the child a feeling of sweet agitation which reflected onto him and excited him to lecheries never before dreamed of. A bit of down attracted his fingers to her abdomen. He suspected he was living one of those unforgettable moments when destiny, stopping its evolution, gives a human being access to ecstasies which blot out everything he had ever experienced before.

He drank in the little girl's abandon as one drinks a glass of excellent wine which acts on the stomach and the mind with penetrating warmth, which prompts one to find everything perfect, everything beautiful.

Agatha, in order to facilitate his task, had placed one foot on the seat and put an arm around his neck, bringing him closer to her. They seemed to have conquered eternity in that silent and voluptuous caress of the masculine hand on the feminine jewel aspiring to rise up from limbo.

A brusque impulse made him pinch the flesh he was fondling. Agatha's first reaction was to bring her legs together, then, before he could stop her, she threw them forward and was standing straight up, saying. "Oh, such a naughty one!"

Blood was throbbing in his temples. He was within an inch of jumping the girl, and raping her. The sound of the neighboring compartment's door being shut brought him back to his senses.

"What is it?" he asked her.

Agatha had peeked out the door after her exclamation to investigate. She replied, "An employee."

And true enough, a few seconds later their door opened and the conductor came in asking for tickets. He didn't notice anything suspect about the little girl standing up, looking out the window at the passing countryside; or about the man reading his newspaper.

Solitude once again surrounded the two travelers.

She had gone to sit in another corner and, acting childishly for the moment, was making faces at Célestin, while peeling an orange.

"Are you hungry?" he asked.

"What a stupid thing to ask! Just because I'm peeling an orange? No, Monsieur, I am a glutton and I love this fruit."

"A glutton for fruit!"

He put down his newspaper and came nearer, in order to look at her more closely without disturbing her most important occupation.

She had the face and attitude of a woman who had stopped growing up, but her features revealed a child, a child who was no longer innocent and who studiously sought to encourage vice.

Her lips took on the expression of mockery and wheedling, one following the other in quick succession; her nostrils were dilated as when at the approach of a desire that was sure to attain satisfaction; and her eyes, oh, her eyes, playing under her lashes made her entire face a poem.

Brutal instincts tormented Célestin. He felt himself flooded by an extraordinary fluid which drew him like a magnet to this child's body! . . .

She was once again seated next to him, offering him her hand that he was caressing in his own. She sweetly obeyed his pressure, bringing her to his shoulder. She didn't pull away her hand when he put it on his trousers, next to the buttons, which he undid once again. She slipped her hand under his shirt without having to lift it as a few minutes before. Then she herself took his prick and held it a few seconds in her hand.

She leaned over to see the virile member and doing so presented to him her blonde, tawny hair, which he kissed.

She rewarded this kiss with a tender pressure of her hand on his prick, then she lifted up his shirt as he had done before and pressed her face to his belly, making him think that she was going to suck him.

She didn't do anything of the sort. She moved as little as he had when he was leaning on her chest. Her hand hadn't let go of his prick, and her eyes were studying it, exploring his manhood.

He respected her immobility, so as not to scare her away, for he knew this was still the best means to obtain what he wanted. . . .

With this young, feminine body pressed against him, Célestin, breaking with his habitual ways, let himself be guided by his impressions. To his great astonishment, his mind was receiving more pleasure than his body was. Not that his body wasn't participating in the celebration, far from that, but because it remained confined to its role of the living affirmation of a desire on its way to material fulfillment.

The little girl's head, flattened against the man's belly, dug through the muscles into the male body's whole structure; this structure culminating in the cock. The latter was completely erect, enraptured by the hand holding it, seeming to read the woman's ardor in the eyes beholding it and quivering from the intellectual communion taking place between the two beings.

Gradually Agatha's head drew nearer and she placed a kiss on the extremity of the prick. The electric spark shook both of them. She straightened up to put her arms around his neck and kiss him. He drew her to him, she gave in to his pressure and found herself astride his knees, with his prick, all warm and vibrating, between her thighs.

What was going to happen? He was already bending her, her young thighs pressed against the glans of the prick were already submitting to its domineering will, and the pussy did not refuse the attack threatening it. Célestin wrenched himself free of the madness which was numbing his reason, lifted her off his knees and said, "Let's be sure that nothing betrays us. Take off your drawers, little one."

Slightly dazed, she hastened to obey without further ado.

Being the precocious little girl she was, once her drawers were off she folded and rolled them neatly and put them in a traveling bag.

This simple action brought a relative calm to the compartment and on the pretext of finding out if the conductor were coming back, he buttoned himself up and went to examine the situation from the door.

She came up behind him, took his hand, kissed it and said; "We're like old friends. You don't have to call me Mademoiselle any more. Let's use first names, Célestin."

Feeling like joking with her, he turned around, knelt down and putting his arms around her replied, "You are as pretty as the most beautiful flowers of creation, my darling little Agatha, I must declare my love for you."

"Don't make fun of me, my dear Célestin. I am not an animal. You're happy to paw me and I am just as happy to do the same to you."

On his knees, he had burrowed his hands underneath her skirts and was fondling her buttocks.

"Oh, Mademoiselle!" he exclaimed, "what lovely curves you have here!"

"Curves? Oh, yes, my uncle adores my fanny."

"Does he, now? And just how did your uncle come to see it?"

"You're too curious! I let you do what he does, you shouldn't complain."

"Oh, the nasty little thing! She knows how to swing her fanny when she's kissed!"

She began to laugh and answered: "You don't have to be kissed in order to move it around. Besides, when girls are alone, they teach each other things. . . ."

Pulled by Célestin, she got back on his knees.

"Little woman, little woman," he said, "you are truly a little woman."

"You're right, let's have some fun; that will dispel sad thoughts."

He sought her lips, she offered them to him; a long caress shook them both to the marrow of their bones, making them cling to one another.

"Célestin, what would you like to do for fun?" she murmured.

"Oh, anything and everything!"

She laughed, her lips against his mouth, and replied: "So would I."

"How does your uncle have fun?"

"He puts me completely naked on his knees—he's completely naked too. But we can't do that on the train."

"Come here, the way you were before."

"Astride you like this?"

"That's right."

She was there in a trice and immediately felt Célestin's cock tickling her thighs. She pressed herself against his chest and his prick slid up the crack of her ass. But this time Célestin's excitement was so great that he kept her crushed in his arms, moving underneath her to masturbate himself by rubbing against her flesh.

She was no doubt accustomed to this, for she herself executed the maneuver and all at once he ejaculated, spattering her up to the navel.

Acting as a woman who knew the value of such things, she let him finish, her head hidden in Célestin's shoulder, no longer moving in order not to disturb him. When he had stopped coming, she lifted up her eyes, damp with pleasure, and said to him, "Oh, the shot was fired! Give me your hanky so I can wipe myself off."

"In a minute."

"Wait, let me lift up my chemise. You wet me so high."

He didn't prevent her from taking this precaution. For several seconds he savored his strange happiness. Then he gave her his handkerchief, she straightened up and he watched her clean herself with consummate skill, wiping off the slightest drops of sperm which might possibly get her into trouble. Once dried off, she opened her traveling bag and took out a bottle of Lubin, poured a few drops on the handkerchief and drenched her parts with it.

Then, very gay, she gave it back to him, saying, "Here, have a souvenir from me!"

In this little girl, the womanly quality affirmed itself in the knowledge of her individuality.

She rebuttoned Célestin's trousers and added:

"I would have thought it would have taken longer!"

"But it's not over with yet!" he cried.

"Oh, yes, it is."

"You wait and see! You wouldn't mind more."

"More! Are you sure?"

"Yes—after the next station."

"Well, nothing would suit me better!"

Once arrived in Paris, Célestin decides not to take Agatha directly to the boarding school, but has her live with him first at his hotel. While there, they continue their sexual activities in greater comfort and security, which allows them to experiment with sex techniques that even Agatha's uncle had not dared to try.

"Do you know, my little friend, that between a man and a woman there is more than these caresses, no matter how delicious they may be?"

"Yes. A man takes a woman. My uncle told me that he buried his whatchamacallit into her belly, that that way he deflowered her and could even make a child."

"Look at the sly one! Just this afternoon she pretended not to know that one inserted the whatchamacallit into the hole!"

"This afternoon I had forgotten," she replied calmly.

"One also buries it into the asshole! Your Uncle didn't teach you that?"

"No, he must have been afraid of making me suffer."

"Are you afraid?"

She left her place on his chest and without getting up from his knees, very seriously demanded:

"Listen, do you really want to pierce me?"

"Do you want me to?"

"I don't know."

"Would you refuse?"

"No. I would never refuse you anything that would please you. But I beg you not to deflower me. I'm too young to have children."

"All right, then give me your asshole."

"You can try, after you've caressed it and caressed it." . . .

He carried her like a child over to the bed, lay her down and slid next to her, taking her back into his arms, kissing her, caressing her, fondling her, saying, "You are my wife, we're married, and I'm going to possess you."

"Oh, yes, I'm your little wife. Possess me."

"Stretch out on your back."

"Like this?"

"Yes, yes, now spread your thighs apart."

"You want to try the front now?"

"Just be ready, be ready."

When he was on top of her, she seemed like such a little thing, despite the fact that she was quite large for her age, that he felt ashamed and contented himself to skim over her pussy with the tip of his prick. Then he slipped between her thighs and gamahuched her. She abandoned herself ecstatically to his caresses, and he softly said, "You're too young to be deflowered. We're going to try your asshole. Turn around."

She obeyed, offered her buttocks to his warm licking. She then felt that he was climbing up her back, covering it with his entire body, and she quivered when his prick touched the middle of her crack, but did not balk.

For a moment he didn't move, so as to quiet her fears, then slowly directed the glans towards the hole. She huddled up into a ball. He tickled her clitoris and seeing that she was affected, he separated the hair covering her slit and with his glans exerted a slight bit of pressure.

"Oh, oh," she said, "do you think that it will go in?"

She wasn't rebelling, and that encouraged him. The head was penetrating, spreading the flesh apart, cracking but not tearing the folds. He replied, "Part of it is already in."

"I feel it. Don't push too hard. It seems to me that everything is being crushed inside me. Oh, stop a minute, this is becoming really wonderful!"

He controlled himself with great difficulty. But he respected this little girl who asserted herself so resolutely as a high priestess of voluptuousness. He only progressed gradually.

In spite of that, since his prick swelled as it got to his balls, there came a moment when a rather acute pain forced a muffled cry from Agatha.

He stopped still. It was she who reminded him of the work at hand by saying, "The most difficult part is over with, I feel it, you've pushed in half of it, don't hold yourself back any longer."

Nonetheless, he continued to advance with moderation, earning his victory, without the little girl even coming close to fainting. When he had put his entire prick into her asshole he took her hand and said, "You see, there it is."

"Oh, it's true!"

"Now we'll perform the second half of the operation: to take it out gently so that it won't hurt you. Then we will start over again, up to the time when it will be wet inside."

"Yes, yes, anything you say."

She felt a few more minor pains but she was completely pre-pared when the amorous attack took place. She was nicely buggered with ejaculation and all, and was thus possessed by the gentleman to whom her worthy uncle had entrusted her.

The tremors satisfied both of them. After the final assault, fatigue finally took hold and she withdrew into her own room to enjoy a rest made necessary by such gambols.

When Agatha is finally enrolled and living at the school, she is reunited with a girl friend, Rita, and the two continue their lesbian relationship. Found out by an older girl who is a super-visor, they include her in their affair, making it a threesome. Later on, when Célestin becomes interested in Rita as well, the specter of jealousy beclouds their otherwise idyllic ménage, into which still other people are drawn as time goes on.

The story brings out the Lolita-style seductiveness and precocity of certain pubescent girls who frequently turn out to be the state's offended party in cases of statutory rape or offenses against minors. The Kinsey researchers give one dra-matic example, among many, in their study of sex offenders: The man had taken a calculated risk, engaging in sexual activities with an attractive young girl whom he suspected to be legally under age, but who was always well made up, wore high-heeled shoes, tight-fitting clothes, seductive night dresses, and who behaved in every respect as a young adult. She liked to go to bars, dance, "have a good time," and, in bed, proved to be a reasonably satisfactory sex partner. All the greater was his surprise and shock when, accused of having taken advantage of a minor, he saw the girl again in court, made up like a child: her hair had been braided in pigtails and, to complete the picture of childish innocence, she had been given a rag doll to hold.

L'AMOUREUSE DE JEUNES GARÇONS

We shall turn now to those fantasies dealing with women who prefer young boys for their lovers. *L'Amoureuse de Jeunes Garçons* (*The Lady Who Loved Young Boys*) ("San Francisco:

Fuckwell C. Lewis & Co. Editeurs," n.d., but probably *ca.* 1890).

A young woman, Octavia, aged twenty-two, still a virgin, does not like grown men, but since she does not see the man in young boys she can accept them as her sex partners. In the beginning of the book, she is just getting involved with Octave (notice the play on the similarity of the male and female forms of the name), a boy of thirteen who is taking drawing lessons from her. He tells her how he and his boy friend, Amable, render each other service by performing fellatio on one another. She decides to play the role of Amable and, with Octave's initial instructions to guide her, fellates the boy: "Kneeling between his thighs, sucking him, she was enjoying with this sprouting adolescent those rudiments of the male sex organs which, in the past, she had always found so monstrously revolting." The act completed, the boy confesses that he liked her ministrations much better than those of his friend and begs her to take over all the other boy's functions. She agrees, but only under the conditions that all be kept in strictest secrecy and that he will completely abide by her instructions.

Octave agrees and, as time goes on, she lets him take her virginity, directing each of his childish movements. Next day, the boy appears for his lessons without any new drawings. She scolds him and wonders whether he has lost respect for her as a teacher, since they have been playing "those games." Oh, no, Octave assures her, he has made other drawings, but does not dare to show them to her. Of course, they turn out to be efforts to draw her in the nude and the two of them during intercourse.

Far from taking offense, Octavia criticizes the drawings very objectively, showing him where he has been wrong in his depiction of female anatomy. The last picture depicts him having anal intercourse with her. He explains that a boy by the name of Savinien has proposed to do this to Amable, but that the latter refused, so he (Octave) has imagined how it would be if he did it to her instead. She gives him a lesson in anatomy instead, but gradually they get around to this and other experiments in sex.

The story goes on in this vein until Octavia moves to the

Midi, where, she figures, the children will be more precocious than in the cold north. She is proven right by a ten-year-old boy, Marc, who turns out to be every bit as mentally advanced and physically developed as the thirteen- and fourteen-year-old boys of the northern latitudes whom she had known.

SCHOOL LIFE IN PARIS

Another story of this genre, though with a heavy emphasis on clothes fetishism, is *School Life in Paris*, published in 1897. It concerns a lady who employs a unique method of coming in contact with adolescent boys.

. . . [she] had, it seemed, a passion for small boys and, finding a difficulty in gratifying this lust, she adopted the expedient of sending numbers of telegrams to herself every day. In Paris I must tell you, telegrams are always brought up and delivered to their owner by the telegraph boys in person. When one of these knocked at her door, and was told to "come in," he found her lying in a long easy chair, with nothing on but a thin silk dressing gown, which being carefully left unfastened all down the front, would fly open at the slightest movement, allowing the boy to feast his eyes upon her naked cunt and tiddies. After looking at these for a few moments it generally did not require much persuasion to induce him to take off his regulation trousers, and place his childish prick at her disposal.

If the boy was a novice in the art of vice her enjoyment was of course all the greater, for there is no greater pleasure for a depraved woman than to teach a young innocent boy all the different ways of satisfying sensual passion and to make him an adept of vice.

Later in the book, we read that another young woman receives a fifteen-year-old boy into her bedroom and proceeds to seduce him by all the feminine wiles at her disposal, including a kind of striptease in which she has the boy help her slowly undress. The lengthy passage (told from the woman's point of view) is sensuous and emphasizes the clever use of clothes and the art of shedding them. We shall reproduce it here (although it belongs perhaps in a later section dealing specifically with clothes fetishism) because it conveys with uncanny insight on

the part of the undoubtedly male writer the peculiar attraction
and erotic excitement which the idea of seducing young boys
must have for certain women.

I had only thrown off my hat, which lay on a chair, and was otherwise dressed just as I had come in from the street. My tiny arched
shoes with their sharp points and tall slender heels were thrust
negligently out of a frou-frou of white petticoats, which were
pulled up high enough to disclose the skin of a dainty pink ankle,
peeping through the windows of a black open-work stocking.

I saw his gaze wander gradually up from there to my very
tightly corseted waist, above which my bust stood out most voluptuously, being lifted up by one of the cushions on which I lay, in
such a manner that not only the big round globes but also the sturdy
little "pricks" showed plainly and attractively beneath the thin well-
fitting corsage. My hands were gloved to the elbow in spotless
lavender kid that fit without a wrinkle, and the slight disorder of
my hair did not, I fancy, serve to make it look any less attractive.

From his increasing blushes I saw that he was somewhat
troubled in the seat of his emotions, and so I asked him to sit down,
and chatted with him on various topics, leading them gradually
round to the paper I held in my hand, the illustrations of which,
being mainly of pretty girls, all in attractive forms of undress or no
dress at all, were calculated to increase rather than diminish the
vague desires with which he was beginning to burn. When I could
see from the flash in his lovely eyes that he was beginning to feel
really naughty, a fact which my sly glances at his trousers fully
confirmed, I suggested that he should help me to take off my gloves,
as it was rather hot.

The voluptuous feeling of the soft kid, warm with the glow of
the feminine hand it had so tightly clasped, caused him such exquisite thrills of pleasure and desire that he lingered a long time over
this evidently delightful task.

I laughingly complimented him on being so excellent a lady's
maid, and suggested that perhaps he would like to take off my shoes
as well. His sensuality was now so thoroughly aroused that he took
the tiny slipper in his hand, and having gently and caressingly
drawn it off, he imprinted a long lascivious kiss upon the rosy
instep, which stood arched up beneath its flimsy covering.

In doing this to the second foot, he lifted it so high to his lips
that he caught a glimpse of the pink and black satin garters clasping
my leg above the knee. "May I not take off those as well?" he asked
with a still more violent blush; to which I of course replied, "Cer-

tainly not, you dreadfully naughty boy." But as I smiled at him while I said it, and at the same time gently pulled up my skirts so as to give him a full view of these dainty circlets, being a youth of sense, in spite of his innocence and shyness, he took this as being the permission it was meant to be, and in a few minutes the garters were off, and, having kissed them, he placed one upon his head as a sort of crown, while he continued from time to time to caress the legs from which he had taken them.

Now, it is a whim of my protectress that I should always wear very long opera stockings, reaching right up to my—ahem (as I have become a shameless "Society whore," I was going to say my "arse," but remembering you are so delightfully innocent yet, I have been afraid to shock you, dear!). So, when I had tantalized my pretty boy a little longer I said, "Well, aren't you going to finish the job and take off the stockings too?"

He looked about quite bewildered as to how to begin, so at last I said, "Well, don't you know how to take off a pair of stockings yet?"

"I—I know how to take off my own," he stammered.

"How do you do it?" I inquired.

"Peel them downwards from the top," he answered in a very low voice.

"Quite right," I said. "Why don't you do it?"

His look of puzzled modesty at this was most amusing, and I don't think that I ever in my life felt anything so delicious as my sensations during those next few minutes. Very slowly and cautiously his hands stole up my thighs, expecting every moment to find the stockings come to an end, and going slower and slower, the nearer they got to my love nest, which was by this time getting so hot that the scent of Rhine violets, with which I always perfume it in accordance with the Countess's wishes—and by no means against my own—was wafted so strongly in his face as to almost overpower him with the voluptuous and lustful feelings, which it excited in his innocent and inexperienced mind. For my part, his modesty and blushing awkwardness made the pleasure caused by the soft tickling of his fingers, as they gradually approached my burning grotto, a thousand times greater than if he had been the most knowing expert of vice in existence.

At last, just at the warm spot where the body meets the thighs, his fingers touched the top of the stocking, while at the same moment his hand came in contact with the curves of my overhanging "ventre," and brushed against the soft tufts of down that fringe the entrance to my "pussie." The start which he gave at this quite unexpected discovery showed clearly enough that this was his first introduction to the mysteries of the mechanism of the feminine person.

"What? Still there?" I said, as I noticed that he showed no signs of departing. "Very well; then you must sit down and turn your head the other way, because it would never do for a boy like you to know what a girl looks like when she is undressed." Saying this I turned him round and, after giving him a voluptuous kiss on his rosy lips, sat him down in a chair straight opposite a mirror in which I had been all the time contemplating myself.

Unfastening now the petticoats, I held them up with my hands for a few moments, telling him that he must not look in the glass, as I could not allow him to see me in my drawers. As I intended, this had the effect of making him glue his eyes to my reflection in the glass and as I let the dainty underwear sink to the ground, "Oh dear!" I exclaimed, "I quite forgot that I had no drawers on!" But he had, I fancy, discovered the fact in his previous explorations.

I was now clad in a pink satin corset, clasping my tiny waist over a perfectly transparent chemise of black gauze, through which my long stockings were perfectly visible, while the tinted marble of my *ventre* showed up in voluptuous contrast to the curly home of Venus between my thighs.

Feasting his eyes on the reflection of this in the mirror, he remained absolutely entranced by the sight of this to him quite novel spectacle of female nudity.

My efforts to unlace my very tight corset were of course quite fruitless, and so I had to ask my youthful companion whether he was good at untying knots. At this he turned round, and positively staggered when he came near enough to perceive the intoxicating perfume, half natural, half artificial that exhaled from my warm body.

Presenting my back to him, I could see in the glass his eyes fall lovingly upon my two plump cheeks, while his hands fumbled, not so clumsily as I expected, at the stay lace. Presently it was really undone, and as the pressure on my body slowly relaxed, I unfastened the front hooks, and was left in the most naked of all states of nudity—a transparent chemise.

Luckily for me I knew I had nothing to fear from the loss of the corset, for my breasts stand up as high and firm, and my waist is almost as slender without them, as with them. And as I looked in the mirror I could not help thinking that this lucky school boy was decidedly to be envied in making his first discoveries of sexual mysteries under such unusually voluptuous circumstances.

INITIATIONS VOLUPTUEUSES

Initiations Voluptueuses, which has already been discussed in Chapter 8, "Incest," also contains a fantasy of an older female seducing a young boy. It includes, moreover, a peculiar emphasis on male semen which is another instance of bizarre fantasies. However, it is presented here because of its dominant theme, the relationship of a young boy with an older girl.

This great interest I have in virgin boys and which in fact was the basis of the education I had undertaken to give my children, this interest, as I was saying, makes me very fond of stories about deflowering.

Could there be a more hypocritical or more cynical one than that of how my dear Stanet was deflowered? This is how he told it to me:

I was fourteen years old, shy, didn't know how to masturbate and was madly in love with Daisy, my English governess, a very attractive girl with blue eyes and golden hair. One day, because of something I'd done, she decided to spank me, and started to take down my trousers! She took her sweet time about undoing my suspenders, opening my fly, unbuttoning my shorts. She did it so well that, excited by her fluttering fingers, I suddenly had an erection! Noticing this phenomenon, she told me without the slightest embarrassment, "Oh, Michel, I'm going to milk you like a cute little goat!"

After lifting up her long dress to just above her garters, she took me on her knees and my little system was thus hanging in the void! One of her arms went around my waist, came around underneath. Her naughty hand took hold of my young, very firm pecker and between her thumb and index finger she masturbated me while her other hand, having lifted up my shirt, softly smacked me.

Results were not long in arriving and my discharge made a good sized spot on the floor which the next day earned me a real spanking from my respectable mother who, in spite of my denials, remained convinced that I had spit on her beautiful rug!

Daisy was very upset about this, so much so that I thought she would never want to play that delicious game again! Fortunately, she was a resourceful girl and since the latest women's fad was frilly underclothes, from that moment on it was on her rustling petticoats that she made me strew my offering! And that was only the beginning! Soon it was under her blouse, in the saucy crotch of her buckram britches where she nested my adorable package. It was there, in that hot haven, against her messy fur, that she amused herself every day, playing "little goat" with me!

ANGE DUMOUTIER'S AMOROUS ESCAPADES

The title page of our next selection reads, in translation: *The Little Naturalistic Theater presents: Ange Dumoutier's Amorous Escapades, by Gilles, Printed everywhere and nowhere, but to be found in the backroom of every bookstore. In our year of Grace, 1890.*

This little French play deals with a shy, young fellow of sixteen, who wants to but dares not and knows not, and a thirty-five-year-old lady, who, much in the style of pre–World War I Europe, is glad and willing to teach him.

Dramatis Personnae

ANGE DUMOUTIER, 16, slightly naïve, but sporting a fetching moustache.

MADAME DE REGNETTE, 35, brown hair, still very pretty, even though slightly broad in the beam.

Scene I

(*The stage represents a little salon whose walls are covered in slate gray plush with ruby red silk trimmings. Window drapes and door hangings are ruby-red satin. Variously shaped stuffed chairs. Dim, mysterious lighting, daylight filtered through pink silk puffed shades. Flowers in every corner. Perfume permeating the air. Lazily reclining on a chaise longue, MADAME DE REGNETTE, in a pink cashmere dishabille all cockled with lace, is attentively reading a letter. Monologue.*)

MME. DE REGNETTE: That poor Ange! As if I hadn't known for a long time that he is all afire to receive his first lesson in love. He loves me . . . obviously. He adores me. Yes, yes, I know he does. What he worships right now is not one woman, but women in general. A brunette or a blonde . . . it would make no difference to him. And in a pinch a rubber woman would serve his needs. Oh my God! He's completely mad! Isn't he proposing marriage? In order to have, he says, the right to express unreservedly the sentiments burdening his soul. Ooh, la la! As if one had to get married to do that! (*She continues to read, interrupting her monologue, then continues.*) Oh, he's going to come round. He wants to know if I'm not too angry and to submit himself to the punishment I deem fit to chastise his boldness. Ah, yes, of course he's going to be manhandled, that gamin. He might be all of fifteen! As if a woman of my age . . . ? It's absurd. In England youngsters his age are still being flogged. In France we've lost our common senses—wanting to make men out of these brats as soon as they're weaned! (*She falls silent for a moment, then begins to laugh to herself.*) Still, it must be amusing to study the sensation of a novice, to initiate him, to make a man out of him. A man who knows how to love. That's rare. Nowadays they love . . . but they don't know how to express their feelings.

(*We hear steps in the antechamber and the manservant introduces* ANGE DUMOUTIER.)

ANGE (*Very moved, terribly self-conscious, he glances anxiously at his letter lying on the rug*): Madame! Oh! You're vexed with my boldness! Please be indulgent!

MME. DE REGNETTE (*Looking at him—neither attentive nor mocking*): I really shouldn't forgive you. But you're so young! We shall reason this out together instead.

ANGE (*spirited*): So young! I'm eighteen years old!

MME. DE REGNETTE (*aside*): He's making himself older now. How that will change in twenty years! This furor to plunge into life! (*She faces* ANGE.) Are you sure?

ANGE (*very red*): Isn't it obvious? Look here!

MME. DE REGNETTE: I do indeed see a beautiful little moustache there! Is it your very own?

ANGE (*sputtering with indignation*): How can you doubt it?

MME. DE REGNETTE: I'm more doubting than St. Thomas. Seeing is not enough for me, I must touch. Come closer. (*She caresses the fluffy down covering* ANGE's *lip. The adolescent, completely inebriated, fervently kisses the perfumed little hand fondling his chin.*)

ANGE: Ah! I see you're no longer angry. You're very good to me! (*He kneels down next to the chaise longue and lets his head fall on* MME. DE REGNETTE's *bosom.*)

MME. DE REGNETTE: Look at my cherub, wheedling. (*She dandles him.* ANGE, *who is better versed in theory than in practice, puts one arm around the beautiful, lazy woman's waist and tenderly hugs her, covering her with kisses.*)

MME. DE REGNETTE: Little cherub, you will be punished.

ANGE: Any way you want, but after I've sinned.

MME. DE REGNETTE: Angelot! I want you to confess to me. Don't lie! You've never . . . ? Never?

ANGE (*very humiliated in such a situation, but truthful*): No, never!

MME. DE REGNETTE: Not even with your mother's chambermaid or the cook at boarding school?

ANGE (*vehemently*): Madame! I have other aspirations, believe me, than such lowly loves!

MME. DE REGNETTE: Oh, really! And since one certainly wouldn't like to keep *ad vitam aeternam* one's rights to a crown of orange blossoms, one decides to have designs on the virtue of one's old friend. But just think, Ange, when you were born, I was already old enough to be married.

ANGE (*continuing to furiously kiss* MME. DE REGNETTE): I love you! It's true!

MME. DE REGNETTE (*who is no longer laughing and is beginning to feel slightly nervous*): So do I. I love you, little cherub. Only . . . (*She caresses the young man's locks.*)

ANGE: Say yes, please do! Would you?

MME. DE REGNETTE: What? I don't understand you.

ANGE: Yes, you understand me. Thank God, because I would never dare tell you.

MME. DE REGNETTE (*mockingly, singsong*): If you do not have anything to tell me, pray why come at all?

ANGE: To learn from you how to give happiness to a woman and to receive it from her. To understand the hidden meaning behind that magical word, voluptuousness! In sooth, to become a man!

MME. DE REGNETTE: But I'm so much older than you, I've just told you so, my dear Ange.

ANGE (*impassioned*): What importance do years have when you are so beautiful! When I love you. Be mine, I beg of you, never will you have a more submissive, more devoted slave.

MME. DE REGNETTE (*looks at him and whispers to herself*): He's charming, this little gamin. In fact . . . why not? Were fate to throw him into the arms of some trollop, he would be a despicable lover the rest of his life, since the first mistress's influence remains for so long. I shall sacrifice myself now for the sake of those who will come later. (*Aloud.*) My cherub, come here and speak to me softly. Tell me, would you like to learn how to love?

ANGE (*in transports of joy*): Oh, yes!

MME. DE REGNETTE: Will you be a good pupil?

ANGE: Test me.

MME. DE REGNETTE: In that case, bolt the door. (ANGE *obeys eagerly.* MME. DE REGNETTE *gets up silently, lifts up the door hanging at the far end of the salon and goes into her bedroom.*)

Scene II

(*Very elegant bedroom. Pink shades drawn. In one corner an English style chaise longue. Mirror opposite it. A very majestic, very low bed resting on a velvet dais. Door to the right opening onto bathroom.* MME. DE REGNETTE, *without airs, as though she were playing, pulls the youth near the chaise longue; she puts her arms around his neck.* ANGE, *more and more moved but at the same time very intimidated, doesn't say a word, doesn't move.*)

MME. DE REGNETTE: And now?

ANGE (*remembering his etiquette*): Ah! I love you!

MME. DE REGNETTE: Then prove it to me. Don't stand there like a statue.

ANGE: Have pity on me, and instead of scolding me, help me.

MME. DE REGNETTE (*deciding to be cooperative*): True, what you need is a lesson. My darling, come and receive it. Begin by learning how to adroitly undress a woman who allows you to do so. Here, one unties this way, very gently, her bodice. (ANGE *rushes to do as he is bid.*)

MME. DE REGNETTE: Oh! The impetuous boy . . . these things are done between two kisses. Come now . . . your lips on mine. There. While your hands part the layers. (*Her peignoir slips down and* MME. DE REGNETTE'S *arms and shoulders are revealed;* ANGE, *enraptured, gapes awkwardly.*)

MME. DE REGNETTE: But I'll get a chill if you don't comfort me. Your lips must weave me a breast plate of kisses while your hands remove my corset. Here . . . this way. (*She shows him how to undo the fastener and the corset slips down, her breasts bouncing out of the batiste bodice. Blood rushes to* ANGE'S *cheeks.*)

MME. DE REGNETTE: Not too long ago, you said good-bye to your wet nurse. Remember what you did to her . . . and do the same to me. (ANGE *hurries to her breasts and seizes a nipple between his lips.*)

MME. DE REGNETTE: Gently. Roll them under your tongue lovingly, with delicious slowness. (*While* ANGE *obeys her,* MME. DE REGNETTE *takes his hand and directs it to his trousers; she undoes the buttons.* ANGE, *getting redder and redder, doesn't stop her*

*and soon the unmentionable has fallen around his heels, his
shirt tail is flapping and two juvenile protuberances can be
seen.* MME. DE REGNETTE *sees them reflected in the mirror. She
signals* ANGE *to take off his frock coat and vest. He is so embarrassed standing there in his shirt that he hides his face in*
MME. DE REGNETTE'S *lap. There he remains, daring not to go
any further, not knowing perhaps what to do next.* MME. DE
REGNETTE, *being very kind, takes* ANGE'S *hand again and puts
it under her petticoats, so as to push them up slightly. The
apprentice lover shudders and lets his hand wander over this,
for him, unknown territory. Chance, that great master, guides
him. He touches the delicate point and feels* MME. DE REG-
NETTE, *quiver with joy. Suddenly she grabs him by the head
and makes him burrow under her petticoats.*)

MME. DE REGNETTE: There, there. That little cherry, suck it, my
dear adored one, as you did my breasts. (ANGE *obeys dutifully,
while* MME. DE REGNETTE, *who has taken hold of the adolescent's
very ardent phallus, caresses it voluptuously.*)

MME. DE REGNETTE: That's enough . . . enough. Come here, we'll
have pleasure together, my love. We'll die together. I want to
share this first sensation with you. Come. (*She voluptuously
embeds the instrument as far as it can go into herself and with
a few good thrusts of her behind, communicates to* ANGE'S
member a back and forth motion. She is promptly rewarded.
ANGE *utters a cry and swoons onto* MME. DE REGNETTE, *who
kisses him tenderly.*)

ANGE (*after a moment's silence*): Ah! Now I'm a man!

MME. DE REGNETTE (*smiling*): Yes, and even a man who, when he
wants to, will give happiness to his loved one of the moment.

ANGE: And now at least I know how one must show his love!

MME. DE REGNETTE: You know one way to go about it.

ANGE: Are there more?

MME. DE REGNETTE: Thirty-three, my friend! One more than there
are ways to fix potatoes, but we can reduce them to five good
ones.

ANGE (*dreaming*): Oh, if I only knew . . .

MME. DE REGNETTE: Go into my bathroom and we'll continue our
discussion in a moment. (ANGE *obeys and leaves stage right.*
MME. DE REGNETTE *opens a hidden door in the wall and also
disappears. A few minutes later,* ANGE'S *instructress, who has
thrown off her clothes, comes back dressed only in a flowing
peignoir of diaphanous batiste, held together by ribbons. She
makes her pupil undress completely and takes him over to her
bed.*)

MME. DE REGNETTE: Now, let's get into bed.

(*The couple slides under the sheets and embraces tenderly. Soon the sheets and covers are thrown off and Ange sees his beautiful friend turn around, kneel down, and offer him a splendid fanny, at the same time indicating with a gesture what he should do. Ange understands and executes the movement.*)

MME. DE REGNETTE (*leaning on one of her hands, puts a finger on her clitoris and encourages* ANGE): Faster, my darling. Faster. There, stop. You see how my little finger moves. Follow its rhythm. Now slower. This little pink monticule that I'm tickling is the key to amorous spasm. It will give the signal. Carry on now. Quicker than that, damn it all! (ANGE *obeys, but clumsily, and comes out of the hole!*)

MME. DE REGNETTE (*disgruntled*): Well, all right. I was about to come. Put it back. Now, my cherub, you can do better than that. (ANGE *takes up his position again. The voyage to Cythera is accomplished without impediment. Deep silence reigns in the room for a moment, then a voice mumbles:* "And the third way?")

MME. DE REGNETTE: Oh! The glutton! He wants to learn everything at once.

ANGE: Yes.

MME. DE REGNETTE (*turns around and, without getting up, offers her globes to* ANGE *and grabs his phallus, already rigid and ready to experiment*): No, don't get up, darling, stay the way you are . . . lying down . . . lazily. Gently. Wait, I'll tell you when . . . Ah! I'm coming . . . carry on, carry on. I love you! (*The third experiment terminates.*)

(ANGE, *reflecting a bit, thinks that lips against lips and chest against chest is much better.*)

MME. DE REGNETTE: You're right. Here, look, this way. (*She is facing* ANGE *and without getting up, makes him repeat in reverse the preceding maneuver.*)

ANGE (*completely enthralled*): Oh, this way. It's more to my liking. It's delicious . . . exquisite. Aah! I'm dying. (*He is very pale. He swoons—practically dead—into the arms of his voluptuous instructress and they remain a long time without moving, in spite of the glasses of Spanish wine which had interspersed the love jousts.*)

MME. DE REGNETTE (*coming to first*): Angelot, let's get up. It's almost dinner time. (ANGE *obeys and jumps out of bed, displaying all the splendor of his juvenile beauty.* MME. DE REGNETTE, *who was about to get up, remains seated on the edge of the mattress, gazing at him. The young man, whose desire has not yet been satiated, approaches as though to embrace her, then flips her over on her back, legs in the air. Normally hidden charms are revealed to him. He lowers himself to see them better.*)

ANGE: A woman is so pretty.

MME. DE REGNETTE (*laughs*): As pretty as all that?!

ANGE (*leaning over further, places a kiss at the entrance to the Cytherean grotto*): Yes, yes—it's pretty, pretty and I love you. Aah! I love you. Here, here, look how I adore you. (*He places little rapid kisses on* MME. DE REGNETTE's *clitoris, and she twists and turns under this delicious caress. She is mad with desire.*)

MME. DE REGNETTE (*coaxing voice*): Do you want to learn the fifth way?

(ANGE, *who on that day would have considered Hercules' tasks child's play, indicates that he is ready for anything.*)

MME. DE REGNETTE: In that case, remain standing. (MME. DE REGNETTE *lifts up her legs and crosses them around her lover's loins, so as to make a belt, then seizing his spear, which has already bravely become erect, she plunges it in to the hilt.*)

MME. DE REGNETTE: Now, there. Thrust. Penetrate to the depths of my being. Do you feel how I'm squeezing you?

ANGE (*ecstatic*): Yes, verily. Oh! I adore you, my beautiful mistress. Oh! Oh! I'm dying. (ANGE, *having learned the fifth way and absolutely exhausted, goes into the bathroom where he gets dressed. In her room,* MME. DE REGNETTE *does the same.*)

Scene III

(*In the same salon where the first scene took place, the two lovers, who have just finished a good dinner, are now conversing. They are slightly pale, but very good friends.*)

ANGE: Do you know, my darling friend, that that fifth lesson was very sweet?

MME. DE REGNETTE: And the fourth?

ANGE: Exquisite.

MME. DE REGNETTE: The third wasn't worth it?

ANGE: It was very good.

MME. DE REGNETTE: And the second?

ANGE: No worse than the others.

MME. DE REGNETTE: Did the first displease you?

ANGE: It opened the doors of heaven to me.

MME. DE REGNETTE: For the needs of those who write and paint other ways have been invented. But remember, little cherub, that the true science of voluptuousness rejects most of them, as well as any practices which do not restrict themselves to the realm nature attributed to love exercises. All other vaunted refinements are the expressions of a sick brain and not that of young people physically in love and avid for pleasure.

Stories which have as their dominant theme seduction of young boys by older females have, if they concern the fantasies of male authors, an obviously incestuous undercurrent: the male writer indulges in wishful fantasies in which he, as a young boy, is accepted by an older female—a thinly veiled allusion to the desired mother who remains not only unattainable in practice, but even unacknowledged as the desired object of the fantasy.

The juveniles involved in the sexual fantasies of adults are, for the most part, girls and boys in their mid-teens—say, fifteen and over, with only a few cases in the twelve- to fifteen-year-old group. In other words, the majority of these fantasies involve adolescents who, for legal purposes, would be classed as young adults with few examples of episodes involving minors. Moreover, it is clear from the description of their physical and mental characteristics that even these younger teen-agers must be regarded as being on the threshold of adult life.

This is indeed, as one might expect. More people are capable of imagining themselves in a sexual situation with an attractive teen-ager than with a child. The rare adult who is sexually fixated on children is certainly abnormal, frequently mentally inferior, socially inadequate, and of the amoral, delinquent type who, for one reason or another, is always in and out of jail. Not so, however, with the unfortunate male who becomes entangled in the legal machinery of our sex-suppressive society because he has had sexual contact with a minor or a young adult "under age"—which in some states of the United States is anybody under twenty-one.

In the case of a girl, the well-developed fifteen-year-old, or the average sixteen-year-old, is a biologically fully matured adult: her menstrual cycle is well established, she is capable of conceiving and bearing children, and her secondary sex characteristics (breasts, hair, pubis, etc.) are already clear and unambiguous—the very reasons that men with a definite preference for prepubescent girls are uninterested in this older adolescent group, whom they regard more as little women than as children.

Adolescents of this age group, that is, fifteen to sixteen years old, usually know very well what they are doing when flirting or engaging in sexual activities with adults. They have, by that time, a fairly good idea of what society expects from them, and if they break its official code of conduct, it is because they have decided not to abide by it. To blame and punish the older partner for the infraction is both illogical and unjust. More often than not, the younger person willingly goes along with the sexual proposition made by the older adult, and in many cases it is the teenage girl herself who seduces the older male partner by her provocative behavior and flirtation.

As for older females seducing younger (adolescent) males, we find no special category or mention in any of the Kinsey studies, including that on sex offenders. It appears that such cases seldom if ever come to the knowledge of the authorities. Few people would be concerned about the moral or physical welfare of the younger male in such situations: he cannot get pregnant and be socially disgraced, as is possible for his female counterpart of the same age; he cannot harm the older female partner; and some people even argue that sexual initiation of a younger boy by an older female is good for him or is better than his seducing a girl of his own age. In short, the double sex standard provides a protective cover for such relationships. Quite aside from this fact, situations of this sort are obviously very rare today, even in Europe where it was not unusual for parents in the upper and upper-middle classes to actively aid and abet this type of contact for their sons.

Fantasies about sexual contacts with adolescents are among the most frequent ones encountered in erotic literature, as in clinical practice. This is not surprising, given the high desirability, from a purely physical point of view, of young individuals as sex objects. This physical desirability is heightened by the social taboos against such contacts, which simply stimulate the fantasies even more, as do all sexual taboos.

10

Bizarre Fantasies

Many of the fantasies we have considered were bizarre enough, but they do fit into certain over-all categories. A number of other sexual fantasies fall outside these categories and we have therefore classed them together under this general heading. Even so, only a select number of bizarre fantasies can be included. We do not cover here, for example, fantasies concerning necrophilia or coprophilia, although they are psychologically important.

The bizarre fantasies in this chapter can be grouped into three categories: dildoes, animals, and fetishism. These we shall briefly take up first. Other bizarre fantasies defy any such classification or are better discussed in the context of the whole sequence of fictional events in which they appear. These are discussed in Chapter 11.

DILDOES

Almost all erotic novels include fantasies involving the use of a dildo. Most are rather stereotyped and repetitious, but a few are clinically instructive. The reader might review, for example, *Le Diable au Corps* in Chapter 3, or *Gamiani* in Chapter 4.

SCHOOL LIFE IN PARIS

The following is from *School Life in Paris* (see Chapter 9) and involves lesbianism, dildoes in various sizes, and the gradual taking of virginity by the different sized dildoes.

From a pocket inside the opera cloak, one of the girls produced a large morocco case, which, with smiling permission from Madame, she proceeded to open. The contents consisted of three rods of ivory of various sizes, rounded at one end, while to the other end were attached two indiarubber balls, like small tennis balls.

I was at a loss to imagine what these could possibly be, when my friend Bertha exclaimed, "Oh, Madame, you have brought the dildoes! How charming of you!"

At this you may be sure I pricked up my ears, for Bertha had several times explained to me the nature of a "dildo," which is nothing more nor less than an artificial model of a man's "dolly."

The smallest was only about three inches long, was not much thicker than my forefinger, and had a much sharper point than the others. This I gathered was nicknamed "the Baby," for it was evidently not the first time the girls had seen and handled these treasures.

The next one, known as "the Schoolboy," was about half as large again, being covered all along its length with obscene carvings in low relief, the object of which was to cause a greater amount of tickling than a smooth surface would have done.

The third was "the Captain," which was twice as long and more than twice as thick as the Baby, being covered like the last with carvings, while the balls were of a considerably larger size.

Bertha, after a short consultation with Madame, darted off to the latter's bedroom, whence she returned, bearing a lighted Etna, which evidently contained some steaming liquid.

Under her arm she carried another leather case, this time looking like a large pistol case, at the sight of which Madame pretended to be much displeased; but she nevertheless opened it, and displayed its contents to all of us, the astonishment of the girls clearly showing that this, at any rate, was something they had never seen before.

It was a dildo, made exactly like the Captain, but of such gigantic proportions, that it positively took our breath away. It was at least ten inches long, and quite as thick as my wrist, the balls being about the size of cricketballs.

"Surely, Madame," said one of the girls, "no one in the world has a cunt large enough to admit that?"

It gave me rather a shock of surprise to hear her use such a naughty word as "cunt" in speaking to Madame, but I soon found out that the latter could be the smuttiest of us all when she felt inclined, as it was evident she did on the present occasion. She only smiled at the question and said:

"It comes from South America, where the women are accustomed to being poked by Negroes, who, as I daresay you know, have far bigger pricks than European men."

"But surely no European girl could use it?"

"That all depends on the way in which it is done," she answered. "Of course, if a girl in cold blood were to thrust this into her cunnie, she would simply fail to get it in, in the first place, and in the second she would about kill herself if she succeeded. But if the cunt had previously been excited, first of all by Lesbian kisses, and then by an ordinary dildo, you would find, I think, that with the help of some Vaseline and a good deal of pressure, 'the Giant,' as I have named it, would not only go in, but would cause the most exquisite pleasure to the pussy, in which it would undoubtedly be a most amazingly tight fit!"

While she was saying this, Bertha had taken out the Schoolboy, and had filled the balls with the hot liquid, which, I gathered, was a mixture of milk and gelatin.

I had forgotten to tell you that each of the dildoes had straps attached to them for fastening them round a female's body, so as to make her resemble a man. The Baby was fastened to one girl, while Bertha made herself into a pretty boy by means of the Schoolboy.

"Now, Blanche," said Madame approaching me, "as we do not allow virgins in this society, we are going to take your maidenhead."

I was laid on the bed, my tiddies were kissed as before by two of the girls, while Madame herself, putting her head between my legs, began, with a far more expert tongue than Bertha's, to tickle my pussy. Her tongue several times touched my membrane of virginity, which was to be pierced by the Baby.

When Madame had excited me sufficiently, the Baby-girl, climbing on me, as a man would have done, slid the instrument into my cunt causing me an exquisite sense of pleasure, which made me clasp her towards me with all my force, and in a moment I felt a thrill, half of pleasure and half of pain, and I knew that my virginity had gone.

As soon as Madame perceived this, she signaled to the Baby-girl to come out of me, so as to make room for Bertha, who, with the larger dildo which penetrated into regions which were now entered for the first time, gave me the liveliest pleasure, and caused me to come, from the enjoyment I had felt when girls had kissed me down there, and which I now experienced for the first time. When she saw that the supreme moment had arrived, Bertha gripped the balls between her legs, and squeezing them again and again, squirted the hot liquid through the tube in the center of the dildo, so as to produce exactly the same effect inside my cunt as if a man's sperm were being poured into me.

What is especially interesting in the above is that the smallest of the three dildoes is called "the Baby," and that in this case, as opposed to birth, the "baby" enters the (virgin) vagina. Noteworthy too is the totally unrealistic ease with which the virgin is deflowered, given the fact that the dildo had to penetrate her hymen. In reality, this would cause much more pain and trouble than appears in the story, especially as the defloration is effected by a hard instrument like an ivory dildo, which does not have the natural flexibility of the male sex organ.

In view of the high incidence of sexual fantasies involving the use of dildoes in literature, it is of interest to check to what extent these fantasies reflect actual sexual behavior in women and to what extent they are simply the figments of wishful male imagination.

Turning to the Kinsey study on *Sexual Behavior in the Human Female* (Philadelphia and London: W. B. Saunders, 1953), we find that only a small minority of women in their sample had ever used any kind of object for insertion into the vagina during masturbation. Not very many women had even inserted their fingers for that purpose—at least not beyond the vaginal vestibule, or entrance to the vagina. Of course, it is the vestibule (and not the interior of the vagina) which is, aside from the clitoris, best equipped with sensory nerve endings. The Kinsey figures may have been somewhat depressed by the stress on hygiene in American culture, which might prevent a somewhat greater percentage of women from inserting their fingers into the vaginal cavity than in less hygiene-conscious cultures.

Cultural inhibitions also seem to have depressed the Kinsey figures on the use of objects for vaginal insertion during masturbation. Phallic-shaped objects for female masturbation are not only relatively common in African and other primitive cultures, but have also been popular in China and especially Japan until recently. A number of Japanese paintings and woodblock prints from the seventeenth to the twentieth century depict women masturbating with dildoes and even with a phallic mask. Nor are dildoes infrequent in the erotic art of the West, particularly in that of the eighteenth century. One might say, in keeping with the Kinsey interpretation of their findings, that these pictorial representations exhibit—like the references to dildoes in erotic literature—just so many male sexual fantasies and nothing more. However, it seems to us that dildoes were more popular in the past with both men and women than at present. We have, for instance, in our collection several Japanese dildoes from the seventeenth and eighteenth century which were definitely manufactured for the benefit of women and not for decoration. One of these objects is still in its original lacquered and silver-decorated box, which bears the inscription, "Property of Her Ladyship's Wardrobe Office," indicating that the item belonged to a lady of importance. Made of hollowed buffalo horn, these dildoes were meant to be immersed in hot water before use, to render the horn more supple. Being hollow inside, they could, of course, also be filled with warm water (and the water prevented from flowing out by placing a stopper at the open end). However, Japanese dildoes, or *harikata*, were, to our knowledge, not fashioned to contain and eject a liquid to simulate the male ejaculation like their European counterparts. On the other hand, *harikata* usually have washboard-like parallel ribs just below the glans, similar to but more exaggerated than the natural male sex organ. This feature may show that the Japanese were aware that the effectiveness of such a gadget depended on stimulation of the nerve endings in the vestibule and the upper anterior part of the vagina, rather than in the upper or inner part of it.

Still, it is obvious that many of the sex fantasies involving dildoes are projections of a typical male overestimation of the role of the penis with regard to the female sex response. We have discussed this matter in greater detail in *The Sexually Responsive Woman* (New York: Ballantine Books, 1965). Nevertheless, the Masters and Johnson study (W. H. Masters and Virginia E. Johnson, *Human Sexual Response* [Boston: Little, Brown & Co., 1966]), has shown that effective stimulation can be provided by sufficiently prolonged coitus, since it does involve indirectly the nerve endings of the clitoris, and more directly those of the vestibule. In the Masters and Johnson experiments this stimulation was frequently effected by artificial coitus, that is, by a mechanical penis fashioned of nonrefractory and sufficiently strong glass to allow for cinematography through the artificial penis and safety through the relative nonbreakability of the glass.

Summing up these sometimes seemingly contradictory observations, we would say that the role of the penis as well as that of the dildo has been greatly exaggerated in male fantasies. With regard to the dildo, cultural factors appear to have favored its popularity in the eighteenth and into the nineteenth century, but militated against it in more recent times, both in the West and the East. Today, the electric vibrator has more or less supplanted it, and its effectiveness in penetrating through its vibrations even the deeper vaginal and perineal areas, as well as stimulating the clitoris by direct contact, makes a return to the old-fashioned dildo most unlikely, at least in actual human behavior.

ANIMALS

The majority of animal fantasies in erotic literature concerns dogs, the species that lent itself particularly well to domestication as household pets. Typical of this fantasy are the following excerpts from *Le Keepsake Gallant*, an anthology of erotic writings published in France at the turn of the century.

DOG'S TONGUE WITH SPECIAL WHITE SAUCE

The chambermaid got up, but her mistress remained in the same position, even more indecent, her snatch open even wider, the moss glistening around her glowing cherry waiting for a second fete.

Grace had disappeared, but she came back almost immediately with . . . Mirza, her pet greyhound bitch. . . .

The greyhound was very well trained and knew just what was expected of her. In two leaps and with a joyous snapping of her jaws, she jumped on the exposed twat, plunged her wicked muzzle between her mistress's thighs and ran her thick tongue, long and wide, over the throbbing cunt. The resulting pleasure must have been atrocious, because the baroness screamed and twitched in her easy chair, her mouth salivating, as the chambermaid rudely rubbed her nipples.

CORALIE AND RÉGINE

They were face to face when Régine said, dropping to her knees:

"Come now, Coralie, now you're hot, look how well it goes in. Help your lover if he can't find your hole."

Coralie turned to her mistress and replied:

"There it is! It's true, it's fabulous! You look fine there, with that dog on your back!"

"Of course! Dogs have beneficial effects upon the kidneys and they fill up your cunt in a highly satisfactory manner!"

"Ooh! Ooh la-la! Ooh! His sliver is just as good as a man's!"

"Long live dogs!"

"Long live the love of a dog!"

LA FEMME AUX CHIENS

Another story, "La Femme aux Chiens" ("The Dog-Woman"), also from *Le Keepsake Gallant*, tells of a dog performing anal intercourse on his somewhat reluctant mistress.

She hunkered down on her heels once again and the animal burrowed in deeper with his seesawing movement. Instinct told him that there was a change in tactics, and no matter whether she held her ass high or low, he clung to her with his forefeet, harpooning her around the waist, on the shoulders, whacking his belly against her buns, between which he stealthily slipped his sliver. He worked to such good purpose that finally his ding found the road to Damascus into the crack and stabbed through the hole. Before she could even think of protesting, Régine was buggered for a second time.

She had a narrow aperture, she struggled to get rid of the machine, but only succeeded in getting it further embedded. The slight pain she had felt as his sliver entered her waned and she let Fido work on her, which he did quite expertly. He came gloriously, and when it was time to get out of the hole, there was a lot of heaving and pulling.

Her ass squeezed tight, Régine contracted as the dog increased his efforts, and remained stuck there, coming like mad, running over like a fountain, and she felt as though her ass would forever be riveted to the animal's. Foxie was going round and round, whimpering softly, trying to detach Fido with licks of his tongue. At last the organs returned to their natural state and the two lustful wrestlers finally broke their hold.

GAMIANI

In this passage from *Gamiani*, the narrator (Gamiani) tells about a girl named Sainte, who had lost her maidenhead in a special way, an incident for which she had been shut up in the convent where Gamiani made her acquaintance.

By dint of racking her brains, this nymphomaniac friend of mine remembered that the ape is the animal which most closely resembles man. Her father, as it happened, owned a magnificent orangutan. She went to look at it, studied it closely, and as she lingered a long time examining it, the animal, aroused no doubt by the presence of a girl, suddenly developed to dazzling proportions. Sainte jumped for joy. At last she had found what she had been seeking every day and dreaming about every night. Her ideal had appeared to her in concrete, palpable form. And oh crowning delight! the unmentionable jewel thrusts itself forward more firmly, more ardently, and more threateningly than in her wildest dreams. She devoured it with her gaze. The monkey moved closer, clung to the bars and writhed about so energetically that poor Sainte lost her head.

Urged on by her folly, she bent one of the bars on the cage, and the lewd animal immediately took advantage of the opening. Eight clear inches jutted delightfully forth, bold as could be. At first the maiden was terrified by such a rich treasure. However with the Devil goading her on, she plucked up her courage and took a closer look; she touched it with her hand, then began to stroke it. The ape was all aquiver and was making dreadful faces. The horrified Sainte imagined that she was face to face with Satan. Fear held her back. She was about to withdraw when one last glance at the flaming wick aroused all her desires. She immediately grew bolder, raised her skirts with determination and stooping over, bravely backed toward the fearsome spear. The struggle began, the first thrusts struck home, the ape had become man's equal. Sainte was bestialized, devirginized, and monkeyfied. Her joy, her rapture burst forth in a chorus of ohs and ahs so loud that her mother heard and came running to find her daughter thoroughly impaled, writhing, struggling, and spewing out her soul.

LE DIABLE AU CORPS

One of the most fantastic fantasies concerning animal contacts is the following passage from *Le Diable au Corps*, by Andréa de Nerciat. The author's critical intent with regard to the aristocracy of the time is obvious. The piece is primarily social satire, similar to Rochester's play *Sodom* or the anonymous nineteenth-century play *Prince Cherrytop*, which is discussed in Chapter 11.

COUNTESS: People have strange ideas about good and bad taste. They don't really know what they want or the difference between ugliness and beauty, charm or ridicule. (*The* DONKEY *brays.*) There's that singer again! He worries me sometimes.

MARQUISE: What do you mean?

COUNTESS: Well, for example, I've often wondered, reading "The Maid," what really happened with Joan and the holy donkey.

MARQUISE: Oh, gracious! It's just a poet's fancy. It couldn't have happened.

COUNTESS: That's easy enough to say, but I'm not so sure. Everyone has heard about the escapades of the gods appearing as rams, bulls, horses, and other quadrupeds. I can take a hint. I know what we women are capable of doing. I'm quite sure that those so-called gods were really down-to-earth bulls, stallions, and so on, that those ladies had the whim of using. When rumors started to fly, in order to avoid scandal and cut short commoners' gossip, they blamed some god, who let himself be slandered without the slightest protest. Why don't we try to find out if, by any chance, your donkey is some modern-day half god?

MARQUISE: Gracious, Countess! You certainly do have an imagination!

COUNTESS: It's funny to see you acting so reticent when you've just swallowed to the hilt a foot-long tally whacker!

MARQUISE: But a man is a man.

COUNTESS (*angry*): And a donkey is a donkey! Certainly much superior to man for our purposes. Come now, Marquise, enough of this prudery. Take heart, let's find out what's what. . . .

MARQUISE: It's so dark in here, let's go back to the salon.

COUNTESS (*holding her back*): Let's not and say we did. We'll have some lights brought in. (*The* DONKEY *brays.*) There, did you hear that? Fate decrees that that devil of a musician will not stop bothering me today! Thanks to our hideous Neapolitan man, a dark cloud passed over my imagination. The spark for a beautiful caprice has just been extinguished and there, just as if the donkey had intelligence, he's forcing me once again to think of him. There's got to be a secret attraction between that animal and the two of us.

MARQUISE: Let's not exaggerate!

COUNTESS (*joking*): Think whatever you like, Madame, but since the word has been said it doesn't bother me at all to divulge to you my innermost weaknesses. Be aware, Princess, that I have designs on your donkey and that with your permission I would like to have the pleasure of his company. Do more than concur—share at least half the experience with me! Let's go!

MARQUISE (*after a moment's hesitation*): Let's go!

COUNTESS (*herself again*): That's more like it! How are we going to go about it? I wouldn't mind going to the stables to fetch him, but where are they?

MARQUISE: I know where. But I warn you—I don't like manure piles!

COUNTESS: We'll send Joujou. He's discreet.

MARQUISE: Fortunately. But I feel reluctant to involve a child in such goings-on.

COUNTESS (*impatient*): You're always finding obstacles!

MARQUISE: Why don't we send Philippine? She's just as discreet as

Joujou. Besides I know how to make her keep quiet—if we manage to use the donkey's resources, she's going to want to try too, I'm sure of it.

COUNTESS: That's true. Since we have to induce her, I think I have a plan. We'll discuss the situation with her. I'll be for the possibility and you against. We'll make a bet, and she'll stand to gain.

MARQUISE: Excellent idea. That will entice her, and the rest will naturally fall into place. I know my Philippine. (*She rings the bell.* JOUJOU *appears.*)

MARQUISE (*to* JOUJOU): Tell Philippine to come here immediately. . . .

MARQUISE: Do you recall that the holy donkey is the one who finally deflowers the heroine?

PHILIPPINE: Yes, Madame.

COUNTESS: What do you think about that?

PHILIPPINE: What do I think, Madame? But . . . it must be true because it was printed that way.

COUNTESS (*to the* MARQUISE): I told you that Philippine would agree with me. She's an intelligent girl. (*To* PHILIPPINE:) Isn't that right, my dear, that a donkey can very well render a courtesy to a woman?

PHILIPPINE (*slightly embarrassed*): Well, Madame, he at least has what it takes.

MARQUISE: Correct. I have nonetheless wagered ten louis with the Countess that if one of the three of us, for example, wanted to make advances to my donkey, he wouldn't pay any attention. The Countess believes that he would respond and agrees to the wager. We would like to know, Philippine, who would win. You stand to collect all the money.

PHILIPPINE (*simpering*): Oh, you're very good to me, you really are.

COUNTESS: Yes. If Philippine is in agreement, I will not renege. Here are my ten louis. She will be so good as to go fetch the donkey and present herself to him.

PHILIPPINE (*amazed*): Who, me, Madame?

COUNTESS: Of course. If he refuses, your mistress will have won. But whatever happens, the money is for you. Does that suit you?

PHILIPPINE: But, Madame, you must be joking. This must be to test me. My liking for money is not enough to make me go through the shame of offering myself to Madame's donkey. Besides, he would probably only snub me!

COUNTESS (*smiling*): I would bank more on his *savoir-vivre*. Come, come, Philippine, bring him in anyway. And to prove to you that all this is not sheer debauchery, but rather a way to satisfy our curiosity, we'll draw lots to see which one of us will be forced to sacrifice herself.

PHILIPPINE: Well, since you put it that way, I agree wholeheartedly! (*She goes out.*)

COUNTESS: All courtesy aside, my dear, would you like to go first?

MARQUISE: No, I'd rather not.

COUNTESS: So much the better. I'm the more determined one, you'll see. When Philippine returns, you suggest we draw straws. I'll get the short one, so I'll be chosen for the "unpleasant" task. Here's our actor.

PHILIPPINE (*brings in the* DONKEY, *who is well groomed, well built. He stops at the door and she encourages him with a slap of her hand, saying*): There, there, don't be afraid, we only want the best for you. (*He comes in.*)

COUNTESS: Very good. Now you must go outside and make absolutely sure we won't be observed. (PHILIPPINE *goes out to make the inspection.*)

MARQUISE: But darling, you'll maim yourself!

COUNTESS: That is nobody's business but my own.

MARQUISE: And if you conceive a little foal?

COUNTESS: Me? I don't conceive anything. (*She caresses the* DONKEY.) Come here, little one.

MARQUISE: I would never have had such an idea.

COUNTESS: But you'll reap the benefits nonetheless. I'm quite sure that starting tomorrow the donkey will have two good grooms in this house.

MARQUISE (*gaily*): That remains to be seen.

PHILIPPINE (*closing the door after a scrupulous examination*): Nobody can see a thing from outside.

MARQUISE: Good. Now let's draw straws.

COUNTESS: Well said. (*She holds out matchsticks.*) Take one, Marquise . . . and you, too, Philippine. I'm so unlucky! I drew it! Oh, well, that's the way it goes. I must resign myself! (*To* PHILIPPINE, *who is laughing:*) What are you laughing about?

PHILIPPINE: Look, Madame (*the* DONKEY *is not excited at all*), do you think you have the right material to experiment with over there?

COUNTESS: Don't worry your head about it. Just put your hand around there. You'll see.

PHILIPPINE: No thank you, Madame! I didn't draw the short straw . . . and besides, the donkey might kick me!

COUNTESS: Chickenhearted girl! Do you believe that donkeys are so uncivil as to mistreat someone who's trying to give them pleasure? Watch! (*She rubs her hand over the* DONKEY's *sheath, who, titillated, immediately shows signs of sensitivity.*)

MARQUISE: Remember my money! This is no longer the same business as a few minutes ago, Countess!

PHILIPPINE: Look at those wretched black spots!

COUNTESS: When this is nested, what difference does the color make? Come, help me, the three of us will work him into shape. (*They gaily begin to do so and soon the* DONKEY *is in a beautiful, excited state.*)

MARQUISE: You have to admit that one could get used to that object.

COUNTESS: I think she-asses really have good taste.

MARQUISE (*to the* COUNTESS): Well, it's now or never. How should we place you? He probably won't help much!

COUNTESS (*taking the member*): He has at least this . . . let me . . . (*She puts two stools next to each other and wants to place herself on them, with a pillow under her head. But this position is hardly suitable for the* DONKEY *to enter her, and besides the beast now steps backwards, doesn't seem at all cooperative.*)

MARQUISE: I won!

COUNTESS (*trembling slightly because she has already felt the tip of his terrible machine*): I'm not even close to losing! Philippine, stand behind him so he won't back up.

PHILIPPINE: He won't kick?

MARQUISE: There's a better way. We'll tie his hind legs together, leaving a bit of leeway. Then we'll put the forelegs on one of the stools. (*To the* COUNTESS): And you, you'll figure something out to find the space you need to put yourself neatly within his reach, as a she-ass would.

COUNTESS (*changing position rapidly*): Of course! She's right. I know what to do afterwards.

(*There was some trouble with the animal, but he finally let them tie his hind legs. They made him put one foot, then the other, on the stool, all the while fondling his dong, thus keeping him in a glorious state. He finally felt against his stomach the warmth of a rump that was worth that of a she-ass. Then he seemed to like the thing. His machine started to make superb movements. The* COUNTESS, *inflamed by increasingly violent desire, says:*) Philippine, direct it to its goal! (*To the* MARQUISE:) And you, darling, stay behind. When he's inside, you push him slightly so that he enters; by doing it rhythmically maybe he'll catch on. (*The* COUNTESS *then groped behind her thighs for the dong, which gave her a good clout on her fingers.*

PHILIPPINE, *kneeling to the right, grabbed the tool and directed it to the opening; the* COUNTESS, *feeling it at the entry, backed up her rump to meet it and made it penetrate. The* MARQUISE, *her two hands placed above the* DONKEY'S *prick, got ready to push, but her help was not needed. The* DONKEY *himself did what was necessary. In fact he conducted himself marvelously. The* COUNTESS, *all her wishes gratified, screamed:*) Aaahh! Fuck it! He's fucking me! What a delight! A thousand gods! No more men, fuck it! More! (*This extraordinary scene threw the* MARQUISE *and* PHILIPPINE *into an indescribable state—consuming desire coupled with amazement. The* DONKEY *was moving more and more and the* COUNTESS *was responding furiously. The* DONKEY *seemed radiant. The* COUNTESS, *in her delirium, and feeling the pump gushing wild blasts inside her, cried:*) A thousand happinesses. My darling! He's . . . flowing. I'm being drowned . . . I'm dying! (*She had lost her voice, lost her strength, and fell, practically unconscious, from the stool. The* DONKEY, *released by this tumble, was still blowing torrential jets of his prolific liqueur.*)

To what extent, if any, do animal contacts play a role in human sexual behavior? Going back to the Kinsey studies, we find that in certain rural areas animal contacts are not at all rare. Some 50 per cent and more of the farm boys in these areas were found to have had some sexual contact with farm animals to the point of orgasm, and for the entire male farm population, the percentage was still quite large, 17 per cent

With women, the percentages of such contacts are lower. Moreover, the incidence is no higher in the country than in the city, the reason being that almost all of these contacts are with family pets, such as cats and dogs. With women, contrary to male behavior, the majority of animal contacts consists of oral stimulation of the human genitals and only rarely of intromission and coitus. The percentage of women in the Kinsey sample who have had such experiences in pre-adolescence was somewhat less than 2 per cent, in addition to somewhat less than 4 per cent who have had them after adolescence. This gives a total of something less than 6 per cent, a low figure, compared to the young rural males' involvement with animals. However, to this we might add the 1 per cent of women in the Kinsey sample who admitted having fantasied such contacts and another 1 per cent who reported sex dreams about such highly taboo activities as this.

We would agree in general with the Kinsey interpretation of their findings that the mental involvement with animal contacts on the part of men is considerably higher than that of women. Only we would qualify this statement by pointing to the much stronger degree of sexual repression in women, not just with regard to animal contacts, real or imaginary, but in every way. Most primitive cultures seem to have some kind of taboo against animal contacts. Nevertheless *some* women are able to accept animal contacts. Among the Kinsey subjects there were, for instance, six women who had each reached orgasm more than 125 times, and one woman who had reached orgasm 900 times in that manner. We take this as another indication that the female sex potential is culturally much more suppressed than that of the male. This view is strengthened by the fact that in a sample of some five hundred unusually liberated women whom we interviewed and observed, almost all of them found fantasies of animal contacts erotically stimulating and a large number of them had actually had such experiences. In addition, almost all of the female painters and graphic artists who have done erotic pieces have at one time or another depicted sexual contact between women and animals. Apparently, uninhibited, imaginative women are indeed capable of fantasizing about such experiences. Nevertheless, it is clear that under normal conditions of life and in the absence of unusual deprivation from human sex contacts, animalism will always play a very minor, though perhaps psychologically significant, role in human sexual behavior.

FETISHISM

As one might expect, there is considerable emphasis in erotic literature on sexually exciting female apparel and underwear. Until the turn of the century, corsets, kid leather gloves and boots, garments featuring lace or feathers had special erotic significance. They have since gone out of style, but other materials, for instance, transparent plastic, black leather with wide, shiny zippers, together with chain belts, crash helmets, and similar gear, have taken their place. Times and fashions change but the tendency of the human animal to invest certain objects and materials with special sexual significance does not seem to change; it merely seeks and finds new forms of expression, depending on technological and social conditions.

It goes without saying that erotic literature would also emphasize the erogeneous zones and secondary sex characteristics of the female, such as the breasts, buttocks, the hair of the head and the pubis, etc. In this respect again, changing social customs have brought about shifts in emphasis. At one time, women's feet and ankles—to say nothing of their legs and thighs—were almost universal male fetishes in Europe. Long female hair, emphasized by the fashions of the day, was likewise an object of much male admiration and not infrequently of fixation. The early sexologists, such as Krafft-Ebing and Stekel, had much to report on all these fetishes, devoting studies to such things as corset-, boot-, and hair-fetishism, which today are extremely rare.

In general, one might say that fetishism is no longer as much of a problem or a thrill as it was in the past. Even the plastic materials and the gadgetry and paraphernalia of the motorcycle cult cannot compete with what was once an almost common and socially accepted preoccupation with some of the mentioned fetishes. This is so because a fetish can only exist in the presence of a strong cultural taboo which calls attention to the specific anatomy and the clothes which are designed to hide it. With the new freedom in women's dress, greater equality between the sexes, and closer contact, much of the artificial mystique and preoccupation with female apparel and female anatomy has naturally disappeared.

In this matter, we take a middle-of-the-road stance. We feel that there is a place and a need for apparel which underscores the sexually attractive aspects of the female and male anatomy. Velvet, satin, lace, and transparent plastic are obviously more sensuous and suggestive than, say, wool jersey or linen (though these materials may have their own specific erotic appeal, if used in certain ways). Today we have seen a nostalgic return to the fashions of the 1920's and 1930's, or of the *belle époque* before World War I, which is a sure sign that people are looking for something more in clothes than functionalism.

One can easily understand this trend as a healthy reaction against the drabness of the work-a-day world and the uninspired and almost deliberately anti-erotic styles in both men's and women's wear which, together with the old fetishes, are happily on the way out. We are under the impression that contemporary society will develop a new style in fashion which is functional and erotic at the same time. But, with the relinquishing of one old taboo after another, we think it most unlikely, nor would we consider it desirable, that Western society should ever return to the fetishes of old or become equally fixated on the new ones— which, to be sure, are present, but just enough to be the spice of fashion instead of its *raison d'être*.

In the light of these reflections, let us consider some of the fetishistic fantasies of erotic literature, especially from the period prior to World War I.

SCHOOL LIFE IN PARIS

We have already encountered clothes fetishism in connection with a passage from *School Life in Paris*, which features, among other things, an episode about a lady who specializes in seducing young boys. Although the fetishistic aspects of the story remained tangential to our discussion then, they actually pervade the whole book.

Clothes are very important to the writer of this book. Speaking through the narrator, a girl named Blanche, he compares the dreary clothes the girls have to wear in an English boarding school to the fashionable dresses and dainty underwear which is the order of the day at the French school Blanche is now attending.

It makes me quite shudder now to look back upon the awful shapeless garments, the hideous cotton gloves, and the low-heeled, broadtoed boots which we used to wear [at the English school].

The headmistress here [is] a tall, handsome woman, of about thirty, exquisitely dressed in the very height of fashion, and in such a way as to show off to the very best advantage her really magnificent figure. When I was first introduced to her, I was quite overawed by her grandeur; while she, on the other hand, was, I think, horrified at my ill-fitting and unfashionable clothes.

When the new headmistress finds out that Blanche has at her disposal sufficient funds, she immediately sets out to have her outfitted "in the latest Parisian style," starting, of course, with the obligatory visit to the *corsetière*. There it is revealed that, in spite of Blanche's ill-fitting clothes,

the waist beneath them had been carefully laced in, ever since I was ten years old, so that I was easily able to wear the smallest and most long-waisted pair of corsets that the *corsetière* had in stock. This I found caused the greatest delight to Madame who takes a special pride in having all her pupils as small-waisted and as tightly corseted as herself. She accordingly ordered a pair with a considerably smaller waist measurement to be especially made for me, assuring me that, after a little training, my figure would easily bear the constraint, while she pointed out that all the other girls in the school would be mad with envy, as, in spite of their enthusiastic efforts, none of them could hope to attain to such a tiny waist for a long time to come.

The fetishistic emphasis on corsets, binding, and the so-called wasp waist which was popular at the time, came close to being the Western equivalent of the Chinese custom of foot binding. Although the foot-binding custom went much further than even the wildest excesses of European tight-lacing and corseting, the remarkable thing is that women were willing to endure pain, discomfort, and even crippling due to foot binding or organic damage due to exaggerated constriction of the midsection, all in the interest of catering to some conditioned male fetishism.

At that period there was another curious fashion in vogue,

he so-called *ventre*, artificial belly, to be worn under the skirt, accentuating the female abdomen and suggesting, as it were, a nonexistent pregnancy. "The other point of difference," Blanche writes, "in the French and English women's figures is that in England women always try to keep the stomach in as much as possible, and have their corsets made so as to force it in, out of sight, if they can. In Paris, however, a prominent *ventre* is as much admired as a big behind, and just as we used to wear bustles to make the latter look unnaturally large, so some French women actually wear a small cushion in front, if their *ventre* is too flat by nature."

School Life in Paris also contains instructions on how to dress for men:

. . . if you are entertaining a man in your boudoir, you should lie on a sofa or on a long chair, and let him sit in a low chair at your feet, when by a little thoughtless lifting of the knees, etc., you will give him a view of quite a different, but no less charming, portion of your person.

Another thing the Countess has taught me is, in dressing for a ball, to wear plenty of soft frothy petticoats, but no drawers: for when a man's hands begin to wander gently up your leg towards the garters and higher—as often happens to me when I am at a ball and am sitting out a dance with some nice fellow in a quiet corner—he loves to come in contact with the delicate texture of luxurious petticoats, but is sadly disappointed if his fingers cannot at last find the cave of delight which they are seeking.

THE MODERN EVELINE

While the above examples are still within the limits of normal sex play, with only mild fetishistic overtones, there is a passage in *The Modern Eveline* which reflects true foot and shoe fetishism. We find the narrator, Eveline, visiting her special bootmaker—a man who has evidently found the right profession.

"How could I keep waiting my most beautiful client?" [the bootmaker addresses Eveline].

"Let us try them then."

He led me into his back room, beyond which was his *atelier.* I seated myself in the large chair. Dalmaine produced the boots from a glass case. He held both pairs up for my inspection. His little eyes danced with pleasure as he scrutinized the glossy black *peau de chevreuil* and the exquisite work of his skilled assistants.

"They appear perfect. I trust they are not too tight. Not like *souliers de vingt-cinque*—you know, Monsieur."

"They are the correct fit for your lovely foot, Mademoiselle. I know not your *souliers de vingt-cinque*. What are they?"

"They are *neuf et treize et trois*, Monsieur Dalmaine; consequently they are *vingt-cinque.*"

"Ah, *mon Dieu!* Now only do I understand you! It is too good! *Neuf et très étroit! Mais c'est splendide!*"

He sank down at my feet. He removed my boot. He inserted my toe into the new one. I pushed my other foot against his apron. The cucumber was already in evidence. I could feel its magnificent proportions. Meanwhile, without noticing my proceeding, the artist in ladies' boots became wholly absorbed in regarding the elegance and the delicate fit of his darling study. He no sooner had my foot in than he commenced the lacing in the most exact manner, his face beaming with smiles as he drew the silk cords together. Not a sign escaped him to show that I had ever permitted any undue familiarity. Nothing marked his conduct beyond the most respectful attention to do credit to his employment.

"I think you had better put on the other boot also, please, so as to make sure there is nothing amiss."

He trembled with delight as he beheld the pair invested duly into office. He molded them. He fondled them alternately. I pushed my right foot towards the cucumber, now evidently getting beyond control.

"Ah, chère Mademoiselle! It is too much! You make me so bad! It is not possible to resist. You are so beautiful."

He pushed his hand up my leg. He lost suddenly all his reserve. His other hand was engaged in releasing his member. He turned up my dress as carefully as if he was my own maid. I saw him fix his gaze upon my thighs. His fingers pressed on higher yet. He met with no restraint. Suddenly he bent forward, his face pressed upon my naked legs. He pushed on until his head was quite buried beneath my clothes. He found his way to the central spot of his desires. I felt him seize on the coveted spot with an exclamation of rapture. I pressed his naked limb between my feet. I parted my legs to give him room. His large tongue was now rolling upon and around my clitoris.

The appeal of leather gloves and their smell also find their place in the seductive repertoire of *The Modern Eveline:* "I leaned towards him. I caressed his hand in mine. Under the pretext that his white dress tie required arrangement, I put my gloved fingers under his nose. I could see his nostrils dilate as he sucked in the perfume of my glove."

LES TABLEAUX VIVANTS

Les Tableaux Vivants (originally published in French in 1870, and in English in 1888) is a sort of fictional sex guide which illustrates various sex techniques by making them part of the story. In it we read of another form of foot eroticism.

Rosine and Nana pulled down my trousers obediently. Coralie took and commenced to roll between her two feet what she rightly called my lovely member.

Are you not aware that the women of Corinth were renowned for their exquisite knowledge of the art of provoking with their feet the venereal orgasm of their Athenian or Boeotian lovers? Coralie's feet were as prettily shaped as they were agile. They seized my member between their two satiny soles.

She ordered her two maids of honor to range themselves on either side of her, one on the right, the other on the left, and commenced tickling one with each hand. Her two pretty little hands disappeared in the black pussies of the two girls. Her two feet glided, flew; turning themselves round my enflamed prickle, they scratched sweetly with their nails on the balls which contained the divine liquor [and] adventured from the tip of my member even into the passage of Sodomy.

DEVERGONDAGES, SOUVENIRS EROTIQUES

One of the most fetishistic books we know is a French novel entitled *Dévergondages, Souvenirs Érotiques,* by "Spadely," published "A la Fontaine des Nymphes." It contains almost every type of fetishistic fixation.

Nothing is more exhilarating, wicked, lascivious, or libertine than a woman's feet as you fuck her. I'm not talking of naked feet but of feet charmingly shod in high-heeled shoes or in long-topped half-boots gripping the ankles and half the calves in their soft glove leather. . . .

In order to enjoy the erotic mime show of the feet through which pleasure's entire soul seems to pass, you must throw the woman on her back on the edge of the bed and take her standing up. You lift up her legs, joining them together vertically in such a pose that the vulva juts out from the strangled buttocks, thus making its access as narrow and as difficult as possible. . . .

And while you're fucking, you wear as a breastplate the backside of her thighs hoisted on high and the exquisite curve of her two calves in their shimmering stockings where your mouth leaves a trail of caresses. Under your eyes you have the delicate joint of her ankle with its graceful, sloping line, at the end of which the gallant shoe adds the final spicy touch of unspeakable lewdness.

You must concentrate all your attention on this shoe as the banging of your loins against her buttocks sets the supple mobility of the little foot in motion. True, in order to relish what is languorous, naughty, or smutty about a shoe, you must have a subtle, analytical mind, a keen imagination, an acute sense of smell, a visual touch of extreme sensitivity, able to penetrate the secret meaning of things.

Then everything is erotic sensation in that shoe or little boot whose elegance first of all heightens your pleasure in fucking a fully dressed woman. In such a position this perversity is highlighted by the shoe behind which the entire woman is masked, betraying her delight only through the twitching of her feet above your head. At that moment her whole life seems to be focused on the feet and to display her happiness to the subtlety of your senses through the foot's dainty leather, velvet, or satin encasements which tremble, shudder, and cringe with ecstasy under your eyes.

Lying on her back at the foot of the bed, dressed in a silk robe with enormous black flowers patterned on a white background, I took off her little pink silk panties and having raised her legs perpendicularly to her ass, she planted my rod between the lips of her cunt and I speared her with all the partiality that I felt toward her lovely vulva, so narrow and so discreetly turfed.

I still feel the cool sensation of her buns and her thighs against my belly which harrowed her softly while I reveled in running my lips over the silky tepidness of her gray stockings.

I was holding her legs by the ankles and as I played with them, opening and closing them in suggestively erotic ways, following one kiss with another, from the bend of the knee upwards, I arrived at the gallant little shoe which was pointing its pretty little black satin snout and jiggling up and down under the effect of pleasure's breakers.

I don't know what sort of sensuality seemed to be emanating from the shoe's elongated, refined charm, from underneath the taut cloth, from the arched instep under her ankle straps, and the exaggerated recess of her high Louis Quinze heel, so arrogant and perverse. Was it the sinuous suppleness of its lines, was it that I was affected through it by the charm it gave to her gait, was it a confused masochistic desire? I can't say what irresistible lure I gave in to, but I was strangely eager to soil my lips with the little buskin's dust. What is this erotic sortilege shoes have?

I went from one foot to the other, I kissed the shoes' vamps, the contour of their heels, their interior recesses, with the same voluptuousness with which I would have tasted the most secret recesses of the body. An insane excitement began to rise in me as I caressed and sniffed the shoes, an excitement which a few seconds later broke out into one of the most intense spendings I've ever experienced with Renée.

I don't think that I ever liked her cunt better than that day when my rut was entirely engrossed in her high-heeled black satin shoes. I can still see myself pinned to the naked flesh of her small, dark-skinned buttocks, under her brown-haired fleece, clasping in my arms her coupled silken legs, long and thin, at the top of which the perverse shoes seemed to be rendering the ecstasy which shook her gentle cunny.

The author goes into a eulogy of his main fetish—women's underwear, and soiled underwear in particular.

Oh, mirage of women's linen, where does your bewitching magic come from?

Consider Georgette, one of our friends, a rather insignificant person. I would never have thought of fucking her if, one day in the room where she was waiting for my wife, and under the pretext of fastening a garter, she hadn't displayed most indecently her exquisite underpinnings.

I can still see her elegant hands, wearing glacé-kid gloves, her two fingers spreading apart inside the flap of her lace drawers the edges of her cunny, already wet, waiting for the licks of my tongue. . . .

. . . dirty underclothes and I took the two drawers that the girls had worn all week. I was an old hand at this little bit of larceny. They were made of sturdy percale with wide, gathered flounces done in feather stitching with large lace scallops. I settled down in the little salon to enjoy at my leisure those cast-off clothes whose symbolic cut fired my imagination as much as the very flesh which had dirtied and creased them.

I drank in the smells of virgin ass and cunt. I warmed up the drawers with my breath so as to revive their exciting bouquet. And when, by means of these odors, my imagination had transformed that wide opening in the drawers into the real life opening between a pair of thighs with my face between them, I masturbated. I took the two edges of the flap, I sheathed my rod with them and maneuvered until ejaculation. Then I plastered the percale with it, feeling as though I were discharging my jissom upon Lucie's ash-blonde fleece and, moreover, coating her drawers with my pitch.

While resting, I recreated the height of my desire by smelling their hung-up dresses and the delicate bouquet of their blonde armpits. Lucie's smelled slightly of shallots, whereas Louise's odor had a pinch of seringa to it.

For a choicer tidbit and for the more tasty pleasure of my repeat performance I had reserved Louise's favors, who was much more to my liking than her older sister.

With this one I wanted to create a more complete illusion of possessing her and of imposing upon her the shame of my defilement. I took one of her dresses from the closet, a watery-green silk one, which she had worn to a wedding party recently and which suited her golden blondeness to a tee. I slipped it over a batiste petticoat with Valenciennes lace flounces that I had seen her wearing the same day, and under these two garments I slipped the pair of drawers which I assumed were hers. I put the ensemble on the bed as though I had reversed her there, backside up, at the edge of the mattress.

I let down my trousers all the way in order to give my flesh the full sensation of the petticoat turned back over the spread-apart legs of her drawers. For a short while I mimed a scene of gamahuching as though in earnest, by sucking the acrid scent with which her cunt's wetting had soaked the edges of the opening in the percale. Then, when I thought I could feel Louise swooning under my mouth, I straightened up. I joined my naked abdomen to the flap, and passing my hands under the Valenciennes petticoat, I made my fingers, between the back ribbons of her drawers, into a tight girdle.

I pushed my prick into it and, standing up, with a thousand passionate words to stimulate my dream, I possessed my cousin until I came. I shot my jissom onto the bottom of her drawers, feeling as though I had filled up her virgin's vulva with it.

When I had put everything back in place, I noticed that a large drop of jissom had tinted opal the hem of her dress.

Do I dare tell you that I experienced a perverse thrill in leaving a visible trace of the double defilement: the humiliation of which I had, unbeknownst to them, inflicted on Lucie and Louise's modesty, whose silliness deprived me of finding my joy in them as I had found it in their most secret linen? . . .

This morning in my study where I have been transcribing these gallant souvenirs, my mind wandered from the image of a handsome ass to lick through a flap of panties, to a beautiful cunt to spear. And since I heard our maid, Faustine, coming and going in the next room, a terrible itch came over me. . . .

Hadn't I seen her two days before . . . masturbating herself through her skirts, next to my desk, as she leafed through my adventures with Marguerite which I had just finished writing?

She rubbed herself furiously through the material and she came that way, plunging her hand into the hollow of her dress between her thighs. . . . Ah, the bitch! Did she ever excite me! It was only the arrival of my wife that stopped me from jumping her. But this morning, she would not stop me. Martha was still asleep in bed, tired out from last night.

Indolently, Faustine let herself be dragged into my room.

"Come here, so I can give you a poke!"

"But, Monsieur, you're not being reasonable. If Madame were to appear!" Terrified, she was straining to hear if anything was moving in the hallway.

"Never mind." . . .

Bent in two against me in her effort to protect her snatch against my attacks, her resistance which was not at all faked whipped up my bestial desire and besides, there was also some sort of lustful curiosity for her flesh and her underclothes—the underclothes into which she released her come, the whore! I hoped she hadn't changed her chemise in the last two days!

Then, à propos, she said, embarrassed: "Well, you know . . ."

"What is it?"

"I haven't washed this morning and my drawers are hardly clean!"

"Yes, that's what I thought. You wipe yourself with the edges when you piss! That's precisely what excites me! Show me . . ."

Against her will I lifted up the front of her skirts and the sight of her drawers, completely reduced to pulp along the length of the flap between her thighs made my head swim. And there, in the opening, I saw upon her upturned chemise a patch of come looking like starch paste. A highly exciting odor escaped from there which intensified my erection.

"You're dirty! The smell of your piss gives me a cockstand! Come over here!"

I pushed her against the sofa, slipped two cushions under her buttocks to place her ass at the right height and made her sit down.

"Oof! You're a real villain, Monsieur! And if Madame were to surprise us like this!"

I flipped her over, brought her thighs towards me and placed her legs on my shoulders. I tossed back her skirts, and from the flap of her drawers I took out her chemise all pink-stained with urine and come.

Under the thick turf of her ebony black hair, the deep slit of her dark red cunt appeared. Driven by my famished rut, I plunged my entire member inside with one sole thrust of my loins.

In these sex fantasies, there is a gradual and sometimes imperceptible transition from a "normal" interest in female attire or from the typical male preoccupation with female anatomy, to the obsessional fixation of such attire or aspects of the female body.

The question is, what constitutes a fetish and what distinguishes it from normal sex preferences?

In general, the more remote the object of sexual interest from its original genital source and goal, the closer we are to fetishism. Likewise, the more exclusive the specific interest in a given part of anatomy, article of clothing, or whatever it may be that has become associated with sexual arousal, the more the interest is in the realm of the pathological and deviant. The man whose interest in female anatomy is focused on the posteriors is no more deviant than the one whose interests are centered on the breasts. But hair, feet, and hands, for example, are already one step further removed from the genital area and therefore that much closer to fetishism. The same holds for articles of clothing. Panties, garter belts, brassieres, and other items of intimate female attire which are in direct contact with the genitals, the breasts, or at least the skin, are more "normal" objects of male interest than, say, gloves, hats, or handbags.

The degree of fetishism also depends on whether a man is

capable of responding sexually to females in the absence of specific stimuli, or whether they are absolutely essential to arousal. This concerns the principle of exclusivity which is, perhaps, the most accurate criterion for sexual deviation that we possess. For example, fixations on whips, high-heeled shoes, boots, heavy leather belts, or leather outfits in general, all suggest a more than average interest in sadomasochism. The more a person depends exclusively for his sexual arousal on such details, the more specific is his sexual conditioning, and the more "abnormal" by definition we have to consider it.

To say that all these preferences are merely a matter of conditioning and that therefore nothing can be called truly normal or abnormal in sexual behavior seems to beg the question. Every neurosis is a matter of conditioning, and yet we do distinguish between relatively normal and essentially neurotic behavior (and by more or less the same clinical criteria).

We hasten to add that by insisting on a clinical definition between relatively normal and abnormal sex interests and behavior, we do not attribute any *moral* significance to such a distinction. Any moral judgments and inferences based on observations of this kind would, of necessity, be ill conceived, irrelevant to the real problems involved (i.e., the origin, development, and effect of such fixations on the individual), and apt to lead to social abuse, personal discrimination, and legal persecution of "sexual minorities," such as is still the order of the day.

The most outstanding characteristic of fetishism is that it is almost entirely a male phenomenon. The Kinsey researchers, for instance, found only two or three women in their sample who could be "regularly and distinctly aroused by objects that were not directly connected with sexual activity." Of course, male fashions over the past couple of centuries have been so drab and unexciting that it is difficult to imagine anyone becoming erotically fixated on them. In addition, advertising, literature, and the mass media of our day have stressed the female form and female apparel to the almost total exclusion of the male. (The fact that this traditional trend is presently changing cannot as yet have had any long-range effects, such as a reconditioning of the female sex response, which depends, like all sexual conditioning, on reinforcing experiences over longer periods of time.)

Nonetheless, we know that whenever social conditions have made such conditioning possible, women have responded by developing fetishistic attachments to certain types of male apparel—for instance, uniforms, leather (even the smell of leather), and riding equipment (again, including olfactory cues). Likewise, with regard to male anatomy, women have been known to become fixated on certain physical types of men, on large male genitalia, and even on such specific stimuli as chest hair, circumcision (or non-circumcision), and on the personal body odor of a particular male. If all of this does not amount quantitatively to more than a mere fraction of the number of fetishes men have, it still does not lead us to the conclusion that women are necessarily more resistant to sexual conditioning than men. That they are so in fact is undeniable; whether they are so by nature seems to be highly debatable.

11

Miscellaneous Bizarre Fantasies

HARLEQUIN, PRINCE CHERRYTOP

This satirical play from the late nineteenth century, subtitled *New and Gorgeous Pantomime, entitled Harlequin Prince Cherrytop and the Good Fairy Fairfuck, or the Frig, the Fuck, and the Fairy,* is a cynical commentary on court life and royalty and, we think, an extremely humorous sexual fantasy focused on obsessive masturbation.

The leading characters in the opening scene are:

MASTURBATION, a demon, opposed to the Fuckwell Dynasty; nervousness, indigestion, blushing, distaste for society, involuntary emissions, etc., his attendant imps.

FAIRFUCK, a benevolent and wise Fairy, the patron of the Fuckwells.

Other characters in the play include:

FUCKWELL THE FIRST, King of Rogeria.

CHERRYTOP, his only son and heir to the throne.

GAMAHUCHE, wife of FUCKWELL, Queen of Rogeria.

PRINCESS SHUVITTUPPA, betrothed to CHERRYTOP.

PRINCESS SYPHILIS, daughter of King Bubo.

GONORRHEA, wife of Bubo, Queen of Rapia.

CHANCRE, a witch, godmother to SYPHILIS, and favorable to the Bubo Dynasty.

MERCURY, a benevolent deity with healing power against venereal disease.

In the opening we are told that the evil Demon of Masturbation in the Island of Spermatorrhea, who has been snubbed by King Fuckwell, has put a curse on the whole Fuckwell court, and especially on Prince Cherrytop, to make both the men as well as the women, and even the animals around them, engage in obsessive masturbation.

DEMON: The Monarch has rejected, spurned my aid,
    Ha! Ha! Revenge, no matter, as I've said,
    A time will come, nay has come; in this hour
    Prince Cherrytop is bound beneath my power.
    I, in disguise, the palace did approach,
    And found the Prince as sound as any roach,
    I touched him with my wand—I spake his curse,
    And he is ours, for better or for worse;
    To frig himself he's bound beneath my spell
    And make all others near him frig as well.
    His father, mother, sister, aunts, and cousins,
    Courtiers and maids of honor by the dozens;
    Nay, even lower animals indeed,
    Who meet with Cherrytop must waste their seed.
    But he himself, chief victim of my ban,
    Must all day long pursue the frigging plan:
    Soon shall consumption waste his blooming youth,

He'll die, still frigging, prick in hand, in sooth.
And when his wasted corpse fills up the grass hole,
Ha! Ha!! Perdition catch his Ha! Ha! Ha!! Soul. . . .
Cunt fuck, front fuck, he shall never once begin it,
Crumb fuck, bum fuck, nor another peaceful minute,
Breast fuck, best fuck, Cherry's prick shall ne'er begin it

Hand frig, stand frig,
That's the sport of him.

At this point the friendly Fairy enters and challenges the
Demon, pledging to save Prince Cherrytop because his father,
many years ago, when still a stripling prince, had met her, disguised as a peasant-woman, had asked how much she wanted for
a fuck, had put her on the ground and fucked her three times in
a row, and had paid her every penny of the bargain.

The first scene opens in the royal gardens of the Fuckwell
court, several courtiers and maids of honor are lamenting the ill
effects of the Demon's curse.

LADY CLARA CINDASIFTA (*addressing a male courtier*):
About your woes you need not make a fuss,
'Tis, I assure you, just as bad for us;
This morn I stood behind the Queen's armchair,
When down to breakfast came the son and heir;
In came the hope and glory of the nation,
As usual in the act of masturbation.
Ladies and Queen turned crimson as a rose,
As all their right hands dived beneath their clothes;
The courtiers flashed their pricks, some spent, some couldn't;
Over the table-cloth, into the tea-pot,
If spend they must, why can't they use a P-pot?
The flies and wasps forsook their jam and honey,
To frig like courtiers—tiny pricks and cunny,
The large Newfoundland dog, the Prince's pet,
Embraced his knees, and rubbed till he was wet;
The cat bestrode the pillow on the sofa,
And rubbed until she got her passion over,
The goldfish swimming round so calm and dreamy,
Spent in the bowl and made the water creamy;
The parrot, double decency to shock,
Frigged 'gainst the bars, while crying "What's a cock?"

Time, the destroyer, quite quiescent stands,
While the clock frigs itself with both the hands;
Many such incidents I could relate,
Of how we all are forced to masturbate;
But as I hear the Prince approaching near,
We'd better bolt before he finds us here.

(*All run off Left. Enter from Palace the* PRINCE, BISHOP, *and At-
tendants, frigging.*)

The Fuckwell court is indeed in serious trouble, but the
good Fairy has arranged it so that the curse will be lifted when
Prince Cherrytop comes of age and marries Princess Shuvittuppa
—an event which the whole realm awaits impatiently. At last the
great day has arrived. But a serious complication has arisen—the
neighboring King Bubo wants to marry off his daughter Syphilis
to the Prince, and the youth must make a choice between the
two girls:

(*Enter* PRINCE. *All begin to frig. Enter* FAIRY FAIRFUCK. *All cease
and blush.*)

KING FUCKWELL: Now, which d'ye fancy, sonny? Do not linger.
PRINCE: One moment, father. Bishop, pull my finger. (*Farts loudly,
then goes up to both princesses and examines their cunts.*)
Both have such elegantly moulded twots,
I really can't decide, so let's draw lots. (*Draws paper with
Shuvittuppa's name on it.*)
Dear Shuvittuppa, will you be my bride?
PRINCESS SHUVITTUPPA: I must first see your prick ere I decide.
(PRINCE *shows it,* PRINCESS *sneers.*)
D'ye call that thing a prick, so worn, so flabby?
I've seen a better penis on a baby. (*Puts his hand into his
trousers and pulls his balls up from his ankles.*)
And these you think are balls, they're like peas;
(*Contemptuously*): I'd put the whole lot up my arse with ease.
Take him away.
FAIRY: Not quite so fast, my dear,
You quite forget there's been enchantment here;
In opposition to the potent spell,
My magic wand another tale shall tell (*produces large rod*).
Take down your breeches; kneel before the Princess.
(*Lets him have it.*)
How d'ye like that, my lad? See how he winces.

Now, girl, behold a nine-inch penis stands.
You scarce can span his balls with both hands.
D'ye spurn him now?

PRINCESS SHUVITTUPPA: Oh, Prince, how I adore.

PRINCE: I wish my bottom was not quite so sore
But still the birch has made me very lewd.

PRINCESS SHUVITTUPPA: Hush! Make love prettily, and don't be
rude.

FAIRY (*presents birch to* PRINCESS): Here, take the wand, wher'er
you find him flagging,
And disinclined for after-dinner shagging;
Give him three dozen, dear, with all your might,
And he'll be fresh as on his wedding night.

Bad Chancre, however, threatens dreadful revenge and consequences if Princess Syphilis, her protégée, is spurned:

PRINCESS SHUVITTUPPA: For all your threats I do not care a fuck
I'll never leave my darling princely duck,
My Cherrytop, will you desert me now?

PRINCE: My love, my life, I'm buggered if I do:
Hook it, you damned old bitch, be that your answer
You can't hurt me.

In this dilemma, Queen Gonorrhea suggests that Prince
Cherrytop marry both Princess Shuvittuppa and Princess
Syphilis, if the latter could accept being his second wife. Every-
body seems happy with this "downright smart suggestion," as
King Bubo puts it, including the Princesses, the Prince, and the
Fuckwells. However, the good Fairy, more moral than the rest
of them, will not hear of the plan:

(*Enter* FAIRY, *disguised.*)

FAIRY: Bigamy, blast me! Upon my word,
D'ye think that I have not this project heard?
Altho' I much regret to spoil your plans,
Most noble Kings, I must forbid the banns,
Oh, mighty Potentate! Oh, cove most regal,
Ain't you aware that bigamy's illegal?

King Bubo, disgusted with the old lady's interference and
not recognizing the Fairy, makes the fatal mistake of giving her

a kick with his foot. But that is just what the good Fairy has had in mind: by striking her, he loses all of his own magic power— he has smitten the whole Fuckwell court with secondary syphilitic symptoms because of the trouble the Fuckwells have given him with his daughter, the Princess Syphilis.

With the aid of God Mercury, the good Fairy now heals the Fuckwells of their secondary symptoms and cheerfully addresses Prince Cherrytop and Princess Shuvittuppa:

FAIRY (*to* PRINCE): You Prince, relieved from solitary vice,
    May now enjoy each hole you fancy nice;
    Your spots for spangles now you shall exchange
    As nimble Harlequin the world to range
    And lest your letch should leave you in the lurch
    As magic wand retain the fairy birch.
    (*To* PRINCESS SHUVITTUPPA:)
    You, fair Princess, shall by your charms excite,
    Each lad who sees you on the stage tonight
    But, Pit and Gallery shall scratch their balls,
    Cockstands be at a discount in the stalls,
    When they behold thee, sweet goddaughter mine,
    Hot, wriggling, moist-lipped, fucksome, Columbine.

All's well that ends well, and Prince Cherrytop and his Princess Shuvittuppa live happily ever after.

LE SURMÂLE

A completely different fantasy is involved in the story *Le Surmâle*, by Alfred Jarry (in Volume III, *Oeuvres Complètes* [Monte Carlo: Editions du Livre, n.d., but published 1900– 1910]).

A variation on the folklore theme of the superpotent male, it has additional elements which make it unique. The Supermale, André Marcueil, has accepted the challenge to top the record set by an "Indian mentioned by Theophrastus"—seventy orgasms in twenty-four hours. The experiment, to be scientifically supervised by Doctor Bathybius, was originally to have been conducted with the help of a dozen young women taking turns.

However, the athletic American adventuress, Miss Ellen Elsen, has donned a mask, and with the complicity of the Supermale, who is made up as an Indian for the occasion, she is to replace all ten.

The clock struck midnight and Ellen listened: "Has it finished? . . . Then it's all ours, master."

And they fell into each other's arms; their teeth rang out as they met and, because they were so exactly the same height, their chests stuck loudly together like suction cups.

They began making love, and it was like a departure on an expedition to some far-off place, a long wedding trip which took them not through cities but through all the stages of sex.

When they first came together, Ellen had difficulty repressing a cry and her features contracted. To stifle her acute pain, she had to have something to bite, and she settled for the Indian's lip. Marcueil had been right to claim that for some men, all women were virgins; Ellen had painful proof of this, but although wounded, she did not cry out.

They drew apart at the very point at which other couples cling even closer together, for both were concerned only with themselves and had no wish to prepare future lives.

What is the point of that when you are young? Those are the precautions one takes—or stops taking—at the end of old age, on one's death bed, after making one's will.

Their second embrace gave deeper satisfaction; it was like reading a favorite book for the second time. Only after several more was Ellen able to detect a note of pleasure deep in the Indian's cold, sparkling eyes; she had the impression that he was happy to see her happy to the point of suffering.

"Sadist!" she said.

Marcueil roared with candid laughter. He was not one of those men who beat their women. There was something in him that was far too cruel to them for it to be necessary for him to add to it.

They went on, and each of their embraces was a port of call in a different land, where each time they discovered something different and always better.

Ellen seemed determined to be happy a bit more often than her lover and to reach the goal set by Theophrastus before he did.

The Indian was exploring and revealing sources of agonizing pleasure within her that no lover had ever so much as touched upon.

At ten she leaped nimbly out of bed and went to fetch a cute little box made of mother-of-pearl from the dressingroom.

"At ten, master, you said we would soothe our wounds with certain balms. This is an excellent balm distilled in Palestine."

"Yes, *the shadow creaked*," whispered Marcueil. And gently he rectified: "At eleven. Later."

"Right now," said Ellen.

The frontiers of mortal strength were left behind the way the familiar landscape of a city suburb vanishes through the window of a moving train.

Ellen turned out to be an expert courtesan, but this was only to be expected, for the Indian looked so much like some idol carved from unknown, pure materials, each part of which became the purest as it was caressed.

All the rest of the night and all the next morning, the lovers took neither respite nor repast. Were they waking or dozing? They could not have said. They nibbled on cakes and cold cuts, and drinking out of a single glass was but one of the thousand ways they kissed.

By noon the Indian had almost reached, and Ellen had long since gone beyond Theophrastus' figure. Ellen began to complain a little. "I'm so warm!" she said, pacing about the room, her hands cupped over her tense breasts; "I'm not naked enough. Can't I take this thing off my face?"

The Doctor was peering through the window at them.

"When shall we take it off?" Ellen asked again.

"When the shadows under your eyes can be seen around the mask," said Marceuil.

"Oh, I hope it will be soon!" wailed Ellen.

He took her in his arms and she hung there like a scarf crumpled into a ball; he laid her on her back on the bed like a child and drew the bearskin over her feet while he declaimed with comic pedantry, to make her laugh: "Aristotle says in his *Problems:* 'Why doesn't it help to have cold feet when you make love?'"

And he recited some of Florian's fables to her:

> "A little she-monkey
>   Picked a walnut in its green husk . . ."

Suddenly they realized they were hungry. They lunged at the table on which a gargantuan meal was laid out and began to eat like poor people in a charity kitchen—poor people who had previously made room in their stomachs with rich people's appetizers.

The Indian devoured all the meat and Ellen all the pastry; he did not drink all the champagne, however, because she took the foam off the first glass from each bottle, munching it as though it were meringue.

Afterwards, she would kiss her lover, so that his red makeup was glazed with sugary things all over his body.

Then they made love twice more. They had plenty of time: it was only two in the afternoon.

They fell asleep. At 11:27 P.M. they were still sleeping like the dead.

The nodding doctor was just about to doze off himself as he wrote down the total which had been reached by then:

70

and put his fountain pen back in his pocket. Theophrastus' figure had been equaled but not topped.

At 11:28, Marcueil awoke, or rather that part of him which constituted the Indian awoke before he did. When he embraced her, Ellen cried out in pain and staggered to her feet, one hand on her throat, the other on her sex; she darted her gaze about like a sick person looking for her potion or an etheromane her Lethe.

Then she fell back on the bed: her breath escaping through her clenched teeth made that same faint hissing noise produced by crabs, those creatures that may be trying to hum the tunes they heard the Sirens sing.

With her body still feeling blindly for the means to forget that deep-felt burn, her mouth found the Indian's . . .

And she no longer knew pain.

They had 30 minutes left until midnight, plenty of time to run once more through the range of mortal strength, taking into account the ground previously covered.

82

wrote Bathybius.

When they had finished, Ellen sat up, arranged her hair and stared at her lover with hostile eyes: "That wasn't a bit amusing," she said.

The man picked up a fan, opened it part way and slapped her with it as hard as he could.

The woman jumped up, drew a long, sword-shaped pin from her hair and, bent on immediate revenge, aimed it at his eyes, which shone forth on a level with her own.

Marcueil let his strength act for him: his eyes defended themselves. Under their hypnotic gaze, the woman fell into a cataleptic trance just as she was about to strike.

The arm and its steel projection remained in a horizontal position.

Marcueil lay his index finger between Ellen's eyebrows and woke her immediately, for it was time.

Jarry's story has strong sadistic overtones. The sex act endlessly repeated becomes an ordeal—much more to the woman than to the man. It is the Supermale who here revenges man against the sexually overdemanding woman. The fact that she is an American makes the situation still more poignant, since at that time American women were reputed to be especially frigid and, at the same time, demanding.

The story illustrates one of the sources of much sex hostility: female "frigidity" and the resulting male frustration and resentment, on the one hand, and the paradoxical male complaint about the sexual insatiability of woman, on the other. Though not without humorous aspects, the story reveals the depth of the understanding which has traditionally bedeviled the relations between men and women.

The ending of *Le Surmâle* contains a striking reference to blinding as the punishment for sexual aggression, as in the classical Oedipus myth, where it is more specifically the punishment for incest. In Jarry's story, the woman is paralyzed in her attempt to blind—i.e., castrate—the Supermale by the latter's hypnotic gaze.

LE DOCTEUR LERNE, SOUS-DIEU

We have already had examples of the role of magic and hypnotism in erotic fantasy, especially in several of the folkloristic stories and in *The Power of Mesmerism* (see Chapter 8). In this connection, we must cite a strange novel by one of the most important precursors of modern science-fiction, *Le Docteur Lerne, Sous-Dieu* (*Doctor Lerne, Demigod*) by Maurice Renard (Paris: Mercure de France, 1908).

It is difficult to summarize this complicated story, but very briefly: the narrator, Nicolas, has come to spend the summer in the isolated mansion of his uncle, Doctor Lerne, the eminent biologist. There he meets the scientist's lovely young ward, Emma, of whom her guardian seems inordinately fond. Nicolas and Emma soon become emotionally and, above all, sexually involved—Emma is something of a "nymphomaniac"—and Lerne is quite put out about this, since his own advances seem to have been spurned. The good doctor, it appears, is experimenting with ways and means of putting animals' brains in people's bodies and vice versa. (Actually, Dr. Lerne no longer exists: his German assistant, named Klotz, has placed his own brain in the Doctor's body.) At the point in the story at which the following excerpt occurs, "Lerne" has gone beyond the stage of surgical interchanges and seems to be experimenting with exchanges or projections of the personality through electrical remote control and some sort of hypnotism—as Nicolas is about to discover.

One evening, passing as usual through the downstairs apartments on my way to Emma's room, I heard a chair being dragged across the floor over the dining room, in my uncle's bedroom. It was unusual for him to be moving about at such a late hour, but this insignificant detail made little impression on me. I went on my way, making no attempt to muffle my footsteps, for my expedition was not clandestine: I had the Doctor's permission.

Emma had just finished putting up her hair for the night, and along with the sweet, feminine aromas in the room, I could smell the scorched pieces of paper on which the iron had been tested, as though the Devil had symbolically mingled his scent with the perfume of a pretty girl in underclothes.

In the next room, all was quiet now. As an added precaution I shut the little bolt on our side of the door that let into Lerne's room. Now we had no need to fear that my uncle would make an impromptu entrance which might have proved embarrassing, though certainly not dangerous. No light shone through the keyhole. Never had we been so cautious.

Emma, all aquiver in a muslim shift that was as silky as her flesh, drew me towards the bed. . . .

At first, Emma wanted to be caressed. Then, having decided that the prelude had lasted long enough, she shifted to a more valiant position, indicating that tonight, as on so many previous nights, she wished to play the role of the equestrian in our wild, amatory ride. However, as she galloped toward the abyss of satisfaction with all the skill of a Valkyrie, an amazing and terrible thing occurred.

Instead of climbing the slope of pleasure toward the climax that I craved, I seemed to be sliding downward, dropping from one degree of pleasure to a lower one, gradually slipping into complete indifference. I was still performing heroically; in fact my body seemed to be actuated by an increasing ardor, but the better my performance, the less enjoyment my mind derived from it. The slenderness of my results was beginning to worry me. And then suddenly, this feeling of worry itself began to shrink. I tried to bring my accursed anatomy to a standstill. Pfftt! There was nothing to be done! My willpower had diminished to the point of impotence. I could feel my faculties shrinking and subsiding, while my soul, now of lilliputian size, was as incapable of controlling my muscles as of receiving any impressions from their activities. I was only barely aware of the movements of my body, but I noticed that they were exceptionally lively and that Emma was obviously enraptured by them.

In hopes of putting a stop to this phenomenon, I brought every ounce of my authority to bear, but all to no avail. It was as if someone else's soul had forced its way into the space allotted to my own, controlling my behavior as it saw fit and relishing impure pleasures through *my* nervous system. That other personality had driven my own ego into a tiny corner of my brain; an intruder was making love with my mistress, deluding her with an infamous disguise! . . .

These were the microscopic thoughts that wracked my dwarf-like soul. It became so small when the couple reached their apotheosis that I feared it might vanish altogether.

Then it began to expand; it grew and blossomed out, gradually taking over its rightful domain once more. My thoughts assumed their proper dimensions. I experienced that intense, satisfying fatigue which is the rear guard of Eros . . . and I felt a cramp in my right calf. A contact on my right shoulder soon became a pressure: in her inevitable ecstasy, Emma had lain her head there, and the two soft mounds of her bosom were pressed against my chest.

It took a long time for me to regain possession of myself. My eyes were not even blinking: they were staring at a certain spot, and now I realized that all during those incredible moments, my gaze had been fastened on Lerne's keyhole; I still could not tear it away.

Then suddenly I could. I withdrew from the embrace of my useless lover. A chair creaked on my uncle's side of the door and I heard someone stand up and tiptoe away from it. The keyhole resembled a dark little window leading straight into Mystery.

Emma breathed a sigh: "You outdid yourself tonight, Nicolas. Let's do it again, shall we?"

I fled without answering her.

We are obviously dealing here with a fantasy which has strong and unmistakable paranoid overtones. The ideas of inter-changeable brains and thought-influence and thought-control are in the paranoid direction. However, when young Nicolas during intercourse with Emma speaks of feeling as if "someone else's soul had forced its way into the space allotted to my own," one is tempted to re-read the phrase as "someone else's *penis* had forced its way into the *vagina* allotted to me." And when he speaks of another soul "controlling my behavior as it saw fit and relishing impure pleasures through *my* nervous system," the paranoid delusion is complete.

Freud had called attention to the fact that paranoid ideation can frequently be traced to denied and repressed homosexual interests which are then turned into delusions of persecution ("I do not love him [her]—he [she] hates me and wants to destroy me," etc.). Likewise, in the story above, the homosexual element is unmistakable: Nicolas fantasizes that another man is making love *through* him, "using" him, and even sharing the same vaginal space with him (provided one accepts our interpretation). This homosexuality is then turned into ideas of influence and persecution in the manner of classical paranoid mechanism.

It is amazing to what extent paranoid ideas have influenced erotic fantasies in literature. Perhaps this is less true today than it used to be, due possibly to the greater tolerance toward for-merly less acceptable sex interests, especially homosexuality. But it might also be that men who write about their erotic fantasies tend to be more paranoid than others, or a combination of both. Some of the most interesting erotic fantasies in literature are those which are not devoid of paranoid ideation. But then, the paranoid process of thought demands a great deal of intelligence and paranoid patients tend, as a group, to be of rather superior intelligence.

LA FEMME ENDORMIE

The striking erotic fantasy which follows is exactly of this paranoid type—*La Femme Endormie* (*The Benumbed Woman*), by "Madame B____, Avocat" (Paris [?]: J. Renold, 1899). A shy recluse, Paul Molaus, asks an artist to make him a lifelike female doll who will be in all respects like a real woman. The artist provides him with such a doll, but, jealous of his precious creation, he surreptitiously enters Paul Molaus's house, when the latter has gone out, and continues the sexual relationship with the doll which he began before turning her over to his customer. At first, this relationship is clandestine, but then it becomes known and tolerated by her owner—the two men even leaving anonymous notes for each other in the most intimate recesses of the doll's underwear.

Paul Molaus, a well-to-do man in his middle forties, had gone through every possible disappointment with his mistresses, and had come to the point where he only saw a woman in an emergency. In such conditions, good-bye to flourishes, good-bye to delicacies.

A brutal ride, a lick and a promise as it were, and he was back with his household gods, crestfallen, sick at heart, practically despondent.

Then ideas started flowing again. In a corner of his mind more than naturalistic fantasies began to accumulate. He dreamed of an imaginary, will-less creature who would submit ecstatically to his obsessions and his lewdness.

Day and night he dreamed of this being.

Suddenly, inspiration struck.

Why not buy one of those magnificent statues which display their incomparable nudity in the annual Beaux Arts exhibition?

The marble of such a loved one couldn't be any colder than courtesans' hearts.

However this Pygmalion love, this love he would vow to a modern day Galatea, would demand purely spiritual worship and would not attain the desired goal.

He wouldn't mind a statue, but only on the condition that that statue would perfectly, in every way, replace a woman.

The idea of desecrating the marble made Paul's blood run cold.

Having taken this tack, our rake's inventive mind immediately started examining a thousand new combinations and at last, came the light. Like Archimedes he shouted: "Eureka!"

A kindly soul had invented the dildo for women deprived of male contact; for the pleasures of brave Captain Pamphile, someone had brought forth the rubber woman, for our hero, a deft craftsman, an artist, would invent a miraculous Phrynée he would be able to manipulate at will—she would always be compliant and silent, no matter how lewd the act he chose to perform.

Money overcomes all obstacles. Paul had plenty of it.

He unearthed a man who consented to create the desired marvel. The creator did it for a very stiff price, because he suspected what dream his eccentric client cherished.

The artist outdid himself. A more exquisite work of art had never been created by human hands.

She was an admirable woman with very uplifted, very firm breasts, outstanding, appetizing, hips, extremely well-shaped buttocks, divinely curved loins, flawless thighs, well-rounded calves. All of this topped off by a most suavely shaped face, her golden hair royally coiffed. Her flesh was so white and smooth it was almost real, and all her joints were flexible. She was sent in a crate, marked "fragile," to M. Paul Molaus, Financier, Bois-Colombes.

An explananatory note accompanied the shipment:

"The extraordinary doll that I've conceived and executed," said the artist, "doesn't differ from a woman, except in one respect: she can't speak. I paid particular attention to her interior, which is fitted with three basins, several boxes and cylinders, and a number of little ducts, so as to permit the circulation of all sorts of products that it would please the experimenter to introduce into the silent goddess's body. By pulling certain curls of her hair, her eyes and lips can be made to move. One can place her in every imaginable position: standing up, seated, kneeling, lying prone, lying on her back. By pushing the navel, one provokes undulations in every part of her body. Her sexual organs are as perfect as those of any live woman. To warm up her body, all one has to do is to pour boiling milk or hot water in sufficient quantity into the different receptacles located under her head, behind her breasts, in her buttocks, stomach, legs, etc. One can also warm up a certain part of her body while leaving the rest only lukewarm. The liquid runs down through a series of tubes in her legs to the heels where a small peg is located. Just turn this peg to empty."

There followed instructions to keep the interior clean by means of a mechanism which opened the neck, the back, the thighs and the calves.

Paul read all of these directions attentively before unpacking the mistress of his dreams. He was alone in his country house at Bois-Colombes, sheltered from any indiscreet observers. His heart pounding at the thought of finally being in possession of a mistress who wouldn't betray him and who would refuse him nothing, absolutely nothing, he opened the crate.

The crate lay open in the middle of the elegant bedroom, voluptuous in the half-light filtering through the heavy drapes. Paul sat down in front of the box and gazed for a few seconds at the thick fabric, which hid the idol.

Flushed, his hands throbbing feverishly, Paul hesitated, glancing nervously about him. He cast a sidelong glance at a good-sized sofa where he intended to install his Dulcinea. He was in ecstasy thinking about the sensuous things he would offer himself, not yet knowing which one he would begin with. He looked around to see if his surroundings weren't hiding any jealous rivals.

Perfume phials and boxes of perfumed powders were scattered on a stand; in the fireplace, milk and water were boiling.

Was she naked underneath the fabric?

He would have liked to find her dressed.

Abruptly he came to a decision and threw off the fabric hiding his strange beloved.

A cry of admiration escaped from his lips and he fell on his knees, his hands joined together.

His madness began that very moment.

Chastely enveloped in a blue satin wrapper, Galatea lay on her back, smiling. Only the beginning of her bosom and the tip of the most charming little foot in the world showed.

Expression had been so well captured in her face and body that one could have believed the statue was alive.

"Oh, marvelous one, oh, divine one," murmured Paul. "You belong to me, you're mine!"

He ran his hands over her body. It wasn't cold, as he had feared it would be.

Lifting her carefully in order not to remove the wrapper, he carried her to the sofa, laid her down, and slowly, avidly, gazed at her from head to foot, as little by little he drew back the corners of the wrapper.

He owned a really womanly woman.

The statue kept smiling and Paul told her softly: "You like that, don't you, my sweet? You love the impudence of my hand already approaching your divine treasures. Tell me, will you love me?"

He pushed his index finger near her notch, started, then putting his hand to his forehead exclaimed: "It's as warm and soft as that of one of Eve's daughters!"

Getting up, he walked around the room, not paying attention to the trunk which got in his way.

"Ah, what beautiful things, what feats of valor I'm going to perform! I wasn't cheated. A marvelous creature has been delivered to me. Anything that comes into my head I will act out until I get satisfaction. I'll never hear another screeching voice jangling my nerves, shackling my virility. Never will I have to cope with a gesture of tiredness. She's so beautiful! More than beautiful—superb! There is nothing missing in that divine body, and it certainly won't suffer from want of adornment. She will have dresses fit for a queen; she will have the most beautiful, naughty dishabilles of all. I'll give her anything she wants. Beg pardon, anything I want. Shivers are running through my loins. This is just the time to celebrate our honeymoon! Our wedding night! And say, why not begin by offering her a bride's trousseau? That's it exactly. I'll do it first thing tomorrow. I'll just have to take her measurements. Well, well. I'm going to get married to a doll. But I'm not going to wait for the wedding night to enjoy my rights! She would be offended. Oh, oh! What a plaything! She's just as good as the most fantastic courtesan! She'll also play that role, by the way. What fun we're going to have. Let's come a little closer, undo the wrapper and admire her in all her nakedness."

No sooner said than done.

The statue, negligently stretched out on the sofa, displayed in front of Paul's dancing eyes her breasts, her rounded stomach covered with thin down, her slightly parted thighs, all the harmonious lines of her body.

"You will be called Mea," he said, "because you are really mine and I want to gamahuche you in order to prove all my love. Here, Mea, exquisite perfumes for your lovely body. Voluptuousness, here we come!"

His tongue went directly to the artificial cunt and his hands were delicately directed to her buttocks.

Fever overtook him.

"Egad! What's this!" he exclaimed after a few seconds. "Am I imagining things? Look, did you really spend, you devil, or am I going mad?"

He slid his fingers between her thighs and, dumbfounded, ascertained the presence of a few little whitish drops.

The doll, flopped on her back, her arms swinging at her sides, her head tossed back, abundant masses of hair flowing all over, belly sticking out, breasts pointing straight to the ceiling, indeed looked just like a woman who had dissolved into bliss.

Paul couldn't resist.

Disrobing in a flash, he bounded onto the irresponsible prey and possessed her wildly. He entered her cunt which, warmed up by his own heat, hardly differed from that of a real woman's, so well had the internal and external work been done. He finally withdrew, after having thought that he would never stop spending.

Sated, he sprawled out on a chair and looked at her in a daze. The statue remained in its former position, hardly disturbed by the fury of his possession, the same smile on her lips, the same fixed stare, the same immobile attitude.

He had come in that thing, and that thing now was flouting him with her glacial indifference.

Now that his desire had abated, he was sorry about the promptitude of his action.

If he was going to be carried away by passion instead of sampling the thousand promised sensations, it was not worth it to possess an inanimate being!

Then, too, why not master one's emotions?

It was that lewd trollop's fault. She deserved to be flogged.

"Slut," he shouted, "you didn't want me to spend my time looking at you, studying your postures, feasting upon your various poses, reveling in your cunt, your asshole, your tits, your calves; you didn't want me to cram my cock between your lips, between your breasts; you didn't want me to sprawl over the curves of your buttocks, or rest my head there. Wretched whore, you acted like a bitch, taking advantage of your body, and you drove me to spear you straight off so as to get rid of me quicker. Here, you harlot, come here. I'm going to whack your bottom to punish you for my stupid behavior."

He threw her onto the rug, turned her over like a bag of dirty laundry, kneeled down next to her to spank her and, at that moment, noticed, planted in the crack of her buns, a little piece of paper. Intrigued, he pulled it out. It was a letter and it was addressed to him. . . .

Paul was stupefied. He didn't believe in witchcraft.

There was no doubt about it. He knew the handwriting; it was that of the artist who had created the masterpiece.

That man therefore wasn't ignorant about the purpose of the doll he had ordered.

In spite of his debauchery, he blushed to the roots of his hair. He felt ridiculous. He wondered if he would ever dare appear in the streets of Paris again.

A moment of reflection reassured him.

He had only found the note after coitus. If he hadn't been in such a hurry, if he had taken his time to examine his new marvel in all her aspects, he would have found the note without feeling ashamed by the fait accompli, ashamed at the thought that a perfect stranger suspected him.

Since he hadn't yet spent, he would rush to have it out with the artist, or else he would have a laugh with him over his missive.

He admitted that he didn't have enough courage and composure to approach the question in that manner. In the wrong—if a wrong had been committed—he flinched from the thought of facing a man who had so well divined his extravagant whims.

Besides, why should love for a doll cause as many worries as love for a woman? No, no, and no! He was a man, he was master of himself, he didn't have to account for his acts to anyone, he wasn't that artist's friend, he hadn't had any dealings with that obscure worker, he wouldn't see him any more now than he had before. The devil with irrelevant thoughts. Back to that trollop who's waiting for her spanking.

No. He would pardon her this time. In addition, he had to carry out the indispensable hygienic measures.

Following the instructions stated in the letter, he opened her back with scrupulous attention and was amazed by her inner workings. An entire system of little boxes, connected one to the other, of little basins, of tubes, appeared before his fascinated gaze. All this rested within an elegant frame, lined with multicolored satin, silk, velvet, etc.

The breasts, shored up internally by circles of high quality steel, were prolonged inside the chest and connected by two pipes to a cylinder placed just about in the exact center of the neck. On this cylinder Paul read that only boiling milk should be used to fill it.

In the hollow of her stomach was a square container fitted with wire netting and various tubes going in all directions. In this container one could burn those small bits of charcoal used in foot-warmers, in order to diffuse heat to all the internal and external parts of the doll, and to keep the juices lukewarm.

Her belly and buttocks were divided into two basins, which one filled with milk.

Between the two cheeks of her buttocks, inside, Paul noticed a point jutting out with the letter X on it.

Consulting the instructions, he realized that by pulling a lever underneath, the two buttocks split apart, opening like double doors.

Having done this, Paul's admiration for the work executed for him was boundless.

The well-padded fleshy parts made the illusion complete. He discovered the anus, preceding an inner tube made of wadded half-rubber, which led to a sphere of unbreakable glass, fastened by strings attached to the tubes surrounding it, like so many points of a star. This stationary piece of glass could be removed to be cleaned in case the sperm, traveling all the length of the drainage duct, happened to fall there.

At the bladder level there was a basin for milk. Next to the cunt's orifice there was a tube analogous to the one in the buttocks, with a tapered extremity which penetrated into the uterus by a sort of recoil operated under external pressure. Having entered the womb, the tube plunged into a mixture of milk, vinegar, and egg white, sucked it up and, under the effect of the heat, returned it outside, thus producing the illusion of spending that had surprised Paul.

Sponges around the vagina were expertly placed to absorb the semen, and Paul noticed traces of his recent coitus.

He then understood what hygienic measures he should take, and proceeded with them.

Empty the liquids, clean the containers and the cylinders, take out the charcoal ashes, wash the sponges, perfume the inside. Paul took great pleasure in carrying out these tasks, and when he was finished his wrath had dissipated, sparing Mea her promised punishment.

It was getting late. He got dressed to go back to the city before nightfall.

Just before leaving his villa, where he was to return the next day, he looked for a place to leave his prized doll.

On the floor? Wouldn't he risk having some insect deteriorate her? Lay her down on the sofa? That might give rise to malevolent suppositions, in case some stranger accidently entered the house before he came back. Put her in his bed? Same inconveniences there as on the sofa.

He decided to put her back in the chest, postponing until the next day the decision of what lodgings to give her.

The next day, Paul Molaus woke up dejected and somewhat battered.

Zounds! For a man past forty to use so ardently an artificial woman doesn't go without consequences.

His ideas, less randy than the day before, persistently evoked thoughts of the artist, and this fact tormented him.

Then, all of a sudden, a feeling of revulsion, a violent sensation of anger at the creator trying out love-making with his creature welled up in Paul.

And why not? That boor, that lout, that mercenary, that proletarian who had guessed Paul's lewdness, had wanted to taste the fruit, and had devirginized an article belonging to him. Exclusive possession of a woman seemed indeed impossible, even when she was a fictitious being!

Jealousy had bitten him. He was the second to grind the beautiful doll. And who knows? Maybe during his absence the slut, discovered by some neighbor, was being used for the satisfaction of other sensuous appetites.

That he would not put up with!

He would lock her up in a special trunk that he was going to order especially for that purpose. He would deck her out in that famous Middle Ages chastity belt, he would don her with monastic robes, with hoods. No one would ever see her.

His jealousy reawakened his lasciviousness.

He came back to normal.

He wasn't going to renege on his promise not to go back to Bois-Colombes that day. He went out to buy a wedding trousseau for his mistress.

He went into a large lingerie store, and having described what he wanted, Mademoiselle Lucile was assigned to take care of his needs.

Mlle. Lucile was a ravishing brunette, twenty-four years old, erect carriage, gracefully shaped, with a nipped in, coquettish waist, a pert but gracious face, an engaging smile, one of those exquisite Parisian girls who know perfectly well how beautiful they are, how to best complement it, and who take every man for an admirer.

She greeted Paul pleasantly and asked him: "What you need,

Monsieur, is a complete trousseau—stockings, chemises, petticoats, drawers, morning wrappers, neck scarves. What price did you want to pay?"

"Money's no object. I want the best. End of the nineteenth century, that lingerie is sheer poetry. Do you understand?"

Mlle. Lucile smiled and answered:

"Very well, Monsieur. We shall certainly please you. Oh, if Madame had come with Monsieur, that would have helped me in the choice of our . . . perfections. A particular type of beauty is very inspiring. What looks good on brunettes doesn't go on blondes. Depending on the person, we give her shorter or longer garments, revealing or less revealing, etc. A thousand nuances come into play. You understand, Monsieur, that we are here to satisfy your tastes."

The glance accentuating these words embarrassed Paul. After reflecting a few seconds he replied:

"Madame lives in the country and cannot come to Paris."

"Very far?"

"Bois-Colombes."

"That's right next door. We could send someone."

"That won't be necessary. I have her measurements and I know what I want."

Transparent shifts, flower-wreathed chemises, silk stockings of every possible color, starched petticoats, surah and satin petticoats, bodices of batiste, chemises long and short, tight and puffed out drawers, garters of every sort, elegant morning wrappers, etc. Paul bought everything they presented to him, to the great wonder of Mlle. Lucile, who didn't understand why he didn't take just an assortment.

Then they discussed dresses. The store had ready-made dresses. Paul asked that they be shown to him. He decided two of them might suit Mea: a plaid one and another in blue and yellow satin for evening wear. He bought them both.

Mlle. Lucile told him: "If there are any alterations, all you need do is write us and we'll send a seamstress."

"Thank you, Mademoiselle, I shan't forget."

All of it was to be sent the next day. The only items he took with him were a chemise, two petticoats, a pair of stockings, and a corset.

"What an eccentric," said Mlle. Lucile as soon as he had gone.

"I hope," commented the proprietress, "that you took good care of him and that he'll come back to us."

"I should certainly think so!"

After leaving the shop, Paul got into his car and was driven to a famous shoemaker, where he bought boots to go with the dresses, slippers for at home, and a few pair of low-heeled shoes.

Once these purchases were made, he was in a feverish sweat.

The very thought of dressing his Mea already had him dizzy with a thousand lustful hallucinations.

The next day had hardly begun when Paul was up and running to the St. Lazare station and into the train which would take him to his villa.

His heart pounding, as if he had a gallant rendezvous, he opened the trunk and uncovered the doll with the ardor of an adolescent. He found her even more beautiful than before.

Throwing back the satin covering he filled the various containers of his Dulcinea, somehow receiving a certain pleasure from this far from poetic task. He then sat her on a settee, kneeled down, and put on her silk stockings—black with gold stripes. They looked ravishing on her.

"Well," he exclaimed, "aren't we beautiful, my Mea, and you will love me well, won't you? You're mine alone, you have not belonged to anyone else! You'll tell me everything, won't you? We're now going to put on this pretty chemise. Will you ever be saucy in this! Quick, give us a buss, little coquette."

He kissed her smile and remembering the instructions for moving the lips, he reached under her hair and pressed an almost imperceptible button.

Her mouth closed instantly, opened again with slight, repeated gestures, responding to the pressure of his fingers on her hair, thus seeming to react to his caresses.

He touched the area commanding the eyes and in the same manner they opened and closed at his will.

"Wonder of wonders," he exclaimed. "I lose my reason in your arms. I belong to you as much as you belong to me."

He kissed her lips and her closed eyes, as though she were sleeping, and slipped the chemise over her shoulders.

He expertly arranged her breasts outside it, tucked the chemise around her body, stretched out the doll on the settee, her head resting on a pillow, and marveled at length over the beauty of the forms showing under the transparent chemise.

Her darling nipples fascinated him at the same time as her calf, showing under the stockings, plunged him into a thousand lascivious desires he could hardly control.

Oh, he didn't want to rush anything!

With trembling fingers, he decided to attach the garters above the knee, then, lecher to the tips of his fingers, he turned back the edge of the chemise to midthigh, and pushed Mea's hand into the gap thus produced, as though she felt like amusing herself all alone.

He was so enchanted by this scene that he dropped to his knees a few feet away, murmuring: "Oh, extraordinary, extraordinary, extraordinary! She's just as alive as I am!"

He dropped to all fours in order to see the hand of the doll playing with her cunt. He had the illusion that that hand was moving with little fluttering motions and, still on his knees and without approaching the settee, took out his prick, by now quite on the horn, and held it between his fingers saying: "Dear Mea, shall we come together, at the same second, each of us masturbating like this? Just look at me the way I'm looking at you and the deed is done!"

The doorbell rang, making him jump, tearing him away from his extravagant whim. [It was Lucile, who had been ordered to deliver personally Paul's wife's underclothing.] . . .

Once Lucile had gone, Paul, replete, came back to the doll's side.

He considered her scornfully for several long seconds.

"You're made out of rubber, my beauty," he said, "and I was on the verge of being jealous of your attractive skin! What a nincompoop! But I must be magnanimous. Thanks to you, I now have the most gracious of women ready to accomplish anything I want. I won't need to fill her stomach and belly with milk and water beforehand. That reminds me—I must clean you up. Here we go, oop! Let's get rid of this chemise and those stockings, Madame. Turn over on your back. Move along now. Oh, the poetic task! We'll open Madame's back and fiddle about with her intestines. Just look at all those containers! My heavens! There, let's not damage anything, one never knows what may happen. All this work, and I haven't even fucked this idiot. Silly one, you don't speak, you don't reason the way that irresistible Lucile does. Wasn't she nice to grant me my every wish? No embarrassment, no hesitations. She just took the right position. And you, heap of rubber, you're going to serve me too! Oh, what a difference!"

Her back closed again after he had removed all the liquid she was holding, the top half of the doll's body was lying prone on the sofa, her legs extended along the floor, her buttocks sticking out.

"My, my," he said, "you're just as admirably made on this side as on the other. Lucile certainly would have complimented me had she seen you. What shall we do with you for the moment? I'm going out for lunch. I'm not going back to Paris until this evening. I'll try your dresses on you after lunch. But I'm afraid you'll catch cold in here and I'm going to put you in my bed. That will be amusing. The other girl and I have mussed it up, so you can lie in the disorder. Before leaving I'll put away all your dainty little clothes in the bedroom. You can admire my generosity during my absence. What's this, Madame? Your legs are tired, you can't walk? Up you go then. Over my shoulder and night-night."

Paul lifted up poor Mea in his arms, carried her into the bedroom, and put her down on the bed.

"You don't look so bad there," he said looking at her, "and it's true, you deserve the benefit of a disheveled bed. I don't want to shirk my gentlemanly duties. I'll put your chemise back on and you'll sleep better while I'm gone."

When he had done this he went down to the first floor salon to fetch the dresses Lucile had brought him and draped them as well as the other pieces of clothing he had bought over the bedroom chairs.

"On my way back, my dear," he said, "I'll stop by Commissioner Bertin's, to see if he's received the packages from the store and if so, I'll bring you your trousseau. Good-bye, beautiful child."

He jeered at her, the ungrateful man, making fun of the woman created expressly for him.

All of a sudden, he stopped, stupefied. A cold shiver ran down his spine and he felt his hair rising.

The doll had moved a leg.

"Gads!" he exclaimed after a few seconds of panic, "am I batty or am I going batty? What is the meaning of this? She moved or I dreamed she did, or I saw double, or I've drunk too much—but no, I know that's not the case. Let's not be childish. Let's examine things carefully."

He went to the side of the bed, leaned over the doll, and broke out laughing.

"How ridiculous can one be? I was shaking like a four-year-old child. I had put one of the legs on top of the other, and the effect of this position made the upper one slip down. Just you wait, sweet girl, till I put you to bed in my own obscene way. When I return, I'm going to fall into ecstasy in front of your little ass, since up to now I've only had the pleasure of looking at your front."

He laid her down, her face turned toward the wall, placed her half on her stomach, flipped the chemise back over her loins, revealing the admirable curves of her buttocks, clucked his tongue in appreciation, gave her a good whack on her bottom and left, saying: "There you are, Madame, that's to teach you to be good in our absence. I'm not too worried about you making me grow a pair of horns, but it's always better to warn women, even rubber ones, that one will not tolerate breaches of conduct and that if they don't walk the straight and narrow road of virtue and fidelity, they'll be sure to pay for it in the end. Do not forget that your ass and your cunt, as well as the rest of your charming person, are my legitimate property. No one has the right to use them without being guilty of theft. I will see you soon, my sleeping beauty." . . .

Anastasius [the artist] quickly learned how to profit from Paul's absences to get into his park.

Mea's master's servants never left Paris, and the care of the villa was left to a gardener of the region who came once a week.

Once in the garden, Anastasius wanted to get into the house. Without the slightest scruple, acting just like anyone in love, he didn't hesitate to take the impression of the keyhole of one of the doors opening onto the park. With this impression he had a key made. He had this key with him that morning.

Surprised by Paul's early morning arrival, but on the other hand understanding his desire to see the doll again, Anastasius was sorely upset by Lucile's visit.

He watched, feverishly impatient, first one, then the other leave. His shadow was outlined on the wall as Paul left.

The happy owner of Mea had no sooner turned the corner of the road when Anastasius, using his new key, strode into the house, completely empty of all living beings.

He had to get his bearings. After inspecting the ground floor, he climbed to the first floor and immediately found himself in the room where Mea was lying on the bed.

Seeing her uncovered buttocks, her chemise pulled back over her loins, the disheveled bed, he had no doubt whatsoever about the cause of these three things.

"Oh," he muttered, "he really loves her!"

That was all.

He was petrified before the perfection of form and flesh which his hands had fashioned.

He examined the setting, noticing the dresses and lingerie, smiled blissfully, and sauntering up to the bed, leaned his elbows on the side, his face opposite the uncovered ass and said: "Bella, tell me, we'll cuckold your keeper, won't we? You want to, don't you? You will allow me, your creator, your god, to do it with you, won't you?"

Caressing her with the palm of his hand, he kissed the entire length of her crack and continued his monologue: "You're so cold, my darling. I want to warm you up."

He climbed onto the bed, took out his phallus, clasped the doll in the position she was in, and delicately began to bugger her, fondling her breasts, pecking at her neck, crumpling the lace at the top of her chemise.

How well he knew this little hole manufactured by his genius! Tenderly, slowly, he penetrated it, seeking out the caressing rims, arranged in tiers inside in order to tickle the gland as it went in and out. He pressed against the plump globes of her backside which bent delicately under the pressure of his stomach, his fingers were running up and down her crack, edging toward her cunt whose hair was quivering under the effect of the thrusts he gave to her body. He kneaded her navel and Mea seemed to come alive in his arms, to return the passion that she inspired in him.

He came inside her, his arms clasped around her neck, his fiery dart embedded to the hilt in her asshole, and the statue followed his jerkings, buckling under his attack, sinking under his weight—better than any woman would have, for in this strange act a personality split took place within the male who was imbued with both the male and female fluids and transmitted to the machine a double desire condensed into one.

Anastasius retired from this bout of love in a collected frame of mind. Readjusting his trousers at the foot of the bed, he said: "Bella, my love, we'll see each other very often, I swear it. I have a hunch that your lord and master will be coming back soon, and he musn't catch us together. Keep my sperm for that bastard; I want him to clean you out. So, until later. Maybe tonight! Good-bye my adored one!"

He left without thinking that he had changed the doll's position, that instead of being lazily lying on her side, she was now lying on her stomach, her buttocks pointing to the ceiling, her body still bent in the position of supreme possession. . . .

Paul headed straight for Mea's rump, buggered the doll furiously, deliciously, jerking and jumping on her body, pawing her all over.

What an occasion! What copulation! The thought that his inanimate lover aroused passions threw him into a wild spasm of amorous rut and he possessed the dummy as he had never possessed any woman. Mea responded to his every movement, contorting herself into any position he wanted. It made his mind reel.

Panting, still mad with sensual rapture, he suspended the flow of his tenderness and, no longer insulting his beautiful dispenser of love who lay exhausted on the bed displaying her treasures in a lascivious pose, he murmured while getting dressed: "Precious day, precious day! I've just turned twenty! Thank you, my adored one, I will never forget the ineffable moment I owe you! You surely do bring me good luck. You enliven my existence and, not satisfied to supply me with voluptuousness as the most divine lover ever, you also got me a charming mistress. I promise you the most beautiful finery in Paris and we will have high times together very often, you can count on that."

Completely dressed, he reflected upon the intruder who had cuckolded him. "Let's take a good look at the problem," he said to himself. "Let's see if I've been a victim of some hallucination. Since I have to clean Mea, I'll find out just what this is all about."

He opened her back to clean the passageway and, if necessary, the glass. The condition of the latter removed all his doubts. The liquid was there. His medical school experience told him that the contents represented the contribution of two men.

"Oh, oh, oh," he muttered. "Very strange."

He rapidly put everything in order, then sat down in an easy chair and continued his monologue. "Someone has entered this house! How and what for? Not to steal from me. Nothing has been touched, apart from Mea." . . .

Blue satin slippers completed the transformation of the doll into a housewife.

Satisfied with his work, he lay her down in a lazy position on a sofa, her head resting on her arm, as though she were dreaming, then stepping back to better admire her he said: "If I were jealous, my darling, I would put padlocks all over the house, and no one would get into my place without being guilty of house breaking. But I'm magnanimous. I won't come back to see you for another three or five days, depending on how I feel. I'm no longer a young man, and I must repair my forces in order to make love better, isn't that right, little one? And then your rival would perhaps like his ration too! According to my experience in life I suppose that Lucile and I have met at the right moment. Oh, you won't be neglected, oh no. And since I'm a cuckold, we'll look on the brighter side of things. But just in case your lover comes to see you, I'm going to leave a little note that you will give him with your white hand. Rather clever idea, don't you agree?"

Warming to his subject, Paul wrote the following lines:

"My darling, the last time you visited me, you forgot to wash me. You know that the state of my health prevents me from speaking or occupying myself with such menial tasks. So when you leave me after having had your fill of all the obscene things you love so much, please be so kind as to not neglect those duties of cleanliness that you yourself recommend. You'll find instructions for this operation on the stand. I kiss you, hoping to be kissed by you soon.

"Your little Mea

"P.S. My cuckold knows about your visit and he didn't get angry. He buggered me after you. Only don't mess up the house.

"A thousand caresses for you—you'll give them back to me, won't you?"

With a mocking smile, Paul put the note in the doll's hand and left for Paris. . . .

The first thing Paul noticed when he came back to his villa after a five-day absence, was that the note he had left with Mea had been taken. The second thing he noticed was that Mea was in a more than indecent position; the third, that one slipper was lying three feet away from the bed and that the stocking of the shoeless leg hung in folds around her ankle. In these folds was an envelope.

"Ah hah!" he cried, "the lover came and didn't hide. He has taste, that beast! He's a brother. What a pity we can't meet! But if we knew each other we might not like the relationship. La Mea is jolly tempting in that position!"

The beautiful doll lay half on the bed, half on her back, her naked thighs open wide. The surah petticoat and another petticoat were lifted above her waist; her drawers were open and exposed the velvety down shadowing her cunt; she exhibited herself like a real temptress. The morning wrapper, pushed aside, framed the spectacle. One leg rested on the rug and the other was halfway up the bed. In this position she revealed the act of possession that had been carried out on her person.

Paul didn't think twice. He crouched down, planted his nose on her cunt and stated: "He heeded my advice. Her position was set up after the act. He perfumed the quim, which does not betray a trace of male contact. Let's read the billet-doux."

He pulled the envelope out of the stocking folds and read:

"Generous master of this paradise, a grateful heart will from now on only swear by your honor! May the fairy of this home render unto you all the delights experienced in her arms! Your instructions scrupulously carried out, you have at any moment a woman as pure, as chaste as when you last visited her. Fuck, you who allow others to fuck; the sacred fire dwells in the imagination as much as in the emotions. This will be proved to you as a token of friendship. Exercise your happiness without fearing my indiscreet peering. We will keep watch for you and we will warn you, should intruders approach while you are plunged in your voluptuousness.

> "Your servant,
> "MEA'S LOVER

"P.S. Congratulations on the name—it suits both of us."

The disguised handwriting prevented recognition of the author of the letter.

"It's a neighbor," thought Paul. "He'll be on watch, and he'll know the hours I spend here. The beast will see Lucile. That lovely child won't be long in passing by. I promised to show her my so-called wife from a different angle. Let's hurry to arrange the subject. The subject! I'm really wise when confronted with such riches, and with the depraved desires I'm feeling! I say depraved for the sake of the imbeciles. Society has them in such abundance! I have such a mad itch in my thighs that I risk not being in good shape for Lucile. It would be playing a bad joke on her. What a pity that yesterday we didn't taste the cup of drunkenness! Let's see, mustn't be too hasty. Should I undress Mea, or simply turn her around? To undress her would take too long. Let's carry her to the salon and there we'll figure out how to best present her."

After having adjusted her stockings and refastened her garters he took the doll in his arms and transported her into the salon.

"Oh," he said, "I'm going to kneel her down, her head leaning against the sofa, as if she were sleeping that way. I'll tuck up her clothes in the back like this, and expose her bloomers which I'll keep spread open over her buns with pins. The view will only be more rakish. Let's try not to forget any detail of the *mise en scène*."

The doll was flexible in all her joints, just as the instructions had stated, and as subsequent trials had proved. She didn't offer any resistance to her lord and master's plan.

He placed her kneeling down in front of the sofa, her body slightly bent over, her head resting naturally on one arm and the other arm at her side. Tucking up her clothes didn't present any problems either. Her open drawers exhibited her entire backside and with a sudden flourish, Paul brought the free arm to her loins, thus attributing to the doll the maliciousness of having tucked up her clothes herself.

Paul gazed at this tableau from a short distance, with a triumphant, gay smile on his lips, and mumbled:

"If Lucile doesn't imitate you, my beautiful Mea, I'll give you a good kick in the ass to punish you for not having inspired her. I'm counting on you, little chickadee."

His heart was beating wildly as he went downstairs to let in the young girl. He was no longer afraid. Mea's bottom had inspired in Master Phallus the most bellicose of dispositions.

Lucile had brought the things he had ordered.

Paul took them from her arms, removed her hat, kissed her on the eyes, took her two hands in his and asked point blank:

"Are we nice and smutty today, Mademoiselle Lucile?"

"Gracious! The naughty boy, to use that wretched word," she replied, blushing.

"Are we nice and smutty today, Mademoiselle Lucile?"

"Oh! He's so mischievous, he even repeats it!" . . .

"Let's go down and unwrap your wife's clothes [Lucile says later]. Since she's still sleeping, you can let me look at her again. No, don't put your hands there. You'll burn your fingers. Rest for a minute. Then we'll begin again and you won't be disappointed."

Still embracing her, Paul undid her bodice and freed her breasts, proceeding to suck them like a gourmet.

"Say," she said, "take me to see your wife's attire. Then in front of the door, you'll kiss them like this. That will be funny, don't you think? Do you want to do that?"

"Yes, you angel, you devil, let's go."

They left his room and went to the threshold of the salon where Mea, still crouched over, displayed her buttocks through her open drawers.

At the door, Lucile took her breasts in her hands and whispered to Paul: "Suck them, darling. Yes, yes, that's right, that's the way. Lower your head so I can see your wife's rump. One would swear she's dead or made of wood. She doesn't move at all. Sweet, come to my knees. I want more. There, kiss my navel, kiss me lower, kiss me everywhere. Ah, you kiss me so endearingly! To think that you're kissing my pussy in front of you're wife's bum! And, you blighter, that doesn't even bother you. The other side now. You're going to lick me all over in her presence. Let me turn around. There, I'll lift up my skirts, suck where you've made me wet. Oh, you mucker, you big mucker, how I adore you! Yes, my adored one, I allow you to dry your machine on my buns, but let it not be too bold. I'm shedding tears too, I am. Rub harder against me. You are a love of a man. Enough, enough, no, we're not going in, the door is closed. Enough, let's go downstairs."

She let her skirts fall and as light as a feather, rapidly descended the stairs, followed by Paul. . . .

It sounded as though a bed was being shaken.

Lucile got nervous.

"Paul," she whispered, "your wife is awake!"

"No," he replied softly, "I don't think so, but it's sure that something very strange is going on. Don't fear. If someone were making a cuckold out of me, I'd have a good laugh and it would be far from a tragic situation."

Stupefied by this reply, Lucile, reassured by her lover's calmness, followed him as he sped upstairs, four at a time.

The noise was coming from the bedroom, and the two lovers found out that Madame was no longer in the salon.

The bed shook under repeated attacks.

The bedroom door wasn't closed, and they could see for themselves what was taking place. Paul and Lucile saw beautiful Mea completely naked, stretched out over someone who was holding her around the waist. She was shaking with the spasms of possession.

Thanks to the position of the two bodies, the only thing Paul and Lucile could distinguish of Monsieur was his shaft submerged in Mea's cunt.

Hypnotized by this scene, they watched the entire performance without making a sound.

The rump bounced with regular movements, the unknown man's rod plunged in and out of Mea's cunt, her hair inundated the entire bed, hiding the head of her ravisher, who kept his two arms entwined around her body, lifting her above him by his incessant attacks.

Paul's hand took Lucile's. They were both trembling.

The sighs of Mea's lover got shorter and faster. The cunt's lips were stretched wider, his cock was appearing less and less outside, the moment was near, when a sudden idea came to Paul. He dragged Lucile into the salon and without giving her time to think, roughly undressed her (she helping too); she guessed that some sort of lascivious mood had come over her lover and she accepted it in advance.

When she was naked, except for her stockings and half-boots, he undressed also, took her by the hand into the bedroom and there shouted: "Don't mind us, children, where there's room for two, there's room for four!" . . .

His hand caressed her loins and buttocks and he whispered: "Oh, my incomparable siren, they have invited us to lunch. Well, both of us will go and I will honor you because your lord disdains you. Come, my love will not fail you."

He jumped out of bed, delicately took her in his arms, inspected her to see if her cunt still had some traces of copulation, ascertained that the sperm had all gone in, and only powdered her sexual organs, saying: "We'll leave the thorough clean-up for later. This will do for now—you'll be no worse off than your neighbor, that strapping wench, that hot bitch, judging by her manners."

Lifting her in his arms, he went downstairs. He appeared on the threshold of the dining room as the other two were finishing their meal.

Paul was teasing Lucile, who stood in front of him, her back against his chest, amusing herself by turning her head around and puckering up her lips with utmost grace, while with one hand stopping Master Phallus who was trying to venture into the crack of her buns.

"Oh!" exclaimed Lucile when she saw Anastasius carrying Mea, "My goodness! It's really true that your wife is semiparalyzed. What a terrible thing!"

Anastasius solemnly placed Mea in an easy chair at the table, opposite the place reserved for Lucile.

The doll's eyes were half open.

Flopped in the chair, splendid in her nudity, one could really think she was ill, practically unconscious, despite the telltale marks of her good health and strength as seen in the perfect regularity of her curves and the magnificent tint of her flesh.

Lucile, still standing, couldn't decide to sit down.

She looked stealthily at Mea, slightly embarrassed by the fact that she found herself in the presence of the mistress of the house, incapable of protesting against the scene imposed upon her, slightly defiant in front of the imperturbable placidity she was being confronted with.

Her eyes only left the doll to dart from one escort to the other, and of course to their rods.

Anastasius left his place, approached Mea's chair, straddled her thighs, clasped her by the neck, and seemed to whisper something in her ear.

Standing in back of him Lucile, shameless in her nakedness, spiced by her half-boots and stockings, let herself be titillated by Paul, who slid his prick over the different parts of her body.

Anastasius ran his hand through Mea's hair, seesawed on her and with her, then slowly straightened up and, setting her on her knees, he addressed the two lovers: "Push away the table, bring your chair over, Mr. Molaus, and I'll guide Mea's head toward your thighs. I'll be hanged if she doesn't suck you off!"

Lucile's eyes opened wide. She couldn't understand anything any more.

She helped Paul execute Anastasius' directions.

As soon as Anastasius saw that his host was installed in his chair, he took Mea to her so-called husband, carrying her under her arms.

The doll's mouth opened at the pressure of a finger behind her head and Paul's prick penetrated between her lips, which were jerking back and forth.

Leaning above, Lucile curiously watched this game, her back-side beginning to form a superb arc. Anastasius, who had stepped back, noticed her in this position, and suddenly clasped her from behind and darted his staff in the direction of her asshole.

She turned around and thrust him off saying: "Oh no, I don't want to be taken that way! Having a good time is all right with me, but I will only be Paul's mistress."

Absentmindedly she put her hand on Mea's shoulder and cried out, horrified:

"That's not a woman!"

The two men couldn't help laughing out loud and Paul replied: "Then what is it? Touch her."

"That's not flesh! Now I understand everything. Oh, the curs, the despicable curs! They're even worse than I thought they were. They've invented a woman to do their dastardly acts upon!"

She looked sweet enough to eat, she was so astonished, so indignant—and full of admiration too.

Paul interrupted the doll's sucking and said:

"You've guessed the gimmick, my treasure. Before knowing you, I had given up hope of meeting a woman who would understand and satisfy all my desires. I ordered a woman made, one that I could mold to my own liking, and who belonged to me and me alone."

"And this woman, even though not constructed of flesh and bone, even though not feeling voluptuousness herself, was unfaithful to you and it served you right, too! You didn't deserve my giving in so easily, you wretched blighter! Go ahead, lick her the way you licked me!"

"Wouldn't you believe it?"

"Look at her, Mademoiselle," the stalwart Anastasius intervened, "and confess that I knew how to conceive a masterpiece. It was solely love of women and the healthy admiration they inspire in me that allowed me to create her, to produce her and to deliver her."

"You made her?"

"Ask your friend."

She nodded her head, examined every detail of the doll, fingering her shoulders, her breasts, her hair, confessing her kindly disposed surprise by her staccato sentences.

"Yes, yes," she finished by saying, "a masterpiece, to be sure. There aren't many women in the world as perfect as she is. I don't think I'm ugly—far from it—I would be lying if I said so, but she certainly surpasses me on several points. Ah, Monsieur, you are a great man! I wouldn't blame you for having enjoyed your marvel! And you, Paul, have you made love to her, too?"

"Of course, my pet. I only wanted her to wallow in my obscenities."

"Even after you started having a good time with me?"

Paul hesitated before replying. Anastasius did it for him. "He wasn't betraying you by using his toy!"

She made a little face, looked Anastasius straight in the eye, turned her back to him, leaned over to put Mea's mouth back on Paul's prick and bent over further to better watch the artificial sucking game.

Anastasius understood that he was authorized to carry out any brazen act he pleased. . . .

Paul and Anastasius were alone.

Through the window they watched in silence as gentle Lucile walked away.

When she had disappeared, Paul extended his hand to Anastasius, saying: "You guessed what I was up to, Anastasius, and I can understand the love which bound you to a work as perfect as yours. In your place I would certainly have acted in the same manner. Thanks to Mea, heaven gave me a little woman, just the one I was looking for. I asked you to partake of this exquisite dish. Voluptuous pleasure reunites more than it divides. Shall we be friends?"

"You have a sincere and loyal nature, Paul, your friendship honors me and warms my heart. Count on me any time."

"It would pain me to separate myself from such a perfection as Mea! However, I will obey Lucile's desire. Friend, I am going back to the city. Make yourself at home here. Take the keys and use Mea whenever you want. You know better than I how to take care of her. Watch over her, I would like to keep her. With a woman made of flesh and bone, it would be childish to hope for a long future of bliss. Sooner or later the true character is revealed and spoils the voluptuous fruit. Perhaps one day Mea will be my consolation.

Therefore she will remain the queen of this house and I ask you to guard her for me."

"Thank you for your confidence in me—you won't be deceived. I will go on working to discover improvements, and pleasure will be living right by your side."

The homosexual implications here are clear. The owner of the doll and her inventor enter into a quasi-sexual relationship with each other *via* the doll which they share, neither one nor the other bothering to remove his "rival's" physical traces.

ADOLLIZING

A fantasy in rhyme from the mid-eighteenth century tells about a man, Clodius, who, spurned by his lady love, fashions himself—half in spite, half in despair—a lifelike doll in the girl's likeness. The poem is entitled *Adollizing, or a lively picture of a Doll-Worship*. In the Preface we read: "The title of this poem is of too singular a nature not to say something by way of Preface in justification of the freedom taken to introduce a new word into our language. I do moreover assure the reader . . . that the groundwork, from whence the term of *adollizing* was taken, is a real fact, known to many others as well as myself. The simple fable is this: A person of high distinction failing in his attempt on the virtue of a young lady of great beauty and merit, resolves to enjoy her at any rate, and thereupon has recourse to the extraordinary method here attempted to be described."

> Woman, cries he, when man's neglect denies,
>   With mimic art the real thing supplies:
>   When of dear copulation she despairs,
>   At once a dildo softens all her cares.
>   O thou creative pow'r! whose fertile thought
>   Can raise a solid entity from nought,
>   Do thou some kind expedient point to me,
>   May lessen CLARABELLA's cruelty;
>   Make more supportable my rigorous fate,
>   And in some measure her disdain defeat.
>   'Tis found, he cries, the lucky thought is hit,
>   Strait let me put in act th' inventive wit.

With this, a *Doll,* by new mechanic aid,
As big as life, he artfully has made;
Resembling CLARABELLA's every grace,
In stature, shape, in dress as well as face:
For this, a groupe of different trades employ
Their various skill to frame the curious toy,
While that dear fortress all delight to storm,
A LATIAN artist undertook to form.
  On the arch'd mount, just o'er the cloven part,
A tufft of hair he fixes with nice art,
Of CLARABELLA's colour, golden hue,
In sweet abundance tempting to the view.
A seven-inch bore, proportion'd to his mind,
With oval entrance, all with spunge he lin'd,
Which warmly mollify'd, is fit for use,
And will the sought-for consequence produce.
  Fir'd with th' invention, CLODIUS, eager bent,
Instantly tries the sweet experiment:
Stretch'd on a couch he CLARADOLLA lay'd
(For so he call'd the figure newly made).
Her cloaths uplifted, bare her legs and thighs,
And all expos'd, he feasts his ravished eyes:
Prostrate before the secret seat of bliss.
The room resounds with ev'ry ardent kiss;
And fancy fir'd, all CLARABELLA's charms
He thinks he now possesses in his arms.
With this, fierce back the supple joints he flings,
And his proud matter to a level brings,
When after the injection as above,
With eager efforts he begins to move:
Then breathing quick, lust rushes thro' each vein,
And for that time concludes the filthy scene. . . .

"Henceforth," he cries, "no longer shall I prove
The poignant tortures of despairing Love!
There is the remedy, the certain cure
For all that wretched Lovers can endure!
My CLARADOLLA yields me kind relief,
And puts a period to my future grief:
What CLARABELLA glories to deny,
She, thrice more bounteous, shall my wants supply:
With pleasing surety not to ask in vain,
From her, no coyness, fickleness, disdain.

> Whatever liberties with her I take,
> No silly scruples will she idly make,
> But unresisting and complacent still,
> Be all obsequious to my wanton will;
> Nor know you scarce the real from what feigns,
> When the hot blood runs boiling thro' the veins."

The inventive lover soon finds, however, that he is beginning to tire of his fantasy ideal, the real woman Clarabella, and wants to change her (or rather his fantasy about her) for another masturbation fantasy (for that is what his "Adollizing" really amounts to). To this end, he decides to exchange parts of his doll to remake her at will into the likeness of whatever woman he wants to fantasize about at the moment.

> CLODIUS, thus baffled, started a fresh theme,
> How to improve the CLARADOLLA scheme.
> "May I not gratify," enquiring he,
> "That darling passion, sweet variety?
> Is there a toasted beauty, if I please,
> I may not ADOLLIZE with equal ease?
> Change but the heads, fresh VENUS's will rise,
> Not, not to IDOLL, but to ADOLLIZE.
> A whole Seraglio will I then prepare
> Of the most celebrated BRITISH fair:
> By thund'ring JOVE! there's not a charming face
> But shall my gall'ries, and my closets grace;
> A prime collection will I order strait,
> In just revenge for CLARABELLA's hate."

The idea of manufacturing and using an artificial woman has actually been put into operation more than once. The Japanese have a long tradition in the art of fashioning such lifelike puppets which, in times past, were taken along by sailors on long sea voyages. We are told in Tokyo that to this day certain Japanese expeditions to uninhabited areas are not undertaken without the presence of at least one of these substitutes. In fact, we were recently offered a puppet fashioned by a master craftsman, at the price of about five hundred dollars, complete with real hair wherever hair is to be expected on a live female, electric heating to body temperature, and an artificial vagina with special suction aparatus. (The price was about two hundred dollars lower without the optional "extras.")

Inflatable or foam-rubber vaginas have also been manufactured, and still are, both in the East and the West.

For example, we have, from the late 1890's, the following advertisement from a French magazine:

FEMALE BELLY
With Artificial Vagina

Designed to give the man the perfect illusion of a real woman by providing him with just as sweet and voluptuous sensations as she herself.

Outwardly, the apparatus represents a woman's abdomen, minus the legs.

The secret parts, the pubis, covered with an abundance of silky hair, the labia majora, the labia minora, and the clitoris offer themselves to his covetous view in as temptingly rose-colored manner as the female love temple itself.

The contact is soft and the pressure can be regulated by a pneumatic tube.

Furthermore, [the apparatus includes] a lubricating mechanism, to be previously filled with a warm and oily liquid, to be released by pressure into the vagina at the critical moment, just as in the case of the natural female glands.

This female tummy with lubrication is the only apparatus that duplicates exactly the copulatory organs of the woman [and is therefore the only one] capable of giving the perfect illusion of reality.

Being readily inflatable and deflatable, the apparatus can be as easily hidden in the pocket as a handkerchief or any other toilet article.

Complete apparatus 100 francs.

LE BAIN D'AMOUR

Another fantasy of the paranoid type, similar in this respect to *La Femme Endormie*, is *Le Bain d'Amour*, a rare erotic story from the period just before World War I. It traces the sexual development and adventures of Pierre Angelin, from his early masturbation fantasies and first coitus with a woman much older than himself (Madame Irene), through his military service in North Africa, his homosexual affair with another young inductee, Abel Latante, through his return to the farm in France where he meets again with his former wet nurse and her daughter, both of whom he goes to bed with, through his rendezvous with his old lover Madame Irene, who had followed him everywhere, including North Africa, to his absurd, unexpected, shocking death at the hand of his jealous lover Abel Latante, who cannot tolerate the idea of sharing him with Madame Irene and would therefore rather have him dead.

The church clock struck four. Pierre Angelin, who for the last twenty minutes had been sitting on a bench of the old Square, only a few steps from the public washhouse, a book open in front of him and apparently reading it studiously, was slyly studying the bustling washerwomen. When they bent over to fish out some elusive garment from the bottom of the basin, the swaying of their bent-over torsos made their upturned petticoats rise above the knee. Pierre remained seated, hoping to catch sight of naked flesh.

The only thing he had been able to see so far were the shriveled, faded, blackish thighs of a very old woman. But since he was very young, that was enough to arouse many concupiscent thoughts in him. Now, his eyes half closed, he tried to conjure up the gracious face of Louise Granjane, a fifteen-year-old blonde-haired girl for whom he had been secretly nourishing the most burning desires.

He was still a virgin. For in spite of his seventeen years, his robust appearance, his handsome features, and the fact that he had received his school diploma last April, the only things he knew about voluptuous games were the nerve-racking and exhausting emissions he indulged in, usually at night in the secret solitude of his bed—unless it was in the company of a young boy four years his junior, whom, precocious seductor that he was, Pierre had corrupted for this purpose.

He only knew about female sexual parts by hearsay. However, one night—his heart beating frantically—he had dared to look through the keyhole of a toilet behind which a woman was relieving herself. By the light of a candle lit inside the toilet, he was able to distinguish above her white thighs, as she got up, a bushy triangular-shaped shadow at the lower part of her stomach. Then he had to flee.

That night his sheets had been abundantly sullied. Now, at that hour when, midst the luminous vapors floating heavy and headily through the air at the end of a summer's day, when nature seemed languid and exhausted by the burning caresses of the sun, he felt profoundly disturbed by the insane desire to hold a naked woman in his arms.

In his mind he lifted up the chaste petticoats of his friend Louise and tried with all the power of his will to conjure up an exact image of the dusky spot between the lily white nudity of her virgin thighs and stomach and that silky triangle, the mystery of which perturbed him so much. Other feminine shapes passed fleetingly, rapidly, elusively, through his imagination. There was Madame Lemou, the butcher—with her enormous breasts that everyone feared were about to burst out of her strained bodice and her huge buttocks, rocking fom side to side as she walked, created a wide, full swell under her skirts. Village gossip had it that this not overly shy woman easily surrendered her voluminous charms to any wooers foolhardy enough to covet them. There was Mademoiselle Lise, the laundress, a 38-year-old spinster, flat as a pancake, who came once a week to work for his mother. In the presence of men, this woman liked to put on simpering, artless, and dreamy airs, counting on such maneuvers to bring about the improbable barter of her stale virginity.

She used prudish phrases. Sometimes, her eyes raised to heaven, she praised with tart voice the pure joys of platonic love. However, some malicious tongues accused her of consuming a few packages of candles every month in connection with some occult practices.

There was nothing particularly attractive about her, but since she was very dark-skinned, had kinky hair, and there was above her upper lip a thick growth of down forming a mustache, Pierre guessed she had quite a bit of hair in other areas too. That tempted him sorely, he was afire with curiosity, especially since he had been able to see under her wide, floating short sleeves the mossy hollow of her armpits. He wanted to run his fingers over the pilous treasures which this old maid guarded like a virtuous dragon. Next he saw, undressed and inviting, Madame Irene, a close friend of his mother. Of all the mistresses of his dreams, it was probably this last one to whom he most frequently dedicated the brief spasm of his barren tendernesses.

Just at that moment, as the clock again struck four, he suddenly remembered that he had come out with the intention of taking to this same Madame Irene a book which she had asked him for the previous day. He had to wait before getting up because his puffed-out trousers much too obviously revealed his excited state. Then he hurried to the Street of the Singing Well where this lady lived.

Three minutes later, the maid was showing him in. Madame Irene was alone. She gave him a warm welcome.

"How nice of you to come! I was bored and I thought, 'If that kindly Pierre had the good idea of coming by, I would be very happy.'

"And here you are. We're going to have some tea and cakes together, then we'll have a chat. I have so many things to tell you. Is your mother well? I'm happy to hear it.

"Marie," she added, turning towards the maid, "you can go now to do the errands I told you about. Please go by Madame Angelin's house to tell her that I'm keeping Monsieur Pierre for dinner . . . please don't interrupt, Monsieur Pierre, I have already come to a decision about this. I will personally take him home after dinner. You can go now, Marie."

After the maid had gone, Madame Irene made Pierre sit down in a large wicker chair and standing up in front of him, right next to him, their knees touching, one hand placed on his shoulder, smiling with tenderly inquisitive eyes, she asked: "I'm not disturbing your plans, am I? It doesn't annoy you too much to stay with me, does it?"

Then she added, "We shall have a good time, you'll see. I'm a widow this evening."

Madame Irene was tall and thin. Her features, perhaps slightly irregular, were intelligent and soft; her head, which she usually carried in the slightly haughty fashion of the grandes dames of olden days, had a hard, sensual beauty. She was then thirty-three years old and still highly desirable. She was married and led a calm, upright life. Her husband, to whom she had never been unfaithful before (no doubt for lack of a favorable occasion), neglected her to gad about in stupid affairs with low trollops, accompanied by other libertines of his sort.

Calm and satisfied at first with her few conjugal joys, after turning thirty she suddenly began to feel a thirst for voluptuousness that her husband foolishly refused to acknowledge.

That is the reason why she had decided to induce young Pierre to make love to her. He would be a pleasant, docile, and discreet lover, and at his age he obviously couldn't ask for anything better. She wanted him at any price. I believe I've said that she was seductive and pretty. Her glance was as sweet as a sunbeam and her smile was like a flower. She had an opulent head of chestnut hair which, on certain nights, was tinged with flashes of gold. It was exquisitely coiled, framing her high, intelligent forehead.

That day she wore a flowing white peignoir festooned with blue garlands. A very deep décolleté displayed the beginning of the full curves of her bosom.

It was easy to see that she wore no corset, that under the transparent, revealing tissue, no lingerie encumbered her.

The aroma of violet perfume (her favorite) as well as that of her own flesh issued forth from the openings of her garment. Pierre, considerably affected, a bit hazy-eyed, replied, "On the contrary, Madame, I'm delighted." Then, trying to look a little less self-conscious, he added, "I brought you the book that you asked me for the other day."

"The book? Oh, yes, I know. Thank you. I'll read it later. You're really too kind. I want to kiss you for your trouble."

And leaning over him, her arms thrown about his neck, enveloping him, the warm odor of her burning flesh penetrating him, she brought him to her and their lips met in a long, amorous kiss, all honey and roses; then suddenly straightening up she flitted away.

"I'm going to make some tea."

Under the effect of such an unexpected caress Pierre practically fainted. Remembering that he had that very morning put on a clean shirt, he had a moment of panic, thinking he had soiled it. Instinctively he brought up his hand . . .

But just then Madame Irene returned, carrying a teapot, a sugar bowl, and two cups on a tray.

"The cookies are all ready," she said and, smiling, added, "I felt sure you would be coming today." And as she placed the snack on a small table, mentally she reviewed her plan of attack, for she knew that with this inexperienced and naïve boy she would be forced to make all the advances, and she couldn't help feeling a bit embarrassed. Even though she had decided in her mind to carry the seduction through to the end, a nagging fear, an eleventh hour feeling of modesty clung desperately to her natty little bourgeois soul. Alas, she was a woman. She was not long in getting rid of such scruples. Besides, she had already taken the first steps. As she put the plate of cookies on the table, nothing could hold her back any longer. Underneath the thin cloth of her chemise, she felt the impatient, lively flower of her tingling belly palpitating, already damp.

Seated next to him she then proceeded first of all by gradually setting his nerves on edge, by brushing against him, with the intention of immediately putting the boy in a terrible state of excitation. Pierre didn't really need that. He was ready, had been quite ready for a long time for the most manly tasks. However, he still remained immobile and embarrassed, not daring even to move his hand, which he had unconsciously placed on his trousers, on the place where it was burning, to cover up the trembling projection. She thrummed with nervous fingers on his thigh, saying some vague phrases whose meaning escaped her and which he didn't even hear. She also said, "Aren't you happy to be here, next to me?" And putting one arm around his waist she murmured, thinking to kindle his senses even more, "If my husband came back now!"

He drew back. She corrected herself immediately. "No, don't be afraid. I've taken precautions." That was a direct confession. She got still closer to him, "What is he touching there, this naughty boy?" And pushing away his hand, she replaced it with her own. Then she drew him to her heaving breast, while her fingers furrowed under his clothing, searching for the young, desperately stiff member. Then he understood and grasping her in his arms he stuck his greedy lips against those of the woman and they exchanged long kisses, their ardent tongues as one between parted teeth. Then, attracted by the heady odor rising from her décolleté, he discovered her breasts and kissed them delightedly. When the peignoir was thus undone, the chemise started climbing up. Madame Irene spread her legs apart and slipping her buttocks along the edge of the chair, she stuck out her stomach, to facilitate to the exploratory hand of the young man the discovery of her mysterious rose, which a sweet dew was moistening. When Pierre felt the curly hair under his fingers, then when his finger had penetrated into the eager, damp slit, he had a spasm, a shiver that rent him. Not being able to control himself any longer, his eyes frenzied, breathing heavily, his teeth embedded into the soft breasts, he unleashed the hot jet of his sap under the hand caressing him and it flooded over the thigh of the woman who, spread out against the back of the chair, was beginning to spend. She didn't stop and, grabbing his hand, placed it between her lower lips, trembling and dripping from joy. With a nervous, rhythmic gesture she showed him the movement. He soon understood and with the tip of his finger he began conscientiously to rub the pink button. She was already swooning away when the idea came to him that to put his mouth on that other one which he felt so ardent and joyous under his caress would be a lovely dessert. So he kneeled down, plunged his head between his mistress's wildly opened thighs, and slipped his tongue into the slit between the silky bush, his tongue eager to unite with the vibrating little tongue that he felt turgid with the delicious juices her flesh was secreting.

His fiery breath infused now, more intense ardor which caused inebriation, voluptuousness, ecstatic joy, to burst like a jet of flame throughout Madame Irene's entire body. She squeezed her thighs violently around Pierre's neck. He drove his tongue even further into her sex, as though to find a refuge there, and avoid losing one single drop of happiness. She went through a succession of sharp little spasms and, her head thrown back, eyes closed, inert and languid, she collapsed into a faint.

Pierre got up, exalted.

A slamming of doors announced the maid. Both of them stood up, worn out but overjoyed. And when the maid entered after a discreet knock on the door. Madame Irene was pouring the cold tea into the cups. They drank it abstractedly.

During dinner, because of the servant they could do no more than exchange furtive caresses, and when Pierre arrived home, escorted by his mistress, he was still as stiff as a rod. That night, however, he didn't masturbate.

Madame Irene remained invisible for four days. After her first sin, so copiously consummated, a few days of respite were called for to allow the body to rest, the soul to repent.

During those four days Pierre endlessly prowled about the house on the Street of the Singing Well, not daring to go in. He hoped she would give him some sign. His mother now only saw him at mealtimes, and at night, once dinner was over, he went to lock himself up in his room. . . .

She closed the wicket gate behind her.

Pierre got up and with extended arms, and greedy lips, stepped up to seize her. But she put a finger to her mouth and stopped Pierre in his tracks, bidding him to be silent. For an instant, their eyes locked together, she bent her ear, attentive, holding her breath. Then, reassured, she slid silently over the floor and immediately abandoned herself, smiling, to Pierre's passionate kiss.

They were in a sort of narrow, high-ceilinged cage, open on the side facing the altar, and protected by a shutter which allowed those inside the cubicle to be able to see everything happening in the church without being seen. Standing side by side, their arms around each other, their heads bent together, their hair mingling, they followed for a while with a certain curiosity (and also with the confused and unuttered want to put off until the culminating point, until the insane faltering of their souls vanquished by rut, the love-lock they both craved) the religious ceremony taking place before them in all its pomp.

They pretended to take an interest in the floating, shimmering whiteness of the young girls; in the glowing brilliance of the altar; in the officiating priests; in the serious, dignified bishop seated on an elevated chair under the heavy, sumptuous folds of the hangings which framed his throne; in the splendidly attired altar boys. As though carried on the fully spread wings of the hymns, the penetrating, intoxicating incense fumes wafted up to them.

On the altar, in front of the tabernacle bedecked in white silk, the heavy monstrance was ablaze. A deep silence fell over the church. Madame Irene slowly knelt down. Two by two the communicants climbed the stone steps—covered for the occasion with a thick carpet—and, their right hand raised above the pages of a big Bible lying open on the marble top of the baptismal font, solemnly renewed their christening vows. Their feeble voices, so pure, so sweet and disturbing, flared up in the silence. Pierre remained standing, immobile and worried, next to Madame Irene, whom he thought had been suddenly overtaken with piety and perhaps even remorse. But his mistress, not saying a word, took his hand and squeezing it, invited him to kneel down next to her. As soon as he was on his knees, she directed the docile hand under the tangle of her underpinnings, which were of very high quality linen and adorned with lace.

Before long he felt between her thighs the damp, tepid flesh opening.

She had meanwhile unbuttoned the young man's trousers. An inebriating heat enveloped him, a violent desire to fuse his ardent flesh with this feminine flesh overwhelmed him. He couldn't resist. With an awkward, brusque hand, he violently flipped up the jumble of petticoats and, having thus exposed the white, broad, round rump of his mistress who obligingly bent over even further to help him in his task, he placed himself so as to penetrate her profoundly. His arms were linked around Madame Irene's drawn-in stomach, clutching her tightly. Feeling joyous, blessed, even, in this atmosphere impregnated with mystical voluptuousness, she offered herself up with relish, she reached for him the way the tiny mouth of a baby avidly reaches out for the nipple of her nurse, and was fainting from Pierre's embrace, who was exploring the most inaccessible depths of her sex.

Down below, the last little girl communicants, whose turn it was to march after the boys, were finishing their pledge: "I renew the vows of my baptism and I swear to renounce Satan, his pomps and his deeds . . ." Soon, the little girls having regained their pews, the singing was resumed and swelled, thunderously majestic, up to the two lovers on the threshold of ecstasy. Pierre instinctively began to follow with his gestures of love the increasing tempo of the music celebrating the glory of the Lord.

And midst this sound, midst the tumult of intermingling voices, midst the dazzle of the altar lights filling the nave in front of their wavering eyes with the maddening glimmers of a conflagration, their short and harsh breathing as one since the woman, convulsed, had tipped her head back to glue her lips to her lover's, as the priest, standing straight and solemn on the steps of the altar raised the radiant monstrance, the glorious monstrance, the dominating monstrance above the heads bowed in pious adoration of the faithful crushed under their love and gratitude for the God-Man, for the Redeemer and Liberator of the Sins of the World, they there on high, they the damned, the ungodly, the blasphemous, their flesh ablaze, their flesh strained and bursting with joy, they came with all the might of their profane but very humane, but very sincere, but very true love. Madame Irene gave a last cry and, crushed by their spent pleasure, emptied of their substance, they keeled over.

The ceremony had finished. The bishop, priests and acolytes, incense bearers, all servants, dignitaries, officials, and priests of the episcopal court had resumed, either one by one or in groups, depending on the rite, their pompous, decorous procession. They had all disappeared behind the altar, the brightness of which dimmed with their departure. Armed with long candle snuffers, sacristans, aided by a few altar boys divested of their precious surplices, nimbly blotted out the flames joyously floating over the forest of garlanded candles and tapers cluttering the ridges, the altar, and the choir. The mass of the faithful, accompanied by the last soughings of the organ, trailed out slowly. Soon the church was empty, dark, and silent.

Madame Irene and Pierre who, in the rumbling confusion of the finishing of vespers and the departure of the participants had remained entwined in each other's arms in a delicious torpor with the impression that their bellies, damp and gooey with carnal secretions, were stuck together, gradually came back to their senses. Pierre got up first.

"Everyone has gone," he said. . . .

Madame Angelin was dozing off, her head leaning on the back of her easy chair, and the conversation of the two lovers became more intimate. They were speaking in low voices, leaning close together, their legs brushing against each other.

Pierre, slightly hesitant at first, began to run his hand over Madame Irene's thigh underneath her thin dress. She smiled, and so, gaining courage after one last glance at his mother, he stole his hand under her petticoats, climbing slowly and cautiously up the length of her expensive stockings first of all, then slipping under the cuff of her drawers, happy to touch naked flesh. There he lost his way. Madame Irene, with a mock frown, put him back in the right direction. Once the drawers were opened he soon attained the tenderer flesh he was seeking. Once there, and continuing to murmur, the better to cover up the dangerous boldness of his act, he set about masturbating his mistress. Pleased and excited, she let him, in turn caressing the young man's fly. He had quite an erection and Madame Irene, leaning back, panting, was beginning to spend, when Madame Angelin, who was not asleep and having caught them in the act, stood straight up, incensed, in front of the two who were blushing with shame.

It caused quite a scandal. After having exchanged several scathing insults, the two women separated, Madame Angelin taking away her son, who didn't dare say a word. . . .

[Pierre has just arrived in North Africa, to do his military service.] They saw a woman lifting up a tapestry door curtain and grinning at them with all her beautiful white teeth. The door hanging fell back and Pierre, imitating his friend, sat down on a piece of matting placed on the floor and watched with some curiosity the two women who, standing up, seemed to await their orders. They were not at all ugly. One was even pretty, fresh and lithe, her complexion light brown, her lips very red, large, very black eyes, sweet and submissive, hardly tattooed, just a few blue marks which gave her face a piquant and different charm. She wasn't yet thirteen. The other one was older, sixteen at least, already chubby and much more knowing. The senior soldier politely let Pierre have first choice and he took the younger girl. They squatted down in front of them; an old woman entered, carrying a tray with four little crockery cups, into which she poured boiling coffee, and left. Alone again, the veteran interpreted for Pierre. It was very simple.

"Show us your ass," he said, and docilely, the two women simultaneously lifted up the flap of their *gandomahs*. Pierre was amazed to see that their lower abdomens were shaved. This amused and arose a perverse desire in him. He had the impression that he was going to possess a maiden. The couples were formed. The veteran and the chubby girl remained on the matting and Pierre was given the honor of the very high bed in an alcove at the back of the room, covered with eiderdowns and cushions, enclosed by a veil.

An antique lamp made of baked clay in which a wick of rolled up oakum was burning in oil, shone down on them with its wan light. . . .

Pierre arrived at the disciplinary company, was given a uniform and assigned to a section commanded by a corporal who didn't seem to be too mean. Placed among these new comrades, who affected a carefree jauntiness and a valiant breeziness, within a few days Pierre began to feel better, and slowly, intimately, began to hope again. After all, there was some drilling, and fatigue duty wasn't all that disagreeable. True, in the evenings he heard, told in low voices, tales of barbarity and cruelty inflicted by sergeants and other almighty lower grades—Corsicans for the most part—on some men of the battalion who were more rebellious or simply badly looked upon by their superiors. However, not yet having seen any examples with his own eyes, he wasn't wary, thinking most of it was exaggeration. Another thing was preoccupying him: without frankly admitting it to himself, his acute, attentive, perverse curiosity rambled, constantly spying on the attitudes, gestures, and the slightest comments his comrades made among themselves. Especially at night in the barracks, when the men, at the tired and somber hour so well attuned to their feelings, stretched out on their beds or perhaps in groups of five or six, or three, or two, talked in low voices—he watched them closer than ever. He hadn't found out anything yet, but he was waiting.

He had noticed that a very young soldier in the disciplinarian company, fresh faced and blond hair, pink and rather pretty in a young girlish sort of way, with huge blue eyes, amazed and naïve, seemed to be seeking out his company. He was always full of attentions toward Pierre; he didn't impose himself, was rather discreet, but with ever ready solicitude and forethought as only a sister, a woman—or so it seemed to Pierre—could have for the man she loved. He couldn't quite figure this out, but he sensed it; and after all, that sweet and delicate attention blossoming in this environment of brutality, pain, and vice, secretly flattered him, and he was gradually attracted by it. The young boy was barely nineteen and his name was Abel Latante. He was his bunk mate. Like Pierre, he was from a good, honest, bourgeois family, well brought up and with a university degree. They started exchanging confidences. Soon they turned into stories about women. Oddly enough, Abel didn't like women. He had nothing but cold, disdainful looks and scathing words for them. One evening, after strolling for a while around their barracks square, they lay down side by side in a retired spot drowned in shadow. "But you must," said Pierre, "have gone to bed with a woman. Didn't you feel any pleasure in it?"

"No. It disgusted me. You can never trust them. Not even during the most ardent moments of voluptuousness. No."

"Well, my friend, I'm certainly not like you, no sir, not at all. And during the rotten long days that I have to spend here, that's probably the thing that worries me the most. I have a mistress—the one I told you about—who had come to join me in Blida and who is partly the reason why I'm in a disciplinarian company right now— she writes me every other day.

"They're love letters, passionate, mad letters; they're recollections, evocations of past joys and I can clearly see, especially at night when I'm alone in my bed, her adorable ass offering itself to me and I can't grab it. Her firm breasts which filled my hands, her round, sweet belly, her twin buns, her warm armpits, and I see, I see at the end of her belly, where her thighs spread open, the pink, damp, throbbing secret of her welcoming flesh below the very dark, silky shadow of her fetchingly curly hair and I feel her prying hand sliding and creeping over my thighs to grab . . . but . . . what are you doing?"

Sure enough, he felt a hand running up the length of his leg, under the fatigue coat, into the unbuttoned fly. It sneaked in and now he had the cheering feeling of a warm tickling pressure keeping down his swollen wand. And Abel's smiling face was right next to his, looking at him with shining, questioning eyes.

"What are you doing?" he repeated. "Leave me alone, you bastard!" But his voice wasn't convincing; it had a consenting tone.

"Let me do it, my darling, it's very good, you'll see. I will be your little woman, we'll love each other well. I'll belong only to you, and you to me." And so saying, he masturbated Pierre with agile, caressing skillfulness.

All at once Pierre cleared up the mystery that had been troubling him since he arrived in that company.

Like a flash of lightning, a violent, complex feeling raced through him. It was revolt, surprise, disgust, and a kind of obscene, perhaps immoderate joy, but a profoundly exciting one. And the more tender young Abel Latante became, the more caressingly he performed his part, the more his joy increased. Seeing that Pierre offered no resistance, he replaced the pressure of his hand with the sweeter one of his lips. For a second the women he had known— Madame Irene, the young Arab girl, others still—flashed before him, naked, desirable, and supplicating. But this only excited him more. Besides, he was about to spend. He was already straining his loins and squeezing his arms even harder around the head of his comrade when the latter, suddenly turning around, his trousers down, stuck out his buttocks with a practiced gesture. "Here, put it in me here." And he directed to the entrance of his anus Pierre's stiffened wand, completely moistened with saliva. Pierre hesitated.

"Come on, stick it in!" panted the other one. "Harder. Bugger me, I love it." So, resolutely, Pierre entered into his friend's buttocks. That was the first time he had buggered anyone of his age. At first, in spite of the fact that Abel was no newcomer to this sport, Pierre met with considerable resistance in penetrating the collar of the sphincter. "I'm a bit narrow," murmured the other boy, "but that's all right, carry on, you'll see in a minute."

And indeed, as Pierre gave a powerful thrust with his loins he penetrated him to the hilt. Once past the collar, it was wide, deep, and without walls. He felt as though he were falling into a well. Meanwhile Abel was quivering happily under his hold and seemed extremely pleased. "Masturbate me while you're at it," he advised Pierre. Pierre didn't wait to be told again and grabbed his rod which was enormous and had reached the bursting point. Pierre was amazed.

"You're wound up like a donkey, you old swine," he said, laughing and panting as he accomplished his act. Finally, when he felt the wand swelling up even more in his hand and spewing forth a long discharge, he let fly with his own copious and scalding geyser into those docile buttocks. Their raucous, prudently muffled sighs were as one.

When Pierre got up he felt a little ashamed. Abel Latante, exultant, didn't give him any time to collect himself. "I love you, I'm yours, I'm your woman. Come on, we're going to have great times."

And as a matter of fact, it was a perfect set up. Pierre no longer had to do anything. His pack was always in order. Abel saw to that. Their love, and we can call it that, bloomed with the same phases as any normal love. Joys, pleasures, scenes of jealousy.

Sulking, passionate reconciliations—nothing was missing. But there were several times when Pierre had to exchange blows with other men in the company who, in what he considered a too obvious, offensive manner, had coveted his queen. Besides, there was the example of his other comrades openly paired off; the example of his superior officers practicing the same sport, without reserve and unashamedly. He felt somewhat excused.

This lasted for eleven months, up until the day when, having been unofficially warned, he reported sick. . . .

As he came down from the room assigned to him to satisfy a physical need, he saw in the courtyard old Mariette, dressed in just her chemise, who, buns in the air, was placidly pissing in the starlight. Since it just so happened that at that very moment he had a tremendous cockstand he called out to her, "Hey, old woman, if

you could find what I've got at the same place, I assure you that
you'd make less water." And since he too was wearing only a
chemise, he lifted up its edge and displayed his rampant cock.

The old woman burst out laughing and instinctively—I think
this is the right word—stretched out her hand to grab what she
hadn't seen in a long time. Pierre let her do it. It was spring. Perhaps
an old unsatiated desire still lingered in her. Her old, wrinkled, dried
up hand was already fondling the willing wand. She took it between
her lips. Pierre couldn't hold himself any longer. He pushed over
the woman and uncovered her flacid belly. Her flesh wobbled, gray
hair hung down lamentably, seeming to cry over the cold sex as the
branches of the willow trees weep over a dried up spring. He inserted his fingers there and her flesh woke up; warmth began to
spread, then the dampness of desire began to flow along the lips; it
was the entry to a woman's sex and Pierre, who hadn't seen such a
thing for many, many months, flattened himself ardently against this
stomach, his lips against those limp lips, and into that ancient, faded
hag he introduced his young thresher. She soon felt flooded. In
spite of all his efforts she still hadn't spent and now as Pierre was
withdrawing, she was still violently excited. "Wait," she whispered,
and picking up a shovel from a nearby manure pile she inserted the
handle into her backside, while sucking the still dripping shaft of
Pierre, who continued to let her work. Under the wan light of the
moon shining down on their amours the hag must have looked
hideous; the gnarled wood of the shovel was ripping her apart, she
was panting raucously from her tardy joy, her teeth were biting
Pierre who had started to get stiff again; then she finally came and
Pierre, wounded, hollered out loud.

She came hideously: arms crossed, haggard eyes, dry mouth,
open thighs, with her flabby belly black and wrinkled, now disgusting with all sorts of dirt. And since Pierre had thrown her on
her back with a violent shove she was now shrieking and wallowing
in the mud, in the dung, in the garbage, looking like some fantastic
witch shaken by hysterical madness.

Her screams woke up Madame Leru. Worried, she came downstairs, a candle in her hand. The old hag fled and Pierre hid behind a
hay wagon. Old Lady Leru was a strapping woman and had plenty
of cheek. She had been beautiful when she was young and was now
a strong, hairy, vigorous woman, still desirable because of her firm
flesh that one could guess was ready for pleasure—because of her
thick red lips shadowed by down, because of her huge black eyes,
which were still beautiful, shining and caressing. She had consciously made her husband one of the well-known cuckolds in the

county. And to tell the truth Monsieur Leru hadn't been any the worse for it.

Dressed in a chemise, holding the candle high, she searched the dark corners of the courtyard, ready to jump on the tramp she thought she would find there. When she was only a few steps from Pierre, he called to her: "Say, Old Lady Leru, what are you looking for?" At first she was amazed to see him, then started to laugh. "Ah! You mucker, I've caught you! You must have been after a servant girl, isn't that right?" Now she was right next to him and mockingly tapped his stomach with her hand under his floating chemise.

"No I wasn't," Pierre replied, "I was all alone. But if I did find one, I won't tell you what I'd do with her."

"You don't have to," said the wet nurse, for she had found Pierre's tool, swollen and stiff under her fingers, "there's no need."

She grabbed it. The young man didn't lose a minute. Immediately he began inspecting the area between the thighs of his wet nurse; her bushy slit was already damp.

"Will you get out of there, you bounder. Aren't you ashamed!" But she didn't let go of what she was holding. Pierre tried to throw her over on her back. She offered only token resistance. Then said in a low, slightly panting voice: "Not here anyway. Come with me." They entered a hayloft where she immediately kneeled in front of him in such a way as to be able to watch the courtyard. When he saw her this way, with her big rump extended and hot against his belly, he felt a slight twinge of modesty at the thought of releasing his sap into the sex of the woman who had nourished him with her milk not so long ago. So he restricted himself to buggering her. Since his sojourn in Africa, he was quite expert at that game. When Madame Leru felt her anus being penetrated she defended herself: "You're making a mistake, you big boob, that's my ass."

"I know," replied Pierre simply and continued his obscure task, shoving his root in as far as he could. "You're hurting me, get out of there, you're ripping me, and it's dirty, get out!" But he held her firmly. She didn't dare cry out and soon, as Pierre was masturbating her with an experienced finger at the same time that he buggered her, she came to recognize the merits of this new pastime. A few instants later, she was saying with faltering voice: "Yes, go, still more. It feels good, that does, my darling, it's wonderful!"

She gradually felt pleasure, a new and intense pleasure which she had never experienced before spreading over her; her lower lips were drooling abundantly; Pierre's wand had disappeared into her buttocks up to the hair and he was still pushing, as though he wanted to ensconce his entire body in hers; and he let loose a great quantity of his hot liqueur, flooding, burning, and filling with pleasure all of Old Lady Leru's flesh who collapsed under him in a supreme convulsion.

They remained as they fell, tumbled onto the hay, for several minutes before they regained their senses. . . .

His cock was standing so straight he could hardly walk. In the basement, by the flickering light of a lantern, he saw Jeannine squatting in front of a barrel. She turned her head when she heard him and jumped to her feet in front of him, chest thrust forward, arms hanging down, proffered lips.

In the darkness of the basement, her dark-skinned face had taken on a passionate beauty. Pierre heartily embraced her, crushing against his teeth the pulp of her lips which he had seen bleeding a few minutes ago.

The young girl went limp and abandoned herself to the arms clasped about her waist. Pierre pushed her back over a barrel and the vacillating flame of the lantern projected against the wall their oversized shadows in a fantastic leaping and bounding ballet.

Jeannine's body was bent double. Her torso was stretched out over the casks and her legs were dangling above the ground.

Pierre had a hard time penetrating the depths of the sex which desire nevertheless was spreading open. The girl wasn't a virgin, but she doubtless hadn't been possessed more than once or twice and the entrance was too narrow for Pierre's vigorous member.

Pierre was trying with all his might to insert completely his spear as quickly as possible. He felt the semen ready to spurt forth and feared he would have to let the salutary liquid escape before he could give to Jeannine a pleasure equal to his own.

The small lips became wet, thus giving Pierre the means needed to overcome the last bit of resistance. Jeannine then encircled his loins with her two skittish thighs and drew him to her with all her force. Suddenly his cock plunged into Jeannine's burning flesh; the sperm shot out, giving the man acute pleasure and drawing from the woman a luscious sigh which her lover plucked from her lips. The same spasm shook them both at the same instant. Pierre, putting his arms around Jeannine's waist, set her on her feet without breaking away from her.

But their absence might seem suspect. They separated, already restless with returning passion. Pierre ran back to his place at the table. Old Lady Leru wasn't there yet. Jeannine even had time to come back and sit down before the farm mistress reappeared. When she did, she glanced at the two young people suspiciously, but feeling Pierre's feet seeking hers under the table, she forgot about everything else but locking her legs tightly with the boy's until dinner was over.

Two hours later, Old Lady Leru and Pierre were in the barn. There, on the bundles of hay where the farm mistress's body left its imprint, he possessed the mother while still vibrating with the memory of the daughter and felt a perverse pleasure in comparing the two.

The farm mistress was insatiable. Her widowhood had long deprived her of the joys of love, and she would have liked to make up in one night for all the wasted years. Pierre passed on to her all the desires that the possession of the daughter had left in him. But he was exhausted; the farm mistress couldn't know that he had possessed a farm girl in the alfalfa fields and her daughter over a barrel and she kept exciting him. As soon as his member became limp, she used every possible means to enable him to give her renewed joys.

When the young man was slow in having an erection, the insatiable vixen tickled him with blades of grass picked out of the hay. These caresses frayed his nerves and gave him new vigor, and so once again he penetrated the sex of the woman, her semen-drenched hand guiding him peremptorily to the spot.

The next day Pierre went after the two other farm girls whom he had not yet possessed: Rose and Louise—both of them blonde and merry. Rose was the youngest and she put up some resistance to Pierre's advances, but Louise gave him free reign, not preventing his hand from making incursions under her skirts.

"What's wrong with your girlfriend," Pierre asked Louise, "to make her so aloof?"

"She's a virgin," declared the servant girl.

"Well, in that case, bring her along with you tonight behind the hedges. We'll have a good time and teach her what it's all about."

But that night Pierre wasn't able to carry out his plan. The passionate widow didn't let him out of her sight right up to the moment of their rendezvous in the barn. Every night the young man had to douse the fires of the incandescent farm mistress.

He would have liked to taste again the intoxicating raptures he owed Jeannine, but Old Lady Leru kept a jealous eye on the two of them. . . .

"Now that I've found you, I'll never leave you, because we are still in love, isn't that right, my darling young man, and we're going to keep house together."

Pierre let this rush of words run its course. Their meeting was not so pleasant to him as it was for the other. Abel, with his tenacious and exclusive love, worried and frightened him.

The former soldier of the African battalions never let Pierre out of his sight. He had dinner with him, showering him with attentions and in the evening Pierre could not but take him to the hotel where he had told Madame Irene he would be. His first mistress was to come to see him the next day.

They shared the same bed. Hardly had Pierre stretched out when Latante began masturbating him and offering him his buttocks: "Come on, buddy, show me that you haven't forgotten the way to make use of this."

Pierre, obliging him, reviewed the whole string of his mistresses: Madame Irene, enticing and perverse in the odor of her petticoats and the perfume of the incense; his mother's maid, docile and virgin; the Algerian women with their shaven bellies; then old Mariette masturbating herself with the handle of a shovel and presenting to him the hideous spectacle of her witch-like contortions; Old Lady Leru and her untamed passions; her daughter with her firm, vibrant flesh; the three farm girls, lewd and rustic.

With these souvenirs haunting him, and with the help of Latante's skillfulness, he experienced a bitter and burning pleasure.

But the next day, he wasn't able to get Abel out of the way and the latter didn't allow him to go out. Latante had guessed that Pierre was waiting for a woman.

"In that case," he said, "don't count on my leaving—I'm going to stick to you like flypaper."

Finally it was four o'clock and Madame Irene came in, filling the entire room with her exciting perfume and the odor of love enveloping her. Abel Latante took his friend to one side: "She's too beautiful," he told him. "I won't have her. Throw her out."

Pierre wanted to rebel, but he was overpowered by the tyrannical jealousy of his friend.

Abel gave Pierre such a significant look when telling him that he would regret his disobedience that Pierre gave in. However, Abel Latante gave Pierre permission to possess his mistress once, on the condition that he would be present and that he would himself prepare his friend. Under the threat of his stare, Pierre promised and set about carrying out the orders of this man who had once more gotten such a hold on him.

He excused himself to Madame Irene and pretended to show his friend out. But the two men stopped inside the door and dropped their trousers.

"Masturbate me," ordered Abel.

When Abel's member had enlarged under the rubbing of Pierre's hand, he introduced it into Pierre's asshole, whispering exciting words in his ear.

"I love you more than I've ever adored you. We belong to each other for life. Do you feel how I'm making you spend? I can feel it coming now."

Abel grabbed his friend's rod and pumped it vigorously, then told him, "Call in your whore!"

Madame Irene came running in at the sound of Pierre's voice. She threw herself into his arms but immediately tried to move back when she saw that he wasn't alone. Pierre, mad with desire and excitement, had seized her with one iron arm and pulled up her petticoats from which a heady odor was escaping.

Madame Irene tried to flee, stepped back as far as the wall, but Pierre was still clutching her, and when she was backed up against the wall, he violently entered the slit shadowed by a silky down, himself being shoved ahead by Abel who was furiously, eagerly, buggering him. The three of them remained this way, swooning and panting, a human cluster: Abel buggering Pierre and Pierre fucking Madame Irene.

Abel finally shot a fiery stream into Pierre's anus, saying: "Pass this on to your neighbor."

No sooner said than done.

When Madame Irene disengaged herself from this monstrous coupling, she quickly threw her arms around Pierre's neck and said, "Come, I love you as much as the first day, but let's escape from this man."

As Pierre made a gesture as though to send his friend away, at the same time joining his lips to those of the woman, Abel came nearer: "So that's how it is! So be it, but let me bid you farewell."

Kneeling in front of Pierre, he kissed his member dripping with sperm, then ferociously cut it off with a chomp of his teeth.

"That will teach you to keep your promises, traitor!"

He got up while Pierre was writhing on the floor, screaming horribly and Madame Irene, spattered with blood, looked on, her eyes rolling around in her head like a madwoman. . . .

The screams coming from Pierre didn't sound human. In a few minutes they had attracted the hotel personnel. There was a doctor among the guests who pronounced the case desperate.

"Nothing to be done," he said, "except to assuage the pain of his last moments."

Under his direction a special bath was prepared with a potion for which he furnished the formula. The wounded man was carried to it and seemed to partly recover his senses and to be experiencing less pain.

The bleeding had slowed down. The flow of the precious liquid was reduced to a trickle which gradually tinged the water in the bathtub red.

The hemorrhage had abated so it was no longer painful; and the substance added to the water bathing the open sore acted as a powerful aphrodisiac—so well did it work that all those looking on the agony of the unfortunate man saw, stupefied, a radiant expression appear on his face, gradually replacing the contractions of fiendish suffering.

It seemed to Pierre that he was possessing Madame Irene, whose luscious sight filled his eyes at the very moment when his friend inflicted that horrible and mortal mutilation on him.

He thought that his absent member was introduced into his mistress's vagina and that the sperm was coming slowly, very slowly, endlessly, perpetuating and multiplying tenfold his pleasure. He thus had the illusion of transforming the spasm's rapid jolt into a voluptuousness so slowly distilled that it was becoming eternal.

This dream didn't deceive him, for the end of that supreme pleasure would coincide with his death.

When he no longer had one drop of blood left in his veins, when the bathwater had become as red as the lips he had so often kissed, he leaned his head on his shoulder and his hand sought the area of his prick as though he wanted to masturbate.

Madame Irene had gone stark raving mad, and the shrill screams she let out pierced everybody's ears. The agonizing man recognized her voice and believed, in his dream, that she was crying out from pleasure. His limbs shook with a supreme spasm. When he drew his last breath, he looked as though he were giving a kiss and his bloodless body sank to the bottom of the purple bath, to the bottom of the bath of death and love.

LE KEEPSAKE GALLANT

This excerpt from *Le Keepsake Gallant* contains an unusual fantasy centered on the idea of erotic urination by a woman (female urilangia), in connection with bathing in hot water and the application of hot laundry and towels to the body (skin eroticism):

"Yes, yes, put it there, between the lips, back and forth. That's right, there, lovely. Enough, enough of the sponge, into the water now." Oof! Aah! That hot water all over is fabulous—the ass in hot water, the snatch in hot water, everything, everything in hot water. And her cute little paw, so sweet, so delicate, rubbing me, tickling me. Oh! The hot laundry now, the scalding laundry . . . set fire to me all over!

She got out of the tub, I immediately applied the boiling laundry over her wet parts, sponging, wiping off, drying her, as she had just done to me.

"Aah! Yes, yes, that's wonderful, wonderful, and that warms the cockles of my heart. Take the other one now. Yes, yes, that's the idea. Push, press down, all the way. Oh! It burns! Oh! My heart! Oh! Oh! Oh! Aaah! It's so marvelous. Gertrude, help! Help! Don't go away, don't leave me, don't leave me. I'm pissing, I'm pissing."

I don't know whether she was really doing that, but the laundry was all wet and when she revived, she had to take a second bath on the bidet, but this time, she sponged herself.

Another excerpt from *Le Keepsake Gallant* also deals with an erotic urination fantasy.

She was convulsed on the carpet, arms and legs flying in all directions, tearing at her flanks and breasts. With an ecstatic smile on her face she muttered:

"Come on, you girls, all of you—all of you piss on me, flood me! Let me drink you and kiss you!"

Lucienne, who had left the couch, was the first to jump to the order. She kneeled over Raymonde's face and a steaming jet burst out, splashing over her nose and lips, her chin and neck, her breasts. Raymonde, clutching the other's thighs, opened her mouth and drank.

Josepha locked her belly between Raymonde's thighs and shot out her urine on her navel, her feminine jewel. Standing up in back of Josepha, Pascalina aimed for Raymonde's triangle.

It was an indescribable spectacle and in no time, adorable Raymonde, dripping with urine, rubbed herself against her girl friends, covering them with it too. Like raving bacchantes, they ran into the bathroom to wash, wipe themselves off, powder themselves, lust making their blood boil.

Two baths had been drawn and they jumped in to have a preliminary washing and, naked, they smelled each other all over, to see if any odor lingered, giggling all the while.

The products of elimination are one of the prime sources of sensual pleasure to the infant. Instead of the later developed, learned revulsion toward waste matter, the human young— contrary to other animals—experiences intense pleasure from direct skin contact with feces and urine and does not object to remaining for prolonged periods of time in this state of pollution.

The fantasy which combines urination with heat eroticism (the application of scalding hot towels on the girl's bare skin and bathing in hot water) illustrates the clinical fact that the infant's first experience of heat (as distinct from the warmth of the normal body temperature) is derived from skin contact with his own urine and feces which are, of course, warmer than the external body temperature. Because of their acridity, they may actually cause burning sensations. Ernest Jones and several other first generation pioneers of psychoanalysis (including Freud) have called attention to the significance of these experiences for the psychosexual development of the individual. And they may well be the kind of imprinting, to speak in more recent psychological terminology, that is responsible for the later sexual preferences and interests of the adult individual.

THE ROMANCE OF LUST

Some of the most intense sexual fantasies in literature, including a strong interest in urilangia, are contained in a number of letters from the year 1859 from Count Rochefoucault, at the time attaché at the French Embassy in Rome, to his mistress, Lady Cavendish. They became the source of a social scandal when they were produced by Lord Cavendish in his divorce suit against his wife in which he named Rochefoucault as the corespondent.

These letters became, undoubtedly on account of their strong erotic content, an appendix to the first English edition of *The Romance of Lust; or, Early Experiences* (4 vols; London: 1873–76), though they have nothing to do with the rest of the book. Their inclusion in this famous erotic novel was a happy accident, for it saved them from oblivion. The letters, written by the Count to his lady friend during her absence from Rome, reflect the feverish imagination of a man totally obsessed by the erotic images he describes.

When I shall have undressed my adorable little mistress it will be nine o'clock; she will be mad with desire, delirious from passion and rapturous exactions (*exigences*), her maddening look exciting me in the highest degree will arouse all the strength I possess, and enable me to exhaust her so completely that she herself will attain the height of happiness; the greater the refinement and delicacy of my caresses the greater will be your happiness, the more languishing will your eyes become, the more will your pretty mouth unclose itself, the more will your tongue become agitated, the more will your bosoms, firm and soft as velvet, become distended, and their nipples grow large, red, and appetising; then will your arms grow weaker, and then will your angelic legs open themselves in a voluptuous manner, and then seeing ourselves reflected on all sides in the mirrors, shall I take you in my arms in order to excite you (*branler*, frig) with my hand, whilst your little rosy fingers will similarly excite me with vigour, and I shall suck your divine nipples with passion. When the agitation of your little legs, of your lovely little bottom (*derrière*), of your head, and those murmurs of pleasure prove to me that you are at the point of emission, I shall stop and carry you to a piece of furniture made to sustain your head, your back, your bottom, and your legs, and having near your cunt (*con*) an opening sufficiently wide to allow my body to pass erect between your legs; then shall I fuck (*enfiler*) you with frenzy with my enormous and long member, which will penetrate to the mouth of your womb; being squeezed by your pretty legs, which will bring me closer to you, I shall wriggle (*remuerai*) my strong pretty member, which you love, with more vigour than ever; my private parts (*organes males*, testicles) will touch your little bottom, and this contact will provoke such an abundant flow of the essence of love in your little cunt that I shall be as if I were in a bath.

How I fear to leave off there! But we shall see. Do not write to me by the night post, it is useless!

I do not wish to have any other woman spoken of, they all disgust me, even to look at them. You know it, and you know that there is nothing, absolutely nothing, in you to disgust me, but all that belongs to you maddens me, and I love and adore all; it has become a madness, and you know it; for when you are kind you give at least the idea by letter of that which you would not do if you had the slightest doubt.

You know that I have sucked you between the legs at those delicious moments when you made water, or when you had your monthly courses, and that my happiness will be complete when you will allow me, and when circumstances will allow you to let me lick (*passer la langue*) at that ineffable moment, when your little love of a jewel of a bottom has just relieved itself. In you everything appears different and pure, the purity which reigns in your every feature, the excess of refinement which exists in your whole body, your hands, your feet, your legs, your cunt, your bottom, the hairs of your private parts, all is appetising, and I know that the same purity exists in all my own desires for you. As much as the odour of women is repugnant to me in general, the more do I like it in you. I beg of you to preserve that intoxicating perfume; but you are too clean, you wash yourself too much. I have often told you so in vain. When you will be quite my own, I shall forbid you to do it too often, at most once a day, my tongue and my saliva shall do the rest. . . .

I shall still have lavished the following caresses upon you, angel of my delight, were I a little calmer. I had a dream, such as it was, about it last night, and only remember it just now by way of explanation of my mad excitement of this morning. I saw you as I was asleep, you were by my side frigging me with your fingers of love, and you heard me say to you, "I see you there." You are as lovely as Venus, your lusciousness and lasciviousness are at their very height, your body is completely perfumed with your urine, in which I forced you to bathe yourself for my enjoyment, so that I might lick you. You have painted the most seductive parts of your person. Your shoulders are white, your rosy bosoms reveal themselves through a rose coloured gauze, trimmed with bows of the same hue. Your thighs, as well as your navel and your heavenly bottom, are revealed through a heavenly gauze, your legs are clad in rose-coloured stockings. The sperm flows; but how much I needed it! This is true, for my testicles were swollen in an alarming manner. . . .

It is two o'clock in the morning, I have violated and well worked you, kissed, frigged, licked, and sucked you, obliged you to yield to my desires, the most debauched, the most shamelessly degrading during the whole of the afternoon. All the afternoon, too, I have got you to suck my member and my testicles. I have made you pass your tongue between my toes and under my arms. I have compelled you to paint your body, to drink my urine. I was almost on the point of getting you sucked and licked by a pretty Lorette, perfectly naked, between your legs, and to make you piss into her cunt in order to make the depravation more debased than ever. I have had discharges from jealousy. I have discharged at least forty times; and when, after having left you to go to my club, I returned home, and finding you fast asleep from exhaustion, I awakened you and insisted upon your frigging me with your rosy fingers, all the while licking my several parts. You implore me. You are wearied, but I am intractable. You must do it in order to excite you as much as I am myself excited. I suck your breast with frenzy. The sucking that I have given your bosoms, and the fear you have lest I should fetch a young girl to violate you with her breasts in your cunt, filling your womb with her milk to excite your senses, and then you hear a voice whose sound alone so pleasingly tickles your womb, saying to you, "My pretty mistress, I implore you to abandon yourself to me. I will love you so fondly. I will be so kind and gentle, I am so handsome, I will do all you can possibly wish. I know so well how to have and suck a woman, my member is enormous, it is beautiful, rose coloured, large, long, hard and vigorous. Yield yourself to me."

Tell me if you like this one.

When you are ready you will call me so that I may come and say my daily "How do you do." You will begin by taking my —— out of my trousers, then half opening your gown, you will lift up your pretty chemise with one hand, and will pass your other arm, soft as satin, round my neck. I shall embrace you tenderly, then I shall lick your snow-white shoulders, your bosoms, which seem to be bursting from the imprisonment of your rose-coloured stays embroidered with lace. I shall lick between your legs, over your divine little bottom, your nymph-like thighs being at that moment on my knees; then you will place your angelic little feet, with your stockings on, one after the other in my mouth. After this you will send me into the dining room, in order to get rid of the servants, and, by this time, filled with an amorous and impassioned languor, each of your movements breathing forth the frenzy and voluptuousness of passion, you will come and join me. There will be only one chair, and the table will be laid for only one person. We shall each of us have only one hand free, I the right, and you the left; then you will sit upon my left leg, which you have found means to make naked; you will have unfastened your gown in such a way that it will hang down behind, and your right hand will caress and stroke my enormous prick, which you will have taken between your legs without putting it into your angelic cunt, whilst my left arm will wind itself round your lovely waist in order to bring you still nearer to me.

After breakfast, which will have lasted till half-past twelve, and which will have given you strength, we will go into the little rose-coloured boudoir. I shall place myself in a low narrow chair, and as I shall be very much excited by your enchanting looks, my enormous member will come out of its own accord from its prison, and you will sit astraddle upon me, introducing, with the greatest difficulty, my pretty and vigorous prick into your pretty girl-like cunt, when wriggling about from sheer enjoyment will stop its movements every time I tell you I am on the point of discharging, so as to increase my desires and my transports of happiness. Then in half an hour's time you will get up and place yourself upon the sofa, whilst I, at your desire shall slip off all my clothes; then you will get up from the sofa and take off your dressing gown, only keeping on what you have underneath. In my turn I will stretch myself on the sofa, getting every moment more delirious with passion, for your dress, betraying the delicious outlines of your figure, without revealing them entirely, will render me almost beside myself, and will make my prick so long and so stiff that you will hardly be able to sit on its point without being fucked, in spite of its size, which will force from you sighs and murmurs of rapture. At last, when once seated, fucked by my manly and powerful prick, you will throw yourself backwards. I should lean my enraptured legs against your bosoms, in order that you might lick my feet, while you would pass your amorous and divine legs, softer, whiter, and more rose-tinted every day, over the whole breadth of my chest, placing your tiny goddess-like feet in my mouth. As our desires would augment at every moment, you would allow me, would even ask me to take off your garters, your pretty stockings, and your slippers, in order to procure me the luxury of licking every part of your body there, and of realizing in the most perfect manner the intense enjoyment arising from the contact of the most delicate, the most woman-like, the most voluptuous member of your body. My hands would frig our little love of a member, my manly prick would kiss your celestial womb, and my thighs would caress your delicious bottom. When I have worked you in this way for an hour, ceasing every moment you were on the point of emission, I should, as I withdrew my member, let you at last discharge, and then an immense stream of love would flow into my mouth, which, suddenly and as if by enchantment, would find itself in the place of my member, while your bosoms would be covered with that white essence of which you are the only source in my eyes (I had never known it before Homburg), and which would escape from my amorous member.

Every day after dinner, reclining voluptuously on a couch, you would snatch a few moments of repose while I was taking off all my clothes. When I had finished, and when I, filled with love, had shown myself to your contemplation, you would give up to me your place upon the sofa, and assuming the most seductive, the most coquettish, and the most graceful attitudes, would come and play with my member, whose vigour would arise solely from the sight of your pretty costume, which, I am convinced would render you more delicious than the most graceful fairy. You would love me so deeply that I should cease to have any power of will, you would have exhausted me, sucking me completely dry, nothing would remain in my prick, which would be more full of desire, more enormous, and stiffer at every moment. My languishing eyes, gentle as love itself, surrounded by large dark blue circles caused by your look, your tongue, your bosom, your cunt, your member, your heavenly little bottom, your legs, your fingers, and your angelic little feet would tell you how complete was my happiness, my intoxication, my extasy, and my faint, exhausted but happy voice would give you the same assurance, would murmur with rapture in your ears—"Oh! how I love you, my lady love, my divine little virgin, caress me yet once more, again, still again, it is a dream. Thank you, oh, thank you, and yet again. Oh I am in heaven, do not pause, I implore you, suck me harder than ever; lick me well; oh! what rapture; ask me what you will, it shall be yours. You are my mistress, no other but you in the whole world can transport me in this way. Frig me with your knees. Oh! oh! oh! I am going to discharge," and my half opened mouth would prove to you my enjoyment, and the thirst I had for the bliss you could confer.

Then, more full of passion than any woman lover had ever been, enraptured as you listened to my voice, so completely beneath your sway, listening only to your own love, you would raise your little coquettish petticoat, and pressing your dear little loves of calves more closely together, for you would be on your knees, resting upon my little blue veins, you would frig me in this manner, with greater vigour than ever, sitting down every now and then upon your tiny little heels, in order the better to release my beautiful prick, perfectly straight and rudely swollen and inflamed with passionate desires from between your divine thighs, as soft as satin, and as white as snow, to better introduce the wet tips of your lovely and velvet-like bosoms into the seductive little hole of my member, whilst my knees raised slightly behind would gently caress your bottom, so as to give you some little satisfaction in your turn; and at last, unable any longer to retard the moment of emission, you would bend forward, resting upon both your hands, to increase my desire, and keeping yourself back a little distance from me, while your petticoats would now cover my head, and act almost like an electrical conductor upon me, you would intoxicate me with the perfume exhaled from your legs, from your member, from your cunt, from your bottom, and lastly, you would slack my thirst and complete the celestial transport by pissing, with eager rapture, between my burning lips some of that woman's nectar which you would alone possess, and which, emanating from you alone in the world, is worthy of the gods. It would be half-past eight.

You cannot form any idea of my excitement at this moment. I hope you will like this, and will answer me prettily. Am I sufficiently in love? And do you believe there will be another woman in the whole world besides yourself for whom I shall have any desire. Oh, how wild is the longing that I have for you at this moment; and this nectar I have spoken of, from whom else could I care for it, could I endure it even, whilst from you what mad delight! Tell me, do you believe this? You know it perfectly well, I am sure; these are not mere words. Tell me that you will piss into my mouth again when I ask you. I am now going to try to sleep, but what chance of doing so with this love that consumes me. I must await your pretty letter of to-morrow morning, for it is that alone which will excite the flow and stream.

At half-past eight you would like to conform to the usages of this room of mirrors, and as your desires have become greatly inflamed by my own state, and by the soft and sensual temperament of our bodies, you would ask me to undress you, in order that, being completely naked, I might the more easily overwhelm you with my most passionate caresses. I should then strip you of every thing, except that in order that your feet might not come into immediate contact with the looking glasses upon which we should be walking, I would slip on your feet a pair of tiny little slippers, with little silk soles, at a distance they would hardly be visible.

Some one is coming. Adieu till to-morrow.

And larger and stouter than that of my little darling, and so indifferently shod with shoes. (Their boots are pretty.) . . .

I would take you for a drive either in a pretty barouche or in a phæton, your toilette would be beautiful but simple. I would only insist upon your wearing a veil, for my love and happiness would render me somewhat egotistical with regard to others. We should not be serious all the time of our drive, for at every instant I should steal a kiss, and your feet would be resting on mine.

We should return home about half-past five to dress for dinner. You would change every thing, and without paying any attention to what our servants might think, I should put on a loose pair of trousers, prettier than what I had worn this morning, but, like them, opening in the front. As for you, my own love, I should insist upon your dressing yourself as a ravishingly pretty little danseuse, with some little difference, however, in my favour. Your hair would be in curls, falling all round your head, upon your beautiful naked shoulders. You would crown them with a pretty garland of flowers, such as I like for Aimée. You should wear a light-coloured muslin dress, very low and very short, up to the knees, your arms bare, and the skirts exceedingly full (the body of which would be transparent, and refine and reveal the divine shape of your angelic bosoms), your legs, perfectly naked, would be visible amongst a mass of folds of muslin, and would be covered by little openwork stockings of rose-coloured silk, fastened at the instep by bows, like the dress, and on your tiny virgin feet you would have little satin shoes, without soles. To pass into the dining room, so as to avoid catching cold, and also to prevent the servants revelling in the sight of my treasure, you would envelope yourself from head to foot in a long veil. During dinner I would try to remain tolerably quiet, so that you might eat and strengthen yourself for the evening, which would be a fatiguing one. Our servants would have directions not to enter until we rang; during each course you would open your veil, and turning towards me (for you would be on my right hand), you would place your pretty legs across mine; immediately my manly prick, which your love would render daily more and more delicious, would display its vivacity, and you would caress it with your lovely satin-like calves, your chair enabling you to do this, being tolerably large, with only one arm on the right, while mine would be much lower, that would not fatigue you much, and this is what you would say to me, "Am I not bewitching and delicious? Do you not think me voluptuous? and regard me as your mistress, holding you under my entire subjection. I am very happy to please you in this way." And I should answer, "Yes, I am your slave; you give me the greatest enjoyment that can be had; there is not a woman in the world who possesses the attractions you have; you make me do anything, you are the queen of voluptuousness, of enjoyment. No one knows how to make love as you do." At last at the dessert you would glide gently upon my lap, allowing your petticoats to flow behind. I should suck your bosoms, for as the servants would be getting their own dinners, I should have thrown your veil off, and you would then appear enveloped in all your many charms. Then I should give you your dessert, which would consist of a biscuit moistened with that white essence which you alone in the whole world have known and know how to produce in me, and for my reward you would allow me to take my wine for dessert. I would then place my wine-glass between your legs, opened voluptuously wide and you would let that delicious urine flow into it. The intoxication that this flagrant liquor would produce, would be the signal for my most passionate caresses. You would begin by placing yourself astride me, and I should thrust with the greatest difficulty my virile member between your legs. In this position we should leave the dining room, I carrrying you along by the stiffness of my member, while every step I took would make you wild with excess of enjoyment. We should go into a pretty boudoir, the floor of which would be completely covered with looking glasses, and filled with furniture intended by their shape and softness to augment the voluptuousness of our embraces. No costume whatever would be put on in this room. Nudity alone would have a right to remain there. There would be pieces of furniture to excite the senses and whereon to recline, others enabling us to suck each of our members, to lick, to frig, to kiss, to enjoy, to complete our performance, to discharge, to fuck, in one word, to supply and promote the extremest refinements of the most celestial and most perfect of all enjoyments.

The continuation on some future occasion. My fear of exciting you will depend somewhat upon my letter of this evening or to-morrow, and particularly upon the frank and sincere reply for which I ask you for the day after to-morrow.

Send me back the beginning.

You cannot have the faintest idea of my dread when one of these sheets is on its way.

Why do you trouble yourself to pay so much attention to style and writing—that takes time. I never read mine over, and that is so much time gained.

ENGLISH TRANSLATION OF THE LETTER WRITTEN BY THE COUNT ALMOST ENTIRELY IN CIPHER

Here is the response of my heart, my beloved adored one. Thou shall have it as soon as I shall dare to send it to you.

Thou shalt belong to me entirely one day, perhaps in eighteen months, and then here is the existence which thou shalt have the grief to be compelled to lead.

In the apartment which I depicted to you the other day, and with the toilette that I require my beloved lady, my lady mistress to render herself every day between eleven o'clock and noon.

She will find there thy loving husband, all fresh and in every respect desirable (*gentil*), clothed in a dressing gown of very light texture.

From noon until three o'clock this is the programme.

At noon thou wilt stretch thyself on the easy chair, thou wilt loosen a little thy girdle and open thy pretty dressing gown. I on my bent knees at your side shall lick you with my tongue, while my arm shall encircle thy divine waist and thy two naked arms shall encircle my neck; afterwards softly widening the virgin legs thou wilt cast aside all that which hides from the eyes, and you will place me between those divine legs.

Successively I shall lick with voluptuousness thy neck, thy shoulders, under thy arms, thy breasts. I shall suck with force those chaste little bosoms, which by their swelling would desire to escape from the pretty little rose-coloured stays; then passing to thy intoxicating cunt, I should suck it with such an amount of frenzy that thou wouldst discharge for the first time in my mouth.

This done it will have so much excited me that, taking thy place, it will become your turn to mount between my legs, and licking all my chest thou wilt finish by frigging with passion my prick, which will become longer and straighter than ever.

As soon as thou shall feel the enjoyment coming thou wilt cease, in order to lick the parts adjoining.

At one o'clock thou wilt want to make water, then my mouth adhering between thy legs, thou wilt allow me to swallow all, then lying down again on thy little belly, I shall lick with fury thy bottom so voluptuous, and thy delicious legs.

Afterwards it will be thy turn to continue thy caresses upon me.

At two o'clock both of us elevated in a supreme degree, lifting up thy little chemise in front we shall do the business, that is to say, that surrounding me with vigour with thy legs, thou wilt make efforts in order to fuck thyself (*enfiler*), but my member will be to such a degree enormous that we shall have all the trouble in the world (the delights corresponding to the efforts). At last, once entered thou wilt procure, by my movements and my pauses, such enjoyments that I shall hear you uttering the softest murmurs of thy voice, and so that thou wilt wriggle thyself on my ravished prick which will still further augment thy transports.

Thou wilt enjoy thyself thus three times. At the third time I shall suck thy breasts with such passion that thy eyes depicting a heavenly languor and a divine abandonment, thou wilt empty out upon me thy delirium causing seminal fluid.

That will last until half-past two o'clock, then we shall sleep together thus until three o'clock, and at three o'clock thou will go to dress thyself in order to go out or to receive visits.

Behold, the following part shall come to you if the commencement pleases you.

The Count's fantasies exclude little in the realm of erotic fantasies: foot fetishism, odor fetishism, every possible and impossible form of sexual intercourse, and especially urilangia, are described with passion and lucidity. It would seem, from these excerpts alone, that the role of urination in sexual fantasies (and perhaps in human sexuality in general) has been underrated. It has also been our own clinical impression that many more people than is commonly believed have such fantasies, either in connection with masturbation or sexual intercourse.

SEPT PÉCHÉS

Similarly underestimated is the role of the male ejaculate, both as a fantasy and in actual sex behavior. In *Sept Péchés* (*Seven Sins*), a novel from the turn of the century, there is the extraordinary sex fantasy of using human sperm for the preparation of jam, and of mixing donkey sperm with honey.

M. de Saint-Grattelon began to give poor Mireille a thoroughly detailed course in anatomy, explaining why she had nothing to fear. When he felt the discharge arriving, he had immediately withdrawn and had let loose at the entry to her pussy, thus lubricating the pink lips of her sex.

In short, after quite a bit of time had gone by, Mireille was absolutely reassured by M. de Saint-Grattelon's explanations which were, indeed, quite true. So much so that she promised him she'd be at the same place, same time, the next day.

All the way home Mireille saw in front of her eyes that

enormous chunk of flesh, and especially that warm liqueur which had left gluey streaks on her hands. Was it good? Oh! To know the taste of that whitish stuff! To suck for hours that member with its incredibly soft skin! Right at that moment, as she was opening the gate to the alley leading to the house, her snatch and the top of her thighs felt all moist. She couldn't do anything about it then, though! As she walked through the dining room on the way to her room to wash she was attracted by a bowl of fruit—cherries and bananas. She took a banana and entered her room, locking it firmly behind her. As she lifted her skirt to run a wet towel over her young pussy she noticed the banana she had placed next to her. A malicious smile spread across her face. She looked at her pussy, still moistened by the semen and sperm remaining at the entrance of the womb. Mireille peeled the fruit and ran it over the entrance to her sex, then inserted it. She left it there for a moment, pleased to feel such a thing in her burning cavern. Then, slowly, she pulled out the fruit, all hot and moistened with M. de Saint-Grattelon's sperm and lovingly enjoyed the banana. Never, certainly never had any fruit tasted as good! To make sure that she didn't miss a drop of the dew and jissom clinging to her thighs and her fleece, Mireille, after taking a bite of the banana, rubbed the rest of it on and around her pussy. She did such a good job that she didn't even need to use a towel that day.

A few minutes later there was a knock at the door and opening it, she found a cousin of hers.

"What do you want, René, my little one?"

"What do I want? Well, I want to see you. I want to say hello."

"So come in. Sit down."

"No, Cousin Mireille, not right away. I feel like I have to wee-wee."

"You do? Well, that's easy—here, do it in the pail."

And she helped the lad to undo his little fly and to take out his little pecker. Mireille mentally took note of the difference between M. de Saint-Grattelon's huge rod and this pretty little thing! Could thick, white liqueur come out of this one too?

"Look at it, Cousin, it's nice, isn't it?" said the gamin all of a sudden, as he noticed Mireille staring at his little member.

Mireille caressed it with her hand and finally, not being able to contain herself any longer, she grabbed it with her mouth. Alas, suck as she would, nothing came out.

The next day Mireille was on time for her rendezvous. But M. de Saint-Grattelon, fearing an interruption by some intruder, was content to kiss the lips of the country girl from Provence. However, he convinced Mireille to come to see him at his home. Nobody would be there, all she had to do was come in through the garden. There was not a chance of being seen.

Half an hour later, Mireille was in M. de Saint-Grattelon's bedroom. It must be said here that the gentleman knew the fetching sin of the young girl and he had placed on a small table some cakes, jam, and other delicacies. Not without some difficulty M. de Saint-Grattelon was able to undress her completely and admire the beauty of her young, well-rounded body. He ran his tongue over her skin which smelled so sweetly of Provence, until he arrived at her pink *motte*. Then expertly, slowly, he licked her sex, all of which fitted into his mouth and soon Mireille melted and came. As he was getting up to wipe off his lips, Mireille grabbed him, wanting to taste the dew still clinging to his mouth. Then brusquely she moved away, her hands fondling his shaft until its slight trembling movements announced an imminent discharge. Bringing the jam jar near her chin, Mireille then dipped the enormous rod into it, loaded with jelly. She then put it once again between her lips, nervously squeezing the member, almost choking her. Finally, there was a prodigious ejaculation. Mireille sucked, sucked gleefully, satisfying her gluttony and her gourmet tastes at the same time. She thought she was eating the food of paradise: currant jelly and sweet, slightly tasteless sperm—what a marvelous combination!

Finally, having literally drained the beautiful instrument, the latter having lost its haughty rigidity withdrew of its own accord. M. de Saint-Grattelon then went to get a damp towel in order to wash Mireille's little monkey face, all smeared with jam, when the clock in the adjoining room began to chime.

"Oh! Six o'clock already?" Mireille exclaimed. "I have to go home!" Before she left, M. de Saint-Grattelon had wanted to put some perfume between her breasts, but Mireille stopped him saying, "How could I explain having perfume on me? That would be a dead giveaway!"

M. de Saint-Grattelon left the next day for Cannes. But he asked Mireille to write to him in case anything happened while he was away.

The day after that memorable afternoon, as Mireille, alone, was walking and dreaming under the olive trees, she passed one of her father's farms and was surprised not to hear any noises. The family must be helping out on another farm, she reasoned. She was going to continue on her way when she spied a kind little donkey that she was particularly fond of.

"Hello, Martin. So you're all alone today?" The animal, recognizing his little mistress, swished his tail from side to side.

Mireille was caressing Martin's underside when her hand ran against the animal's member. Slightly surprised, she looked closer. There was the machine in all its glory! So big, so long! And those nuts! Her hand stayed on the member. Martin stiffened on his hind legs. Mireille mentally calculated how much it could hold! Taking a quick look around, realizing that nobody would appear, she made up her mind. She practically ran into the kitchen, discovered a pot of honey, put it in her apron, and hurried back to the donkey. After making doubly sure that there was no one around, she grabbed the member again, caressing it up to the balls. Quite content, the donkey offered no resistance. Driven by her gluttony, she dipped the tip of Martin's machine into the honey pot and smeared it copiously all around. Then she went down on her knees under the animal's stomach and brought her lips to his dong. The enormous extremity barely fitted into her mouth. That didn't bother Mireille however. She made one effort after another, and succeeded so well that the gland soon disappeared into the hot prison. With her hands Mireille caressed the silky skin of the plunger even more. But the donkey, not knowing just exactly where his member had entered, tried to embed himself even further. Fortunately, Mireille was a strong girl and all the while she was squeezing and remounting the dong, she had enough strength to keep it in place and to prevent it from entering too far! Finally, incredible jolts shook the machine, dragging Mireille's blonde head with them, her mouth tightening more and more around the imprisoned member. Then a formidable geyser of sperm spurted into her mouth and throat, completely filling them up. Mireille continued to avidly pump out the divine liqueur whose taste blended so well with the taste of honey!

A few days later, she obtained permission to go to Cannes with a girl friend who under a false pretext was going to meet a lover. M. de Saint-Grattelon, whom she had notified, was waiting for her in a small house which he shared with a good friend on the outskirts of the city.

We can imagine the passionate embraces they exchanged. That night, Mireille, her lover, and his friend had an intimate dinner. The beautiful girl from Provence, although not really drunk, was feeling quite tipsy.

They were having dessert and Mireille had in front of her a plateful of *crème à la kirsch*. M. de Saint-Grattelon's friend had just got up to go to another room. Mireille's lover also got up to place a long kiss on the head of his young mistress. She put her hand in his fly, quickly brought out the robust spear, which she directed to her plate. Then, increasing the pressure, she deftly made the member discharge right in the middle of the dessert, practically emptying the prized tool, while Saint-Grattelon's friend, back at the table, beheld this charming scene. Noticing his presence, the country girl glanced at M. de Saint-Grattelon in silent supplication. He understood her plea and, smiling, nodded his head in agreement. Abandoning the now empty instrument, Mireille turned towards the friend, unbuttoned his trousers so quickly that he didn't have time to react—he didn't put up any resistance, however!—and took out an attractive member which was just as large as M. de Saint-Grattelon's. Then, masturbating him, gently at first then ever faster, she had the satisfaction of seeing a large discharge of sperm shoot forth onto her plate of sweet cream to join the previous one. She refused to give the member back until it had completely lost its stiffness. Like a true dilettante, she stirred her special dessert of cream and sperm as it should be done—with a small spoon—and was finally able to enjoy her delicious dish. For two days and two nights our three friends thus varied their pleasures, one as tasty as the other.

Sometime later, M. de Saint-Grattelon, unable to live without feeling those delicious lips pump him dry, married beautiful Mireille.

Madame de Saint-Grattelon could then give free reign to her gluttonous instincts, spending the rest of her life pursuing her passion up until the day when the following epitaph attracted the attention of those passing by Mireille's grave: "Here lies the most divine and the greediest of all gluttons . . ."

LA LIBERTÉ OU L'AMOUR

The excerpt below, which also deals with male ejaculation, is taken from *La Liberté ou l'Amour*, by Robert Desnos. For our translation we have used the first edition by Kra, 1927 (?), which was mutilated by police. The book was later republished by Gallimard in 1962. In this story we read of a Sperm-Drinkers' Club, a vast organization that hires women to masturbate the handsomest men all over the world. Each sample is sealed in a tiny phial or crystal, glass or silver, carefully labeled and shipped with great precautions to Paris, the headquarters of the Club. Connoisseurs also relish a mixture of male sperm and female lubrication. The activities of this extraordinary Club are reminiscent of the Beggar's Benison and other old English "hell-fire" clubs.

The Club's agents are staunchly devoted to their duty. Some have lost their lives on dangerous missions, but all carry out their task enthusiastically. In fact, they vie with one another to see who will have the most brilliant ideas. One will collect the sperm of a man who dies under the guillotine in France or on the gallows in England, for these emissions acquire the taste of the water lily or the walnut, according to the method of execution. Another will murder girls and fill his phials with the seminal fluid which their lovers release under the shock of anguished surprise caused by the terrible news delivered by the agent in person. Still another, employed in an English boarding school, will gather the evidence of a girl boarder's excitement when, having reached the age of puberty without the knowledge of her schoolmistresses, she commits some trivial offense and is whipped, skirts up and panties down, in the presence of all her classmates and perhaps that of a schoolboy who happens to be there, the god of amatory pleasures. The founders of the Club were the last exponents of occultism; they met for the first time at the beginning of the Restoration. Since that day, the association has perpetuated itself from father to son, under the double auspices of love and liberty. A poet once expressed the regret that the society had not been founded during the last days of the ancient world. For then it would have been possible to collect the sperm of Christ and Judas and, as the centuries passed, the sperm of Charles Stuart of England, that of Ravaillac, the corporeal tears shed on her way to Chaillot by Mlle. de Lavallière under the influence of the sensual trotting of the horses that drew her carriage, those of Théroigne de Méricourt on the Terrasse des Feuillants and all the splendid sperm that flowed onto the revolutionary platforms during the Red Terror, as surely as the blood with which it mingled. Another poet always regretted the loss of the divine brew that must certainly have resulted from the Duke de Clarence's drowning in a vat of Malvoisie. . . .

A new arrival: "Gentlemen, I want you to visualize the excitement of a sturdy, proud, haughty, and fairly tall woman who has been rendered helpless and is being carefully sodomized by a young man. He has not undressed her completely. Her petticoats and skirt are rolled up between her belly and rump. Her panties are down around her knees and her rumpled silk stockings provide a charming disorder. In the front, her clothes hang almost normally. At the point where they begin to rise, there is a glimpse of white flesh to be had and, in the shadow of the rumpled underwear, it is possible to distinguish the outline of the buttocks. After lubricating the firm flesh, the young man spreads the buttocks. He penetrates slowly, with steady tenderness. The patient is wracked with a new kind of excitement and the moisture betokening pleasure begins to appear. A little girl daintily collects the sacred tears with a silver spoon and puts them in a small jar made of red sandstone. Then, because of her small size, she is able to slip almost entirely under the couple's legs, and none of the semen frothing about on the writhing member escapes her. When the superb tango of love has become a storm of cries and sobs, she collects the warm, sweet-smelling snow that forms on the lip; when the orifice is well defined, she applies her mouth to it like a tiny red suction cup. She sucks a long time, mixing the fluid thoroughly with her saliva, and this mixture goes into the sandstone jar as well. Finally, the woman kneels down and lets the child collect her tears of shame, rage, joy, and fatigue.

Pornographers of all times have always, and correctly, stressed the importance of the male ejaculate. Why it should have this special significance may not be clear at first glance. However, the male ejaculate represents to the unconscious the source of all power, potency, health, and welfare. This accounts for the proscriptions, from Biblical times to our own, against wasting it and the exhortations of preserving it and its life-giving strength.

Thus the eating of semen may be regarded as a symbolic act of incorporating its inherent life-preserving power, such as the unconscious, archaic layers of the mind take it to be. Psychotic males not infrequently can be observed in the wards of mental hospitals to do just that and, if verbal, are apt to comment on the act in terms of "preserving their vital life force," "putting it back," or "keeping the power inside." Moreover, skin contact with the ejaculate is experienced (regressively) as extremely pleasurable by many ("normal") individuals, to say nothing of the earlier mentioned connection with latent homosexual interests, which can find vicarious gratification through contact with the sperm of another man *inside* the woman.

Bizarre as many of the sexual fantasies may be, it is well to remember that even the most shockingly deviant forms of human sex behavior can be explained if we know the person's background and the kind of learning experiences and conditioning he or she has undergone. It is clear today that the many sexual deviations—sadomasochism, pedophilia, homosexuality, transvestitism, etc.—are no greater mysteries than one person's preference for blonds and another's for redheads. Both are conditioned or learned responses to certain stimuli and associations between sexual feelings and certain events. These connections are, more often than not, forgotten, repressed, or otherwise inaccessible to the person's conscious mind (and, hence, to his volition and control).

Sexual learning or conditioning is no different from any other kind of human learning or conditioning experiences. Through the accident of environment and upbringing, the individual may come to associate sexual arousal with a number of specific stimuli—say, leather, certain smells, sounds, particular musical scores, certain lighting, specific colors, and so on. If these associations are formed very early in life, that is, prior to the full functioning of the symbolic mental processes and language, they are, of necessity, inaccessible to the person's conscious mind and recall. Such very early sexual conditioning has been called imprinting by some students of animal behavior, but it is equally applicable to the human situation.

In the case of such early imprinting, the individual's sex preferences are usually extremely pronounced and inflexible and are apt to appear to the outsider, as to the person himself, totally inexplicable and bizarre. They do not seem to be in harmony with the rest of his personality or correspond to his known sex history. In short, early imprinting tends to produce the most rigid, the least influenceable, and the most specific sex preferences, such as object fetishism or a particularly high degree of specialization on certain physical or characterological types of sex partners, aside from which sexual arousal simply does not occur.

However, the usual kind of sexual conditioning is based on somewhat later learning experiences, when the cognitive processes of the mind are already more or less operational. These are more easily traceable and can be brought to recall under certain conditions, such as by free association in analytically oriented therapy or by hypnosis. Also, the resulting sex preferences are much less marked, specific, and inflexible. These sex preferences, say, homosexuality or a tendency toward sadomasochism, are therefore more readily influenced by psychotherapy.

Whether re-education and reversal of sex preferences is desirable depends, of course, on the particular circumstances of the individual and his desire or absence of desire to change. In and by itself, we see little reason why such people should be encouraged to undergo the time-consuming, costly, and to a certain extent psychologically painful process of re-education if they themselves are happy and comfortable with their sexual preferences. However, the stronger and more pronounced the sexual preference, the narrower the range of stimuli which may lead to sexual arousal and gratification. Any strong sexual preference constitutes a definite limitation on the person's capacity for sexual response and is theoretically less desirable than the capacity to respond to the widest possible range of sexual stimuli that may present themselves. But these are ideals which are seldom meaningful in actual practice, and rare indeed is the individual who has the drive and ambition to make the most of his mental, emotional, or sexual potential.

A great deal of sexual conditioning occurs, as the Kinsey researchers have stressed, through the human animal's capacity for communication through verbal and pictorial symbols. There is no doubt but that we are all influenced (conditioned) by what we see and read. Humans are able to share their sexual experiences and fantasies through the printed word and pictorial representations, and thereby influence and condition one another.

What does this signify in the case of the many erotic works we have examined in this study? What effect, if any, do we expect them to have on the reader?

One may safely assume that many of the fantasies will prove sexually stimulating to a certain number of people. They may have fantasized similar situations as the ones described and respond to them sexually. However, if the sexual fantasy communicated is too alien and finds no echo whatsoever in a person's own sexual experience or fantasies, he is not likely to respond to it, or only to a very minor degree. The more bizarre the sexual fantasy, the less likely it is to have any effect on others, aside from its literary and intellectual merits. Of course, the closer the communicated fantasy may be to commonly experienced fantasies, the more likely it will evoke a sexual response in a greater number of people.

For the vast majority of people, the experience of vicariously sharing the sexual fantasies of others through the printed word or pictorial representations is likely to evoke sexual behavior which is channeled through the habitual, preconditioned outlets that are typical for that individual. Once these channels for sexual release are firmly established, nothing the person reads or sees or hears is likely to significantly alter that pattern of response. If the communicated fantasy happens to correspond to the person's own favorite sex fantasies and sexual interests, the communication would tend to reinforce the *already existing* interests. Such was apparently the case in the English "moor trials," in which a young man and woman team of sex criminals sadistically abused and killed a number of children, using as one of their literary sources of inspiration the writings of the Marquis de Sade. To conclude from this, as the press and the police did, that they were led to commit the murders by the literature is, however, a gross misunderstanding. It would be more correct to say that they were responding to Sade's violent sex fantasies because they were already so inclined and were using them to confirm their existing inclinations along these lines.

It is even highly doubtful whether exposure to deviant sex fantasies would have any effect on young individuals in the way of conditioning them in that direction. What is needed above all for such conditioning is much more direct learning experiences during the most formative years of psychosexual development in the person's childhood environment. Once these experiences have occurred and the preliminary conditioning established, any vicarious sharing of fantasies in that direction would, of course, tend to reinforce the tendency. One might even go so far as to say that there is a possibility—albeit a non-proven one to this day—that certain predisposed individuals may be triggered off to the acting out of antisocial fantasies by the vicarious sharing of similar fantasies of others. Nevertheless, this risk is counterbalanced by the fact that an even greater number of people do have an opportunity for vicarious satisfaction by mere mental identification with the characters in these stories, without any further need for actual acting out on their part. Still other therapeutic advantages derive from the reduction in guilt and shame reaction. The fact is that most people do have sexual fantasies and impulses of which they are ashamed and which are morally unacceptable to them. By realizing that they are not as rare, deviant, aberrant, and abnormal as they may have thought, they will find considerable relief and comfort. This, in turn, reduces the likelihood of guilt feelings becoming so overpowering that the individual has to adopt drastic psychological countermeasures. These usually take the form of reaction formations which frequently lead to paranoid ideation or even to the persecution of those whom they suspect rightly or wrongly of the very tendencies on fantasies which they themselves are unable to admit.

If there were no printed pornography, people would simply make it up themselves—the walls of our public toilets give ample evidence of such spontaneous sharing of sexual fantasies on the most primitive level of personal communication.

We are therefore diametrically opposed to every form of official censorship. We hold the free flow of ideas, even noxious ideas, infinitely preferable to any form of censorship control, a control, moreover, which, in the absence of any objective guide rules, by the nature of its enforcement is bound to do considerably more harm than good.

We would like to make a strong plea for tolerance of deviant sexual behavior (as distinct from fantasies), as long as it concerns consenting individuals, capable of making up their own minds, and does not present a clear danger to individuals or infringe on the rights and privacy of others. Fortunately, most sexual deviations fall into this category; and few, indeed, are the persons who have so little ego control and whose minds are so twisted and truly perverted that they can find no satisfaction except in harmful, antisocial sex activities, such as murder and rape.

We do not advocate, as some clinicians do, the censorship of violent and openly antisocial ideas and fantasies, such as our senses are daily bombarded with from news reports, television, the cinema, and similar media of mass communication. It is, of course, tragic to us that impressionable youngsters should be exposed to such saturation propaganda glorifying violence, warfare, and the law of the jungle. But even this seems preferable to us than to admit the possibility of official censorship in any area of communication and with regard to any subject matter at all.

Instead of censorship, we recommend, therefore, a program of voluntary education and therapeutic community guidance which would attack the evil at the root, rather than aimlessly and ineffectually flailing at the branches. Here the role of parents, the schools, and other educational or devotional organizations is to help the individual sort out and distinguish the good and constructive from the bad and destructive. If that is done, we need not worry about what goes into print or is sold on the newsstands. For an enlightened citizenry does not fear printer's ink or movie screen. It has its moral values and will not be misled by violent or otherwise antisocial propaganda. And those are the only real safeguards a civilized community has at its disposal.